# GROWTH AND THE ECONOMY: *Principles of Economics*

# GROWTH
# and the ECONOMY
## PRINCIPLES OF ECONOMICS

*David McCord Wright*
UNIVERSITY OF GEORGIA

CHARLES SCRIBNER'S SONS · New York

# *Preface*

In this book I have sought to merge the familiar approaches to the study of economics, usually found in introductory college courses today, so as to produce a more coherent and understandable pattern. Macro-economics and the theory of the firm are not sharply separated but instead the topics are grouped in a sequence by which they mutually illuminate one another. The book begins with economic growth, and growth, change, and adaptation form the connecting thread of the whole. As these inevitably imply both business policy and government attitudes toward employment and income theory, the various individual threads are easily gathered together. The analysis ends with a discussion of international trade, and some of the more urgent of economic problems.

The new arrangement represents a complete re-thinking of the analysis which I wrote earlier and which appeared in *A Key to Modern Economics,* published by Macmillan in 1954. I am grateful to the Macmillan Company for letting me use here some subordinate material which first appeared in that volume.

Acknowledgments are especially in order to my colleague Professor William Miller of the University of Georgia who read the whole manuscript in draft. I am also obliged to the other members of the Georgia economics faculty for help and material. Any errors in this final version are my responsibility, not his or theirs. Acknowledgments are also due to my students at McGill University, the able and responsive subjects of many experiments in teaching during my seven years in Canada. I am also grateful to publishers who have permitted the reprinting of their materials and to Fordham University Press for the use of several figures from *The Keynesian System,* written by myself, and published in 1962.

David McCord Wright

*Cotuit, Mass., June 1964*

# Contents

# Figures

# GROWTH AND THE ECONOMY: *Principles of Economics*

## Part I

# ECONOMIC ORGANIZATION AND ECONOMIC GROWTH

+ + + | + + +

## What Is Economics?

Economics is a way of understanding a special set of problems—some of the most important problems in the world. Pick up any newspaper. There you will surely find items about taxes, or strikes, or unemployment, or inflation, or gold "outflows", or farm prices, or poverty, or wealth—dozens of similar items, constantly repeated—and all of them "economics"!! They are "economic" because they are closely tied up with two main problems: What to produce, and who gets it after it is finished. Any set of social arrangements which tries to solve these two problems for a nation we call an economic system.

There have been many attempts at more exact definition of economics. "The science of man in the business of earning a living" writes one author. "How the goods and services we need get produced and distributed" writes another. Yet a third approach speaks of economics as an analysis of "choice" —the choices whereby we allot our limited productive powers among their many possible uses. All these ideas are important and we will come back to them later, but the basic idea remains: What to produce and who gets it after it is finished. These are the basic questions of economic science.

Yet economics is not just a way of getting understanding. We also study it in order to get help. What shall we DO about unemployment, or to get more housing, or to "defend the value of the dollar," to name a few problems at random. Economics tries to answer these questions too. It is not enough for most

*1*

of us to know that a given nation is, say, poor. We also want to know what might possibly be done to make it better off. When we are merely seeking understanding of economic problems we call it economic "analysis." When we are trying for solutions of economic problems, we call it economic "policy." Either way, if we charge in without thinking, we are likely to get into trouble. Either way, whether we are dealing with analysis or policy, we will be within the field of this book.

## What Are We Trying for in This Book?

A modern economic system is not just a lifeless balancing of mechanical pulls. It is a process, a change, a becoming. Modern industrial societies are always on the move. Something new is always being added. Every modern, growing nation—capitalist or socialist—lives in a perpetual technological revolution. If we do not understand our economic world as a process of constant change, we will never understand it at all.

But an economic system has another side. It is also a process of adjustment. People become conscious of new methods, new wants, new ideas, and try to adjust to them. We can't just focus on the fact of constant disturbance if we want to understand what is likely to happen. We also have to know the logic of adjustment. Why does the manager adopt one method and reject another? What sort of goal has the consumer vaguely in mind when he spends his money? What analysis can we employ? If we can't answer these questions, we, again, will never understand our economic world.

Accordingly we get the first two aims of this book: (1) To understand the modern economic system as a process of constant change; (2) To understand the economic system as a process of adjustment. But there is more work to be done.

We have just said that the aim of economics is not only understanding but also help. There are plenty of economic problems. We have already mentioned two of them, unemployment and growth, but that is only the beginning. Can we make our society more stable? Can we make it more secure? Can we help the "under-privileged?" Finally can we do all these things without stopping the total process of change? Questions like these bring us to the second set of aims we have in mind: To supply the fundamental apparatus needed in looking for a solution of economic problems.

## Choosing Economic Policies

Notice that we say help in "looking for" solutions. In this book we are not trying to do your thinking for you, but only to help you think more clearly.

Furthermore, debates over economic policy, or over what to do, are often really not debates over economic analysis at all but debates over political ideals! By and large, for example, people do not want *merely* to curb inflation or cure unemployment. What nearly everybody wants to do is either to curb inflation or unemployment within the framework of a given economic system, or to curb inflation and unemployment *and* bring on a different system—one they think is much better because it happens to fit their ideas of what is "right" more than the present one does. In selecting an economic policy we have to choose among social aims, just as in spending our salaries we have to choose among a quantity of different products. But this is where the trouble often starts.

A simple example will give the main point. Suppose two doctors are called in to treat a very sick patient. One doctor is extremely anxious to keep the patient alive. The other thinks the sick man is in such bad shape he had better be allowed to die. The first may prescribe a stimulant, the other merely a pain killing drug. Yet both men may be equally good doctors, and there may not be the smallest disagreement between them as to the nature of the disease, and what might be done to cure it. Their *aims* are different that is all! Economists often find themselves in the same position, though often without realizing it. One man really does not like economic growth. He prefers a peacefully poor society. Another man is convinced that rising incomes will lead to a better world. They may both be equally good economists, trained at the same school, and yet they will suggest widely different remedies.

The trouble is that economics is like a road map. It can tell you how to drive to Chicago, and it will tell you how to drive to New York, but it cannot, of itself, tell you which town will suit you best. What good then is economics? The answer is "Lots." True the science cannot, of itself, choose your aims for you but it can give you plenty of help. First of all it can warn you off many blind alleys and side roads that would never lead you to any of the desired destinations. But next, and most important, it can give you a much better idea of the costs, or consequences of selecting different aims.

An absurd example will give our points. Suppose you meet a man who offers you a beautiful, shiny gold brick. Well, first of all, you will want to know if the brick is a phony. But suppose it is genuine. "Do you want it?" he says. "Sure" you reply. "Well let me cut off your finger." That changes things a bit. Often the hidden cost of a plausible social aim may be something as serious as losing a finger. The usefulness of studying economics is that it will help us to detect social gold bricks—both as to whether they are genuine or not, and also in discovering their real costs—costs which are often hidden, or which take a long time showing up. The economist does not say "You cannot do this." More often he says, or should say, "*If* you do that you will probably be sorry" or, "do you really want such and such results?" "Look before you leap" will be our motto in this book.

## Economics as a Science

Yet now the question has to be asked: By what right do economists say what they say? How do they know what they say they know? Can economics be called a science at all? To answer these questions we have first to define a science. A science, for our purposes, is a body of knowledge and analysis which enables us, given a particular set of facts, to make a reasonably reliable prediction as to what is going to happen. Now in spite of everything economics does very often meet this standard. Any science, even the most exact, can only predict *if* the data on which the prediction is to be based are given. The same is true of economics. Yet through thousands of years of history we have seen the same forces operate again and again. We have analysed their operation, and we have made mental models of how they must operate. These models, if we remember their limitations, show a high degree of reliability.

But, though economics is a science, it can never reach the practical precision often found in what are called the experimental, or exact sciences. For probably the greatest single obstacle to scientific economic analysis is our inability to use what is called the "controlled experiment." Contrast an economist studying the stock market with a psychologist studying the learning habits of rats. The psychologist can construct the maze he wants and vary it in just the way he wants. Within broad limits he can exclude the smells, sounds, and colors he wishes to eliminate. He can make things hard for the rats or easy. Not so the economist. He is not allowed deliberately to "break" the market. Even if he tried, and succeeded—that is to say, the market did fall—so many other forces would be operating that in most cases the economist could not easily tell whether *he* had really done it or if it were just coincidence. What the economist is forced to do is to study an actual uncontrolled process and try by analysis to work out how it is functioning and which forces are the most important. Naturally there is plenty of room for error.

There is another factor operating here to upset prediction—particularly in institutions like the stock market where expectations are important. That factor is the *consciousness* of the units being studied. Even the scientific psychologist encounters this one: his rats must not be too sophisticated! For example, the reactions of an animal that has been experimented upon may be quite different from those of inexperienced ones fresh from their natural state. It is even more true of human beings: if they do not like or approve of what is going on they can start changing things!

Economic life, in fact, is not simply a mechanical process like knocking billiard balls together on a billiard table. It is much more as if a billiard ball could suddenly stop and say, "I don't want to keep rolling in this direction. No. I'm going to start rolling that way and hit the black instead of the red." On the other hand, electrons (we assume) are not conscious of what is being done to them when the physicist sets off an explosion. The electrons, we presume, do not hold conventions and pass resolutions altering their future behavior. But the economist deals instead with men who are for the most part conscious that they *are* being dealt with. Thus it is a curious fact that, in many cases, if economists could predict the future "accurately," and their predictions were widely believed, the predictions would prove wrong! Why? Because people would react to the prediction and begin to "hedge." Thus, if stock prices were accurately forecast to drop in six months, and if the prediction were believed, many people would sell at once and the decline would be brought forward. Fortunately for practical economics, however, not all economic life is a mere matter of varying expectations. Fortunately also the economist deals generally with cases in which behavior is largely independent of him, and his predictions are not controlling.

Yet, in the matter of human behavior one does encounter an important scientific point bringing the exact sciences and economics closer together. The physicist, after all, like the economist, travels on the law of averages. Modern physics does not pretend to be able to predict the path of individual particles. It deals with the probable behavior under given stimuli of crowds of electrons. So also the economist does not try to predict the behavior of single individuals. He too deals with the probable behavior of large numbers. But large numbers are predictable only if the people composing them have many of the same ideas. In other words an economic law is an expression of an observed pattern of behavior in a large number of people. Some of these patterns, to be sure, grow from the basic physical or mental nature of man. But an extraordinarily large number are rooted in the nature of particular cultures or civilizations. Thus, a prediction that would be perfectly reliable for the inhabitants of Manhattan might be highly unreliable for the inhabitants of Malagasy. Yet, fortunately, it is a fact that the few uniformities of behavior supposed by economics do happen to be very widespread, and if we watch out for these differences of culture, and allow for them, our predictions can often be reasonably well adjusted. Thus through the historical record, careful analysis, and much testing the economist has available a great variety of extremely useful knowledge.

## Our Plan of Attack

We have now reached a point at which we give a broad overview of this book. Our aim, we have seen, is to understand our economic world both as a process of constant change, and as a process of constant adjustment. Our aim, furthermore, is to analyse some of the problems of economic policy, and to show some of the costs and choices involved in deciding what to do about various problems. What thread can we find to organize all this material? Where can we start?

Fortunately there is one idea which can be used to tie the whole set of problems most conveniently together. That idea is growth. While there is still plenty of argument as to the best way to "raise living standards" almost every-one today thinks doing so would be a good thing. Furthermore, even if you don't agree, it is still true that practically all the important modern economic problems are rooted in some way in growth. Unemployment is often the result of a failure to grow fast enough. Instability of the economic system comes from growing too fast. Are you worried about economic uncertainty? Stop growth and you will get rid of most of it. The list could be extended indefinitely. Thus we take growth as our starting point and we commence with its basic require-ments, as broadly stated as possible. In other words we begin with dynamic process.

Yet, next, we have to remember that growth in our society takes place under the institutions, and pushes and pulls of a particular system. We move, therefore, from growth in general to a discussion of the general working of the capitalist market. Yet even this is not sufficient. We go on to recall that total expansion is the result of a multitude of individual decisions to expand. Why did an individual unit decide to expand? What reasoning did they use? The problems involved are first presented in non-technical fashion by a chapter on "managerial economics", and are followed up by a simplified review of the tools of abstract economic theory. In this first part we are laying the ground-work for an all out analysis of the basic functioning and problems of modern society.

Yet there is still one more set of preliminary ideas to learn. These concern the institution of money—at once one of the most important and one of the least important aspects of economics. We will have to learn to see it both ways, and then we will be able to take on such problems as unemployment, business cycles, and economic stabilization. Following the trend of the modern world we do not treat these by themselves but tie them in with international trade and the general problem of international relations.

Our concluding section will apply the ideas we have so far learned to spe-cific problems such as agriculture, monopoly, labor unions, comparative eco-nomic systems and so on. Throughout, we will relate the practical problems to the questions of political and philosophical standards that lie behind them. What we will be aiming for throughout the entire study is not to present a series of independent, isolated, problems and topics, or a disconnected set of analytical tools. Rather our aim will be to obtain a picture of economics, and the economic system, as it actually is: an enormously diverse and yet interrelated whole, seeking adjustment by definite rules and yet never getting there, constantly throwing itself forward into the unknown, and ever bearing on with it the hopes, the fears, the energy and the aspirations, of the crowding generations of mankind.

+ + + || + + +

# The Expanding World

All streams run to the sea; but the sea is not full; . . . What has been is what will be, and what has been done is what will be done; and there is nothing new under the sun (Eccles. 1:7, 9, RSV).

## The Change in Expectations

If we live today in a time of danger, we also live in a time of hope. Up to a couple of hundred years ago, the human race, if it thought at all of a better world here on this earth, looked backward to some mythical Golden Age and not forward. Human history was thought of as a process of decline, not as a process of improvement. Men talked of the "good old days," not of the hopeful future. Things are different now. In spite of all our upheavals, we are neverthe-less constantly presented with more and more glowing possibilities. The thing which distinguishes our period, with all its shortcomings, is still that surging process of experiment and hope which shows itself, among other things, in eco-nomic development. Each recent generation has found its horizon larger than the one before, until now the process of expansion and discovery has been built into the very fabric of our culture. It is impossible to understand modern society without thinking of it, first and foremost, as a continuing process of change, adaptation, and growth.

It is this process of change and adaptation that makes economics worth studying, for if there were no technical change or no expansion, economics would not be a very interesting or important subject. We would merely be think-ing of how best to repeat a fixed routine. It is not by accident that the develop-ment of scientific economics sprang from attempts to analyze, to bring about economic growth. Adam Smith's *Wealth of Nations* is, in fact, much more a book about the growth of nations. The French eighteenth-century economists called "the physiocrats," from whom Smith learned much of his analysis, were likewise concerned primarily with the growth of their country. So were the "mercantilists" who preceded them. As early as 1819, the great English econ-omist David Ricardo was making remarks about the cultural obstacles to growth which read today as if they had come from some United Nations release. At the moment, the systematic merger of economic growth and economic analysis is going forward rapidly.

## Growth and Change

Few subjects are more important. If we hear a lot in current speeches about the "revolution of expectations" and about the great new world which we may possibly have, it must be remembered that it is one thing to expect wealth and another thing to get it. Economic growth is not just an automatic process. Fortunately, the broad universal elements of the process are now pretty well recognized. We will first state them with as little reference as possible to particular economic systems. This is far from saying that one economic system is as good as another, but it does help greatly to learn, first, those universal requirements which are conceded by practically everyone, before going into the problems of our special society.

The first thing to realize is the principle already mentioned, and which we will constantly be referring to, namely, that growth comes through change and causes change. One country, it is true, will grow best by developing one industry and another by another; and some countries, for example New Zealand, may even become wealthy without any great amount of manufacturing at all. Nevertheless, the one thing common to all of them is that, as their output increases, the pattern of production and the pattern of wanted goods will keep changing. All change does not make for growth, but all growth does make for change. We cannot talk of one without talking of the other.

## Growth and Production

Economics is full of surprises. You might think that if we wanted to increase output by, say, ten per cent, all we would have to do would be to order that each plant and each industry in the country make a ten per cent expansion. In fact, this is quite untrue for several reasons. On the simplest level if you want to double output, you clearly would not want just to take a blueprint of the old factory, multiply all the feet and inches on your drawing by two, and let it go at that. Would it make any sense to multiply every dimension? Clearly not.

## The Problem of Scale

First of all, it would be a terrible waste to make the doors, windows, and ceilings twice as high for no particular reason. But there is something more complicated at work than that. The whole general pattern of the machinery must be redesigned if output is to be doubled permanently and efficiently. As the sizes of the different parts of a machine or a building or a boat are changed, the balance of forces is changed within them, and with it all the stresses and strains. Engineers will tell you that even when the most careful model is "blown up," that is to say enlarged by some fixed factor, many unexpected difficulties will crop up. Quirks of this sort have been discovered in all lines. For example, when the Salk vaccine was introduced, it had been found to be quite safe for large population groups, but from vaccine made in small lots. But then everyone rushed to order the vaccine; and when, without preliminary checking, the attempt was made to produce it in much larger quantities than before, the formula and the margin for safety proved to be no longer reliable, and several deaths occurred. Technical economic language sums all this up by saying that we do not often find "constant returns to scale" in this world. In other words, a simple doubling of everything will not necessarily produce a doubling of total output. An efficient increase in over-all size will nearly always mean a great shift in the proportions of the different parts to one another. For example, if you launch a boat that has been built merely by multiplying all the lengths and breadths of a small boat by two, the chances are that instead of sailing twice as fast it will probably turn over.

### Diminishing Returns

What we have talked of so far refers to any expansion, regardless of whether there are new inventions or not, but there is a further productive problem. A truly continued development needs genuinely new inventions or new ideas; in other words, not doing the same thing in a larger way, even with modifications in the proportions of the parts, but tackling the problem in an entirely different way. New inventions, in fact, and the shifts in production methods which they imply, lie at the base of all continued, constantly maintained growth. For there is another technical expression, "the law of diminishing returns," which says that in an unchanged technological environment growth becomes progressively more difficult. It is true that one can grow for a while quite successfully without introducing any basically new methods, but the productive effect of a simple increase and single modification of known types of machinery will soon begin to reach a limit. Without new ideas and new methods, continual development will be progressively more difficult, if not impossible.

### Growth and the Pattern of Wants

So much for production. Let us shift now to consumption. Again we are in for a surprise. Here, too, you might think that the doubling of over-all output would mean a doubling in the demand for particular goods by consumers. For example, if consumers had used 10,000 turnips, you might expect them now, with doubled income, to want 20,000 turnips. But again, you would be wrong.

Of course, a society could be organized like a prison, in which each man simply had a certain ration doled out to him. But such societies are very rare. Even the toughest dictatorship usually finds it convenient to allow a man a certain amount of free choice. He works better that way.

It follows that even the most despotic society usually allows some freedom of choice as to what to buy and a modern capitalist democracy allows a tremendous leeway to the consumer. But, as freedom of choice increases, shifts in choice become more frequent. The man who used to eat one orange a day will not eat a dozen oranges a day just because he has more money to spend. The man who lived in one small house will not try to live in two small houses because he has more money; chances are he will buy a different sort of house, one requiring more money to buy, but at the same time giving him more space or different space in which to live. As people become better off, they will necessarily experiment in new patterns of consumption, and this would be true if there were no advertising and no attempt to influence their choices from outside. The mere fact of a larger total to be spent produces, of itself, a shift in the pattern of outlay.

We can now see that, for basic and largely technical reasons which have very little to do with any special economic system, the mere process of expansion is also bound to be to some extent the process of reorganization and redirection of economic life. Old towns making old products must give way to new towns making new products. People who have been trained in old skills will have to move elsewhere, or be trained in new skills, or both. Our analysis gives us two fundamental requirements of economic growth for any type of system. While the methods used may be different, an economic system which wishes to keep growing must possess the following two forces: It must have mobility, and it must have enterprise. By mobility we mean the willingness and ability to be moved from one job or location to another and to learn new skills. By enterprise, we mean the energy and foresight which puts through the changes needed to induce effective mobility. Let us discuss both these forces in more detail.

### Security versus Expansion

Mobility is not an easy quality for an economic system either to obtain or to keep once it has it. The basic problems of resistance to change are much broader than merely capitalist organization and turn up under somewhat different forms in almost every society. Even if everybody got the same real and money income and even if everybody worked for totally owned government industry, it would still be true in a modern, sophisticated society that there would be tremendous psychological problems of obtaining industrial mobility. In primitive countries, the problem of transformation is even worse, and becomes at times almost overwhelming. Let us begin with the primitive country and then discuss the sophisticated, modern society.

## The Primitive Society

All of us know that for a sophisticated person without previous training the jungle is a very dangerous place. But what people often do not remember is that a modern city would be just about as dangerous for, say, an African tribesman without city experience as a jungle is for a city dweller. Death in traffic would, of course, be the most immediate hazard, for the tribesman would not have heard of traffic lights; but still more dangerous though slower forces are at work. The tribesman would not know how to stay healthy, or what to eat, or how to protect himself in bargaining, how to find and keep a job. To survive a city environment successfully, all these things would have to be learned. In many cases, initially fine primitive types deteriorate terrifically in city environment even though their wages are extremely high. The reason is they do not know how to handle alcohol, canned food, various diseases, and all the other possible dangers of the city environment.

Experience has worked out for the tribesman in his primitive surroundings a diet and customs in which he could survive. These customs, to be sure, may be rough or cruel or wasteful, yet they are bound to make a certain sense. We know that they have to make sense for the best of all reasons—if they had not had a certain fundamental, practical value, the tribe would have died out long ago. And since the tribesman is shaped by these institutions, which as we have said do have some basic logic, he is safe as long as he stays under their control and as long as external conditions do not change. Furthermore, he feels or believes himself safe and derives a certain psychological support from the unchanging routine of his ancestral environment. But when a primitive community begins to industrialize itself, all this must be changed. The old tribal skills will not do for modern technique. The old system is broken. But then comes trouble.

The tribesman released from his tribal control must worry about the future for himself. Up to now, the tribe had done it. He must find his own amusements, his own friends, his own food, look after his own health, reach somehow his own community function, and status, and feeling of belonging. All these things were automatically managed for him by the tribe, and these tremendous problems must be solved in surroundings which are perfectly strange to the tribesman. Indeed, half of the needs which he had will never be realized by him until it is too late. He will assume, for example, that he will remain healthy until he finds himself struck down by disease. Is it any wonder that, after a brief experience, "civilization" may prove fatal?

Here we meet, for the first time, a problem which we will encounter over and over again in this study—a distinction between a single change and a continuing change. The simple way to meet the problem of the rootless former tribesman is simply to make him a member of another tribe. If a group of tribesmen are absorbed into a particular work town and drilled in a special set of skills, and in the requirements of health and order for that particular industrial community, that will be fine for them as long as the situation lasts, but it does not meet the question of continuing expansion. We can be sure that in a few years that particular industrial town will have to be reorganized to meet new industrial conditions of demand and production. People may have to be switched over to a new plant; certainly they may have to learn new skills and a new order of life. And once more the job of rooting up the new (now old) system will often be unwieldy. Furthermore, in a fully developed, modern-type society, people must learn not just one set of skills or rules, but how to learn or acquire new sets of skills and rules. In other words, they must learn to have a sufficiently intelligent self-reliance to begin to shape their own lives and not simply look for some organization to shape it for them.

## Pressure Groups and Modern Cultures

In modern industrial civilization, many of the obstacles we have just talked of will be lacking. Nevertheless, it is important to realize that the problem of resistance to change is absolutely universal. In capitalist society, the principal objection to the moving of jobs or to the changes which growth makes necessary is found in the fear of losing money. People do not wish to take a cut in salary, and they are afraid that should a new method come in, their jobs will be out of date, and they will be poorer than they were before. But even in the modern society, the obstacles to change are far deeper than mere matters of income. Nor would we get rid of them if everybody had the same money income and if all industry were owned by the state.

It might seem, to be sure, that although shifting around and retraining would always be needed in any growing society, all would be well if this society were planned to avoid interruptions and if everybody got the same income. In such a society, one would think, in which the fruits of growth are by law to be equally shared, each individual man would recognize that he could only be better off personally by increasing the total product. Since no one would suffer a loss of income because of technical change, and since everyone would benefit from the increase which the change had made possible, everyone, it would seem, would be only too glad to move from one line into another. There would be no pressure groups and no obstructions. New ideas would gladly be tested as soon as they were discovered, and immediately and joyfully adopted if the tests proved successful.

## Nonmonetary Resistance to Change

Unfortunately, the problem of resistance to change is much deeper than such a theory would imply. There are at least five important types of insecurity, or five strong human motives, which might lead people to resent and resist the changes needed for over-all growth, even in a completely planned society in which no one's income could be larger than that of anybody else. These basic motives are: (1) love of friends and workmates, (2) love of skills, (3) love of places, (4) love of power, (5) love of conspicuous service. The life of any reasonably happy man is not just a matter of the size of his paycheck, even allowing for possible changes in prices. It is the total dimensions of his existence which he wishes to protect, and the five dimensions we have given represent some of the most important parts of life to most normal human beings. Unfortunately, these are the dimensions which must be disturbed by growth in any type of social system. Suppose that you are the Commissar of Railroads. As Commissar of Railroads, you have a number of decorations from the government; when important events occur you are allowed a seat on the platform near the highest officials, and you are generally a big shot. Next, suppose that someone invents, let us say, flying boxcars, which do away with the necessity of heavy railroad freight and make your job much less important. Suddenly, you find yourself moved from the fifth row to the twenty-fifth row at grand state festivals. The seat which you used to have is taken away from you and assigned to the Commissar of Aviation. And unless you are an adaptable type who can move over to another industry quickly, and a good politician, to achieve leadership equally quickly, you will suffer a personal disaster not at all unlike that of the capitalist millionaire who loses his fortune.

But we must not think that these problems occur only in connection with the leaders. The ordinary workman who likes his job or the group of people with whom he eats lunch, who enjoys the view from the window of his house, and who has come to feel himself a part of the life of a town—he, too, will be deeply disturbed if he is suddenly asked to move to a strange community and to undertake an entirely different calling. The mere fact that he may have an unchanged salary, or even a greater salary, will not always be enough to compensate him for the painful disturbance of his life which growth has involved. In European socialist countries after World War II, there were numerous cases in which all the securities of social welfare could not reconcile populations to the uprooting of their way of life. English villagers refused to move twenty miles to a new village and a new mine, even though they knew that the old mine was no longer productive. Railroad unions struck against the government-owned railroads, even though the representatives of their own socialist government told them that they were jeopardizing the whole socialist experiment and the welfare of their own "class."

Nor need we talk only of industry or of politics. Even in pure science, a man may become so identified with his particular theory that he cannot bear to have it disproved or to have his hypothesis fail. If his ego is too deeply involved, he may even go "over the line" and fake the evidence needed to save his scientific guess. For example, a certain scientist reached the notion that there were bound to be prehistoric remains of an early type of ape man in Piltdown in England, and when he could not quite find the necessary evidence, he faked the bones which would seem to prove his theory and soaked them in a chemical solution which gave them artificial age. For twenty years the "Piltdown man" was one of the best-known examples of man's development, and only in the 1950s was it discovered to be a fake. We thus reach a universal conclusion: Growth comes from change and causes change, to be sure, but growth is always disturbing or painful for somebody; and the people who are inconvenienced or harmed in one dimension or in another will often try to organize to prevent the change which upsets their personal routine, even if the change may be good for the country. It follows that, while some nations may be more mobile than others and some cultures more hospitable to change than others, still always, if there is to be growth, there must be a special class whom we will call enterprisers, or entrepreneurs—men with the energy and determination to overcome the various types of social barriers which we have just sketched in, and carry through intelligent developments.

## Enterprise

The enterpriser, or entrepreneur, as we use the word in this book, is not the same thing as the inventor, on the one hand, or the businessman or public administrator, on the other. What distinguishes the enterpriser is that he "puts across" the new idea, or gets it used, not that he necessarily invents it. Frequently, the pure scientist who hits upon a new combination of ideas may be uninterested in working out their practical implications. Even if an inventor uses some new ideas of pure science to invent a particular practical gadget, he still, even then may not be the type of person who can deal successfully with other men, or carry through the day-to-day use of his invention. Thus the inventor may often be quite happy to sell the application of his invention to some more practical-minded enterpriser or organization of enterprisers. So much for the difference between enterprise and invention.

On the other hand, while a new idea may be put across by a businessman or a government official, it does not necessarily follow that any particular businessman or government official is interested in putting across new ideas. Even if a man is the president of a twenty-million-dollar corporation, he may still not be an enterpriser if he runs the corporation in an unimaginative and routine way, along lines previously laid down for him. The same thing is true of a government official who just "runs in the groove." It will be seen that enterprise, or entrepreneurship, is not the same thing as the possession of legal authority. By enterprise we do not merely mean operating an organization, but rather persuading or forcing the organization to follow new paths.

## Does Personality Still Matter?

In modern corporate business and government life, where so much work is done by committees, it may sometimes seem as if there were no longer any need for special qualities of personality and leadership. The members of a committee, it might seem, would pool their knowledge of the facts, and on that basis a decision would be reached. However, life is not that simple. Though committees may ratify decisions, committees are still made up of human beings. If the people on a committee are all of them timorous and unwilling to take chances, the committee will not often reach daring decisions even though persuasive facts are put before it. A committee decision still takes special qualities of determination, persistence, and insight by some members at least to get a genuinely new policy through. Men, in this connection, may speak of "the" state or "the" government as "doing" something. But it must not be forgotten that the state remains a designation for a group of people, and that to a great extent the state will be as wise, foolish, unenterprising, or as rash as the people who compose it may be.

What most distinguishes the enterpriser is the courage to run risks. Under a capitalist society, if a man backs a dud he may go broke; under a socialist society, he risks his reputation, his power, and his influence. Furthermore, you can see that it is not enough to be willing to back new ideas; one must be able to back them persuasively or forcefully, and to have common sense as to what idea to back. We will see much more about the problems of the entrepreneur as we follow the analysis of this book. All we are trying to do at this point is to sketch the universal basic characteristics that are needed for economic growth in any society. It is clear that enterprise is one of them.

## Growth and Capital Formation: Land, Labor, and Capital

So far, we have talked about broad general requirements for economic growth which anyone can understand without special training. Now, it is necessary to go into the more technical parts of the subject. We have seen that growth comes through change and causes change, and that in order to get these changes adopted people must be willing to shift around and there must be individuals who are willing to put across new ideas. But, although these social qualities are basic, the aspect of economic growth which is most immediately observed is what is called "the formation of capital." Nearly always a productive new idea involves not just moving people or things around, but also the construction of new instruments of production. It is, in fact, the accumulation of machines, the designing of tools, the piling up of equipment, the obtaining of stocks of semifinished goods, which are the most immediately observed things going on in a growing society. These activities are all lumped together by the economists as "forming capital." So important is the role played by capital in economic development, that it often is easy to think of machines and tools—i.e., "capital"—as the only requirements of economic growth; but we have already seen that much more than that is needed. Let us see where capital fits into the entrepreneur's problems and where he gets the capital which he will use.

Suppose we have a primitive economy in which development is wanted. First of all, it will require entrepreneurs, either private or government. But, next, what will their task be? Unless we know the conditions and resources of that particular country, we cannot say specifically what sort of industry needs expansion or what type of tools and equipment, that is, capital, needs to be amassed. But some kind of capital will surely be needed, and we can say generally that the entrepreneurs will want to alter the direction of economic life and the economic methods of production which have been used up to that time. And in this task of alteration, economists have for generations said that the problem—the problem of the entrepreneur—is to put together three things: land, labor, and capital.

## Land

By "land" is meant natural resources. Clearly if a country has no labor (that is, no population) and neither possesses nor can reach natural resources, it cannot develop. But it is important to remember, first, that "natural" resources can be traded for and, next, that they are not very "natural." We mean by this that what is a natural resource or whether one can get it is often a matter of the ingenuity and insight of the people of a region, not just its geography. The North American Indians were roaming through a country teeming with "natural" resources, but there is little to indicate that they would ever have used them. On the other hand, there are some regions like Norway or the British Isles, not outstandingly endowed with minerals or natural wealth, which yet, by technical ingenuity and enterprise, have achieved high place in the roll of developed nations. Again the mere location of a nation relative to others may be a great asset.

### Labor and Capital

"Labor" is not just foot-pounds, nor yet just a matter of nose-counting. The level of *skills* is of prime importance, and it must not be forgotten that these have to be retaught for each generation. Skills, however, lead us on to "capital" or "produced means of production." For it can be persuasively argued that training a man is, speaking technologically, as much a matter of creating a new productive tool as building a dynamo. One thing is clear: our entrepreneurs who wish to initiate change will want to get hold of natural resources, to train and recruit labor, and nearly always they will want more equipment of some sort—in other words, "capital." But where does capital come from?

### Capital and Money

Many people talk as if capital were just a matter of money. You can easily see why men should feel this way. If an underdeveloped country can borrow money from a more developed one it can usually use that money to buy the equipment, training, and other resources that it needs. In the same way, if I get more money from you, I can usually buy more of what I want from others. Nevertheless, if we stand off and look at the economic systems as a whole, we will find that money is not the essential thing.

Let us take, for example, India. For century upon century some people in India have been heaping up treasure. For thousands of years it has been "good manners" for Indian families, especially royal but also people of "standing," to accumulate a family treasure, particularly of gold and silver. Where possible, the hoard is added to. Almost never is it spent. The result is that India now possesses a vast mass of hidden treasure of unknown size. Yet India is a relatively poor country. Suppose all that money were taken out of the ground and put to work—would it do any good? Possibly yes, possibly no.

Of course if the gold were sent abroad to countries which had a highly developed productive structure and could afford to sell goods, equipment might be brought back which would be of the greatest help in Indian development. But suppose, instead, that the attempt were made to spend it all in India? Since Indian production would not at first be any greater, the only effect of trying to spend more would be to force up prices and cause inflation. We will see later in this book that some increase in production might be managed through inflation, but only at the expense of great suffering and dislocation. Let us rule out inflation; then we will see that just spending the treasure would do little good. It would not of itself give more *real* production. Mere money then, considered by itself, is not the basic thing for economic development. What is the fundamental force? The answer is *saving*.

## Saving

By the word "saving" we now will mean forgoing leisure or consumption, and using the energy and resources thus released to produce more capital—that is, more tools and equipment. Usually in modern society the process is handled *through* money, though money, as we have just seen, is not the basic force. Speaking very crudely, one can think of each bit of money as a "ticket" or "vote" controlling a certain tiny portion of the stock of labor and resources available. When we spend our money on immediate gratification we are "consuming" and we are, at the same time, "voting" for the production of consumer goods. When we do not spend on immediate gratification, and the money is transferred to finance production of new equipment, we are "saving," and the money at the same time is "voting" to use resources to produce capital goods. We will see later in this book that the process of saving money and using it for capital production or, as it is generally described, "investing," can sometimes be interrupted, with very disturbing effects upon the economy. But at the moment all we are concerned with is essentials. *Any* economy that wants to grow will need some method of keeping, or persuading people from using all their incomes for immediate gratification, and of transferring the energy released into tool production of some sort. This fundamental fact has nothing to do with capitalism. A socialist state, to be sure, might try to do the whole job by taxing. Taxes might stop consumption, and the proceeds of taxation might be used for tool production, or "investment," but the essence of the problem would be unchanged.

## Enterprise, Capital Formation, and Risk

We see now that the entrepreneur wishing to initiate change will have to put together natural resources, labor, and capital. In the first instance this capital will appear to him as a flow of money, raised by borrowing from others or by his own saving or that of his corporation, or, if he is a government entrepreneur, perhaps by taxes. The flow of money, however, will be of value only if it also makes available a flow of physical and mental resources which can be recombined in the new project. So far as essentials go, money need not be used at all. Villagers, let us say, might be taxed at so many bushels of wheat or days of labor, and the proceeds used directly in the new project, perhaps a road. One factor remains which we have not yet mentioned, but which is well-nigh universal, and that is the factor of risk.

The trouble is that as one moves into new territory, technologically speaking, predictions become less and less accurate. We have seen that, even when careful models have been built, unexpected relationships can emerge as full-scale application is attempted. More than that, it takes money and resources even to build models and do research. Finally, not all research need pay off. The fundamental idea may prove to have been wrong. Nor is error any monopoly of particular economic systems. During the United Kingdom Labour government large sums were spent on African development projects that later turned out to be mistaken. The Red Chinese government has made vast miscalculations in production. So has Russia. On the other side, the world is peppered with the wrecks of mistaken private enterprises, often very large corporations. Thus the process of development inevitably involves risk to individuals and some way has to be found to persuade them to bear them and yet forge ahead.

In a capitalist economy the hope of profit or of interest payments may be sufficient to persuade people to lend money to risky enterprises. It might seem that a socialist state, operating by taxes, would not have a risk problem, but this is far from true. Here the problem falls instead with special weight upon the government servant. It is not his money, to be sure, that he risks in promoting a new idea, but it is his reputation, his responsibility, his career. In China he may even lose his life as the consequence of a bad guess. How then is he persuaded to take risks, to behave like an entrepreneur? Partly through patriotism, but, the world over, the noble motives usually need some reinforcement. The hope of honors is the great socialist incentive. "Conspicuous service" we will call it. Which is best—or works the best—the hope of a million dollars, or the hope of the Order of Lenin? This is a question which we cannot discuss until near the close of this book. All we need to realize here is that special distinctions, differential rewards of *some* sort, appear inevitable if risks are to be borne, capital formed, and growth to continue.

## Organization and Outlook

We have seen so far that growth comes through change, that change, in all systems, provokes resistance, that men must be found to overcome these resistances and to mobilize the land, labor, and capital needed for growth. Finally we have seen that these men must somehow be rewarded for bearing risk and taking responsibility. A final set of requirements must also be mentioned—these concern the social organization and ideas within which the entrepreneur has to work. No matter how enterprising, ambitious, and well rewarded a man may be, if the social process is too hostile to change he will not be able to get anything done. Thus if "peaceful contemplation" is the highest value of a society it is not likely to have a high living standard even if some would-be entrepreneurs are trying to stir things up. Nor will growth occur if waste and display are the chief ends. There will not be enough saving. We will discuss these problems in later chapters. It is enough to realize that one of the basic requirements of economic growth is a favorable social outlook and organization.

## Stability

Emphasis on mobility can be overdone. Many good things are old, and not all new things are good. Again, without an ability to make plans, who would face the future? What we need is a society that is mobile but not too mobile. In the same way we need to study not merely the requirements of economic growth, but also the requirements of economic stabilization. For one can hardly expect the surging process we have sketched always to balance out. And remember the government servant is no more endowed with omniscience than the businessman. Both can make mistakes in predicting the future. Therefore some means of relative stabilization must be evolved. They, too, are needed.

## Summary

In this chapter we have given a rudimentary outline of the major problems involved in starting and maintaining a process of continued growth. The word "continued" should be especially noticed. About 140 years ago the Rev. Thomas Malthus predicted that mankind was doomed to misery. If ever the standard of living rose, he said, population would increase even faster. Soon man would be back on a subsistence level. Malthus' predictions have not worked out for Europe and North America, but only because of the combined labors of the inventor and the investor. In other words, new methods of producing energy have been discovered and implemented faster than the population increased. Yet it must not be forgotten that had we tried to make out with the techniques of Malthus' day his gloomy ideas would have been proved correct. For that reason we have not stated the requirements of economic growth in terms of mere static quantities and efficiency. We have not even stated them in terms of a stock of capital. What is needed is an all-round appreciation of the complicated forces which, taken together, keep society not merely expanding but also creative. Full understanding of the problem will not be reached until the end of this book is reached, but in understanding the rudimentary obstacles to change and growth, at least we have made a good beginning.

+ + + ||| + + +

# Modern Market Economy

So far we have not tied our explanation of economic growth to any particular economic system. We have shown the qualities and activities that all growing systems must have and engage in—for example, mobility, enterprise, and capital formation. But there are many different ways in which such qualities and activities can, at least to some extent, be obtained and coordinated. What is important for us to learn now is how the job is done in our own society. The American economy is all around us. Most of us have known it since our youth. We take it for granted and it seems natural to us. In fact, however, it is one of the most astounding sets of social arrangements ever worked out. Let us stand back and try to take an overview of the whole system through fresh eyes.

## The Amazing Picture

Through and through it is a process of constant change and adaptation. Wants are changing; methods are changing; firms, one way or another, are changing in size. Yet millions of students in our economy go to college each year and pick the subjects they want to study. No government bureau tells them what to take. Millions of people decide to drop one job and take another. Unions and other groups may interfere to some extent, but no government planner orders their choices. Millions decide on their own to move from one town to another; but no one says, "This town is full." No one tries to direct the constant migration of people. And yet, all this motion somehow fits itself together. From these many individual decisions, there nevertheless emerges a certain basic, rationally functioning, coordinating institution. Take New York, or still more remarkable, some near-arctic city like Montreal. Here are great cities, entirely dependent on the outside world to keep them from starving, with thousands of products for sale in their stores drawn from all over the world. Fresh tropical fruits, available in arctic weather! Surely there must be a board to direct all this, to draw up, let us say, an annual schedule of requirements, to settle priorities, to arrange for emergency reserves, and to take care of possible rationing. But not at all. Most of the time, and not just in the cities, the great process runs itself. How?

## The Market Mechanism: A First View

The answer lies in the pushes and pulls of what is called the "market economy." This market economy, as we suggested in Chapter II, can be thought of as a perpetual election to decide what shall be produced. Money is the votes. Advertising is the campaign literature. The election returns, determining what shall be produced and what not, are profit and loss.

Suppose that New Yorkers decide to eat less rice and more spinach. More money will be spent on spinach. Prices will probably rise a bit. Far away, spinach growers will find sales and, probably, profits rising. The chances are they will want to expand. On the other hand, less money will be spent on rice. Sales and profits in rice growing will fall. There will be pressure to reduce the rice crop. Thus the pattern of money spending reflects itself in the pattern of production and, barring special government acts, the citizens of New York or Montreal, in their daily purchases, command the type of planting in distant lands. Yet nobody is arranging the pattern. It arranges itself.

Still more is this the case with different jobs and professions—what people call the labor market. Suppose new ore deposits turn up in Labrador. There is a great new demand for engineers, miners, construction workers, for all sorts of people. But at first nobody may be on the ground save a few Indians or Eskimos. What happens? High wages are offered to work in the new project and people who are earning less elsewhere are tempted to swarm in. Take a more urban example of the market at work. Suppose a new demand grows in industry for mathematicians. Salaries of mathematicians rise. The word gets around in the colleges and schools that mathematics is the thing to study. The flow of young mathematicians rises.

On the other hand, the process works in reverse. If there are no longer so many miners or mathematicians needed, their wages or employment will lag, and some will shift elsewhere or into other lines. By the process of shifts in money-spending, consequent shifts in profits, wages, and earnings, and resulting shifts in the direction of the training and education men seek, the system continually adjusts itself to its continual disturbance.

## Capital Formation

All we have given so far is the simplest of outlines. It will take the rest of this book to work out in detail the general picture we have given. Nevertheless if one holds on to the idea of the market economy as a perpetual election, in which changes in the way money is spent induce changes in prices, wages, and profits, and these changes in turn induce changes in the direction of production and flow of labor, one will have a clue to fundamental understanding which will always be basically helpful. However there is one more task for the market to perform which we have not yet mentioned. That task is capital formation.

We have seen in Chapter II that for a society to grow there must nearly always be a stream of investment—in other words, new plant, machinery, and training must constantly be undertaken. Why do people invest in a market economy? The answer is easy. They do so in order to make money, to obtain a profit. We will see in later chapters that the constant flow of technical change, upon which growth ultimately depends, gives rise to a constant stream of new profit opportunities, new opportunities for expansion. But, in order to expand, one must have resources: money, in the first instance, and, in the second, the real resources that money buys. In a market economy which is working fairly smoothly, one which is undergoing neither inflation nor unemployment, this money for expansion must usually be borrowed from those who are saving it. Yet the flow of noninflationary savings is limited. The result is that those who expect to make money by expansion bid against each other for a share of the flow. They persuade people to part with their money by offering to return a bit more than they have borrowed. In other words, they offer a share in the profits they expect to make. This share, this extra return over what has been borrowed, is called the "rate of interest." It is usually a fixed per cent of the amount borrowed. It serves as compensation for possible risk—for not all the new ideas are going to work out—and to some extent as an inducement to save. Here too we are enormously oversimplifying a very complicated process. But here too let us concentrate on the big idea: capital formation.

In a market economy, capital is formed basically because, on the one hand, the profits expected from growth and change make people want to expand and, on the other, because people in such a society are willing to save and lend money for, among other reasons, a rate of interest or extra income in return. The process does not necessarily work smoothly, and our account is tremendously oversimplified; nevertheless we have given an accurate statement of the fundamentals.

### Basic Elements of the Market: Property, Exchange, Specialization, Money

The modern market economy is so enormously complicated and interdependent that it is easy to lose sight of its basic institutions. We have so far sought a general understanding of how the market works. But now let us see what are the basic institutions that *make* it work. It is a long way from a group of primitive peasants exchanging goods to the stock exchange in Wall Street, yet the same fundamental institutions can be traced in both, and the line of development from the one to the other is easily traced. Any market, we will see, depends upon the following two institutions: property and exchange. If the market is to show any real development two more features must be added: specialization and money. Let us begin with property.

*Property.* The astonishing feature of a market system is the combination of great independence for the individual citizen, or economic unit, with a co-ordinated order which somehow emerges from it. But on what is the independence of the citizen and the economic unit grounded? There are many forces operating; one of the chief of them is individual property. Once grant to an individual some security of property and freedom in the use he can make of it, and society will be well on its way to the development of a general market. It has been found that when each individual is allowed, within wide limits, to keep what he can earn and save, the result is usually both greater independence for the citizen and a greater incentive for production for the group as a whole. Thus in seventeenth-century Virginia and Massachusetts, the first settlers of both colonies set up "communal" economic organizations: all food harvested belonged to the community and was rationed equally among everyone. The result was great inefficiency and lethargy. The lazy were sure of getting as much to eat as if they had worked; while the industrious, resenting the exploitation to which they were being subjected by the lazy, turned sulky and worked less and less. The fundamental method, therefore, by which both Captain John Smith in Virginia and Governor William Bradford in New England saved their respective colonies was to introduce the principles of private property and private ownership. "Give a man a one-year lease on a garden and he will make it a desert," said Arthur Young, the eighteenth-century traveler, "but give him a twenty-year lease of a desert and he will make it a garden." In the same way today, the agricultural development of some of the primitive countries is being held back by social institutions which allow members of a man's family or tribe to settle upon him like locusts should he accumulate anything, or which make it possible for the tribe to take back any piece of land which he, personally, makes unusually productive.

*Exchange.* Private property alone does not suffice to produce either a market economy or a developing one. The next great requirement is exchange. As soon as people begin producing for themselves it is likely that one family or another will find itself with small surpluses of particular goods. The general consequence of this is that they begin trading with one another, each man trading what he can spare for what he lacks. Soon specified times and places come to be recognized for trading to take place and a market is well started.

*Specialization.* But neither private property nor an occasional market are enough in themselves to create a true market economy. The next step in the development of a country's economic life comes with specialization. As people begin trading with one another more and more, they gradually discover one of the fundamental principles of economics—that of the *division of labor*. One man is a good hunter, while another finds he is good at raising vegetables. Gradually they learn that they *both* have more if the farmer sticks to farming and the hunter to hunting, and they exchange products. This notion of specialization is a fundamental principle of economic life which runs all the way from the simple example we have given to the intense and minute specialization of modern times. The division of labor lies, indeed, at the base of the productivity of modern society.

*Money.* Property, exchange, specialization—all these are essential to a modern market economy, but a true market can scarcely emerge without one more element: money. Money makes possible a system of comparison and exchange extending far beyond the confines of a single village or even a nation. Without money, the minute division of labor characteristic of modern society would be impossible. Without money, sophisticated modern social planning has been discovered to be impossible. Finally, it is through money that the pushes and pulls of a free market express themselves. Let us see why money is so important. We will find the key to an understanding of money in outlining the functions which money serves, and the way that types of "money" of widely varying origin have grown independently in many different tribes and civilizations to a very similar final result.

## Money as a Medium of Exchange

The uses of money are threefold: as a medium of exchange, as a store of value, and as a standard of value. We begin with the medium of exchange, for exchange is the use through which the various forms of money seem generally to have originated. As a medium of exchange, the great convenience of money is to save time. In a country in which there is only direct or primitive swapping of goods, an enormous amount of time can be lost in trying to find someone who not only has what you want *but* wants what you have. You may have fish and want milk. But the person you know who has milk may want beads, not fish. Your fish may spoil before you find someone with beads who wants fish. But if money is in general use, you can sell your fish right away, and *then* look for what you want at leisure. Money has thus usually originated in some commodity so generally desired that the man who takes it in a trade can be sure of finding someone else who wants it very quickly. For example, Chinese money originated as knives. They were valuable and generally desired. The man with a good knife would never be left without an opportunity for further trade. But gradually emphasis came to be put not on the usefulness of the knife in itself but on its token value as something widely acceptable. In the course of centuries the blade of the knife entirely disappeared and all that was left was the loop which had once formed the handle. Roman money, on the other hand, originated as herds of cows—easily exchangeable—and wound up (again a loop) as the metal circlets originally placed on a cow's tail for identification!

## Money as a Store of Value

We see what a time-saver money can be in arranging exchanges, but there is another quality of money that cannot be overlooked: Unless the thing being used as money is reasonably *lasting* it won't be efficient. Remember we spoke of selling the goods *you* have and then waiting until you can find the product you want. If your money disappears while you are waiting, it will not be of much use. But on the other hand if the medium of exchange is lasting, it can be used to store value for very long periods. Thus hoards of gold—if they are not stolen, and if people continue to want gold—will last practically forever. But a barrel of flour will soon spoil and a cow will die. Money as we have it today, however, is light, portable, and lasting, and remains continually available. For these reasons money assumes its second function: a store of value. Instead of having to store up for sickness or old age collections of physical things—food, clothes, and so on, which will rot and decay—we can accumulate money in one of its various forms, for example a bank account. The only remaining hazard in most cases is that of loss of value through inflation. We will discuss this later in the book.

## Money as a Standard of Value

So much for a store of value. But money might seem to be less necessary in a controlled or "planned" economy where the state plans production and looks after the old and the handicapped. Even as able a man as Lenin at first thought money was not necessary. But he soon found that to organize a huge modern industrial society there must be statistics, and to have useful statistics, there must be some basis of comparison. The basic difficulty here has been called the horses-and-apples problem. Suppose that one year you have one horse and two apples. Next year you have two horses and one apple. Has production increased, decreased, or stood still? Apparently it has increased—a horse is bigger than an apple. But suppose the horses are sick and the apple is a specially rare and desirable one. Only by the use of some common standard of value can one compare all the thousands of varied things produced in modern society and keep track of their flow. Through money such a standard can be reached—though there are many problems involved which we will develop later in our detailed chapters on monetary matters.

## The Market Mechanism Once More

Let us see once more how the essential mechanism of the market works. The production flows are tied together at any one point of time by the flow of money; and these money flows in turn affect the profit-and-loss situation in each individual enterprise. In so doing they affect expectations as to future wants and prospects, and thus induce shifts in the next period's output. The profit-and-loss situation, indeed, may be likened to the lights on a switchboard. A high profit prospect is like a red light, showing a gap in the desired production structure that needs to be plugged. Barring special restrictive action by groups of some sort, or a great lack of confidence, or great uncertainty as to future price–cost prospects, enterprisers will soon see the need and the opportunity, and begin to make plans to fill the gap. In the same way, as we will see in much more detail later, the rate of interest on borrowed money helps to ration the flow of saving and over the long run to affect its size.

By measuring the money flows, furthermore, statisticians are enabled to keep track of output in a way that would be otherwise impossible. Through money we compile such statistics as "gross national product" and allied measures of output, which we will study later in this book, and without which the economic forecaster would be completely lost. Furthermore, the use of money makes possible a comparison of prices over nearly the whole of the world. Though these prices can be distorted by inflation and controls of various sorts, the modern business society compares possible methods and costs over an area and among a number of commodities almost unbelievable. Yet as the work of the market is done mechanically and usually quietly, the complication of the problems which it handles is only appreciated when, as in war, we try to do the whole job by direct control. It is found then that there are all sorts of interconnections which no one had remembered. The production board will accumulate the fullest available information and issue orders on that basis only to discover that a vital link in the production process has been unexpectedly disturbed.

## Independence

But now we must raise the question once more: How, if the market is so interdependent and so shifting, can there be independence for the individuals within it? Especially do we ask this question when we remember that the modern citizen, unlike the self-contained farmer, is technologically almost completely dependent on society for food and survival. The answer is twofold. First of all, under conditions of pure capitalism and with no government action, people were expected to make their provisions for emergencies by saving for "a rainy day." To take care of these savings and to channel them into productive invest-ment a myriad of institutions came into being: insurance companies, banks, finance companies, and so on. We shall be developing them in more detail as this book proceeds.

In addition there is a second basic source of economic independence, in spite of interdependence. This source is competition plus transfer. As long as there is reasonably full employment and prosperity, most people will have available a number of possible jobs; and if for some reason they tire of one line, and if they have some backlog of reserves available to support them while job-hunting, they may transfer to another. This does not mean that the merely lazy or bad-tempered can keep on being lazy or bad-tempered without paying a penalty. But it does mean that as long as the market is relatively free and prosperous any employer or group is limited in its power over others by the fact that no one is *compelled* to work for or under them. The other side of the medal is shown by Trotsky's remark that under Communism no one would dare disobey the state. *For since the state was the sole employer,* disobedience would mean starvation.

## Government

Yet a consideration of the problems of independence and stabilization leads us to a final fundamental element in the market economy—the role of govern-ment. Even in the most completely uncontrolled economy some government action is necessary in order to preserve health, safety, and order—which includes freedom from robbery. To this list even Adam Smith added a limited group of state enterprises such as lighthouses and other projects which the market economy will not usually furnish if left to itself.

How far the field of government action should be extended is a hotly debated question and one that we will discuss in more detail in the concluding chapters of this book. It will be enough at this point merely to indicate some of the principal modern lines of state action.

First of all, the state is called in today to set rules for the market, Pure Food and Drug acts, that sort of thing. In a village economy the baker, for example, who baked bad bread was speedily identified and dealt with, but in the modern mass market the line between producer and consumer may be so remote that experience has shown a need for the state to impose market standards.

In the second place, the state is often called in to protect natural resources and see that they are not destroyed. Salmon, seals, many other forms of valuable wildlife would all have been lost long ago without the state to protect them. The same is true of the national parks and forests.

Next comes state action to prevent individual groups from becoming too strong—unions or corporations, for example.

Again there is a growing field of social services designed to give the individual a "fair chance" or "decent security."

Also the slogan of "equality" has been used to justify some curb on the size of individual fortunes. This is a hotly debated subject.

But the field in which the government tends to be most active today is in the field of stabilization. More and more, people are unwilling to put up with the instabilities which they attribute to the free market. Yet it is just here that the trained economist must stop and think. It is not enough to say, for example, that there is unemployment. The question is, Why? And, again, it is here that we have to remember that we are not dealing with mechanical units but with semi-independent firms deciding policy on their own. For that reason we must now analyze the growth of the individual economic unit or firm before we go on with general stabilization.

## Summary

In this chapter we outlined the basic manner in which a "free exchange" or "market economy" functions. We began by pointing out what a really astonishing thing such a society is, and how it is only familiarity that dulls our appreciation of its behavior. We next went on to describe the "perpetual election" to decide what shall be produced, and from that to an outline of the vital activity of capital formation so basic to growth. Next we considered some of the basic social institutions of a successful market economy. These were property, specialization, and money. When we reached money we were compelled to go into more detail. We explained the three functions of money: a medium of exchange, a standard of value, a store of value. With money for our background we could then sum up once more the mechanism of the market. Finally we pointed out very briefly some of the relations between the market and personal freedom, and some of the ways in which government is called in from time to time to supplement the unaided mechanism of exchange.

# Growth and Organization
# of the Individual Firm

We turn now from the growth and functioning of economic systems as a whole to the growth and organization of individual economic units. Though the role of government, and government corporations, is much more important today than it was a hundred years ago, it is still true, in our society anyhow, that the larger share of economic life remains in the hands of private (nongovernment) individuals and groups. Accordingly, in this chapter, we will outline very briefly some general principles concerning the organization and growth of individual industrial units, usually given the catch-all name of "firms." For when most firms are growing the economy is probably growing too.

## The Firm

Not all the units which influence economic life are called "firms" by any means. First there are individuals and families. Their spending habits and reactions are clearly of vital importance. We will return to them later. Next there are various government bureaus. Finally one finds a large number of professional men, practicing by themselves. None of these is usually called a "firm." We reserve the name "firm" for business units and partnerships, and it is their action which still accounts for the greater part of economic behavior in the North American economy. But "firm" is a very general word. You and your family run a farm. The farm is a firm. Smith and Robinson running a garage in partnership is a firm. The essence of the idea is that a firm is a business enterprise under one ultimately coordinated management, although a large firm may allow great independence to subordinate units.

There were over 3.5 million American business units in 1964. As long as one thinks only in numbers, the majority type of firm in North America is not the great firms like Ford Motor Company or U. S. Steel Corporation. Most North American firms are short-lived small concerns owned by single persons. Such firms are highly unstable and a majority of them are unprofitable. One-third to one-half of all retail businesses, for example, are discontinued within two years. Yet, though small concerns are well known to be often failures, people keep launching small ventures both for the satisfaction of "being their own boss" and for the bonanza gains that do sometimes occur.

We, however, will be interested here in the methods by which firms obtain the resources to *grow* and the importance for growth of various types of business organization. In this chapter we will study the forms through which the firm passes and what in general it is trying to do. In the next chapter we will bring out some samples of the internal problems of management which a firm must overcome during the process of expansion.

## What Is the Firm After?

Before we can study a firm's growth we must see something of its motives. The usual answer to the question, "What is the firm after?" is that a firm wants to make money. Real understanding, however, requires that we amplify this bald statement considerably.

In the first place, the desire to make money does not mean that the firm will always squeeze every dollar of legally (or illegally) obtainable profit out of a *present* situation regardless of consequences. Most North American businesses are acutely conscious of the value of good will and good customer relations. In order to protect these, they will often forgo advantages which they could enforce had they abided by the strict letter of the law. Because of the failure always to squeeze the last dollar some writers go the other way and say that the firm, particularly the large firm, is no longer interested in profit. That, too, is an exaggeration. The firm is still in business to make money, but it is interested in the stream of *income* over *time*. If a judicious amount of present altruism produces better public relations, that may well produce more income over the long run. Thus altruism is not only for its own sake, but also with some reference to future cash.

Most American firms, however, are interested in more than just income and the enjoyment of income. Most North American firms are interested in *growing*. Unlike the continental European enterprise of a century ago whose owner, having reached a "comfortable" figure, might simply decline to expand, the North American firm usually continues to be interested in the accumulation of assets. Thus much of income may be plowed back into business. It seems fair to say that the prevailing motive of United States business is not so much getting the greatest income stream over time as achieving the largest possible rate of asset-accumulation, or growth, over time.

So much for the motives of the enterprise. Now we must consider the motives of the people who run the enterprise. Firms are run by people—either as owners, employees, or as corporate officials, and people come in all shapes and sizes. There is Mr. A who is mostly interested in a quiet life. He has a good business, but does not much want it to grow, for that would be "too much trouble." It will take a much bigger profit opportunity to get A to expand than would be needed for his friend B, an eager-beaver type anxious to grow. There is C who wants to grow, but "slow and sure" is his motto, whereas D wants a quick large return and is willing to gamble considerably to get it. Again there is E, who is assistant vice president in a large corporation. E, it is sometimes said, is interested in security and status rather than corporate profit; he may well be. On the other hand, probably a majority of corporate officials of E's type are still interested in salary as well as status and since there is a fairly definite relation, over *time,* between salary and allied rewards, and one's reputation as an able growth-inducer for the profits and assets of the corporation, such men are interested in corporate profits too. Finally there is F, who hates bureaucracy and red tape. He likes to be his own boss. Accordingly he prefers the freedom of a small firm to the possibly larger cash rewards of working in a big one. Sometimes F may be consciously sacrificing income opportunities. At other times F may think that if he were free to work out his own ideas in a small firm he would eventually be better off financially than if he stayed in a big one. Thus, cash and profit still form part of his plans.

Perhaps, however, the greatest oversimplification is to think that men work only for *one* motive. Usually there are many. Men work for money and status, or money and fun, or money and creativity, or money and a sense of achievement, let us say. But money is usually the marginal inducement. What do we mean by that? Well, some men will do some work for little, indeed sometimes no reward. But will as *many* men do as *much* work as we want for no cash reward? That is another story. Thus an author might write one book for love, and one for fame, but the third is likely to have a commercial motive. So it is with other types of activity. The last, or marginal, bit of activity often has a large financial inducement. But now let us go on to the actual process of a firm's growth.

## "On Your Own"

For most businesses in North America it is still true that one does not have to ask anyone's permission to go into them—if one has the money to start. Nor does an individual owner usually need legal formalities. You have reached the conclusion, say, that people will buy a special kind of fertilizer. You have experimented and used it on your farm, and you think it will have a wider appeal. Presto! you decide to make it. You get a batch of labels printed, buy a collection of bottles, and set up your "factory" in the empty garage at the back of your lot. You are making "Smith's Grow-Well Fertilizer."

Economists marvel at the number of small enterprises of this type started each year. Why do they marvel? Because of the risks involved. Usually concerns like this, as we will see in a minute, do not have enough money to operate at an efficient size. They stay in business only as long as their initial cash and credit last. But more important than the loss of initial cash is the possible loss of *other* assets. In a small informal firm all losses fall on the owner. If you cannot meet them your creditors can make you sell your house, cash in part of your insurance policy, and generally liquidate your property. Your liability in fact is "unlimited," and except for the minimum reserved by law, everything you have can be seized for debt. If the enterprise fails, you may lose not only what you have put into it, but everything else as well.

There are compensations! You are "on your own." You, and you alone, decide whom to hire and fire, how many men to employ, and how to operate. If you have any money left over above costs at the end of the month, it is yours. You pay income tax on your net earnings, it is true, but there is nothing to stop you from dipping into the business cash balances for a binge if you are so foolish as to do so.

## The Worries of Success

Yet somehow we may suppose that "Smith's Grow-Well" begins to make money. Perhaps it does so by catching local fancy. More often today, a small business grows by dealing with some larger business, say a chain willing to place a large single order. Once this order has been filled and paid for, you feel that you will really be on your way to success. But in the meantime you have to get the order filled—the fertilizer made—and payment is many months away. It is time to think of some way of bringing in more money. Perhaps partnership is the answer.

The reason for looking for a partner will be best understood if we review the general business situation for our rapidly expanding business. Strangely enough, the more business it is doing the shorter of cash it will be. The reason for a continuing shortage is that you have to pay wages *now* and you often have to pay for supplies *now,* but no cash from sales will come in for a considerable period.

Of course the most obvious place to go for help would be to a bank. You can spread out your orders and your accounts receivable on the bank president's desk and you can talk to him of your prospects as *you* see them. But the banker has another responsibility. He has to look after his depositor's money and it is far too early in the game yet for him to be sure that "Smith's Grow-Well" is really going to be a success, or is not just a temporary fluke. He knows that if there is any sort of serious depression small enterprises like yours will almost certainly be washed out. He will probably, therefore, not be able to lend you nearly enough and, even on what he does lend, interest will be high, by one subterfuge or another—such as requiring a sizable minimum balance in your account.

Of course, a bank is not the only way to get hold of money. There are less easy ways of economizing on cash. You might, for example, let your bills to your suppliers run up, or you might go to a personal finance company. But it hurts the standing of man and business not to pay bills promptly. Also it costs money, since most bills carry a 2 per cent discount if paid within 30 days. This will be lost if you fail to take advantage of it. Personal finance companies, too, are expensive. They may charge you as much as 3 per cent a month or 40 per cent a year. You can, of course, mortgage your home and risk having you and your family turned out into the snow. If you are also earning a salary from some other line of work, it may be easier to borrow since your wage can be attached or garnisheed. But the venture is now probably taking all your time.

In recent years two other possibilities have developed. One is the Small Business Administration which makes loans in conjunction with private banks. A good deal of time may be involved here in persuasion and formalities. Some state or city "development councils" or commissions also might give a little help. But such sources are not often likely to be your answer. What you need is somebody (1) with some money who (2) knows you well enough to have confidence in you, and (3) is willing to make an arrangement that will not be too expensive for you. The partnership is often the combination which will best meet this situation.

## Problems of Partnership

Partnership, however, is much like marriage and, financially speaking, very nearly as important. Almost any two or more people can form a partnership. Usually it is more sensible to have a written agreement, but even that is not absolutely necessary. As in marriage the death of any one partner means that the whole relation is dissolved, even though (unlike marriage) as many as 60 or 70 or even more partners can sometimes be involved.

What really makes the partnership (like marriage) so much a matter of personal character is that except in very special cases each partner's *personal* fortune is liable without limit for the debts of the partnership. Even more serious, every partner, acting on his own, can usually bind the partnership (so far as third parties are concerned) for whatever debts and obligations he contracts in the partnership's name. Thus your partner should be both honest *and* sensible and, if possible, healthy. If he is not, you may find that he has gone off and bound the partnership for a half million dollars of debt which you *personally* have to pay (if you can), or that he is too ill to act, or that his sudden death will necessitate a complicated and expensive reorganization, perhaps sale, of the enterprise.

In this connection it is also true that, like marriage in most states, a partnership can be dissolved at the will of either party, and if the partnership is "strictly business" one partner may propose sudden dissolution in order to embarrass another or even seize control of the firm. For often the assets of the firm are so tied up in the business that it is impossible to pay off any one partner's share without wrecking the whole concern. Generally, in such a case some third party will have to be called in—perhaps to buy the business, leaving you in the cold. Thus you can see you want an ethical partner, for there is plenty of room for maneuvering by the unscrupulous.

## The Partnership at Work

Return, however, to "Smith's Grow-Well." Somehow you have found a partner: a brother, or old friend, or brother-in-law—someone, anyway, who you hope meets the requirements we have just noted. The next thing is to agree on terms of partnership. Now *you* have practically no money left and yet the chances are you are asking him to make a substantial cash payment—say $40,000—into the business. In return you might give him a fourth of the business. Suppose you agree that first he is to get, as salary, $8,000 a year and you are to get $10,000. Next, he might agree that after all costs, including your respective salaries, are calculated, one-fourth of the profits might go to him, and three-fourths to you. You make a deal on that basis—why has he done so? Remember *you* have no money left. What is it that enables you to hold out for three-fourths' ownership, a higher salary, and three-fourths of the net profit?

What you have is, essentially, the basic idea on which the project is based, plus a certain amount of insight and "know-how." The importance of the basic idea is often overlooked, but it is like the parable of Columbus and the egg. Anyone *could* have stood the egg up on the table by denting it slightly at one end, but it was only Columbus (or whoever the story is being told of) who *thought* to do so. On a less basic level you have accumulated a certain number of trade contacts, a certain number of customers who will buy "Smith's Grow-Well" regularly. These contacts and customers constitute "good will" and this has a real cash value.

Because, therefore, of the fundamental policy insight which you have regarding your business, plus your, we must assume, reasonably good management, the business now has in it, let us say, a profit *potential* of $24,000 a year over and above expenses, including your and your partner's salaries. This means that your partner will be getting $6,000 a year on his $40,000 invested (supposing the business continues to prosper) or a return of 15 per cent. To get that income from safe 4 per cent bonds he would have had to put up $150,000 capital. So by sharing in the income opportunity you have created, he gets a much larger income from his capital than would otherwise be the case. But don't forget he also gets a lot more risk.

### The Hungry Fledgling

Still the business grows. Fundamentally it must be growing because of some real or fancied advantage which customers think your product holds over its rivals. But as you grow other forces help you along. With a larger, more steady volume of sales it becomes possible to plan production more efficiently and to buy in cheaper wholesale lots. Next you can begin to advertise more, and hence your product will become more widely known. Finally you can begin to buy up the plant and good will of other small competitors. You can begin to make some of your own materials, and last but not least "Smith's Grow-Well" can be supplemented by "Smith's Kill-Well," a weed killer, and a line of other allied products under the Smith name.

But if all these changes have taken place your business must really be growing phenomenally, and so far as cash goes, your first partner's $40,000 will probably have come to seem a drop in the bucket. You are again just about as pinched for cash as before. The demand of the business for cash will seem as ceaseless as that of a fledgling for worms.

One method of obtaining funds will be the "plowing back" of profits. You and your partner may well have become tremendously enthusiastic about the growth prospects of your business and you may decide not to draw out all your profit but to put it back into the business. Yet even reinvestment of earnings, or "plowing back" profits, will scarcely meet the capital needs you are likely to be encountering. You may want to build a larger factory, or to buy one. Perhaps most of the money can be raised by one or more mortgages from a bank or insurance company. Or the seller may take notes, mortgage secured. Yet even so, this saddles the company with a considerable fixed obligation and should your sales falter great trouble might ensue. For you will have to keep paying interest whether you are making any money or not. You are probably big enough now, to be sure, and sufficiently well known to be able to borrow from a bank, both to tide you over the busy season (say spring) or perhaps for a longer period. Nevertheless here too a "fixed" obligation is being created which may be awkward if business or prices begin to drop off.

A final method would be to take in more partners. And indeed there are firms in the United States with a very large number. But we have seen that the partnership is a very personal relation and a somewhat unstable one. It is not therefore usually capable of indefinite extension. Time now to think about forming a corporation!

### The Bird Takes Wing: A Corporation?

Incorporation is in most lines today almost a necessary accompaniment of any sort of economic maturity. The corporation overcomes most of the difficulties that are raised by a partnership. A corporation, for example, can last as long as the government unit granting its charter permits; thus the death of an individual will not have the same disrupting legal consequences (though if he has been the "brain" of the corporation it may still disrupt management). Since the corporation exists as a separate legal "person" its employees, the president, vice presidents, etc., are bound by rather strict limits as to the extent they can commit the corporation to binding contracts—unlike the extremely broad powers of most partners. Finally, and most important, there is usually "limited liability," that is, the corporation alone and *its* assets alone are usually liable for corporate debts. A man buys a share of stock in a corporation and the corporation goes broke. He loses the money he put into the stock. But he is not usually liable for anything more to meet unpaid corporate debts. In other words, the personal property of the corporate executives is not endangered by bankruptcy of the enterprise—and only in very rare cases would stockholders be called on for any further contribution. Thus the individuals concerned in the enterprise have far less risk.

From a tax point of view, however, the corporation has one serious difficulty. The government taxes the returns from corporations twice. First it taxes corporate profits before dividends. In wartime the tax went as high as 80 per cent. In peacetime, until 1964 it was about 52 per cent. Then the government turns around and taxes what is left, when it is paid out as dividends, as part of the *receivers'* income. However, as long as dividends are not declared, the profits earned (after corporate income tax) can be accumulated to meet reasonable needs of the business without paying personal income tax, though this cannot be overdone. Many people find such accumulation a convenient form of saving. Again in a closely held corporation a certain amount of personal income, in reality—though not in name—can be paid out to officers and interested persons as "expenses." Here, too, the Internal Revenue Bureau is always on the watch.

### Starting the Corporation

You have weighed all these pros and cons and have decided that your business has really got beyond the partnership stage. So now you start to form a corporation. Forming corporations used to be a very serious business requiring all sorts of special state action, if not particular acts of Congress or the state legislature. Today the job can be handled by a lawyer for a small fee. But raising the money is a different story.

First of all you decide to issue 30,000 shares of stock—10,000 to you, 5,000 to your partner, and 5,000 to your wife. This keeps a majority of the stock in your hands and since corporate decisions are made on a majority basis, not by unanimity, that means your group (your partner and yourself) has retained "control." Of course your partner, unless restricted by special agreement, might still "sell out" to a third partner. Or people may refuse to buy stock if the control by one group is still so strong. Usually, however, the fact that the corporation has done well will make new stock purchasers willing to accept the present control. Once more we may ask what have you and your family done to "rate" so much stock? And again the answer is that you furnish the idea, the good will, and the know-how. But today any large stock issue is looked over by the Securities Exchange Commission to see that you have not overvalued this contribution.

You are now offering one-third of your shares to the public. You are hoping for $15 a share purchase price, but to save trouble you call your stock "no par" stock. That is, in effect, merely saying that no particular value is indicated on the certificate. Because you are a small firm you will probably have to go to a local investment banker rather than to one of the bigger companies. An investment banker is a "middleman" dealing in securities. He knows people who have money to invest and he keeps in touch with businesses who want to raise money by selling securities. His profit comes from the difference between the cost of the securities to him (what he pays you) and what he sells them for to his customers. Like all profits its size tends to be proportioned to risk. For a large corporation the investment dealer often "underwrites" a stock issue. That means that he pays the seller for the shares immediately, and if he is unable to sell all of them the loss will fall on him. Also, for many large companies, the margin between the investment banker's buying and selling costs may be very small—for the issue will almost "sell itself." But you are not in this happy condition. The investment banker may offer you $12 a share and hope to resell at $15. Also he may not "underwrite" but instead merely agree to use his best efforts to sell. Let us, however, suppose that he does sell all the securities. The money is turned over to you. You are now running a corporation.

## The Corporation

Once the enterprise reaches the corporate form methods of financing become more standardized and it will pay to understand the main forms of financing. We deal here with finance and postpone for the moment the general problems of management, that is, of operating and controlling a large corporation. Corporations, it is enough to know, are theoretically run by their presidents "controlled" by a board of directors "elected" by the stockholders. In fact the real seat of power may be located in any one of several different places. And in the small, close-held corporation, the whole apparatus is largely a formality. Let us, however, at this point merely go on to examine how the corporation raises money and the various types of securities which corporations can issue before we close our outline of the firm. These securities take many different forms and are capable of almost endless complication. However, they come under three main heads: bonds, preferred stock, and common stock.

### How Corporations Attract Savings: Rights of Security Holders

A bond is really a promissory note in which the corporation issuing the bond promises to return the bondholder's money after a certain number of years (when the bond matures) as well as to pay the owner of the bond a definite amount of income every year. This income is called "interest." The bondholder is in a relatively secure position because he has first claim on the earnings of the corporation. That is, holders of preferred and common stock cannot receive anything until the bondholders have received the interest due them. In fact, interest on bonds must be paid whether the corporation has the income to do so or not. (If you are wondering how a firm might pay interest when it has lost money, you will be happy to hear that corporations, like other firms, keep some of their assets in the form of cash or securities which can be sold and used to pay the bondholders.) In case the interest payments are not met the bondholders can declare the bonds due and "foreclose their mortgage"—that is, they can begin legal steps to go against the assets of the corporation and, if the amounts are insufficient, to have it declared bankrupt. When bankruptcy occurs the bondholders have first claim on the assets of the corporation after certain wages and taxes have been paid. But frequently this prior claim on assets is not too meaningful, because if the firm is dissolved and the assets are sold their total value may not equal the amount which the bondholders originally paid for the bonds and expenses of the liquidation. Often, also, there are many different bond issues each with special claims on particular pieces of property. Elaborate problems of "priority" and division of the assets may then occur.

The next main type of security is preferred stock. Preferred stock gives the holder a claim to annual income equal to a specified percentage of the value stated on the security ("face value" or some definite amount of money). But of course the owner of preferred stock does not receive the income due him unless the bondholders receive their interest first. Usually, if the preferred stockowner does not receive the income due him, no lesser claims (such as those of the common stock discussed below) can receive any income until the back payments on the preferred are made in full. When the preferred stock has such a priority it is called "cumulative preferred stock," because the dividends owed accumulate over the years and the common stockholders get nothing until all the accumulated dividends for previous years on the preferred stock are paid. In addition to having first claim on the income of the corporation after the interest on the bonds has been paid, the preferred stockholders have first claim on the assets of the corporation, after the bondholders, in case of reorganization or dissolution of the firm.

After the bondholders and the owners of preferred stock come, as we have already seen, the common stockholders. They do not have the same assurances which the owners of bonds or preferred stocks enjoy. The common stockowner is the last to get income and the last to share in the assets of the corporation should it get into difficulties. On the other hand, we have already seen, the stockholders do have the control.

But common stocks are risky investments because of what is known as "trading on the equity." Trading on the equity means in effect that the common stockholder (often called "the equity") is made to bear most of the risk as compared with bondholders and holders of preferred stock. For example, if the total interest on a corporation's outstanding bonds is $5,000 and the total payments for dividends on the preferred stock is also $5,000, and the firm makes but $10,000 in that year, then the common stockholders will not get a cent. But if next year the firm makes $20,000, and all the corporation's earnings are paid out as dividends, then the common stockholders will receive income of $10,000. Yet if, in the following year, the corporation should fall back to earning only $10,000, the common stockholders would again get nothing. In this example you can see how trading on the equity creates a situation where a fluctuation in the earnings of a corporation causes a much greater fluctuation in the dividends received by the common stockholders.

This discussion of trading on the equity shows one reason why corporations often prefer issuing relatively large amounts of bonds and preferred stock compared to common stock. Because the risk attached to the ownership of bonds and preferred stock is less than that pertaining to common stock, a corporation will not need to offer the potential investors as high rates of return on their investments as they would have to show if they were trying to sell common stock.

In addition to the advantage of not having to show as high a rate of return when selling bonds and preferred stock, we should also note that an existing group of stockholders will avoid sharing the voting privileges in the corporation if they merely sell bonds and preferred stock. The fewer the common shares outstanding, the fewer votes are needed to control the corporation. For if strangers buy additional new stock, this will weaken the control of those who already have shares. The problem of control may be of great importance when an existing corporation wishes to expand its operations but finds itself short of funds. If the existing stockholders want to maintain control of the corporation, they will not want to issue more common stock, for then they might be outvoted. The alternative is to issue bonds and preferred stock, though sometimes a special security called "nonvoting common stock" is issued.

Against the advantages of being able to sell bonds at a lower rate of expected return, and of avoiding a sharing of control, lies the fact that the interest on the bonds is a fixed charge and that when the business has a poor year those interest payments must be met or the firm will get into trouble—possibly leading even to dissolution. Such problems are quite important to the management, who may lose their jobs altogether. In consequence a corporation heavily burdened with fixed claims for bond interest may be seriously hampered where risks need to be run. On the other hand interest in bonds is a deductible expense which may reduce the net "income" of the corporation for tax purposes, and put it in a lower tax bracket.

## "Smith's Grow-Well"
### Balance Sheet (in dollars)
### Dec. 31, 1964

| Assets | | Liabilities and Proprietorship | |
|---|---|---|---|
| *Current Assets* | | *Current Liabilities* | |
| Cash | 40,000 | Accounts Payable | 40,000 |
| Inventory | 120,000 | Notes Payable | 50,000 |
| | | *Long-term Liabilities* | |
| *Fixed Assets* | | Bonds Outstanding | 100,000 |
| Equipment | 260,000 | | |
| (less allowance for depreciation) | | *Proprietorship* | |
| Buildings | 180,000 | Preferred Stock | 100,000 |
| (less allowance for depreciation) | | Common Stock | 200,000 |
| Land | 60,000 | *Retained Earnings* | 170,000 |
| | 660,000 | | 660,000 |

## Summary

In the course of this chapter we have followed through the financing, growth, and development of a single enterprise. The aim has been to present the forms of industrial organization in terms of the *problems* which call them forth. Just as we have sketched the problem of social growth, as a whole, so also have we tried to show the usual types of business activity in the light of the growth process. But now it is time to draw together the threads of our analysis. Let us aim at a final summary and description of the problems of the economic decision unit before we begin to study the analyses and tools which economic theory has made available for handling these problems.

# Managerial Economics:
# A Summary and an Introduction

Throughout the preceding chapter we took for granted the growth of our sample firm. We described some of the problems which this growth raised in obtaining money, we vaguely mentioned the fact that the founder of the firm had a "good general idea," and we touched upon some of the problems of finance and "control"—how the man who originated the idea might act to retain direction of the project. But we said very little about the problems faced in the internal management of the enterprise. We just assumed that correct decisions were somehow being made.

### From Management to Theory

It is time to do something more specific. We need to learn a little of the problems of the decision unit for two reasons. First, in the general pattern of this book we have seen that in all societies to some extent, and in American society especially, general expansion in most cases comes about only through decisions by individual units to expand. Why does any decision unit decide to expand? Clearly we must know something of the reasoning that leads to such a decision even when we are trying to predict total output. Second, economic tools are apt to seem extremely remote and abstract if we do not first see something of their practical application. Economic analysis or "theory" was not just dreamed up in an armchair; on the contrary it was built up, among other reasons, for dealing with precisely the problems of "firm" policy, including expansion, which are here involved. Accordingly, this chapter on managerial economics will bridge the gap between individual production decisions and general growth and also will show, practically, some of the down-to-earth questions which economic theory tries to solve.

### The Economic Production Decision Unit

An economic production decision unit, whether it be a capitalist firm, or a socialist guild, planning board, or other productive unit, can be thought of in the following terms: An organization in which human beings come together to use "labor" to operate "plant" to process "materials" into final "output." Our description fits such varied units as "Smith's Grow-Well" Company, the Tennessee Valley Authority, and a Russian collective farm. It is general enough to apply to all economic activity save purely personal and family consumption. Of course there are some decision units, such as planning boards, whose only output is decisions themselves. In such cases it is primarily information which is being processed by "labor"—of many sorts and names—into decisions, or conclusions, or forecasts. Sometimes the durable equipment of "plant" of such a unit may not be very important—though the rise of computers of all sorts has changed this picture greatly. Nevertheless, our formula of *labor* working on *plant* to process *materials* into *output* is a universal one, and as we turn it over in our minds we will see that it implies five basic problems for all units: namely, *what* to produce, *how* to produce, how *much* to produce, who *directs* production, authority and transfer, how to deal with *other* units. Let us review them in turn.

## What to Produce

The first thing each decision unit has to do is to decide what to produce. Clearly you cannot run your company if you do not know what you are making, nor could a collective farm get along very well if it did not know what it was growing. In some socialist states, decisions as to who shall make what are reached by a board at the top, which also decides upon quotas to be aimed for, and production schedules for each individual plant. Such minute supervision, however, is far from universal. The socialist manager is sometimes granted wide discretion. Yet the widest reaches of socialist management are nothing compared to the enormous range of choices confronting the usual capitalist business. The capitalist business will not merely be trying to meet a production target or only producing a standard good. On the contrary it will probably be trying to differentiate its goods from others, to invent new and "improved" types, or to start wholly new products, if that seems reasonable.

## How to Produce

Furthermore, just as there is a vast range of choice in what to produce, so also there is an enormous range of possible methods of production. Here too the economic unit under socialism frequently has its methods set from above, though it is difficult to tie down the local organization completely, since "emergencies" will occur. But in matters of production, also, the most independent socialist unit seems circumscribed compared to the capitalist manager. The student must not think a firm's knowledge of how to produce is limited to the method actually in use today. The method in use today is only the particular one, out of many *known* alternatives, which seems desirable at a given time and with given circumstances and expectations. A change in prices, or in the type of raw material, or in wages, or in taxes can change the method very quickly. We will have much more to say about this later on.

## How Much to Produce

Again we cannot think that each plant has one, mechanically set, volume of production. In business policy the capitalist firm balances alternative types of product, methods of production, and amounts of output before reaching a final decision. The socialist unit likewise, at the very least, shifts its methods to some extent as it shifts the amount to be produced. Furthermore, in neither case is the fact that people "want" more of the product—i.e., are willing to buy more of it at the present price—a guaranty that more will really be produced. Costs might rise too fast, for example.

## Who Directs Production

We see that, clearly, a lot of decisions have to be made. The next question is, Who is to make them? In some types of socialist theory a great deal is said about "worker participation," sometimes even of "worker management." The effect of such schemes, in practice, is much as if a ship were to be sailed by a perpetual committee of the whole crew. On a quiet pond, and in good weather, "total" participation might indeed work; but on the ocean, if the crew had to sit around and debate each order before anything were done, the ship would have a good chance of being sunk by a sudden hurricane. Economic life, especially in a growing, changing society, presents similar emergencies. Every time people have tried to abolish management and authority, practical experience has forced them to reinvent it—though sometimes under another name—in order, among other things, to make quick adaptation possible. European socialist and Russian experience show this overwhelmingly.

## Authority and Transfer

There is a great range of organizational possibilities, varying from place to place, as to what types of authority can be permitted and how much, but in *some* form the problem is universal and vital. Ortega, a famous philosopher, put the matter as follows: "The problem of commanding and obeying is the decisive one in any society. When there is doubt as to who should command and who should obey all else goes ill." The orthodox capitalist solution, now being considerably attacked by the unions, is authority limited by transfer. In other words, the typical capitalist decision-maker has full technological and personnel authority *within* his organization. But his possible caprice is limited by the fact that nobody is forced to work for him, and if he behaves in an unpopular way he will find it hard or impossible to secure efficient labor. On the other hand, the manager, under centralized socialism of the usual Russian or Chinese type, has in actual fact much more power over the worker than his capitalist counterpart. For in the first place the Communist manager's decisions can scarcely be questioned by the rank and file. In most cases, so-called meetings are more to tell the worker what has been decided than really to consult him. Next, movement out of a given plant without the manager's consent is extremely difficult. To be sure, the Russians, like all previous rulers, have found that even the most dictatorial government cannot wholly overlook morale. If, for example, you try to kick men into working, you will probably soon find that you have more men doing the kicking than doing the work. Problems like these bring up the whole "human relations" question, which is of the greatest practical importance. We will return to it later in this book.

### How to Deal with Other Units: The Strategy of External Relations

One would think that in talking of what to produce, how to produce, how much to produce, and who should have authority, we had brought out a sufficiently complicated set of problems for any single economic unit. In fact there remains another set of difficulties often even more important in practice: the strategy of dealing with other units. A capitalist decision unit, we will see, sets its price not just with reference to its own costs but also by what other producers are charging. Capitalist businesses set their production plans, for example, by considering in part what others are doing or what a given unit *thinks* others will do. Again the questions of how much a given unit will spend on advertising, what its wages will be, how much outlay on research it thinks desirable—all are largely decided by reference to external "market" forces and how a given business feels its competitors will behave.

You might think that socialist decision units would not be so concerned with interunit strategy. At first glance it might seem that they would obey passively the orders of the central bureau. But Russian and other socialist experience does not bear out this view. It is true that a socialist state has usually much less business advertising. The squares of East Berlin are "decorated" with political slogans—not neon-light advertising. Personal wealth accumulation is also less important, though Russia, for example, allows wide differences in both income and inheritance. But in place of the strategy of wealth, one finds under socialism an immense increase in the strategy of power. Different types of product and different lines of activity compete for scarce materials while administrators, as we saw in Chapter II, compete for scarce jobs, for high position (and its perquisites), for decorations, and for "conspicuous service." The two lines of action intersect. Promotion of a state servant, for example, may depend upon his convincing the higher powers that the industry he administers should be allowed to expand, and therefore be allotted more materials. More unpleasantly, a failure to meet an output target, once it is set, may quite literally mean exile or death to the administrator. Confronted with the possibility of Siberia or execution, Soviet managers have indulged in every sort of intrigue, theft, kidnapping, and falsification to carry out, or seem to carry out, the required task. The socialist decision unit is thus led to put a good deal of time on promotion activity; and even the lobbyist, the "know-it-all" contact man, the representative in the capital of the manager in the provinces, has reappeared in Russia.

## It All Happens Together

So brief an outline of administrative and organizational problems is clearly no more than a sketch to start the reader thinking. One thing, however, must always be remembered. You must not conclude that there are five separate and distinct sets of decisions, which are separately made. Not at all! At one and the same time the decision unit in any system will be balancing together all the choices we have been describing of products, labor organization, prices, policy, advertising, strategy, and so on. The capitalist unit is seldom called upon, for example, to decide in isolation whether or not to increase its advertising budget. No indeed. In practice, the problem usually will appear as follows: Shall a thousand dollars be spent on introducing a new product, or designing a new plant, or buying more advertising space, or trying out a new material, or training men in a new skill, or complaining about one's competitor, say, to the Federal Trade Commission; or, to give a socialist sample, to take precious hours for a trip to Moscow to present one's claim for extra materials? All such problems come up together and are evaluated in one single decision. It is only in theoretical description that we can deal with them separately.

## Practical Examples of the Economics of Business Management

We pass now from a broad, general catalog of management problems to specific difficulties of management in a market economy. In other words, we step from general questions of social organization to "Smith's Grow-Well." "Smith's Grow-Well," as part of a general process of moving change, is going to have to make some of the decisions we have just talked about. Suppose you are Smith's manager. How will you make these decisions? What questions will you have to ask? What tools has economic theory worked out to help in answering these questions? In this chapter we will not actually describe the particular economic tools, but what we will do is to show some of the situations that set men to thinking about them, and some of the conditions in which economic analysis can be applied.

## How Much to Charge

Strange as it may seem, there are some businesses in which the problem of how much to charge never comes up. In such businesses prices are set in mass markets over which the individual producer has no control, and he is obliged to take what the market gives him. Of course, the government may intervene to try to stabilize such markets, with what results we will see later in this book. But even with government "stabilization" the individual producer is still obliged (legally, anyhow) to take the market price if he sells at all. He does not have any problem on setting one of his own. Markets like these exist in cattle, in cotton, in wheat, and in many other agricultural staples. However, once we move into industry and into merchandising, such businesses become extremely rare. It would seem likely that this has always been the case. Even in medieval villages, or later on in the eighteenth century, local prices were much more the result of custom and local attachments than of any impersonal laws of supply and demand. Of course, outside forces would operate in the long run, but for immediate purposes prices were scarcely the result of automatic markets. With most businesses today, in the market economy, price is the result of at least two forces—the outside general condition of the market and the inside special judgment of the particular firm. The decision unit "sets" its price and then watches how it works out. If the manager finds the price has been too high, he will shade it a bit; or if he thinks it is too low, he will try to raise it. But the adjustment is not merely automatic. There is tremendous room for personal judgment and, in modern society and probably throughout the past, business units could be ruined at the start by bad price decisions. Let us begin by taking practical examples from "Smith's Grow-Well."

Suppose you are now back at the early stages of your fertilizer business. You have made up your first packages of your product and you are about to try to sell it. The question is, What price will you ask? Of course, there will be some sort of going price for fertilizer in general, but you are not yet in mass production. Also, you are probably in the "small lot" retail market at first and selling more to garden clubs and housewives than to big farmers. Furthermore, your product either is, or is claimed to be, something different from standard fertilizer. Suppose you have made up a batch of your product, and persuaded a retailer to carry it on his shelves. What price tag shall you tell him to add? This is indeed a vital decision since if you make it incorrectly you may ruin your business before it ever gets started. How would you go about it?

### "Common-sense" Price Calculation

Let us give an example. The common-sense way might seem to be as follows: You have made 500 packages. Well, would it not be sensible, first, just to figure out what the labor cost is that you have paid, what you have paid for chemicals, and add a little for the cost of your own time? Add these figures up, and you might think you had the total cost of your first batch. Now, then, divide this total cost by 500, that is, by the number of units which you have produced, and wouldn't you have the unit cost? Surely, what we have said sounds very sensible, does it not? Let us then add 15 per cent to each unit for profits before taxes. Presto, you have the proper price for your product. The job seems to be done. But think a bit. Have you really done it the right way?

However sensible our common-sense account might sound, a man trained in economics would spot it, at once, as miles away from the facts. In the first place, the costs have not been figured adequately. We will come back to actual cost questions later. But a much more serious omission is involved. What would hit the economically trained man in the eye is that in figuring out how much to charge we assumed that we only had to make and decide on a price for 500 bottles. We have not considered what would happen to the number or amount of units sold if we varied our price. A lower price might increase sales so much that it would make it possible for us to use different and cheaper methods of production. Thus, if we consider the possibility of larger sales at the lower price, a lower price might actually turn out to yield the larger profit. There is a reverse side to this. Sometimes, if a businessman makes his price high, a product will go over better in a small "prestige" market than if it were cheap. Some consumers in these small markets seem really to like to pay out money. Now in either case, there is a tool of economic analysis called "the elasticity of demand," which, if you had heard of it, would at least have reminded you of the possible reactions, on amount, of shifts in price. We will discuss elasticity in the next chapter.

### Cost and Policy

We pass from demand to cost. "Smith's Grow-Well" is probably not big enough yet to be considering the more refined questions of cost and output. But even with your first 500 packages there is one cost which you have obviously omitted. You forgot to say anything about the machinery. Nothing in this world lasts forever or remains up-to-date; and though our first venture in the back of a garage will not be likely to have very complicated equipment, still something has to be said for what is called "depreciation" and "obsolescence"—wearing out, and becoming out of date. In other words, in computing our costs, we have to allow for the fact that the machinery and equipment is wearing out or becoming out of date. Unless we add a little more to the price to permit us to buy new and better machinery as the old wears out, or is outclassed by new types, we will find ourselves after a certain number of years suddenly confronted with bankruptcy.

### Opportunity Costs

There is another common-sense cost that has to be considered before you decide that you are really making a profit. Suppose your neighbor comes in and sees you working away at your new fertilizer combination. He might say, "Look here, why are you messing around with this stuff when you could take an excellent job downtown for six hundred dollars a month?" Your neighbor might not be a trained economist, but he would, nevertheless, be bringing out, in this question, one of the fundamental doctrines of economic thought—the idea of "opportunity costs." For example, if you find after you have run your "Smith's Grow-Well" for a few months that you have about $300 a month left after all expenses, you might think, and your books might show, that you have made that much profit. But to the economist you might actually be losing money. If your neighbor is right and you could be making $600, then your $300 would not be a profit but, in terms of economic alternatives, a loss.

### Sales Volume, Cost, and Profit

But now comes the problem of volume. We have already learned that the aim of a capitalist firm, and of many socialist ones, too, for that matter, is to make a profit. But a mere increase in sales does not necessarily mean an increase in profits. Costs have to be considered, too. If we do not think about costs, we might be like the celebrated young man who bought some shoes for $12 a pair and sold them for $6 a pair. When his friends told him he could not get rich that way, he said, "Oh, but think of the turnover." While increased sales volume helps cost, we shall find there are limits to how far it can be pushed and still yield adequate profit.

### Alternative Production Possibilities and the Cost Curve

The problem of output and costs soon becomes exceedingly complicated. One factor is the problem of choosing what method of production to use. One can scarcely deal with such production decisions without getting into the problem of forecasting. For example, suppose someone says that if you buy a double supply of one of the chemicals that you are using he can give you a very much lower price. But suppose this chemical gradually loses its strength? You clearly have to decide how fast you will need to use it. Let us next consider a less obvious problem. You find at first that you need to combine three chemicals and that they are always used in the same amount. You find also that you need a certain amount of labor and that it, too, tends about to double in amount and cost as you double output. Can you go ahead on that basis? Can you necessarily buy on the assumption that you will always have the same percentage increase in labor costs, and in the quantities demanded for each chemical? If you do, you will probably be wrong. For, in fact, you may find after a while that you cease to need quite so much of one chemical as you have been buying, and you may also find that you need either more labor time or less for the additional output. Here we encounter the problem of "constant returns to scale" which we talked about earlier in Chapter II. Economics has tools of analysis to be applied here, too. They are called "cost curves," and from them we see certain rules as to the behavior of cost. You will need to learn much more about them before you can make intelligent decisions.

## Long Run versus Short Run

Again, costs are not merely "short run" but also "long run." Furthermore, the effects of an increase in the scale of an industry may be quite unexpected. Suppose "Smith's Grow-Well" has so tremendously expanded that you are operating a small mine for some needed material, far out in the jungle. There may be almost no communication with civilization and except for the occasional flights that you make in your own plane, and the long and extensive hauling of the product by land over almost nonexistent roads, there is no communication whatsoever. But suppose that the product catches on and that more and more of it is demanded. If you are flying out enough materials, commercial airlines will come in or, perhaps, even a railroad. More people will settle near the mine. A village will spring up and soon there will be a post office. As all these things occur, many costs will become cheaper, for transportation will be much less difficult. This is only a sample of how costs change as output changes.

## What to Produce and Marginal Cost

How to produce leads to what to produce, for all these decisions, as we have already said, appear together. Repeat the assumption that "Smith's Grow-Well" is flourishing and the name has become well-known. Suppose, as we said in Chapter IV, someone suggests that you add a new line, "Smith's Kill-Well," a weed killer. Right away you must figure costs. At first you may find that practically all the needed items are being stocked by you already in connection with your other product. You find that to produce 500 cans of "Kill-Well" you will need to spend only $100 extra on chemicals and $50 on labels—you will not, let us say, have to change the container style. Yet you think you can sell the product for a dollar a can. It looks as if you will take in $500 while only adding $150 to costs. Clear profit, it would seem, of $350 and well worth it. Yet experience, analysis, and the longer view add many more points to be considered.

First of all, there are taxes—how much of the extra income will go to the government? Also, as we saw, depreciation and obsolescence must be allowed for. But there are more fundamental questions. Is it right to charge all these costs to "Grow-Well" alone and give "Kill-Well" a free ride? Ought not the overhead be charged to both? Leaving aside overhead, won't it take some labor to make the new product? The job can scarcely be done by the men you now have—if they were fully and efficiently employed before. The chances are, therefore, that even if you need no immediate outlay you will need to pay more for labor, either new men or overtime. Add $50. Still that leaves a wide margin for profit. Probably you will put in the line. You decide to expand.

But again, expansion and the long view bring in more problems. "Kill-Well" catches on wonderfully. More and more it crowds into your space and plant. More and more labor is called for. Because the plant is crowded, work is less efficient. In economic terms, "marginal cost" is rising. Here is another economic concept to be considered. What is the addition to costs as output expands? Economics again tries to handle this with a special "curve."

It looks as if "Kill-Well" is no longer a paying proposition. But here economic cost theory would say that it is time to reconsider the whole setup. You would be foolish to drop "Kill-Well" just because it crowds your garage. What about building a factory or renting one? Similarly, what about trying to make, or have made, a "market study" to find out why "Kill-Well" is doing so well, and also which line is most popular in the long run, and whether more outlay on advertising would pay off? Questions like these for small firms are the forerunners of the elaborate research-and-development outlays of larger more technical-minded enterprises. We will see more about this shortly.

## Who Shall Decide? Management and Wage Theory

Even with all the questions named so far we have not yet begun to exhaust the relationships between the tools of pure economic theory and ordinary business policy. Let us take, for example, the question of management. As "Smith's Grow-Well" becomes larger and as you add other lines, how shall you manage it? Who is to do the deciding? Would it be most efficient to have everything run from the central office and to have one over-all set of accounts that deals with the whole enterprise? Some American businesses have obtained vast size under this form of administration. Yet in a great many cases, after so long a time, it has been found that that is not really the way to do things. In the General Motors Corporation, for example, it was discovered that greater over-all efficiency was obtained if one set up a sort of competition inside the firm. The various operations of the corporation were put under separate heads who were allowed a very large degree of independent responsibility, and special accounts were kept for each type of product. For example, if you tried to run all of "Smith's Grow-Well" from New York, you might find yourself making decisions on the telephone which had little real knowledge of the actual situation. Most large American businesses, therefore, now use the General Motors method and divide their operations into independent units coordinated at the top.

But let us turn next to wage theory. In the early days of "Smith's Grow-Well," you hire such men as you can get, at the going wage rate for casual labor. But as your company becomes more and more prosperous and employs a larger and larger number of people, you will find it necessary to make your wage contracts more regular and specific. Suppose your men strike for a guaranteed annual wage. That is to say, they ask that they be guaranteed earnings of a certain fixed amount during the year whether you are employing them or not. Should you accept this proposition or should you not? Economic theory, we will see, has much to say concerning decisions of this sort. We will discuss some of them in the sections on "distribution theory," and others will come later in the chapters on labor problems.

## Broader Problems: Forecasting and Business Cycles

Finally, we do not need to limit the usefulness of economic theory to business simply to the economic theory of the organization of the firm. There is another section of economics which will occupy about a third of this book and which deals with the movement of the business cycle and the theory of general employment and unemployment. Many a businessman who is good at controlling conditions in his own business and who knows his local market may nevertheless go broke because he does not understand the general movement of the business cycle. Suppose, for example, that sales of your "Smith's Grow-Well" business have increased phenomenally, that many people are building new houses in your town, and that things are generally very prosperous. You decide, therefore, to build a new plant. But suppose that your son, who has just come home from college where he took a course in elementary economics, brings up the following points. He says that the outflow of gold from the United States is very considerable and that the Federal Reserve Board has recently raised its rate of interest and its reserve requirements. What in the world have such abstruse things to do with your decision to expand your plant making fertilizer? Strange as it may seem, they may have a great deal to do with the wisdom of the policy you have adopted.

## Summary

In this chapter we did not try to cover the whole immense field of managerial theory and organization of the firm. All we tried to do was to bring out a few practical problems which would serve as an introduction to the fascinating questions which the tools of economic analysis were created to solve. This chapter first gave a very general review of the problems of the production decision unit, under socialism or capitalism. We next went on to more specific, largely market, questions. What price is most profitable? What costs should be remembered? How does output affect cost? How shall authority be channeled in our firm? What wage is "fair"? Which way is general expansion going to go? Will there be unemployment? Many chapters must be covered before we can give even tentative full answers to these problems. Yet in the next section we can at least learn the elementary tools which economics uses to solve them.

# Part II

# THE ECONOMIC THEORY OF PRICE, COST AND DEMAND

✦✦✦ VI ✦✦✦

## Demand, Supply, and Market Price: A General View

We start now on the task of understanding some of the techniques which economic analysis has worked out for the prediction and calculation of economic adjustment. At first it might seem that these tools could not be precise or reliable, for we have just learned that a growing economy is one of constant change and movement. Apparently the necessary fixed assumptions called for by, say, mathematics would be lacking. However, economics has come to grips with this problem, and solved it in a way which is frequently fairly satisfactory. The tool which economics uses most is the "model." We must see what "models" are.

**Economic Models**

By a model we mean setting up a problem in terms of certain fixed assumptions of behavior and relationship, and asking what will result if the assumptions continue to hold. It may be assumed, for example, in a "market model" that men are going to behave according to certain rules, that the prices are given at such and such a figure, and that the supplies produced are of such and such an amount. The economist might then ask how much would be sold under these conditions. Much more complicated models can be worked out. One might assume not fixed prices but fixed *rates of change* of prices, and so on through boundless complications. There is only one assumption from which a model can never escape, which is that the basic conditions will not change or will change only in ways which are allowed for. This "fixity" of basic relations is, of course, restrictive, but the student must not think that there is anything unusual or unscientific about the use of models as such. On the contrary, all sciences use them; the development of physics, for example, has been greatly helped by the use of very complicated models, using extraordinary assumptions. The question is: Can the model be applied to real problems without seriously varying the fundamental assumptions on which it is based? How does economics handle this problem?

### Types of Models: Part versus Whole—Equilibrium versus Dynamic

Economics uses two main types of models: first, those applying to parts of the economy, say a given individual or firm, or a given industry or product in isolation; next, those applying to the economy as a whole or to all the people in a market, rather than to one person. Basic assumptions are made regarding given conditions and the workings of the individual units, and the logically inferred behavior of the model is followed out. In the most usual economic model, conditions are assumed which lead to a condition of general adjustment called "equilibrium." When such an adjustment or equilibrium has been reached, the model will show no further movement; and unless some new force is assumed to come in from outside, the adjustment is supposed to be permanent. But not all models are "equilibrium" models. Some show "endless," dynamic fluctuations. Either way, how can restricted models of this sort be applied to the real world?

### Applying Models

The case of the partial model, that relating to a single firm or industry or product, is theoretically the easiest to solve. For frequently one can realistically assume that a firm or product or industry is sufficiently unimportant as not to disturb the economy as a whole by its movement; and also, of course, there can be intervals in real life when the general movements of the economy will not happen to affect a given small firm or industry. Again, even when we are dealing with a very important industry, we can sometimes realistically assume that, during a short interval, changes in its behavior will not have affected the economy as a whole, though this assumption becomes increasingly difficult as the industry becomes more and more important. However, the most serious problem for the economist concerns models of the behavior of the whole economic system. These, in turn, may either relate to long-run trends or show continuing fluctuation of the "dynamic" type already referred to. "Trend" models, assuming the basic quantities and relations chosen apply to the facts, can often be used with some realism. Small, short-run changes do not affect them. Short-run dynamic models, however, are very tricky, as sudden changes in expectations, or techniques used, can upset them entirely. The assumptions of the model will cease to correspond with the facts, which makes the model useless for practical purposes. But there is another type of general model which is especially hard to handle. That is the model of "stationary general equilibrium."

## Stationary General Equilibrium

We will find later in the chapters on distribution that understanding of basic forces shaping different types of income requires us from time to time to assume a model of a society in which no change whatever is going on for the whole system. Every square peg in it has found its appropriate square hole, and every round peg its round hole. All adjustments have been made throughout the system, and there is no further motion. Some economists have worked out elaborate standards of arrangement and rearrangement for stationary general equilibriums of this sort. However, it should be clear that, in the solving of practical problems, the model of stationary general equilibrium is not very useful. Since a true general equilibrium requires a complete adjustment, while the fact of growth requires continuing change, it follows that the two ideas are, to a considerable extent, contradictory. Again, the word "equilibrium" is also used, we shall see later, in studying *national* income to apply to an instantaneous balance of saving and investment plans in a dynamic model; but this so-called "equilibrium" is a widely different concept from the usual idea of a stable adjustment, which barring outside disturbance, would be permanent. Let us turn now, however, from models in general to the study of specific models, and how they are used in predicting and calculating economic adjustment. We may begin with consumption.

## The Analysis of Consumption

The analysis of consumer demand is one of the most important parts of economic theory. Consumption is important for two reasons. First of all, there would be no point in producing anything if it were not expected directly or indirectly, somehow, at some point, to help satisfy a human desire. Even armament expenditure might be treated as helping to satisfy a need for "defense" or "protection." Next, the study of demand is important because, on a purely practical basis, if economic decision units do not predict the movement of consumer wants fairly accurately, they will not make intelligent decisions. Either there will be a great deal of waste from a social point of view, or the decision units will fail to keep their own firms or families running well. Accordingly, we want to know what models economics uses in attempts to predict consumer responses. As a first beginning of this task, we ask: Where do wants come from?

## Where Do Wants Come From?

There are, of course, a few basic wants with which we are born—for food of some sort, for warmth in a cool climate and coolness in a hot one, generally for some sort of covering, and generally for some sort of companionship. Many people also seem to have an inborn real need for intellectual as well as physical effort, and one could list various other examples. But even the so-called "natural" wants have a well-nigh incredible variety of ways by which they can be satisfied. A man, for example, can satisfy his hunger with dry bread. He can also satisfy it with roast beef. He might think that he has had enough of dry bread, but still feel hungry when someone brings him strawberries and cream. Thus, even our natural wants are highly various and varied. Why do we pick one form of satisfaction rather than another?

One explanation, of course, is the inherited manners and customs of the society in which we find ourselves. But anyone who reads the newspapers today will also be conscious of the fact that the American consumer is constantly being exposed to advertising campaigns to persuade him to buy item A rather than item B, or indeed, to buy something which he has never previously heard of. Knowledge of pressures like these has led some writers to think that the wants of the typical consumer are irrational products of social conditioning, and that therefore "individual" preferences deserve no respect. We cannot give a detailed discussion of so serious a question this early in the book. We will return to it in the chapter on comparative economic systems. Two points, however, may be mentioned.

## Inherited Social Wants

First of all, the mere fact that a want is inherited or customary or derived from the institutions of our forebears does not necessarily prove that it is irrational or artificial. As a great political thinker of the eighteenth century, Edmund Burke, put it, the "wisdom of our ancestors" is based upon a great deal of experience, and one would be rash to assume that everything that came down by custom was necessarily wrong. Take a modern example. When the Russian experiment first began, there was a great attack made upon the family, which was regarded as an out-of-date, bourgeois institution. Yet, within a generation, we have seen Russian manners revert to stanch puritanism, in which the sanctity of the family is strongly protected. Also, in a preceding chapter, we had occasion to speak of the rediscovery by the Russians of the convenience of money, even in a planned society. The Russians have also rediscovered the need for management, for incentives, for discipline in schools, and for many other supposedly arbitrary institutions.

### Forming New Wants

The second point, that concerning new wants or advertising, is even more complicated; but there is one aspect of it that can be spoken of here. Many people talk as if the mere emergence of new wants was, in itself, something bad. But the fact is that the human being can never keep from wanting! He can only change the nature of his wants. Suppose an individual decides to become a hermit and "get away from it all," living in a desert on the minimum of food and water. Has such a man really stopped wanting? Not at all. He has merely substituted a new want—"understanding" or "enlightenment" or "salvation"—for, say, roast beef. A very great economist and philosopher has, consequently, defined progress as "not satisfaction but better wants." Furthermore, we have seen that, even if there were no advertising, as output rises the pattern of wants will change. Thus the mere fact that wants have changed is not in itself bad; the question is, What kind of wants are they?

In this chapter, we are concerned with the down-to-earth problem of predicting consumer behavior. We can therefore, for present purposes, simply conclude that wants are partly natural, partly inherited, and partly the result of the persuasion of businessmen through advertising. All we want to do here is to learn more precisely what tools economics has worked out for forecasting and calculating them. We will begin by assuming that the wants we are studying are not immediately responsive to cash propaganda by the business we are studying, but that they are wants already independently existing in the mind of the consumer. Later on, as our model becomes more dynamic, we will begin to relate changes in wants to changes in advertising. But at this stage all we need to know is that, with growth, wants will change anyway. Why is that?

### Diminishing Marginal Utility

We start out with two tremendously important observed facts. First of all, it has been observed over and over and over again that nobody spends all of his income on one satisfaction. At some point, even the dope fiend takes a little time off to eat. The second point is the one just mentioned—that as output rises, the pattern of wants will change. How can we explain these two known facts?

Economics helps to do so by reference to the principle called "diminishing marginal utility." By "utility" we mean the feeling or satisfaction yielded to an individual by a particular good. It is, in itself, an entirely private and subjective personal experience. Nobody ever saw a "utility" or directly observed it diminishing, though all of us have felt both things. The law of diminishing marginal utility is therefore something economists have deduced from their own feelings and from watching the behavior of others. The basic idea is best given by a concrete example. Suppose you like chocolate nut fudge sundaes. Somebody says he will treat you to as many as you want. Wonderful! You start right in. Yet, the result may be somewhat disappointing. The first sundae will be delicious. The second, good. The third, just fair. And the fourth, if you have lasted that long, will probably make you sick. Experiences like these are what the economists express as "diminishing marginal utility." The word "marginal" means the satisfaction added by the additional or last unit consumed—in our example, the last sundae. Economists and psychologists have found that, for practically all forms of satisfaction, as a stimulus is repeated, it begins to lose its keenness. Like our chocolate sundaes, the last or marginal stimulus of something, which began by being very pleasant, may not yield any satisfaction at all, or may even be intensely disagreeable.

However, before we apply the law of diminishing marginal utility too broadly, we have to understand the qualifications under which it works. First of all, utility will only be certain to diminish if all other circumstances such as the person's taste, income, surroundings, and so on, remain the same. Next, the law holds only for a reasonable time period—that is to say, usually it operates only over relatively short periods. For example, some people eat bacon and eggs for breakfast three hundred and sixty-five days in the year, and seem to enjoy one breakfast as much as another. Does this fact contradict the idea of diminishing marginal utility? Not at all. The reason for no contradiction is that each should be considered as a more or less isolated or separate experience. Diminishing marginal utility, however, would apply quickly enough if anybody attempted to eat three hundred and sixty-five eggs and pieces of bacon at once!

### The Consumption Pattern

Yet diminishing marginal utility does help to explain why consumer wants and expenditures show a pattern of outlay among different goods, and not merely a total expenditure on some one good. Most of us have limited funds, we must remember, and all of us have many alternative possible uses for our money —alternative possible satisfactions. Suppose we start out to satisfy the most keenly felt want. We begin to buy the good which satisfies that want, and as we buy more and more of it the *marginal* utility from each additional purchase of the good drops. But in the meantime there are other wants and other goods to be bought, and *their* marginal utility will not be dropping. We feel less hungry, say, and so we begin to be more conscious that we are cold.

### The Economic Theory of General Outlay

Economists have worked out rules as to the way in which a customer should spend his money, supposing that his income is fixed and that his tastes and other circumstances are not changing. The consumer, under such conditions, should so distribute his purchases that the "utility" derived from the money spent on the last unit bought of each product should be *proportional* to its price. Some things cost more than others so that the exact sum spent is not the same. But theoretically the marginal utilities, from the marginal dollars spent, should be proportional to their prices. When such an adjustment has been reached the consumer is said to have "maximized" his possible utility. Very elaborate analysis can be made here but it is sufficient for us, at this point, merely to get the basic idea. Furthermore, as things keep shifting, in the real world, adjustment must keep shifting too.

Also we must not identify the "maximization" of utility through "rational" spending—which is what is meant by a consumer's "economizing"—with the state of an individual's personal happiness. A man can be a highly "rational" consumer, getting his "dollar's worth" from each dollar spent out of his paycheck, and minutely weighing relative costs—and yet be utterly miserable. Perhaps nobody loves him—or he doesn't like his work. If the writer were asked to define happiness, he would list it as *participation in a satisfactory process,* rather than as just "rational" spending. But this question, again, carries us far afield. At the moment we are merely engaged in studying the behavior of the market.

### Bread and Diamonds: The Substitution Effect—Changes in Pattern

Diminishing marginal utility, nevertheless, enables us to explain one of the oldest paradoxes in economic thought—why people pay more for some relatively useless things than for some more useful ones. Why, for example, does bread cost less than diamonds, though bread is more useful and necessary? The answer is bread can be produced more easily. Since we are, therefore, able to get more of it we carry our *marginal* spending on bread much further. Therefore our marginal utility—and the amount we are willing to pay—is much less for the last piece of bread than for the last diamond. But if diamonds could be produced with the same ease and in the same quantities as bread their marginal utility would drop much faster than bread, and they would be much cheaper.

## Change

The rule for spending applies, as we have mentioned, to a fixed income and a fixed set of surroundings. We have a more immediately practical problem to solve in a growing world. Why do wants change? Diminishing marginal utility helps here, too. Suppose, for some reason, producers raise the price of a given good. This will disturb the *relative* marginal utilities and people will tend to spend more on substitutes. For example, if the price of coffee is raised, more may be spent on tea. In a growing world the matter also works the other way. Growth seldom comes symmetrically. The supply of some goods increases faster than that of others. Yet if consumers are to absorb an increased supply of, say, coffee this must usually mean a lowering of its marginal utility relative to the price formerly charged for it. People are not going to buy all the additional supply at the old prices: probably price will have to drop. And if, as a result of the price cut, the consumer has a net money gain, a net sum unexpended, he is far more likely to buy something else, perhaps wine, whose *relative* marginal utility is *now* higher, than to keep on buying coffee. Here we see one reason why the pattern of wants constantly changes in a growing world. The *relative* marginal utilities are constantly being altered as output increases and costs are changed. Yet a further question must be asked. Suppose some omniscient planning board increased quantities of all things in the same proportion? Would the pattern of spending remain unaltered then? Not at all—there would be too much of some things, not enough of others. To understand the why of such behavior we need a more precise and practical set of economic tools. We start with the "demand curve" and the concept of "elasticity."

## The Demand Curve and the Concept of Elasticity

When we come to the demand curve and the concept of elasticity, we find ourselves learning some of the most useful economic tools so far invented. We begin with the demand curve. It will help in understanding both the demand curve itself and how it can be used if we commence with a specific problem. "Smith's Grow-Well" is a little too small to be useful to us. Let us take, instead, a group of growers of some special fruit who have set up, as they are allowed to do by the law, a cooperative market study institute for research into general market conditions. First they will want to find out what the general "demand" conditions for their product are, that is, how much would be bought at various prices. Of course these cooperative institutes often advertise for their product: "Tangeraps make you healthy," but for the moment we may suppose that they are merely trying to find out how things stand "as is." In carrying out such a study they will call in statisticians to survey the makeup of their market: Who buys "tangeraps" and where? Is the product a "prestige" one, sold in a small luxury market, or has it a broader appeal? Would the lowering of price to invade the mass market be worthwhile? On the basis of these aims and studies, careful questions will be prepared. How many more tangeraps would you buy at a price of 10 cents, 20 cents, 30 cents?

Suppose, next, that our institute has carried through its plan of interviewing, that the questions have been asked and the results tabulated: the statisticians and market analysts of the institute can draw up a schedule or curve. On one axis they might show the number of tangeraps that would be sold, at various prices. On the vertical axis they would show the alternative possible prices. We show such a schedule in Figure 1. Such a graph is called a "demand curve."

Figure 1
THE DEMAND CURVE

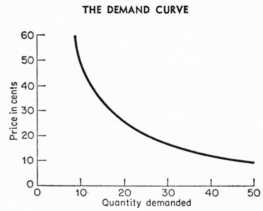

It is one of the most famous and frequently used bits of economic technique. One could learn from it, supposing it to be accurate and reliable, exactly what the effect of a change in prices would be on tangeraps sold.

*Ceteris Paribus*

From the account just given, the student will have a fair idea of what a demand curve means, but before we go further, we must stop and learn a bit of economic terminology—the meaning of the expression, *ceteris paribus*. This formidable label conveys no more than the qualifications concerning the nature of an economic model, with which we have already begun. Common sense will tell you that our curve will be reliable only if conditions did not change very much while the survey was being made. You will know, furthermore, that only as long as conditions continue to remain unchanged can the information given by the curve be trusted. Economists assume that there is no change registered in a demand curve except the two forces of price and quantity. Other things are supposed to remain equal. In other words, the income, tastes, and customs of the community remain unaltered; the prices of competing goods are not supposed to change; and so on. All these conditions are summed up in the Latin phrase, *ceteris paribus,* which means "other things being equal." We will see later on that this *ceteris paribus* assumption is a very important qualification for nearly all economic theory.

## Why Does the Curve Slope Downward?

One of the first things you will notice as you look at the curve in Figure 1 is that it slopes downward. Why should the curve slope downward? There are several forces at work. One of them is our old friend, "diminishing marginal utility." By the analysis you have just learned, you will see that the more tangeraps you eat, the less the marginal utility of the next one is likely to be. You might start out, for example, giving them to your family and eating them yourself; next, giving them to sick friends; and so on. The chances are, however, that beyond a certain point you will begin to feel that you have had enough and that it might be more pleasant to start spending money in some other way. Here we have one of the most important explanations of the slope so far as a single person goes. But the sample curve we have given did not apply to one person but to all the eaters of tangeraps in that area. We have here another, reinforcing reason for the slope. At a high price a few wealthy persons might buy tangeraps, but to reach the lower income, mass-market prices must be cut. So much for the fact of slope. Let us now try to understand the economic meaning of "demand" in general.

## The Economic Definition of Demand

By "demand" the economist means not just the amount of a good that is sold at a single or particular price, but the whole set of "simultaneous possibilities" portrayed in a demand curve. Remember that the demand curve does not in itself show any passage of time. You are not moving down from, say, $7 in March to $5 in April. The demand curve is rather a set of possibilities for March, if that is the month in which you made the survey, in which you plot all the possible repercussions on sales if prices were changed in various ways. Consequently, the demand curve must be treated as a set of simultaneous possibilities. It describes the whole state of people's sales attitudes, relative to price, for a given product at any one interval of time. It is this whole set of simultaneous possibilities expressed in the curve which the economist means by demand. For example, people often say that, because a price has been reduced, demand, by which they mean sales, has increased. But this is not good economic usage. Demand, in the economic sense, would have increased only if the whole curve had shifted upward. By a "shift" in the curve we mean some change in the fundamental data of the problem, say, in the total income of the community in our example, or some other basic force. Thus if a curve shifts upward, some force has changed which would lead people to buy more tangeraps at nearly all or most points of possible prices.

## Elasticity

So much for the general nature of the demand curve. Now we want to discuss the concept of "elasticity"—in other words, the shape of the curve and the type of behavior which it portrays. Elasticity, we have already said, is very important. In the first place, speaking practically, we shall see that it will show the result not just on sales but on gross income of a given shift in prices. But also, as a general scientific proposition, from the concept of elasticity and, as we shall see, different types of elasticity, we will know one of the reasons why the pattern of demand shifts as output rises.

In Figure 2, (a), (b), and (c), you will see three different demand curves of three differing shapes. *Very* roughly speaking, the concept of elasticity is a way of describing the shape of a given demand curve. It means, in effect, the *proportional* response of sales and gross income to price. Once a man is familiar with demand curve analysis, he can usually tell the type of elasticity of a given curve and, consequently, the likely response of sales, gross income, and price almost just by looking at the curve. Skipping complicated mathematics, we may describe the three types of elasticity by referring to the effect upon total gross income of any given price change shown on the curve. By gross income, we mean merely that costs are not being considered here, and that it is only the gross income that is reflected by the curve and not profits.

## Types of Elasticity

There are three types of elasticity. First, "unitary"; second, "inelastic"; third, "elastic." Let us describe them in turn.

*Unitary*. If a demand curve shows that, after a reduction in price, total gross income has not changed, the demand curve has a unitary elasticity at that point. If a demand curve is of unitary elasticity throughout, then gross income will be the same no matter what the price; for the response of sales to price will be such as always to yield exactly the same total. For example, if at a price of $10 five goods are sold, the gross income is $50; and if at a price of $5 ten goods are sold, the gross income will again be $50. In a demand curve which has unitary elasticity throughout, therefore, the total gross income is the same no matter what the price may be.

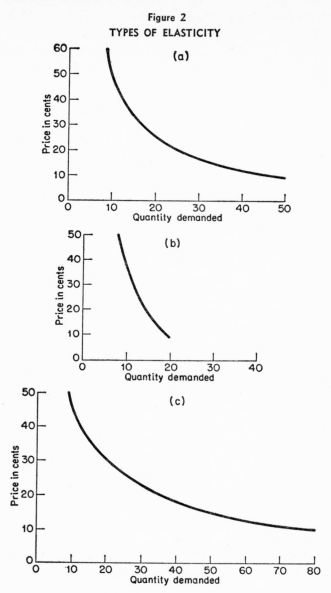

**Figure 2**
**TYPES OF ELASTICITY**

*Inelastic.* If a demand curve is shaped so that as a result of a reduction in price total gross income declines, then that curve, at that point, is said to be inelastic. For example, if at a price of $10 you sold five units, the total gross income was $50; if at a price of $8 you sold six units, your total gross income would now be $48. In other words, your total gross income would have declined. This would be an inelastic demand curve at that point.

*Elastic.* Finally, if a demand curve is shaped so that after a reduction in price total gross income has increased, that curve at that point is said to be elastic. For example, if at a price of $10 you sold five units, your total gross income would be $50; but if at a price of $8 you sold ten units, your total gross income would be $80. There would be a substantial increase, and one calls such a curve an elastic demand curve for that point.

### Changes in Elasticity

Notice, however, that we refer to the elasticity at a given point. A demand curve need not have the same elasticity throughout its entire length. On the contrary, the elasticity may change from point to point. If, for example, a demand curve turned out to be a perfectly straight line at an angle of 45 degrees, the elasticity would vary widely from point to point. The student might find it a useful exercise to try this out for himself and see why it is true.

### Summary on Demand and Elasticity: Some Practical Applications

We have now seen that a demand curve is a schedule reflecting the simultaneous possible repercussions of changes in price upon sales under given conditions, or *ceteris paribus*. We have seen that we can describe the general type of reactions under the concept of elasticity of demand, and we have outlined the three general types of elasticity. Clearly, if a business finds out that the demand for its product is elastic, then if no problems of cost are involved it will probably pay to cut price. Similarly, if the demand is inelastic and costs are otherwise satisfactory, a cut in price would not be desirable. But under what circumstances are demands elastic and inelastic?

Human nature being what it is, there are many unexplained or unexpected quirks in demand behavior; but generally speaking, demand is likely to be inelastic where the outlay on the object is small and your want is urgent, that is, there are not many good substitutes. A perfect example would be salt. Everybody needs a certain amount of salt, nobody needs much salt, and there are not many good substitutes for it.

On the other hand, demand is elastic when a small cut in price leads to a large increase in sales, or when a small rise in price leads to a large cut in sales. It is not as easy to list cases of elastic demand as inelastic demand, because the situation is apt to be more complicated. So far as price increases are concerned, the larger the amount you spend on a good, the more reluctant you will probably be to buy more of it, particularly if there are numerous other substitutes available. For a large response in sales to a small cut in price, which is the other aspect of demand, the good must be capable of extended use. Only a very little salt will give you all you need of it. But an automobile can be driven over a very wide stretch of territory; thus it is possible for the demand for automobile services to be more elastic under proper circumstances than the demand for salt. Although it must not be forgotten that the law of diminishing marginal utility holds good at some point for all commodities.

## Growth, Income Elasticity, and the Pattern of Wants

However, from the concept of demand and elasticity of demand, we now have another reason for knowing why the pattern of wants will change as output changes. Suppose that the elasticity of demand varies greatly for the various articles that make up the national output. We know that in fact this is the case. Yet suppose that the general, equal, proportional change in all types of output that we spoke of earlier were attempted. Such a change violates the *ceteris paribus* assumption of the individual demand curve. But let us say, for the moment, that the different curves are temporarily unchanged. We may suppose, further, that an increase in total output of, say, 10 per cent, is accompanied by a 10 per cent increase in money income. If the demand for some one satisfaction, say food, is inelastic, a very considerable cut in price would be needed to induce more food consumption. On the other hand, the demand for some luxury which people have always yearned for, but not been able to afford, may be very elastic. Indeed the increased income, instead of being spent on food, may cause an upward shift in the demand for that luxury. Its price may not fall—it could even rise. Just at this point, therefore, economists add another type of elasticity— income elasticity—which means the effect of an increase in society's *total* income upon purchases of a particular good, its price being unchanged. Furthermore a very little imagination will show that some consumption experts, or market analysts, will use three-dimensional calculations of income, price, and sales change, but we do not enter on such complications here. We have still a few more fundamentals to review.

## Individual Demand Curves; Firm Demand Curves; Industry Demand Curves

Our explanation so far has enabled us to learn the general idea of the demand curve and of the concept of elasticity; but we have not in our explanation clearly distinguished between three main types of demand curve. Just as there are three kinds of elasticity, so also there are three kinds of demand curves. First of all, there is the individual or personal demand curve. This tells how much each individual is willing to pay for various amounts of a commodity. Next, there is the firm demand curve, which tells how much a given firm can sell at different prices acting by itself. Finally, there is the industry demand curve, in which we take a particular product and see how much of it can be sold at various prices, paying no attention to the individual sales of the particular corporations which are in the industry, but considering the industry as a whole.

## Industry Equilibrium

But with the introduction of the industry, we are brought back to some of the basic models of economic theory; and especially to the concept of "equilibrium which we mentioned in the first sections of this chapter. We have said that when we find a given industry (that is, a set of firms making the same product) which is not being disturbed from outside to any important degree and which does not, of itself, disturb the economy, we can usually talk about an equilibrium of that industry. Provided only, furthermore, that we bear in mind the fact that these equilibriums are temporary and subject to be disturbed at any time, the concept of industry equilibrium is one of considerable value. To it we now turn our attention.

## Supply Curves

For our analysis we will need one more concept—the supply curve. By a supply curve, economists mean a curve drawn up for supply on much the same assumptions and methods as the curve drawn up for demand. That is to say, the supply curve will tell you how much of a given good would be produced at various possible sets of prices, subject to *ceteris paribus* limitation, as was the demand curve. Also like the demand curve, it is a set of simultaneous possibilities and not the record of a movement through time. One further point must be remembered. The supply curve merely says what would be *offered* at the stated price during the interval in question. It does not say a thing about profits, or whether the producers are happy about what is going on. In the next chapter we will discuss the costs of the individual firms that make up the industry, but in this chapter we merely take for granted that somehow there are firms producing the product and that the amount which they produce will vary as the price varies. If, for example, prices are high, profits are likely to be high and more firms will be attracted into the industry, but at this point we are not considering profit at all—we just assume that output is what it is.

## Demand and Supply

Next let us fit demand and supply curves together for a single industry and see how the market price in that industry can be formed by their interaction. Figure 3 gives an example.

A demand curve and a supply curve for the same product are drawn together on one diagram. And in addition to the *ceteris paribus* assumptions already made, we further assume that the two curves are independent of one another—that is, that the responses to price change shown in one curve do not disturb the responses to price change shown in the other. Fitting the two together, we see the idea of equilibrium clearly expressed. Let us follow it in more detail. Suppose we are dealing with the supply and demand for oranges in a limited, independent area in which only one type of orange is being sold. Let us say that when the price is $5, our supply curve shows that people will offer a hundred units for sale. But next we look at the demand curve. How many oranges would people

**Figure 3**
**DEMAND AND SUPPLY**

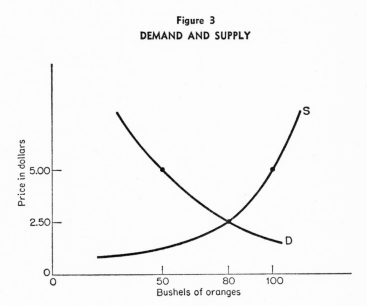

want to buy at $5? Our demand curve shows that they will buy only 50. Obviously, if the price is set at $5, 50 units will go unsold and the producers will find that they have misjudged the market. Suppose the price falls to $2.50. Producers now, let us say, will offer only 80 units for sale since the price is lower. But on the other hand, consumers are encouraged by the lower price, and will increase their purchases to 80. Thus our diagram shows that the two curves meet at a price of $2.50 and an output of 80, and the market is said to be in "equilibrium." Until something happens to disturb the situation, the same price-quantity relationship will prevail; there is no tendency to alter.

### Unstable Equilibrium

It might be thought that when equilibrium had been reached, there would be a natural tendency to settle down at that point; and also that if for any reason the price is moved away from the equilibrium point, there would be a natural tendency for market forces to bring price and quantity back to equilibrium. Unfortunately, this is not always the case, even when we are dealing with a particular industry and in a society which is otherwise undisturbed.

**Figure 4**
**UNSTABLE EQUILIBRIUM**

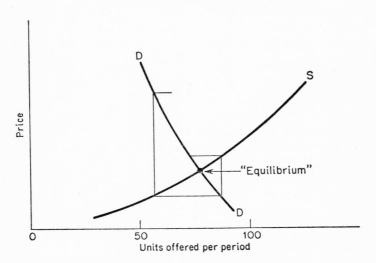

Figure 4 shows a situation in which the equilibrium is unstable, namely, if by any chance the price is set away from the equilibrium one, society will not naturally return to it. Instead, there will be continuing disturbance. The diagram in Figure 4 shows why the situation will get worse rather than better. A higher price will lead to an oversupply. This need not mean an increase in the number of firms, but only in their output. An oversupply will lead to a drastic fall in price. A drastic fall in price, in the diagram, leads to a steep cut in supply. Next the cut in supply sets the price skyrocketing, which in turn produces a worse oversupply, and so on. Behavior like this is often called the "cobweb theorem" because the path of the price and output movement looks like a cobweb. The situation portrayed is not just a pipedream. There are a number of industries in which such conditions can occur for awhile. But it is a useful lesson in the limitations of the demand and supply curve analysis to ask if these fluctuations would grow endlessly worse and worse. In the real world, experience shows that most of the time they do not. Why not? Because we are dealing with people and not just with blind forces. The wild fluctuations portrayed come from the fact that people have paid no regard to past disappointments or experiences and have merely produced blindly with reference to the present price on the assumption that it will not change. Sometimes, to be sure, people are nearly that stupid; but after an industry has burned its fingers often enough, there usually comes, for awhile anyhow, some change in expectations and hence a change in behavior. The *ceteris paribus* assumption will no longer hold good and the pattern of market behavior will alter. Nevertheless, for those industries which do show cobweb behavior, we see here a serious problem—quite independent of the special disturbances of growth.

## Supply, Demand, and Price-fixing

Our diagrams of demand and supply, however, can show some of the difficulties which spring up when a government attempts to fix prices at a point different from the "equilibrium" one. As shown in Figures 3 and 4, if the price is set too high by the government—that is, higher than the equilibrium one for the industry—there will be an accumulation of unsalable goods; unsalable, that is, at the price which the government is trying to maintain. And the government will have to purchase or otherwise remove these goods from the market. Our problem appears today in our agricultural support program. On the other hand, if prices are fixed lower than the equilibrium one, some consumers will go unsatisfied and there will have to be rationing. Rationing turns up in war economics. We merely indicate these problems at this point in order to show some of the practical applications of our concepts.

## Final Summary: The Laws of Supply and of Demand

In this chapter we have outlined the basic elements of the economic theory of consumer response, demand measurement, and the determination of price in a single market by demand and supply. We began by talking of the economic model and the limitations which circumstances imposed upon it. Next we discussed the demand curve and its elasticity. We went on to talk about the difference between personal demand curves, firm demand curves, and industry demand curves. And from there we discussed the meaning of the supply curve, and finally the equilibrium of demand and supply for a given industry in a given market. Our analysis, however, shows two general laws of behavior which have so far not been explicitly stated. They are the "law of demand" and the "law of supply." The law of demand says that, other things being equal, the higher the price, the less the quantity demanded. We will find later that there are certain freak exceptions to this rule, but it is practically never violated, once one remembers that it is subject to the *ceteris paribus* assumption. Similarly, the law of supply has it that the higher the price, the greater the amount produced; and this too is a practically universal pattern of behavior, although it also has certain exceptions. We put the two together to get the idea of equilibrium. But we found in our brief section on unstable equilibrium that sometimes, even when both the law of demand and the law of supply hold good, one nevertheless can have a situation in which a variation from equilibrium would theoretically, anyway, grow endlessly worse rather than endlessly better.

## Some Pitfalls of Demand Curve Analysis: Collecting Data

It might be worthwhile to mention here some of the problems which come up in the application of demand analysis. One point not mentioned so far is the difficulty of collecting data. Since the system is in constant change, it is evident that it is very difficult to find a long period of time in which some disturbances are not occurring. But another problem not so easily realized is that even when we attempt to measure consumer responses by a market survey taking place at a given time, we may run into trouble. Sometimes the consumer does not know his own mind, or at least he does not tell the interviewer what the interviewer wants to know. One example is famous. A certain automobile company sent out interviewers to ask people what type of car they wanted. They also asked them what sort of car their neighbors wanted. As far as their own cars were concerned, the consumers all said they wanted a simple, light car which would get them from place to place, with no fancy fittings and a very low consumption of gasoline. So far as their neighbors were concerned, however, they said the neighbors wanted a big car with a lot of shiny chrome, high power, and speed, regardless of gasoline consumption. The automobile manufacturer assumed that the consumers knew their own mind and produced an economy model. But the model turned out to be premature. It hardly sold at all. And so, for that interval, it was found that following the statements of the consumer might give an entirely wrong impression. A few years later, however, consumers evidently changed their minds, and decided to buy what they wanted, not what would impress the neighbors. And so the economy car came in. This is only a sample of the many practical problems which are encountered in trying to use the demand curve.

## Shifts in the Curve

Another problem to look out for is a shifting of the curve when basic conditions shift. For example, when the first attempt was made to measure the demand for steel, remarkable results were found. It was found that apparently the higher the price, the greater the amount of steel sold. As this contradicted all the laws of economic theory, people were very much disturbed at first. Yet, a little thought soon brought out what had happened. The information on price and output change, on which the curve was based, had been taken over various periods of time, and showed merely the actual behavior of prices and output in the actual market without allowing for national income changes. It was soon realized that the curve drawn was not a demand curve at all, but a supply curve! Why? During the years for which the various changes of price and output were being recorded, the national income had changed greatly from year to year; and each change of national income, bearing in mind our *ceteris paribus* assumption, meant a "shift," or change in the location of the demand curve as income rose or fell. A higher price did not, therefore, mean that consumers really preferred to buy steel when it was more expensive than when it was not. It only meant that in certain years the demand for steel had risen greatly in response to a great change in the level of national income. This is only one example among many of the difficulties encountered in applying a limited and stationary tool of analysis to a process of dynamic change. But before we can discuss general dynamic change, we need to study costs and their relations to profits and prices for the firm.

## Summary

This chapter began the survey of the elementary technical tools of economic analysis. We started with a brief description of economic models and saw how even the best and most complicated of them can never escape from the "as is" or *ceteris paribus* assumption. We nevertheless saw how enormously useful such models can be as long as one does not forget their limitations. From a description of "partial" and "general" equilibrium we passed to a discussion of wants, their source and the fundamental law of diminishing marginal utility. This theoretical concept was immediately given a practical application in explaining some of the reasons for the constant shifting of the pattern of wants mentioned in Chapter II, but we did not stop at general patterns but passed on to the analysis of wants for particular products, and the resulting market demand.

The ground was thus laid for the analysis of the "demand curve" and its "elasticity." Various types of demand curve, individual, firm, and industry, were also explained, and an idea given of their practical uses. From demand analysis it was an easy step to the notion of the general supply curve of an industry, to the laws of demand and supply and the concept of industry equilibrium. However we immediately saw that such an equilibrium might not be stable. The chapter ended with a discussion of some of the pitfalls of our analysis applied to actual statistics.

# Production Analysis: Output and Costs

Most of the preceding chapter was concerned with demand. Only toward the end, in discussing the elementary theory of market price, did we bring in "supply" and even then we merely assumed a supply curve without explaining it. Obviously, however, there must be some relation between the costs of particular firms and the supply conditions for the market generally. Accordingly we now go on to a discussion of supply and costs in much greater detail.

## What Are Costs?

The term "costs" can be used in a number of different ways. There are costs for the individual or firm, and costs for society: money costs and real costs, alternative or opportunity costs, and supply costs—but we will begin with the last two.

## Supply Cost and Opportunity Cost

The word "cost" in economic theory has two principal, allied yet different, meanings. One is supply cost: the value of the efforts and resources which go into producing the good. It is convenient, as we saw in Chapter V, to compute these costs in money, but theoretically they might be thought of in physical or "real" units. The next meaning of "costs," however, is somewhat different. It is the concept of alternative or "opportunity" costs. "Costs," in this sense, means not simply the actual resources going into production in a particular firm but what those units *could* have produced in the best alternative line. An example will make the difference clearer. In the chapter on managerial economics we spoke of some of the problems involved in adding a new product to the fertilizer business—"Smith's Kill-Well." We saw, for example, that the new line might yield $250 net a month. Suppose that instead you had taken a job with some corporation and earned, as manager, $600 in the same number of hours. *That* would be your "alternative" or "opportunity" cost also mentioned in Chapter V. And on the basis of such an alternative or opportunity cost calculation, you would be losing $350, not making $250.

Calculations of this sort can be made for "social" costs also. For example, if a tax is imposed and a magnificent public stadium is erected for "free" exhibitions, the cost would be not just the actual outlay but also whether the tax had stopped the growth of other projects. And the question of whether the project was a net benefit could only be evaluated by asking whether the citizens really enjoyed the "free" spectacles they saw in the stadium as much as the goods they would have bought for themselves if the tax had not been levied. We cannot yet handle these basic problems of social policy. It is enough, at this point, to realize that cost for the individual and the firm includes not just what has actually been recorded as used, but also the alternatives that have been forgone. Thus, for example, we must count among the costs of a business the returns that could be earned on a similar investment elsewhere.

## Short Run versus Long Run

In dealing, however, with the problem of supply and costs, and indeed with economic decisions generally, one of the most important distinctions is between the "short" and the "long" run. For example, we have seen that a corporation may be earning enough to pay its wages and salaries, buy its raw materials, and have a "profit" left over. And such a corporation could keep running that way for quite a while. It is covering short-run costs. But we have seen that after a while the factory will begin to wear out, and if no provision has been made for replacement—that is for the long-run costs of the enterprise such as rebuilding the factory—the corporation will have to close down. From problems like these has been developed a distinction between long-run and short-run planning. But, as the words are now used, they have become a bit tricky, for *the distinction refers to a type of planning, or adjustment, and not to a length of time.*

Let us think back a bit about our fertilizer business. At first you began by mixing materials in your garage. But then came a major step. You decided to build a small factory. Up to that point you had dealt with stopgap, day-to-day, adjustments. But when you built a factory you were *planning for the long run.* Furthermore, if a man after careful consideration of all factors known to him builds a factory, he will not be likely, the very day after completion, to tear it down and start building a new one. Even if he finds out that he could have done somewhat better by using a different design, the chances are that he will try for a while to "make do" with what he has, through various small changes in the way the existing plant is operated, rather than to build a whole new plant.

In the same way, if demand conditions appear to have changed and sales, let us say, have increased, life is still apt to be so uncertain that men will often wait a while to see whether the change is really going to be a permanent one before they try building new plants. In the meantime they will shift things around *within* the existing framework. Those adjustments *which do not involve chang-*

*ing the fixed plant* are called "short-run" planning. On the other hand, adjustments which call for *a general reconsideration of the whole problem including re-erection or extension of plant,* are called "long-run." We can look at the matter either from the point of view of the single firm or from that of the industry as a whole. Thus we speak of the long-run planning of a single business which is deciding to extend its plant. Or we speak of the long-run adjustment of an entire industry, which may be brought about, as we will see later on, by the competitive and uncoordinated decisions of many individual businesses. But in either case the fact that the amount and nature of the fixed plant is being allowed to change is one of the chief things which marks the difference between the long run and the short run in economic terminology.

### Choosing Production Methods: Physical Input–Output Relations

In Chapter V we said that any decision unit could be thought of as a group of men operating a plant to process materials into final product. In our short-run–long-run distinction we have called attention to the problem of long-run reconsideration of the whole project and shifts in the fixed plant. But there are many other problems and relationships to be considered besides fixed plant and labor. In dealing with real life, indeed, it would be helpful to compare the production decision unit with a concrete mixer. For in a concrete mixer one does not just put in a single material, but instead sand, gravel, cement, and water are combined in a mixture of materials to produce the final product. And this idea of a "materials mix" is vital to an understanding of the problems of a decision unit.

For what the decision unit is always dealing with—however fumblingly or unconsciously—is the problem of *proportions.* "How much of this shall be used with how much of that" to get the most efficient output? Furthermore, this problem of proportions is universal. It does not apply merely to short-run problems of the mixture of materials passing through the machine, but also to such questions as the balancing of outlay on one product against outlay on another; the hiring of more labor against the use of better materials; the redesigning and rebuilding of the plant against smaller short-run adjustments; and so on.

### The Problem of Proportions

In the present section, however, we want to show merely some elementary notions about the behavior of the various agents of production as they are combined with one another. In order to explain the very broad and fundamental points we want to make, it will be easiest to stick to short-run (as defined in the last section) combinations of materials and other agents of production. Let us, therefore, concentrate for the moment on the problem of combining one production agent—labor—with a given fixed plant using a given type of material and product. Suppose we are dealing with a newly built cotton mill; all new inventions are ruled out for the time being, and we are asking only how many men are to be hired.

What would happen if we began by hiring only one or two men? The chances are that they would produce hardly any cloth at all. They would have so many different things to do that they would not have time to become expert at any of them. Lots of time would be wasted maintaining the plant, keeping records, and so on. Many of the machines would probably be idle.

But as more and more men were added the chances are that these problems would begin to be ironed out and the output of cloth would rise noticeably. Men could be trained for special tasks. The plant could be kept in regular and full operation.

We must not, however, think that continuing to add more men would continue to raise output as fast as men were being added—or even to raise it at all. For after a while, for example, the men would begin to get in each other's way. To carry the thing to extremes, if we put in more and more men indefinitely there soon would not be even standing room! Nothing could be done.

## The Law of Variable Proportions

What we have been describing here in very simple words is something which economists refer to as "the law of variable proportions." It means that if we rule out all new inventions and consider merely the addition of various quantities of one type of production agent to given *fixed* quantities of other types, output is likely to behave as follows: At first, as the new production agent—say, more labor—is added, output is likely to increase more than proportionately. The return from the additional men will be *increasing*. But after a while things will begin to level off and output will be increased merely in proportion to the outlay of labor—$10 more in labor will give $10 more in product. This is called "constant returns." Finally increases in production will become even more difficult to achieve. It will take more and more labor to give a smaller and smaller increase in output, until at last there may be no increase at all or even a decrease.

Of course we can seldom make comparisons of this sort in real life in so simple and tidy a way. There are usually many different kinds of products. All sorts of readjustments would have to be made as more men are added. And results would probably be different for each plant. But the extremely simplified example just given does help us to understand one very important idea which has been found by practical experience and experiment to hold fairly universally as long as new inventions are ruled out: *The physical output derived from adding more and more of some given agent of production to a fixed quantity of others will not usually show a straight line of increase.* Instead it will show wide variations in proportionate response. Thus efficient production (and efficient policy) requires a constant shifting of materials, labor, plant, and methods so as to obtain the most efficient balancing of these fluctuating proportional changes in products. This is another reason why we had to say in Chapter II that a doubling in production would not involve simply a doubling of the size of everything.

**Total, Marginal, and Average Product**

In order to explain this problem of combining efficiently various productive agents, whose output per unit of input is fluctuating, economists have found it useful to distinguish three types of product: total, marginal, and average. Let us see what these words mean.

*Total* product is the total amount produced when a given amount of one agent of production is combined with fixed quantities of the others. When we vary the amount of the particular agent that we are studying, leaving the rest fixed, we will find that the total product will not remain the same, or change at a fixed rate but varies from point to point.

*Marginal* product means the amount by which total product is increased when we add one unit of the agent we are studying to a fixed amount of the others. You figure marginal product by figuring, say, the total product when 10 men are being employed and then discovering what the total product is when 11 are working. If 10 men produced 90 units of output while 11 produce 100, then, everything else remaining the same, the marginal product of the extra man would be 10.

*Average* product is average output per unit of input. For example, when 10 men produced 90 units, you could say their average product was 9. When 11 men produced 100 units their average product was 9.09 plus.

These rather technical terms—total, marginal, and average—may sound a bit strange and difficult at first but they are really extremely simple and serve to explain ideas which we will find constantly coming up as we go along. The student will therefore find it well worthwhile to take the small amount of trouble needed to understand them.

But now let us see what happens when we apply the total, marginal, and average labels to the law of variable proportions, which we talked about in our last section. First as to total product. If the law of variable proportions holds, total output will at first increase rapidly as we add the productive agent we are studying. Next it will begin to level off, and finally (if anybody were foolish enough to keep on going) the total would actually drop.

We next see what would happen to marginal product. Marginal product would shoot up very rapidly and then fall quite steeply—also finally disappearing. Average product, on the other hand, though showing eventual changes in the same general direction, would move more slowly and less violently. All these ideas are very important in determining the way an efficient manager should balance his various productive agents. The student should also remember that a shift in outside market prices may lead to the substitution of one material or method for another.

These relationships also lie at the basis of the usual or normal behavior of costs, and we may now see how these physical input–output relations express themselves in the cost situation, or cost curve of the individual firm.

### The Short-run Cost Curve: An Introduction

One of the most used tools of economic theory is the short-run cost curve. This is a curve which explains how the costs of a single firm may vary with output. In effect it translates into prices the net effect of some of the physical input–output relations we have just been discussing. But before we explain the curve, we must make clear the extremely rigid assumption under which we will be working. We saw in the previous sections what was meant by short-run planning —that it meant planning which did not consider changes in the fixed plant of the firm. In the same way the curve which we are about to draw is a short-run curve. That is to say, it is based on the idea that both the plant and the fixed money costs undertaken in connection with its construction are not changing. But in addition to the short-run assumption, our curve will also be drawn under a number of other limiting conditions. We assume that there are no new inventions affecting the plant, and further that no important changes are taking place in the economy generally, which would seriously disturb the conditions influencing our plant. Furthermore, we make the usual *ceteris paribus* assumption that the plant itself is so small that changes in its prices and output do not have important repercussions on the rest of the economy. Bearing all these assumptions in mind, let us now try to develop the idea of the short-run cost curve. As already explained, we assume that a given business has a fixed plant, and we ask how costs within this plant are likely to react to changes in output. The usual economic diagram is given in Figure 5(a).

Just as in the case of the demand curve, we mark off the bottom line to show various amounts of output, while the vertical line at the side shows money figures. But whereas in the demand curve diagram the output figures show amounts *sold,* and the money side indicates *prices,* in cost curve diagrams the output figures show amounts *produced* while the money figures show the average cost of producing that output.

With fixed plant unchanged, and under conditions that are otherwise normal—i.e., with full employment and no inflation or deflation—most economists generally assume that the cost curve will have the U shape shown in Figure 5(a). We will discuss shortly some of the criticisms that can be made of this assumption, but for the moment we want merely to see why it is so generally adopted. Some of the principal reasons are indicated in Figure 5(b).

In Figure 5(b) we show two curves. One is marked "average fixed cost." The other is labeled "average variable cost." The fixed cost curve slopes downward as output increases. The variable cost curve slopes upward. The two together equal the average cost (U-shaped) curve just discussed. Let us see what these two curves mean and why they slope the way they do.

It must be remembered that we are dealing here with the short run. That means that no changes are being undertaken in the fixed plant and equipment. We saw, furthermore, that we were for the present making a number of other assumptions. General prices, we will say, are not changing either way, and the money cost of repairs and replacements for the fixed plant is also not changing. Fixed cost, under these conditions, means cost *whose total amount does not change* with changes in output. There are several main types. First of all there may be interest on bonded debt. This will not vary with output. Next, many economists add a figure for "normal" profit, needed to keep the plant in business. This is a slippery idea which we discuss in detail later. Next, the plant, or its site, may be leased under a rental contract. The rent is not likely to vary with output. Finally, accountants will want to make allowance for depreciation and obsolescence—that is, they will want to see to it that the business earns enough to replace its fixed equipment when that wears out or becomes too old fashioned to use. These allowances also will often not vary (or not vary a great deal) with output.

### Why Average Fixed Cost Declines with Output

Once we get the idea that the total amount of fixed cost is not changing, then the slope of the curve of average fixed costs is easily understood. As output increases, the same sum is being spread over a larger and larger number of units. This means that each individual unit will have to cover only a very small part of the total. If the huge Ford plant produced only one car, that car would cost millions merely on overhead. But when the plant produces hundreds of thousands of cars, the amount of fixed costs borne by any one car is very small. Accordingly, we see that as output increases the charges relating to fixed costs get smaller and smaller. This is one of the main reasons why the cost curve at first slopes down.

But now we have to explain the upward slope of average variable costs. By

Figure 5
## THE SHORT-RUN AVERAGE COST CURVE

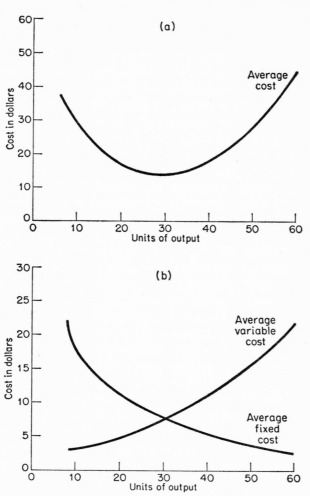

variable costs we mean labor cost, raw materials, and so on. These, under the short-run assumptions we have made, do vary with output, and, for the reasons just described regarding variable proportions, they are likely to rise as output increases, once production from a given plant becomes substantial. In other words, it will usually cost more *on average,* so far as variable costs are concerned, to produce a greater and greater amount. Gradually the rise in variable costs will offset the fall in fixed costs. And so the curve of total average short-run costs shows its U shape.

## Why Do Variable Costs Rise?

But why do the variable costs rise? There are several reasons, some of which refer to conditions inside the business and some to those outside it. The main reason, inside the business, is that a plant is usually designed by its engineer or architect for some fairly specific average "optimum" amount at which it will be most efficient. As we go beyond this point of maximum efficiency the output, as we have seen, tends to become proportionately less and less. We may add more men at the same wages, but the increased output which each additional man is responsible for nevertheless becomes smaller and smaller, and consequently more expensive. The same thing is true of burning more fuel, let us say, or using more materials of other kinds. The second set of reasons refers to conditions outside the plant. If a plant is rapidly increasing its labor force it may have to pay higher wages (or prices) to get men (or materials) out of other lines. Thus variable costs rise.

## Costs and the Industry: External and Internal Forces

Unless we confine ourselves to a single moment of time, we cannot deal with the possible shape of the cost curve with reference just to the single firm. First of all, variations in the *general* business situation will change the shape of the curve. If there is considerable unemployment it might be easy to hire more men without raising wages; the attitude toward work and hence "productivity" of those working might change. Also extra raw materials might be brought without paying a greater price, indeed they might be had at a discount. Thus the marginal and average costs of increasing output might be less and the curve "flatter" during a depression. On the other hand, in time of high inflation and labor shortage, any increase in output might involve very large payments for overtime work, steeply rising prices for scarce raw materials, and that sort of thing. Thus under those conditions the curve might be much more deeply U-shaped.

## Long-run Cost Behavior as Output Rises

Economic theory, however, is not so much concerned with dynamic changes in the general economic situation as with the effect on the costs of the firms within a single industry, of an increase in general output. This requires us to look beyond the single firm and to deal with long-run cost conditions within a single industry as that industry's total output increases. But we will continue to adhere to the *ceteris paribus* technique. That is, we still assume that the industry is too small for changes in its output to upset the general economic situation and we assume that in turn the general economic situation is not changing. Nor are we allowing for shifts in tastes and for major new inventions. Although these assumptions are highly restrictive, they are still useful in obtaining a clear beginning idea.

Figure 6 shows six different expected cost curves for particular firms as the total demand for the given industry of which they are a part increases, the "other things" just mentioned remaining unchanged.

**Figure 6**
**INDIVIDUAL COST CURVES IN AN EXPANDING INDUSTRY**

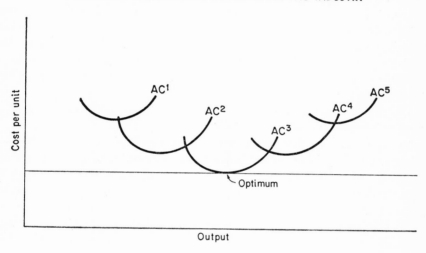

It will be observed that the size of the particular curves and their positions change as the industry expands, also that each curve is at first lower (costs are less) than the preceding one, but that after a while, though the curves continue to indicate larger enterprises, costs begin to rise. We will now examine why the costs increase.

## Economies and Dis-economies of Size

As output for an industry increases there are, for a considerable stretch of output, substantial savings in costs. First, a greater total output makes possible larger individual plants and these may be more efficient. Next, the expansion of the industry *itself* may lower costs generally. It is from this cost saving that one gets the downward-sloping half of Figure 6. Let us consider the industry as a whole, both industry problems and firm problems—industry first.

## Industry

Suppose as in Chapter V you are setting up a new plant for a new product in some undeveloped area. You may find, as there pointed out, that no adequate roads exist; that no steamship, airplane, or railroad lines run regularly scheduled service; that no cities are conveniently near. Also no one may ever have heard of your product. People may regard your industry as highly speculative and you may be able to borrow only at high rates of interest. Finally, there may not be any trained labor available at a reasonable cost.

Suppose, however, that you and other businesses begin to develop the product and the area and that the new product encounters a brisk demand. Very soon, as we saw in Chapter V, cost conditions for you and all your competitors will begin to change greatly. Regularly scheduled transportation service will be set up at great saving in cost and increase in efficiency. The state or province will probably begin to build roads. Cities will spring up nearby. Labor will move in, and the labor force already available will improve in training. As the products become better known it will be easier and cheaper to borrow money. Wholesalers will be more anxious to stock and to distribute your goods. The market for the entire industry will become better organized and more efficient.

Suppose, however, that public demand continues to rise. The condition for the industry will begin to go into reverse. As increased needs for service and supplies cut into other fields, the alternative or opportunity costs—the premiums that have to be paid to attract labor and resources from other industries—will become higher. Bottlenecks may be encountered. If you are dealing with minerals, the easily reached ore may be exhausted and more expensive equipment will be needed if shafts are to go deeper. Forces like these will explain why long-run cost conditions—for the industry generally—will once more start to rise. Hence the general shape of Figure 6.

## The Firm

Let us shift now from the costs of the industry in general to the costs of the firm, as its size increases. There are many obvious savings that can be made. Much more specialization and division of labor will be possible. Mass production processes can be introduced. More elaborate and delicate machinery can be used. The flow of materials through the plant can be fitted together more carefully—also by-products that go to waste in a small plant can become the basis of subordinate industries in a larger concern.

Even when *single* plants have reached their most efficient size, there may still be considerable technological saving from combining several or many different plants in one enterprise. We can disregard for the moment advantages of centralized marketing and advertising, for they, strictly speaking, belong in a class by themselves, though their relation to size is obvious. However, just from an engineering or technical point of view it is still clear that there may be many savings from fitting together a number of plants in one managerial unit. Products of different plants can be fitted together. The flow of materials can be more efficiently planned.

## The Nemesis of Size

All the advantages we have mentioned are true and real. Yet eventually, for all enterprises as we saw in Chapter V, there comes a point beyond which they, too, go into reverse. The trouble is that someone in every business has somewhere to pull the whole thing together. The larger the firm, the greater the specialization. Still more important is the problem of adjustment, of day-to-day replanning to meet unexpected circumstances. In the giant firm there may develop too much red tape, too many "levels" between top management and actual work.

Despite all the advantages of size, therefore, the smaller firm retains some advantages. It can be more adaptable, give more specialized service, keep personal contact. Sometimes big firms that have integrated the production of raw or unfinished materials with their main plants, expecting great savings from "coordination," have found to their surprise that red tape considerably overbalanced the benefits of central planning, and that it was cheaper to farm out production once more with smaller independent concerns. Thus, just as an industry can get too big, and a plant can get too big, so also a large coordinated enterprise can get too big. *How* big is too big, however, depends on the particular circumstances of each individual enterprise. We will return to these problems of management and size later in this book.

## The Optimum

One final point must be briefly mentioned before we conclude this chapter on costs. It is sometimes rather rashly stated by various writers that the point of lowest cost, on the cost curve of the most cheaply producing plant, is the optimum point of production. This, however, involves too great an emphasis upon production-cost conditions only. The economic system and the market also consider *demand* conditions and alternative needs. The true optimum is reached only by considering both demand and supply, and the *general* pattern of wants and production. Indeed older economic theorists usually considered that output would be somewhere *beyond* the optimum. Thus the rising market supply curve for an industry, which we used in the preceding chapter, may be recognized as closely related to the rising half of the industry and plant cost chart given in Figure 6 of this chapter.

## Summary

We have given a brief introductory survey of the apparatus used by economic theorists in analyzing cost and supply. We have learned the two allied meanings of "costs"—supply cost and opportunity or alternative cost. We have also learned the difference between "short run" and "long run" as economists generally use these expressions. Going on to input and output we learned the meaning of the words "marginal" and "average" and we studied the shape of the firm's short-run cost curve and the reasons for that shape.

Our next task was to see how costs behaved and how the size of plant changed as the output, not just of a firm but of an industry, increased—"other things" being equal. This led us to discover both why costs fell at first as the industry grew, and next why they later rose. We also saw why a larger and larger plant and enterprise might reduce costs at first, but later raise them, and we applied all these ideas to the rising supply curve of the industry shown in Chapter VI.

But the optimum scale of production both for society and for the enterprise is not a matter of cost and supply alone. It is also a matter of demand. Accordingly we will now proceed to put our demand and cost curves together to work out a basic theory of output both for the firm and for the industry.

# The Fundamental Theory of the Firm: Output, Cost, and Profit

We reach now a critical turning point in understanding the fundamental, stationary, economic model. In this chapter we put together what we have learned about demand with what we have learned about cost to work out a first elementary model of output and profit. Though the logic of this chapter will have to be greatly qualified when we apply it to the real, dynamic world, nevertheless the model of the firm which we are going to work out here is the ultimate base of all economic logic. Once the student has learned this mode of reasoning he is well on his way to being an economist.

In the present chapter we shall see how pure economic logic deduces the level of output, price, and profit for the single firm, considered alone. In the next chapter we will deal with an entire industry. In this chapter we mostly take the "given" economic model on its own terms. In the next chapter we will begin to make it "jump." But first there are some important remaining definitions and distinctions to clear up.

## Demand for the Firm versus Demand for the Industry

In spite of all that we have said about demand curves we have nevertheless still left an important gap in our analysis. This gap is full development of the distinction between demand as seen by an individual firm and demand as seen by the industry. The assumption is sometimes made that the individual business in the capitalist market has no independent policy of its own, that it does not try to set price and merely reacts blindly to external forces—whatever is happening today apparently being supposed to continue indefinitely tomorrow. If there are any such businesses they are extremely rare. A much more sophisticated and complicated theory is needed for the real world. Economics lays the foundation for such a theory by distinguishing the demand curve as it is seen by the individual business for its output alone and the demand curve for the industry.

## The Single Firm

People often are confused by the distinction between the demand for the firm and the demand for the industry. To give a simple example let us leave such special-labeled products as "Smith's Grow-Well" and talk instead of a stand-ardized product like graded wheat. Research has shown that the demand curve for the individual wheat farmer, acting alone or considering the consequences of his own acts in isolation, would have a very peculiar shape. It would be a straight, horizontal line, or to use the terminology we have learned, it would be "perfectly elastic." Why is this?

The reason is that any individual wheat farmer is so small a part of the total market that as long as he is acting by himself, as long as we think of his single behavior in isolation, he has no influence on the price at all. He can sell all he can produce at the going market price (assuming that he is the only one increasing supply), but he cannot sell above the market price and he is not likely to want to sell below it. So we draw the demand curve for his wheat taken by itself, at any one time, as a perfectly straight line at the market price. We see this in Figure 7(a).

**The Industry**

But does this mean that the demand curve for *all the wheat in the United States* is perfectly elastic—that is, that no matter how much wheat we grow, the price (in a free market) will not fall? Not at all. The demand curve for the wheat industry, that is, for all the wheat growers of the United States together, may have an entirely different shape. We see that in Figure 7(b). In Figure 7(b) the upright line on which the prices are marked is drawn to the same scale as in Figure 7(a). But in Figure 7(b) the line at the bottom on which the amounts sold are checked is marked off on an entirely different scale than Figure 7(b). The same space that stands for one hundred in (a) stands for one hundred million in (b).

The point is that an increase in one man's output of from 10 to 100 bushels of wheat, or even from 10 to 1,000, would be so infinitesimally small a part of the total that it would not affect the market price at all. Therefore Figure 7(a) shows a flat straight line. But an increase of millions of bushels, due to expansion by all the farmers in the United States, would be bound to affect the price. And so the demand curve in Figure 7(b) is shown as less than perfectly elastic. Thus we have an apparent contradiction which often confuses beginners. The demand for the individual firm in the industry may be perfectly horizontal (elastic) *at the very same time* at which the demand curve for the industry as a whole may be steeply sloping (inelastic). But there is nothing really surprising about all this. Of course an increase that runs into millions of bushels will have different effects upon price than an increase of only a few hundred bushels in a vast market running into millions.

Figure 7
DEMAND FOR THE FIRM AND DEMAND FOR THE INDUSTRY

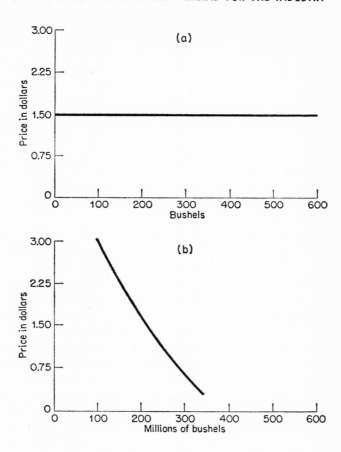

## Pure, Perfect, and Monopolistic Competition

From the distinction between demand as seen by the individual firm and demand as seen by the industry economics works out a series of important distinctions between the different kinds of competition. Especially stressed is the distinction between "pure" and "monopolistic" competition. But we shall go further in this study and show that an equally important distinction involves the difference between "pure" and "perfect" competition as we shall define them. But let us first begin with pure competition.

**Pure Competition**

The easiest way to define "pure competition" would be simply to say that pure competition exists when the individual producer thinks that his individual demand curve is perfectly elastic. But to give more concrete meaning to our definition we have to specify some of the conditions that would produce such a perfectly elastic individual demand curve. They are twofold. First, the commodity produced must be perfectly uniform as between producers. To return to wheat as an example, as long as wheat is of the same grade nobody cares whether it is from Joe's ranch or from Bill's. Second, not only must the product be identical, as between producers, but also there must be so large a number of producers that each one feels that increase in his special output, acting alone, will not affect general price. Note that we use the word "feel." Unfortunately it is not possible to say that, for example, twenty producers would be pure competition whereas ten would not. A great deal depends on the psychology and attitude of mind of the individual producer. The important thing practically speaking is, often, not how many producers there are but whether or not the producers behave *as if* they had, acting alone, no influence on price and could consider price as given no matter what their individual output. Let us now distinguish this condition from what may be called "monopolistic competition." We will find the concept of monopolistic competition a rather tricky one and we will have to examine it carefully.

**Monopolistic Competition and Monopoly**

A market may be said to be "monopolistic" whenever the individual producer feels that his individual output, even when he is acting alone, can really have some influence upon the prices of the things he sells. In other words his firm or "individual" demand curve is less than perfectly elastic. Our definition is broad enough to cover both what is usually called "monopoly" and, second, the much broader and more usual case of "monopolistic" competition. We begin with "monopoly."

**Monopoly**

A man may feel that changes in his personal output will affect the price of his product—in other words that his firm demand curve is less than perfectly elastic—in the very rare case, in modern life, in which he is the only producer of a special, technologically well-marked commodity, with no close substitutes. For example, if one man owned all the wheat ranches in the United States the demand for his wheat, and the demand for wheat in general, would (save for imports) be practically the same thing. Such a situation of single selling is, in fact, what most people mean when they use the word "monopoly." In such a market the demand curve of the individual firm and the demand curve of the product become the same thing. Although there may be commodities whose demand is perfectly elastic for a certain range of output, the analysis of Chapter VI showed that the presence of alternative goods plus diminishing marginal utility makes it certain that past some given point people, other things remaining equal, are not going to buy more of any particular good unless the price is reduced. Thus the demand curve of the single producer of a given well-defined commodity cannot be perfectly elastic indefinitely. The single seller, therefore, is confronted by a demand curve sloping during part of its length, at least, and we will see later in this chapter that this fact profoundly affects the price and production decisions of such a producer.

## Product Differentiation and Monopolistic Competition

The most interesting and usual cases of monopolistic elements or "monopolistic competition" are, however, based not upon sole possession of a single, technologically well-defined field but upon something quite different—the mere presence of a certain range of "attached" buyers, that is, people who feel that one man's product is different from other people's and worth paying a little more for. Let us take as an example the early stages of "Smith's Grow-Well" business. Certainly when you began your first tiny enterprise, mixing your ingredients in your garage, you were a million times removed from what most people think of as monopoly. Yet economic theory would still call it "monopolistic competition." The reason is that you were putting a special name on your can of fertilizer, and probably your chief chance of success would lie either in "Smith's Grow-Well" actually being different (better) from others or in somehow making people think it was. If fertilizer were sold by hundreds of producers in identical packages marked merely FERTILIZER and with no maker's name and no variation in chemical content, that would be pure competition. As soon as the product becomes "differentiated"—i.e., people notice and prefer differences comparing "Smith's Grow-Well" as against, say, "Jones' Garden-Glow"—that is monopolistic competition.

To sum up, the presence of special personal preferences or inducements is the essence of most monopolistic competition. The effect of all such special inducements is to create a greater or smaller number of attached customers—people who are willing to pay somewhat more in order to deal with, say, a favored store than they might have to pay if they dealt with some other. Such attachments may run all the way in rationality from the obvious and genuine convenience of dealing at the nearest place, to a mere desire to see the smile of the young lady behind the counter at another one. But whatever the cause and the special appeal, we express all of them economically by saying that such differences give rise to a *sloping* (less than perfectly elastic) *demand curve* for the individual firm. Such a condition we call "monopolistic competition."

Let us repeat for a minute what we mean by this monopolistic competition. First of all, it has nothing necessarily to do with size or with numbers. All that it means is that the particular business has a certain number of buyers specially attached to it who would, if they had to, pay higher prices in order to keep on buying that same product or dealing with that same store. To the ordinary citizen an independent corner drugstore is perhaps as *un*monopolistic an enterprise as there is. Yet by our special analysis and definition—the existence of attached buyers and a special market—it is a clear case of monopolistic competition.

### What Is a Product under Monopolistic Competition?

When economic theorists began to experiment with ideas like these they soon discovered what businessmen had known for some time: First, that the strategy of a purely competitive business is considerably different from that of a monopolistic one; next, that it is almost impossible to draw a clear-cut line between different products or industries. Let us first consider strategy. Suppose you discuss advertising with a wheat farmer. He will say that he never bothers to advertise his product. The reason will easily be seen. He is producing a "homogeneous" product in a purely competitive market. Any money spent on advertising by him *alone* would be pure waste. For he produces only a tiny per cent of total output and no one can tell his grain from anyone else's.

Again, the wheat farmer would probably say he never worried about "setting" a price or about the repercussions, on other people's prices, of what he was charging. This again is understandable. For wheat prices are set (leaving aside government action) in various exchanges over the country in which brokers deal with one another in an entirely impersonal way. There could be few questions of strategy in such a situation and under modern conditions of regulation.

But let's not idealize pure competition. In the first place, just because a producer, say a wheat farmer, is purely competitive, he need not be poor—on the contrary, he may be operating a tremendous enterprise and be very wealthy. Nor need the wheat farmer be concerned solely with productive efficiency and have no concern with trying to outguess the market. On the contrary, the mere fact that he knows he cannot affect the market, acting alone, does not mean that he thinks the market will always remain the same. He has therefore a forecasting problem. We will see more about this shortly. But he does not have the problems of interfirm strategy that the producer of "Smith's Grow-Well" does.

For "Smith's Grow-Well," however small, has an identified product that people can come to prefer. Nor is its price set in an automatic, impersonal market like a wheat "pit" or commodity exchange. "Jones' Garden-Glow," to be sure, is a close competitor but Smith may think that if he charges more for "Grow-Well" he may attract the prestige market; or he may think of some other sales approach. Furthermore, where does competition stop? Suppose you had all the fertilizer business from one type of chemical, would you have a pure monopoly? Clearly, no. There would be other chemicals. There might even be rival methods of getting more fertility—deep plowing, and so on. Let us switch to more domestic examples. Take refrigerators. There are gas refrigerators, ice refrigerators, and electric refrigerators—besides various other methods of preserving food. All are more or less substitutes for one another. Or take aluminum. Twenty years ago 90 per cent of all the newly produced aluminum in the United States came from one company. Was that a pure monopoly? Not by economic theory! For not only was there a great deal of remelting of old aluminum, but also there were many light metals, stainless steel, copper, tin and so on, all forming a more or less endless chain of imperfectly connected substitutes. Thus in modern society it is difficult to mark off any special area and call it an "industry," just as it is difficult to call any particular thing a "product." More and more we think in terms of individual firms producing goods which compete directly or indirectly with scores of other products often technologically quite different—e.g., gas and electricity—but in terms of consumer demand closely competitive. It is therefore easier to talk about a firm than a "product" or an "industry." In this chapter therefore we will talk about the firm, but we return to the industry in the next one.

**Pure versus Perfect Competition**

One more definition remains to be discussed. So far we have learned the difference between "pure" and "monopolistic" competition, but clear thinking requires a second distinction—that between "pure" and "perfect" competition. By perfect competition we mean in this book that each producer and consumer in a market has both perfect knowledge and perfect mobility. In other words, each man knows *all* the relevant facts, past, present, and future, needed to make a decision, and he can instantly adjust to these facts. Very little thought will show you that such a condition of perfect knowledge and instant mobility is an absolute impossibility in the real world. Always it takes time to get things done, and usually it takes time for the real forces operating in a given situation to be understood. Nor are they ever completely understood by everyone. Again, sometimes what I want to do depends on what my competitors will do—but what he wants to do depends on what I will do. Until somebody breaks down and acts, nobody can have full knowledge of the situation. In view of these complications, why do we bother to set up so unreal a concept as our perfect competition?

There is a very practical reason; and we have already, in fact, indicated it without saying so. In a growing, changing economy one of the most vital problems is accurate adjustment and accurate forecasting. Some industries should be expanding and others should be contracting. But which ones? If there were perfect or nearly perfect competition, producers would know right away. Men could rely on the market mechanism always to work out in the manner indicated in Chapter III. Every producer could know in advance what he ought to be doing, and he could do it. But we have just seen that such perfect competition is impossible.

When, therefore, in the real world, the market mechanism fails to function in a satisfactory manner, we should not necessarily conclude that such failure is bound to be the result of monopolistic forces or of a lack of pure competition. Such a conclusion is quite wrong. Just because a man is purely competitive, that is, just because he has, or thinks he has, a perfectly elastic demand curve, we cannot suppose that he will also have infallible clairvoyance concerning the future! Under the purest of pure competition, it still takes time to get things done. There are still obstacles to perfect adjustment and perfect knowledge. The full implications of this fact will appear in the next chapter, but we must mention it here lest the basic economic model we are about to describe give too idealized a view of pure competition.

### Price, Profit, and Output for the Individual Firm

And so at last we reach the point at which one can set in place what might be called the keystone of the arch of economic theory. That keystone is the determination of profit, output, and price by marginal adjustments. "Marginal," we have already seen, means the "last" or the "additional" unit considered in an economic calculation. The fundamental idea of the analysis we are considering is really very simple. Let us state it broadly as an introduction to the more detailed explanation.

### The General Idea of Maximizing

Economists believe that after a while, in most cases, an expansion in output for a given firm reaches a point at which each unit of additional output is *adding* a greater and greater amount of total cost. On the other hand, they feel that each unit sold will be *adding* a less and less, or at most an equal amount, to total revenue. Thus the spread between costs and prices *at the margin*—that is, for each unit added—is declining. Finally one reaches a point where the amount of cost added and the amount of revenue added in producing and selling the last unit are equal. At that point, in the ideal model, the greatest possible profit has been earned, the last drop has been squeezed from the situation. Profit has been *maximized*. We shall see that if the business goes beyond this point of maximum profit, it will not necessarily be sustaining a loss, but it will not be earning the most profit that it could. Profit, therefore, will not be at a maximum. Thus the ideal manager, under ideal conditions, will be searching for the point of marginal adjustment, the point at which the addition to cost and the addition to revenue just balance. Here, we should see, is the point at which his total profit is greatest. It is on this basis that we work out the theory of price, profit, and output for the individual firm. Our task involves putting together the individual short-run cost curve of the previous chapter and the individual short-run demand curve of this one. Let us begin with a monopolistic firm like "Smith's Grow-Well," and to make our analysis clear we start with two especially useful concepts: marginal cost and marginal revenue. Our model is best understood by an example. Let us say you are Mr. Smith of "Smith's Grow-Well," who wants to find out what output and what price will give him the greatest short-run profit. Long-run considerations, involving the building of a new plant, we will set aside for the moment. How will Mr. Smith go about making up his mind? He may begin by considering his sales.

## Marginal Revenue

The first thing Mr. Smith will want to know will be how much he will increase the total money amount received if he raises or lowers price. He may find, for example, that though he can sell 20 units of "Grow-Well" at $30, he can sell 30 units by cutting price to $29. The number of cans sold is not, however, the basic thing. What Mr. Smith wants to know is how much he would *increase* his total money receipts by making such a change. Yet the increase would certainly not be shown just by multiplying the 10 additional cans sold by their price of $29. For though Smith has sold 10 more units, he has also reduced the price on the other 20 by $1 each. What Smith has to do is as follows: He multiplies the 10 new units by $29. That gives him $290—the gross increase. But then, in order to figure out the *net* increase in the money value of total sales, he must allow for the fact that his former output is now being sold at a lower price. The old output was twenty and each unit of that is now being sold at a reduction of $1. So $20 must be subtracted from the $290 gross. The result is a net increase of $270 in the total amount taken in. This net increase we call the "marginal revenue." It means the net increase in the amount derived from the increase in sales. Usually the net increase is figured unit by unit in standard models. On this basis we get the standard definition of marginal revenue: *Marginal revenue means the net addition to total receipts derived from selling one more unit of output.*

If Mr. Smith is a good manager he will not rest after making only one such calculation. He might next ask what price would be needed to sell 40 units. He might find they could be sold only if the price on all were further cut to $28. In that case the marginal revenue for each of the extra 10 would be $25. For though the 10 additional units would give him $280, the $1 reduction on the previous 30 would cause a loss of $30. If we string together a number of such observations, all made under similar conditions, we will get what is called a "marginal revenue curve." It will show how much the total money sum taken in will be increased, other things being equal, by the sale of each additional unit. Such a curve is shown in Figure 8(a).

But when Mr. Smith has reached this point he has done only half the job. He is not interested in knowing merely how much his total gross income will increase. He wants to know how much his profit will increase. We cannot figure profit without comparing changes in revenue with changes in cost. As long as each increase in sales adds more to revenue than it does to costs, the total of profit is being increased. But if an increase in sales adds more to cost than it does to revenue, then, though the business may not be "in the red," still the total profit will be reduced. So what Mr. Smith now has to do is to figure out how much each increase in sales adds to cost as well as how much it has added to revenue.

**Marginal Cost**

He goes about this in the same way. The total cost of producing 20 units might be $580. But the total cost of producing 30 might be $810. In that case he has added $230 to total cost by increasing output, or $23 for each unit of the extra 10. We call this the "marginal cost curve." This is shown in Figure 8(b). *Marginal cost means the addition to total cost involved in producing one more unit.*

We are now in a position to put our diagrams together and this is done in Figure 8(c).

We have said that as long as an increase in output added more to revenue than it did to cost, total profit would be rising. From this it easily follows that the point at which to stop is the point at which the addition to cost just equals the addition to revenue. If a producer goes beyond this point he may not, it is true, be bankrupting himself, but he will be lowering the size of his total short-run profit.

We can explain our calculation in diagram form by saying that the output giving largest (short-run) profit is the output at which the marginal revenue and marginal cost curve intersect. This is shown in Figure 8(c) as 85 units. In 8(c) the demand curve and its accompanying marginal revenue curve are placed on the same chart with the average and marginal cost curves for the same

Figure 8

**MAXIMIZING THE FIRM'S SHORT-RUN PROFIT**

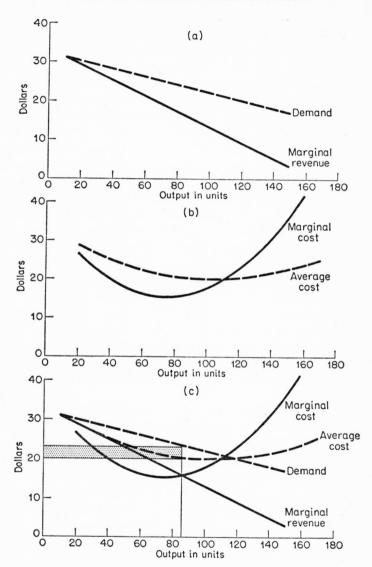

firm. We are thus able in one diagram to follow the effect of changes in output on costs, sales, and prices. The marginal revenue curve (MR) shows the addition to total gross receipts. The marginal cost curve (MC) shows addition to total cost. As long as MC is less than MR an increase in output will add more to income than to cost and hence increase profit. But at 85, the point of their intersection, the last bit of profit has been extracted.

The student is urged to study all three parts of Figure 8 very carefully, and to make sure he understands them. We will have to add many qualifications to the ideas there expressed, but as a shorthand explanation of the basic common sense of economic analysis these diagrams are exceedingly valuable. Before concluding our study of the individual firm, however, and before indicating some of the major qualifications that often have to be made to the analysis we have given, it will help to add a few words of explanation regarding Figure 8.

### The Shape of the Curve

One thing which often puzzles people is why the marginal cost curve is drawn with the shape we have given and why it cuts the average cost curve precisely at the bottom. The reasons are as follows. As output is increased toward the point of maximum efficiency in the short run, the addition to total cost involved in producing one more unit is at first relatively small, and less than the average. But because of the rise in variable costs already spoken of in Chapter VII, these additional costs will probably begin to rise, and after a while they may become very high. This explains the shape of the curve. The fact that marginal cost cuts average cost at the lowest point, on the other hand, is only a mathematical truism. The location and shape of any actual average cost curve can be determined only by a study of the actual data. But the marginal cost curve will always, by definition, come through at the lowest point. Since students are often puzzled by this fact we will explain it in a little more detail.

### Why Marginal Cost Cuts Average Cost at the Lowest Point

The reason the marginal curve always cuts the average at the lowest point may be indicated in the following analogy. Suppose you are figuring the average height of all the people in a room. As long as each new man coming in is shorter than the previous average, the average must fall. But when the new men start being taller than the average, the average will rise. So it is with marginal costs. As long as they are less than the average they lie below the average cost and the average cost curve is falling. When they are higher than average cost, then the level of the average and with it the curve of average costs must begin to rise. Thus the point at which the two types of cost are equal must be the lowest point of the average cost curve. People without mathematical training sometimes find this idea difficult to get at first, but if you think about it a bit it will soon become clear.

**The Size of Total Profit**

There are two further points which must be discussed before we go on to qualifications. The first of these concerns the size of total profit. A little study of Figure 8(c) will show that the diagram can be used not only to show what the point of optimum production is but also to show the size of total profit. This is indicated by the shaded rectangle of Figure 8(c). If we draw a vertical line from 85 units, the output at which MR and MC intersect (the point at which we have seen profit is greatest and therefore the point at which Mr. Smith will want to stop), that line will cut both the demand curve and the average cost curve. Now the demand curve will give the price which is going to be charged for each unit and the average cost curve will give the cost per unit. All we have to do, therefore, is to multiply the profit per unit by the number of units produced and we get the size of total profit. We show this in 8(c) by the shaded area.

**Marginal Revenue under Pure Competition**

The final point which needs to be mentioned is the location of the marginal revenue curve under pure competition. Under pure competition, we must remember, the demand curve of the individual firm is a straight horizontal line. This means that the individual firm, as long as it acts by itself, can sell all it can produce at the same price. The result is that in computing the addition to total revenue involved in selling more units, if the firm is acting alone, we do not need to deduct for any reductions in price. Since price does not fall, the marginal revenue curve under pure competition is identical with the demand curve. The general rule still holds that the point of maximum short-run profit-ability for the single firm is the point at which MR and MC cross each other. But since under pure competition MR and the individual demand curve are the same thing, it will be the intersection of MC and the demand curve which is shown on a diagram.

**Summary and Qualifications Concerning the Theory of the Single Firm**

So far in this chapter we have studied the rudiments of the standard economic theory of short-run costs and of price determination by the individual business. We have learned what is meant by marginal revenue and marginal cost, and we have seen how it is possible to combine the cost curves and the demand curve of the single firm into one diagram which will show both the point at which the largest short-run profit can be made and also how big that profit will be. All these rather abstract diagrams and ideas are given in order to provide the student with the convenient shorthand used by economists in describing real problems. But now we have to point out some of the chief ways in which such diagrams are unsatisfactory.

The cost analysis we have just given is often attacked in two ways. First, people criticize the assumption that businessmen always act to get the greatest amount of immediate profit. Next, people often say that men cannot have full knowledge of all the curves we have talked about. Finally, it must be realized that these curves shift with changing conditions, and that conditions are always changing.

Concerning the matter of profit, we have already pointed out that a businessman often does not take full advantage of a given situation. But this does not necessarily mean he is uninterested in profits. All it means is that an intelligent businessman looks a little further than the end of his nose, and that he considers what is necessary to maintain good relations with his customers and with people generally.

Again, different types of businessmen we have seen are attracted by different types of ventures. One man, for example, will plunge for the chance of a high profit in a risky business, while another will prefer peace and quiet and playing safe. We will talk about such factors in more detail when we get to the specific study of profits and other types of income.

Another criticism often made is that the businessman cannot always know all his costs. So he cannot in the sense, let us say, that an efficiency expert might know them. But he does usually have a general idea of his costs within the range of his operations. In the diagrams and charts we use we show a great deal more of the curves than is necessary for an actual business decision. But this is done merely to make the figures clearer for the student. It does not mean that the businessman is actually supposed to know so much over so wide a range of information. He acts most of the time with reference to fairly small changes. It is in connection with these that he usually must make his calculations.

Finally, many businesses produce many different products from the same machinery. Obviously numerous difficult problems of allocation are involved here which the cost accountant is called upon to settle, often largely by rule of thumb.

But perhaps the most basic criticism of the cost analysis we have just given—just as it is the basic criticism of our demand analysis—is the constant variability of general economic conditions and their effect upon the particular curves. In deep depression, for example, labor and raw materials may be so cheap that variable costs may hardly rise at all as output increases. But when prosperity returns the situation changes. Bottlenecks and scarcities develop and the cost curves become, as we have seen, more and more U-shaped. Thus, when we are confronted with statistics which claim to show that cost curves are shaped thus and so, we must ask not merely what industry is involved but also what set of conditions generally. Statistics gathered during a depression, for example, cannot be reliable indicators of cost conditions in a boom. Nevertheless, as long as the given conditions hold, the shape found statistically will be valid.

# The Fundamental Theory of the Industry: Output, Profit, and Price

The pieces of our puzzle ought now to be falling into place. In the previous chapter we learned the logical steps which the businessman will go through, however fumblingly or unconsciously, in guessing what output will earn him the greatest short-run profit. In this chapter we will learn how the market mechanism will work to limit the businessman's calculations and bring about a different final adjustment. You must not think that profits, in a capitalist market, are set merely by the individual decisions of particular businessmen. No indeed! The level of profit earned by one firm may have reactions upon the output or behavior of others. For example, a high level of profit being earned by one firm may set others swarming into the field. New plants will be built, output will increase, and prices will probably fall. On the other hand, losses by one firm may keep others out of the industry, or cause others to transfer into different lines. If the movement outward lasts long enough, prices and profit may once more rise for the firm which has been losing money. Our job in this chapter is to work out a more detailed analysis of how all these adjustments are made.

## Basic Assumptions

It will be seen that the analysis of this section will differ from the chapter just completed in two ways. First of all, it will be long-run analysis, that is, the total number of fixed plants will be allowed to increase. In the second place, it will be an industry analysis. We will no longer concentrate on the single seller but on the group. On the other hand, we will at first continue on a fairly abstract level. We will assume, to begin with, that we are dealing with a true industry— that is, a group of firms producing a fairly sharply defined, uniform product. Next we repeat all the *ceteris paribus* assumptions used before: i.e., no new inventions except any single one we may be studying, no serious upheavals in the economy as a whole, no disturbance of the general economy by the movements of our industry. On this basis let us proceed to study the effect upon industry, output, and price of a change in profit.

## Static and Dynamic Functions of Profit: "The Marginal Efficiency of Capital"

Before we can understand the functioning of changes in profits we must have a clearer idea of what "profits" are. Unfortunately the word is a mere label covering a multitude of different forces, and rewarding many different services. Speaking very generally, however, we can say that profit has four main purposes: (1) as "wages of management," (2) as compensation for risk, (3) as an inducement to expansion, (4) as a guide to the direction of output. We saw in Chapter V that sometimes the so-called profit of a small businessman was really only his wages of management—the amount he could have earned if he had been a salaried employee of some larger firm. Again it is clear that an industry which has very high risks will usually have to have a higher average level of profit in the firms which remain in it successfully than one which is very safe. Finally, we saw in Chapter III that profit functioned as a sort of red light on the market switchboard, indicating a gap in production that needed to be filled. Profit operates negatively too in this connection. Every firm in the long run must at least make the average minimum profit earned in other businesses of its class. If it does not make the average minimum it will be discontinued sooner or later. For it will not be meeting opportunity cost.

All the distinctions we have been making are important but there is a further one that is absolutely vital. The vital distinction is between the profit you are making on the plant you have now, operating at the scale you have chosen now, and the additional profit you expect or hope to make if you increase output or build another plant. The late Lord Keynes gave the name "marginal efficiency of capital" to this expectation of additional profit from producing more, and as the idea is a useful one we might as well learn the term now. A very little thought will show you that the marginal efficiency of capital is a very different thing from the level of profit actually being earned on a plant already built. For example, one filling station at the corner of an intersection may be doing very well, but this does not mean that if you built three more stations at the other corners you could expect to make as much or even any profit. The reason for distinguishing so sharply between profit earned on existing plant and the marginal efficiency of capital is that it is the marginal efficiency of capital (or as we will abbreviate it the MEC) which is the thing to be considered in deciding whether or not to expand your plant or output. What profit you are already making is not final to your decision to expand. What you expect to make on the addition is what counts.

Figure 9
LONG-RUN INDUSTRY EQUILIBRIUM: PURE COMPETITION

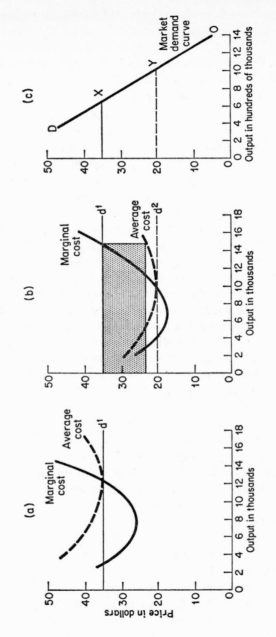

With so many factors operating it is not surprising that there is really only one basic principle regarding profit on which most economists are agreed, namely, the principle that there is no *single* "reasonable" profit rate (say 10 per cent) mechanically and universally applicable to all businesses. The "reasonableness" of profit depends upon the risks and other conditions involved in each individual case. One hundred per cent profit, for example, might not be unreasonable in some terribly risky business; and on the other hand 5 per cent profit, though it sounds reasonable enough, could be excessive in the case of some very secure, stagnant monopolies. Again the profit expectation which would be enough for one man might not be enough for another.

But there is another distinction which is particularly important for the sort of analysis we are about to explain. That distinction is that the amount or percentage of profit necessary to induce continued growth is usually thought to be higher than the amount which will serve just to keep a firm or an industry going without expansion. Accordingly, one level of profit may be necessary to get a continually expanding society. Quite another may be all that is needed to keep it going at its existing output. A stationary society may show a certain amount of profit, but this need not mean that there is any adequate marginal efficiency of capital or expectation of additional profit from increasing output.

One final paradox remains to be mentioned. Conditions in an industry may be such that although no individual firm already in it has any incentive to expand, nevertheless the industry as a whole may be expanding. The reason is that the profit level of that industry may be so high that it will attract new men into the field. Let us now proceed to study adjustments of this sort in detail.

## Profit for the Firm and Long-run Profit for the Industry

We now study the relation of firm profit levels to the expansion of the industry. We will sidestep the question of reasonable profit already mentioned. Instead we will merely assume that we know what is the minimum average level of profit needed to keep the industry going at an unchanged total output. Next we will assume that all the firms in the industry have the same cost curve and produce an identical product. We further assume that, in addition to an identical product, there are enough sellers in the field to give us pure competition. Finally, we suppose, as we did in Chapter VII that the somehow-determined minimum profit level is included in the cost curve as a necessary cost of production. It will not, therefore, show up in our diagram at all. Any profit indicated on our diagram is, by definition, in excess of the stationary minimum and will serve as an incentive to someone to come into the field.

The basic diagram is shown in Figure 9(a), (b), and (c).

In Figure 9(a) we see a firm in an industry in perfect adjustment. As there is pure competition the individual demand curve of the firm is perfectly elastic—that is, a horizontal straight line. Furthermore, as the needed minimum level of profit is drawn *in* the cost curve, and does not show on the diagram, and as the industry is supposedly neither growing nor shrinking, and therefore cannot be earning any extra profit, the price being received by the individual firm must be the lowest possible, i.e., just at the lowest point of the firm's cost curve. We will see the reason for all these statements in more detail shortly.

We suppose, next, that something happens to raise the profit level in the industry. The increase could come in one of three ways. First, demand for the product may increase, and with it the price. That could show on Figure 9(a) as an upward shift of the individual demand curve. But demand is not everything; we will prefer to explore two other alternatives. They are: profit rises because wages have fallen, and profit rises because a new invention or method lowers cost. Either way price at first remains the same but the cost curve is lowered. We see this result in Figure 9(b). Furthermore Figure 9(b) shows, to begin with, a very high level of *extra* profit—that is, profit in excess of the minimum shown in the curve. What happens now?

Figure 9(c) gives the answer to both the elimination of profit and the needed increase in output. The firm shown in Figure 9(b), acting by itself, has no incentive to increase output—not at least from that plant. The point of maximum short-run profit has already been reached. They are "equating" short-run marginal cost with marginal revenue. Perhaps the same people who own the plant in Figure 9(b) might want to build yet another plant. On the other hand, it may be so difficult to run two plants at the same time that it cannot be done profitably. Or suppose that they just do not have the money. Or again, they may not want to bother. They are enjoying very high profits on what they have and are content to stop there. For any or all of these reasons that particular firm will not expand.

But though the people in Figure 9(b) may have no incentive to expand, that does not mean that nobody else has an incentive. Far from it. Since the cost curve already includes reasonable profit—that is, an amount of profit needed to keep that business going—it follows that anything over and above this reasonable amount will serve as a special temptation to other firms to come into the field. Even if they should know that their entry will begin to reduce prices and profits somewhat, they still may feel that remaining profits may be so much higher than what they could expect in other lines that building a new plant will be well worthwhile.

Figure 9(c) shows how this process will work out. Figure 9(c) is drawn, in part, on a different scale from Figure 9(b). The upright lines measuring prices are the same. But the horizontal lines, measuring quantities, are quite different. Just as in Figure 7, the spaces which in (a) and (b) measure thousands, in (c) measure hundreds of thousands. In other words, (a) and (b) show the demand for one firm's production and (c) the demand for all the production of that industry in the country. The firm's demand curve is shown in (a) and (b) but (c) shows the demand curve for the industry as a whole.

Suppose now, as already stated, that all the new firms coming in have the same cost curves as that shown in Figure 9(b). If the process of expansion were to work with mathematical exactitude the effect of an expansion would be as follows: New firms would swarm into the industry, increasing aggregate output for the industry as a whole. Prices would thereupon begin to fall from point "X" on D in Figure 9(c) downward. This process of constantly increasing supply and constantly falling prices would last until the market price fell to point "Y" on D in Figure 9(c)—a point just equal to the lowest point on the average cost curve of the individual firm in 9(b). There it would stop. The reason is not hard to show. As long as prices are a little above the point of lowest average costs there would still be some little bit of special extra profit to serve as bait for new expansion. But when price has fallen to the lowest point, only a minimum profit is being earned, and this minimum amount merely serves to keep the firm satisfied to do what it has been doing and no more. If price should fall below the lowest point, then, of course, everybody would begin to lose money and some of the firms would leave the field. Thus, after some oscillation back and forth, it is reasonable to assume that, barring further disturbances, the expansion would come to a halt with price just equal to the lowest possible average cost.

The process of adjustment we have been explaining can be summed up as follows: Profits will rise for any one of three reasons. One would be an increase in the demand for some product all through the industry, even though there is pure competition; the second would be lower costs from a new invention; and the third, lower wages, raw material costs, or taxes. High profits will attract new businesses from outside. The increased output thus resulting will bring prices and profits down. We have thus shown the elimination of "abnormal" or "extra" profit under pure competition. As Adam Smith said nearly two hundred years ago, the acts of an individual businessman have led to an end that "was no part of his intention." He was looking for high profits, yet somehow he helped to lower them. We need to study this paradox in more detail.

### Once More: Pure versus Perfect Competition

All that we have really done in the last section has been to give a geometrical diagram of something which economists often call the paradox of the "invisible hand." We have seen how businessmen, each setting out to realize on a high-profit opportunity, have somehow managed in the long run to reduce the profit level. The reduction is managed through the invisible hand of market competition. But are business managers really that shortsighted? Is pure competition really all that is required? The answer is No. Truly to understand the problem we must go into it much more carefully, and basic understanding can be reached only if we recall, once more, the difference between pure and perfect competition. The strange contradiction emerges that if the market worked too "perfectly" it would not work at all. How is this?

Professor John Maurice Clark in *Competition as a Dynamic Process* says he was told that at one point in the automobile industry several producers had the same improvement on their drawing boards, but for several years none of them introduced it because they all knew that the others would instantly follow suit. Whether Professor Clark's example was in fact correct the writer does not know, but the situation is a perfectly possible one. Most people would jump to the conclusion that some sort of monopoly or conspiracy must have been involved. In fact nothing of the sort need have been present. There could have been entirely pure competition. The real trouble was that competition in that case was too nearly perfect.

What lured the new entrants into the industry in the last section was the existence of high profits in the firms already in it, and the hope of the new firms that they would share in them. Without the hope of a special reward they would scarcely have gone to all the trouble involved. It is not an easy thing to build a new plant and to venture into a new field. Without some extra compensation the risk would not be taken. Yet businessmen are not mindless morons. All of them have some understanding that high prices and profits in a special field will not last forever. The new entrants into the field hope that the "abnormal" conditions will last long enough, take enough time to correct themselves, for them to earn a sufficient bonus in the *interval*. It is the hope that adjustment will not be instantaneous that leads them on.

We need now, therefore, to ask why adjustment would not be instantaneous. Economists generally explain the fact of delay by referring to the existence of "frictions." What they are really saying, in the terms of this book, is that competition is not perfect. In other words it usually takes time for people to see a new opportunity, time for them to decide to act on it, and time, even after the decision has been reached, to build the new plant. In other words there is not that instant mobility and perfect knowledge which we defined as perfect competition in Chapter VIII. Thus because the process diagramed in Figure 9 does not work instantly, it *can* work, period. If people could not reasonably expect an interval of abnormal profit they would not expand at all into the new industry or line. We have here a practical point of the greatest importance which will be cropping up throughout the remainder of this book. Without friction, or "imperfections," of competition, there would be no marginal efficiency of capital or incentive to expand.

But the imperfections of competition, and the resulting obstacles to a perfect adjustment relate to many more things besides the lapse of time. Not all resources, for example, can be found everywhere. Some countries have one set of natural resources and some another. Some people have more ability in some lines than have others. Not everybody can be everywhere at once, and there are only four corners to Fifth Avenue and Fifty-seventh Street. All these facts are aspects of imperfect competition, as we define it here. They have nothing whatever to do with any conscious monopolies or conspiracies. But the result of their existence is that there are bound to be differences in costs between firms, even under pure competition. The assumption of identical cost curves made in Figure 9 is thus extremely unrealistic. Let us see what happens when we admit differences in cost between firms.

### Long-run Equilibrium and Differences in Costs

As just seen, we must not suppose that even in a stationary state, under given conditions, and even in a world of pure competition all extra high returns above cost would necessarily be eliminated. While the complete understanding of this problem has to be postponed to the chapters on distribution, nevertheless, we can show here something of the basic consequences of differences in efficiency, location, and cost upon the individual firm.

As a firm or an industry increases its output, cost conditions are likely to change a good deal. We have already shown in the analysis of the long-run cost curve of Chapter VII that at first the general level of cost will rise and that later on as output continues to expand for the industry costs will go up.

In Figure 10 we will see an indication of the effects of processes of this sort upon the return over costs of various firms. In Figure 10, as in Figure 9, we assume pure competition, but we also assume that our industry has expanded to a point where it is running into more and more difficulties and costs are beginning to rise. Figure 10 shows three sample cost curves in an industry, under these conditions, which has reached an equilibrium—that is, an industry in which there is no incentive either to expand or to contract. We are supposing that in order to produce as much as is demanded at the market price three plants—(a), (b), and (c)—are needed, and we want to see how their costs might compare in an equilibrium.

The first thing the student should notice is that in the diagram all of these firms are producing at the intersection of MC and MR (the MR is $10 for all outputs, since there is pure competition), that is, all of them are at the point of maximum short-run profitability, considering their costs and market price. Furthermore, there is no incentive for any new firm to come in. No new firms will enter because Plant (c) represents what is called the "marginal plant," which means that conditions are such that any additional plant coming in could operate only at a loss. We show such a plant in Figure 10(d). Obviously it would not pay to build it. On the other hand (a) and (b) are clearly earning very high returns over costs. Yet they too have no incentive for expansion. Our figures might be considered as a breaking down of a possible supply curve into the individual curves that underlie it.

What could explain cost differences similar to those shown? One obvious explanation might be differences in location. Plant (a), for example, might be especially close to its market or raw materials. Consequently Plant (a) would have much lower costs. Plant (b), on the other hand would be further away, while (c) would be so far as barely to earn a minimum reasonable return. Plant (d), still more unfortunately located, might be so far away that only a very considerable rise in prices would enable it ever to break even.

There are innumerable other special circumstances which could create differentials. Perhaps, in fact, the most important idea for the student to get from Figure 10 is the realization that even in a stationary and purely competitive equilibrium there may be wide differences in costs as between firms. However, to complete our analysis we must examine the problem a little further.

If the special advantages of, say, Plant (a) are due solely to location, it would be a mistake to suppose that the balance sheet of the firm would necessarily show a high return. The chances are that nearly all the special yields of the fine location would be paid out as rent for that particularly advantageous space. Of course, if the factory owner also owned the land, there might not be any specific ear-marking of rent, and the profit in his books would be shown consequently higher. But under modern sophisticated accounting practices the chances are that an attempt would be made to separate what was attributable to the location from what was earned by the general business.

Another source of differences in cost, though not necessarily of surpluses, would be differences in the ability of the managers. The president of the (a) corporation, for example, might be an exceptionally able man whereas the head of (c) might be only just fair. Theoretically, however, all the surplus earned by (a) on special ability would be paid to him as salary. Hence, here

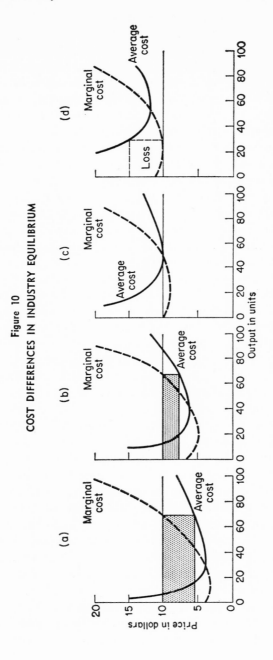

Figure 10
COST DIFFERENCES IN INDUSTRY EQUILIBRIUM

again, the firm's accounts would show no special high return. But in fact the super-excellent manager for various reasons often does not get his full worth. And in such cases also a special high return might show in the accounts. We will elaborate all these problems in the chapters on distribution. Right now all we want to show is that in the real world, even under "given" equilibrium assumptions, not all costs are the same, and returns can vary.

## Long-run Adjustment under Monopolistic Competition

The process by which abnormal or "surplus" profit is eliminated under monopolistic competition is more complicated than under pure competition, yet the essential logic of the process is much the same. We see how the adjustment works in Figure 11(a) and (b).

Figure 11

RESTORING LONG-RUN INDUSTRY EQUILIBRIUM: MONOPOLISTIC COMPETITION

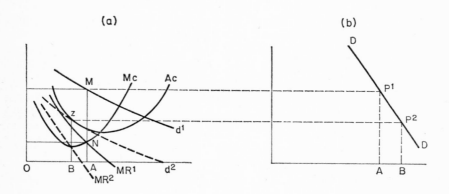

In 11(a), as in 9(b), the marginal and average cost curves (Mc and Ac) remain unchanged throughout. With monopolistic competition however, $d^1$, the demand curve for the firm, is less than perfectly elastic. We must therefore draw a marginal revenue curve $MR^1$. By analysis explaining Figure 8, p. 99, maximum short run profit is reached when $MR^1$ and Mc meet at point N, yielding output OA and price AM on $d^1$.

By the method of Figure 9, we next carry price AM over to point $P^1$ on the aggregate industry curve D, similar to that in 9(c). It will be evident that the price AM (or $P^1$) is far above minimum average cost and yields great abnormal profit.

The model in Figure 11 works exactly as it did in Figure 9. Once again other firms see the opportunity for abnormal profit and once again we assume that they crowd in, but that all the firms continue to have the same level and shape for their cost curves. Once again the demand curve is pushed downward until it touches Ac, the average cost curve, this time at point Z on $d^2$ with price BZ and output OB. Output OB is also that at which $MR^2$ cuts Mc. At this output abnormal profit will have been eliminated and price BZ shows as $P^2$ on D, the aggregate curve. A new equilibrium has been reached. But since $d^2$ is less than perfectly elastic, that is to say sloping, point Z is considerably higher and output less than the minimum point on Ac. This is a matter of simple geometry which you can easily follow from looking at the diagram. But the consequences so far as simple geometry goes, and under given conditions, are quite serious.

The final equilibrium in the monopolistic industry will differ considerably from the final equilibrium under pure competition. Curiously enough, under our assumptions the profit level will be the same assuming the conditions of the two industries to be otherwise the same. But you will see from looking at the diagrams on Figures 9 and 11 that prices will be somewhat higher and output less than would be the case under pure competition. In other words, the existence of differentiated products, with special labels, leads to a higher-priced equilibrium with a reduced output than would obtain under pure competition. On the basis of Figure 11 many conclusions unfriendly to the normal pattern of modern business are usually drawn. For we have already seen that most modern businesses do have special labels and a special market. Yet these differences appear to lead to a higher price and a smaller output than if one had pure competition.

## The Competitive Ideal and the Forecasting Problem: Oligopoly

So unfavorable a conclusion regarding monopolistic competition as we seemed to reach in the last section obliges us to spend some time on the question of what is the ideal form of competition in the real world. Before we can do this, however, we must mention one type of competition which is perhaps the most usual in the real world. That type is "oligopoly." We have so far analyzed three types of competition. First, we mentioned the single seller of a given well-defined commodity. This is the condition usually meant by what people call "monopoly." Second, we talked about pure competition, a swarm of producers of a single identical product. Third, we talked in the last section of monopolistic competition. In the model we have just used there was a swarm of producers, as before, but each one had a certain number of attached buyers and a less than perfectly elastic demand curve. Nevertheless, we tacitly assumed without saying so that we could still talk about an "industry." In other words the diagram of Figure 11 assumed that a fairly sharp line could be drawn between the competitors in the field we were diagraming and other industries. Also, each competitor could still ignore reactions on others.

Real life frequently requires the addition of two more qualifications. First, we speak of oligopoly. Under oligopoly, even when the product is identical, the competitors are so few that each man knows that changes in his price or output are bound to react on the prices and output of the others. In addition he often has to consider if his acts will bring in potential competitors who are not yet in the field. Next, in the real world one frequently cannot speak of an industry, but rather of an endless chain of more or less imperfect substitutes. What is the effect of these changes upon our analysis so far?

First of all, in the oligopolistic case, with an identical product, the individual demand curve disappears. What is left is a set of strategic expectations. "If I do this, my competitor will probably do that." Competition takes on some of the qualities of a poker game. Bluff, psychology, and guesses as to another's temperament play a great part. To try to handle the model by purely rational analytical methods, in fact, often leads to conclusions like that of the mythical donkey which starved to death between two equally attractive bales of hay. He could not make up his mind!

The tendency is, therefore, for producers to try to build up special markets of attached buyers. In addition, since we can no longer speak of a definite industry, the tendency is for analysts to retreat to diagrams of the individual firm, allowing for external forces by the shape of the assumed demand curve.

### Effects on the Competitive Ideal

Economic analysts are often disturbed by the qualifications we have just given because of the vaguenesses and uncertainties that are often implied. But can we say offhand that the world of oligopolistic and monopolistic competition just sketched is necessarily less efficient than that of pure competition? A full discussion of this question must be postponed to later chapters on Monopoly and on comparative economic systems. Nevertheless, certain things can be pointed out here.

First, you must remember that the conclusion that price is necessarily higher and output less under monopolistic competition holds only under conditions of (1) equilibrium, with (2) no further change. But in the real world change is more or less constant and equilibrium if it exists at all, is usually a brief interlude. The test for the real world is thus not what type of competition gives the best equilibrium but *what type deals best with uncertainty and change.* Pure competition, we have seen, does not in the real world eliminate the need either of forecasting or of risk premiums. A purely competitive industry can make just as many mistakes as an oligopolistic one, and it is quite possible that a purely competitive industry may so misjudge the future that it actually produces less, at a given point in the real changing world, than an oligopolistic one. We will discuss these problems later in the chapters on monopoly. One final point however: The introduction of oligopoly, monopolistic competition, and imperfections or frictions does not render the standard economic model wholly irrelevant or useless. Quite the contrary. Resources still move though sometimes sluggishly, with the direction of consumer spending. Abnormal profit still attracts people into a new line and losses still tend to discourage output. The fact that models cannot be relied upon to work with slot-machine exactitude is a long way from proving that they are useless. Let us set about applying them to some specific problems. In particular we must remember that the "market" deals not only with the prices of goods, but also in the incomes and wages of different productive agents. It is time to study them.

## Summary

In this chapter we discussed the "long-run" theory of industry output. Even with the severely limited models used, dynamic considerations began to come in—especially in considering the role of profits. We were obliged to draw a fundamental distinction, which will be often repeated in this book, between "normal" or stationary profit level and the "marginal efficiency of capital" or expectation of abnormal profit which induces expansion. We saw that the fundamental source of such profits lay in change and "friction," and we explained the paradox by which the abnormal profits that induced expansion brought about their own destruction. Yet we pointed out that businessmen would scarcely run the risks and incur the effort involved in expansion if they thought that abnormal profit would be immediately competed away. Here is where the distinction between pure and perfect competition becomes of great practical importance. Competition, we saw, can sometimes be pure, but it is *always* "imperfect," under our terminology. The frictions of imperfection permit the temporary existence of abnormal profit even under pure competition and hence make expansion profitable and possible. "If the system worked 'perfectly' it would not work at all."

At that point we were obliged to explain that even under purely competitive long-run equilibrium all long-run surpluses above cost were not necessarily eliminated. This led to a discussion and diagram of the problem of economic "rent." Following rent we worked through again the elimination of "abnormal" profit expectations—this time under monopolistic competition—and we showed the differences between the purely competitive and the monopolistically competitive equilibrium. Once more, however, dynamic conditions upset the conclusions of abstract equilibrium theory. The student was warned that it did not necessarily follow that the purely competitive producer would have the same expectations as the monopolistic or oligopolistic one. Hence it was quite possible under dynamic uncertainty for oligopolistic or monopolistic output to be higher.

# Part III

# THE PRICING OF PRODUCTIVE FACTORS

+ + + X + + +

## Wages and Rent

Financing "Smith's Grow-Well" is now far behind us in our study. The question of unemployment, on the other hand, begins to approach. Yet we have still a final set of theoretical tools to master before we can make an all-out plunge into the full complexity of the dynamic world. Most of the analysis of the past three chapters has been concerned with "value" and price: why people want things, why they cost what they do, and why a particular amount of them is being produced.

### Valuing Human Action and Natural Resources

But the market, we have seen, also deals in, and ties together, the prices of two other sets of resources: human labor, human enterprise, human saving, on the one hand; natural resources like coal, iron, uranium, on the other. The prices paid for these factors sooner or later become income in someone's hands. Speaking very broadly, the incomes going to human action are called "wages," "interest," and "profits." Those going to the possessors of natural resources, and certain other special advantages (to be defined later) are given the name of "rent" in economic analysis, though the various terms overlap to some extent in practice. What we want to ask here is, What logic or mechanism sets the size of the various incomes? How does the pricing system do the job?

**Once More: The Given Model**

In approaching our problem we meet once more the profound clash between "given" and "dynamic" analysis. The value and price concepts of the last few chapters could most of the time be kept subject to *ceteris paribus* assumptions without involving any fundamental contradiction. Our problems thus treated could be thought of, generally, as either relating to the behavior, in part or whole, of a great system under given conditions, or else as referring to so unimportant a section of a changing economy that repercussions from outside and upon the outside could be neglected. We will see that one can get reasonably far in the analysis of wages and rent while still subject to the same sort of *ceteris paribus* limitation, but profits and interest are a different story. As we find them in the modern world they are nearly always dynamic in origin, and the given assumptions, which are merely uncomfortable in the earlier analysis, become almost nonsense when one tries a full treatment of the interest and profit problem. The two chapters of Part III, therefore, form a fundamental bridge leading from given to dynamic problems. Once we have worked out a basic theory of wages, rent, interest, and profits we are well on our way to the study of business cycles, unemployment, and similar questions of dynamic policy.

Yet there remains the problem of keeping our analysis clear. Clarity of understanding still requires taking things step by step. We accordingly begin, as before, with *ceteris paribus* and stationary analysis. We ask what forces would determine wages and rent in a stationary, perfectly adjusted world— one without growth and change—and which we will assume is purely (though not perfectly) competitive. Next, we ask what vestiges of nominal profit and interest might remain in such a hypothetical society. Finally, in the next chapter, we carry the problem beyond such rigid, stationary assumptions and go on to a full theory of distribution, involving change and growth.

**Employment and Wages for the Single Firm under Given Conditions**

There are two ways of approaching the theory of wages. One is to start with a given wage level and see how many men an individual firm will employ at the level. The other is to start with a given set of men and a given stock of capital, for some particular economic system, and to ask what wage level would give them all jobs. In other words, either we can start with the wage level and try to compute the volume of employment or we can start with the needed volume of employment and available capital, and calculate the necessary wage rate. For purposes of clarity we will begin here with a given wage rate and explain the employment calculations of an individual firm.

We commence by considering the behavior of a purely competitive producer, dealing with a purely competitive labor market, who is getting ready to determine his output and his production methods. His output and production methods taken together will of course determine the employment he offers. We further assume a stationary society in which only our particular producer is making adjustments, or we assume that he is so small a part of the total that he is neither disturbed nor disturbing where outside forces are concerned. The purely competitive producer, we remember, has little concern with price strategy and none at all with advertising. He is merely trying to produce, by the most efficient methods known to him, that output which will be most profitable to him—given the prices he expects to receive and the costs he has to pay.

## Realism versus Analysis

There are two sets of extreme statements often made in wage theory concerning the behavior of such a producer. On the one hand, as indicated in Chapter VII, pure economic theorists sometimes talk as if a producer would always have an absolutely free hand with which to choose among hundreds of alternative methods of production. For example, he may be thought of as instantly free to choose either a large, complicated plant and a small labor force, or a large labor force and a small, simple plant. If he were a farmer, for example, he might be considered as immediately deciding whether to use more labor and less fertilizer or, say, more fertilizer and tractors but less labor. Our producer, furthermore, might be thought of as extremely sensitive to price changes. A very small increase in wages, for example, might be supposed to lead him to buy more machines or redesign his layout, and vice versa. In pure theory an intense sensitiveness to price and an almost complete flexibility of methods are apt to be assumed.

On the other side is what appears to be the severely practical approach. This approach points out that once a man has built his plant he is not going to rebuild it the next day; that often a plant seems to call for exactly so many men, no more, no less; that it often costs a lot of money to lay off men; and so on. In extreme forms it may be thought that there is only one available method of production, using one absolutely fixed and invariable amount of men and raw materials, and totally incapable of being changed. Tied to this point of view is apt to be the idea that every plant has some fixed definite figure called "capacity," neither more nor less.

Truth in the real world lies somewhere between these extremes. If we think merely of a single plant, for a short time, then it is true that only at the beginning does the businessman have even some approximation to a free hand. The present policy of every producer is always somewhat influenced by the past costs he hopes to cover and the past mistakes he has to live with. On the other hand there is always a certain amount of shifting that can done while, as the plant wears out and depreciation allowances are available to be expended, drastic reorganizations and even relocations can be managed. Thus the actual determination of output, production methods, and prices in any given case is a mixture of long-with-short-run considerations, of habit with conscious decision, of more or less unalterable factors with those that can easily be changed. The mixture varies from man to man and from industry to industry, but all the elements listed are always present to some extent. Most of the time, if one is willing to pay the cost, a little more production can be coaxed from an existing factory. On the other hand, there are always some rigidities which temporarily at least have to be taken as "given."

## The Search for Efficiency: The Substitution Principle

But, though the facts just stated show that we cannot apply pure theory with slot-machine exactitude, it remains true that on the average every producer, to the extent that he is efficient, is trying to achieve the best, i.e., the most cost-saving, combination of productive elements in the light of general circumstances. In making such a decision mere technical considerations are not enough. Price (present or expected) has also to be considered. If we were guided by technical ideas only, we would probably try to find the production method which would give us the greatest possible physical flow of output per unit of time. But the producer is not interested merely in output. He is also interested in profits. The best technical method might be so inordinately expensive as to be ruinous. Thus, when the price of one factor rises, businessmen will tend, over time, to *substitute* some cheaper agent or method. The process of regrouping is endless as an economy changes.

In Chapter VII we compared the individual firm to a concrete mixer. We did this to stress the idea of a "product-mix"—to show how all-pervasive was the problem of balancing "a little more of this against a little less of that." We also saw that when a manager applies more and more of one type of agent of production—say labor—to a fixed amount of other agents there would be a tendency for proportions to vary as between the amount of additional input and the resulting amount of additional output. In other words, the ratio of marginal inputs to consequent marginal outputs would vary greatly. Finally, we said that economists usually assumed that under pure competition most firms would be making calculations in the zone of "diminishing returns." But, in addition, we see that price and price changes are also considered. All aspects are balanced together in a single decision.

## Combining Productive Agents

Bearing in mind this idea of balancing, as output increases, a lot of shifting proportions against one another in order to get the greatest total output, economic plus mathematical and engineering studies can show a number of very interesting relationships. In particular it can be shown that, if the amounts of other agents of production are held constant but the amount of some single further agent—say, labor—is being increased, then the intelligent producer will add the agent which is being increased until the cost of the last or "marginal" unit of that agent added is just equal to the value of the last unit of final output produced by adding that agent. Of course, in practical fact, one must allow for "lumps" and "discontinuities." Some things, in the short run anyhow, can only be had in given sizes, for example. But theoretically and often practically these various values and costs are compared by a series of small adjustments. An example will help. If, adding two more men to a plant increases costs by $10 an hour, and if the value of the added product is $12, the men will be hired. But if the added cost is $10 and the added value is only $9, the men will not be hired. The producer will try to set employment so that the cost of the last man added and the value of the last bit of output (produced by adding the man) will be equal.

## Not Just Addition: Rearrangement

Calculations of the sort we have just described are not usually made for one agent only, with the amounts of all others held constant. Instead, in theory and to a considerable extent in practice, there will be a recalculation, as output increases, of the amounts of all the agents which are being combined. Furthermore, if there is a change in the relative price of any one productive agent, the physical proportions in which they are combined will sooner or later be changed—for the cheaper agent will tend to be substituted for the more expensive one. If machinery, for example, becomes very costly and labor cheap, the result will be (other things being equal) that an attempt will be made to economize on machinery while using a lot of labor. Contrariwise, if labor becomes more expensive it will give a special incentive to the increased use of labor-saving machinery.

## The Fundamental Wage–Employment Calculation

Applying this analysis to the theory of wages, let us take a single more or less homogeneous type of labor—that is, a type in which the individual differences among various men are not especially important so far as the work they are doing is concerned. Let us further take the wage rate that prevails in the market, and ask how many men will be hired by any given producer. It follows from the analysis we have just described that each producer will hire more men until the values of the addition to total product, given by the last man added, will just equal the wage of that man. We see this calculation in Figure 12.

**Figure 12**

**WAGES AND MARGINAL PRODUCTIVITY: PURE COMPETITION**

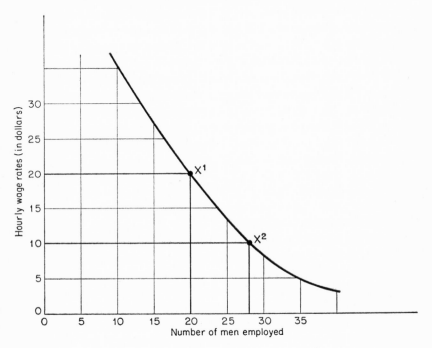

In Figure 12 we assume that the fixed equipment of the plant is unchanged. We further assume that there is only one known set of methods and rearrangements available as output is increased. All other factors of production are held constant and the only change being considered is how many men to employ, given the market rate of wages. It is further assumed that these men are, for production purposes, interchangeable—that is, that the labor force is homogeneous. On the upright axis of the figure we show money wage rates. On the horizontal line we show the number of men employed. The curve shows the value of the total product produced as employment is increased. It should be remembered that we are dealing here with pure competition; in other words, the price of the goods sold (as long as we speak only of changes made by one firm) does not fall as output is increased, and remains the same. Under monopolistic competition the situation is much more complicated, but as this chapter is concerned only with bare essentials we stick to the purely competitive case. The curve of total product slopes downward because of the law of diminishing returns, already explained.

Given all these conditions it is clear that it will pay the firm to hire additional men as long as the increase in the value of total product is greater than the wage of the added men. The optimum, that is the most profitable, amount of employment for the business is reached, as we have already seen, when the wage of the last man employed is just equal to the value of the product which he adds. In the Figure, this equilibrium occurs when the wage is $20 dollars an hour, at the employment of 20 men, and labor's total income is $400. Suppose now however that we want to employ more men, or that the wage rate drops to $10. In that case equilibrium is reached at 28 men, *but* labor's total income has dropped to $280. We see therefore that, given all our assumptions, the volume of employment is a direct result of the wage rate.

## Aggregate Wages in a Purely Competitive Society: A First Model

Though we have given some of the steps by which a particular firm determines how many men it will hire at a particular wage rate, we have not yet worked out any theory of general or aggregate wages. In other words, we now have to turn the problem around and to look at it from the point of view of an entire economic system rather than of a single firm. Instead of assuming a fixed rate, and asking how many men a firm will hire at that wage, let us assume instead that we have a certain number of men to employ in an economy, and we want to know what wage rate will be needed if they are all to have jobs. Instead of dealing with one firm we will suppose that there are many doing the hiring. But we stick to the remainder of the assumptions of Figure 12.

The problem of a general wage rate is an extremely difficult one to explain realistically because, in practice, it is so often tied up with the question of full employment, total output, and aggregate demand or consumption levels. So far we have not handled any of these problems though we will come to them in Part IV. Yet we must still, at this point, keep to our technique of taking one step at a time in order to prepare for an eventual "total" discussion. We will here, therefore, only approach the problem of the general wage rate under some very special conditions. We will assume that society has only a fixed amount of plant and other equipment available for use, that there are no new inventions, and that there is no saving or investment going on except what is necessary to replace the equipment being worn out. People will consume all final output as it is produced. Let us further say, in order to keep the argument simple, that all labor is homogeneous and that there is pure competition. What would then determine the general wage?

The answer is that, under the very special conditions we are here dealing with, the general wage would ultimately be determined through the same type of calculation that we have just described in connection with the individual firm. If, for example, a given wage rate was so high that, after the individual firms had made their employment calculations, some men were still unemployed, only one thing (remember we are talking of pure competition) would be bound to occur. The unemployed men would bid against each other for jobs and the wage level generally would fall. On the other hand, as the wage level fell, employers would bid against each other for the additional men whom it was now (at lower wages) profitable to employ. Thus—remembering that we have assumed away all the problems of net saving, growth, and demand—the general level of wages would be bound to come to rest in our example at that point where, given the amount of equipment, the size of the labor force, and the technical relations between the two, the general wage rate would be set just equal to the marginal product derived from using the last man hired—that is to say, the value of the amount added by employing him. This last man, of course, does not mean any particular man, but simply refers to the calculations by which employers determine how much would be added to product by various sizes of the labor force.

### Labor's Share and the Quantity of Labor

We are now in a position to state some simple but important conclusions. Still disregarding the whole problem of net savings, growth, demand, and the problem of how a society would behave in moving from one stationary adjustment to another, and supposing (as we will discuss later) that a stationary adjustment is ever possible, we can nevertheless say that under conditions of stationary adjustment with no technical change the share of labor in the total output of society would depend on its quantity relative to the amount of equipment and other capital items.

For example, under the conditions to which we have been limiting ourselves, if there were still no increase in the amount of machinery and equipment, but population increased—with the result that a still larger number of men would need jobs—then again only one thing could happen if full employment were desired. Wage rates would have to fall again.

## Reversing the Problem

But the analysis we are giving does not show only why wages may fall. Let us turn it around. Suppose we say that the quantity of labor is fixed, but that the amount of machinery and equipment relative to labor is allowed to increase for a while. Suppose that the expansion then levels off, so that there is no longer any net saving and investment, but only replacement; and suppose as before that we set aside all problems of demand. What will happen to the level of wages and the relative share of labor? The answer is that both must rise. For now labor is scarce as compared to equipment. Employers will be bidding against each other for a scarce labor supply to use with their new plant, and while the marginal product of the last unit of equipment will have fallen, the marginal product of the last man hired will have risen.

## An Iron Law of Wages? Equilibrium Wages versus Subsistence Wages

The very general conclusion emerges that in full employment, stationary, purely competitive equilibrium, the wage rate will be set by the marginal productivity of the labor force. Furthermore, labor's relative share—relative, that is, to other income claims—will depend upon its scarcity or abundance as compared to the amount of capital and other equipment. But there is one final question to be added. Is there any necessary standard of living at which the stationary equilibrium wage must be set? Some of the older economists often talked as if there were. They talked of an "iron law" of wages, and of minimum subsistence levels, etc. Their idea was that, if the standard of living rose above the minimum level just necessary to sustain life, people would proceed to have so many children that population would outstrip the means of production. Because of the competitive process we have already explained, living standards would once more fall to the bare minimum needed to sustain life.

We now know that the subsistence idea does not necessarily follow. Particularly in America and Western Europe, population, while increasing enormously, has not begun to absorb all the gains from additions to the stock of equipment and the productiveness of new methods. Thus the standard of living has risen far above subsistence and has remained there. We do not need, therefore, to suppose that the minimum equilibrium wage called for by economic analysis in a stationary society is merely a subsistence one. However, it remains true that in the last analysis the standard of living depends upon a race between the inventor and investor, on the one hand, and the "stork," on the other. If population grows unchecked, while new inventions are increasingly hampered by pressure groups, and if investment, the construction of additional equipment, is made more and more difficult, a fall in the standard of living is inevitable. Thus in some Oriental and African countries the iron law of population increase has operated almost literally for thousands of years. Nevertheless, the student must keep the two points separated: *The equilibrium wage of economic analysis has no necessary relation to a subsistence or iron-law limit.* Economic analysis shows that many different wage levels are possible. The iron law merely shows the result of *one* set of assumed factual conditions.

**Capital's Share—Introducing "Rent"**

The preceding sections, despite their simplification, do nevertheless give us the fundamental wage model. We will add many complications to this model, as our study proceeds, especially in the chapters on labor unions. But those complications are not necessary now. What we want to do here is to turn to the analysis of the incomes which make up capital's share. You will notice that capital's share, in Figure 15, is marked R.I.P. These mystic initials stand for "rent," "interest," and "profit"—the three capital incomes. Let us begin with rent.

By "economic rent" in this book we mean payment for the use of an agent of production whose supply is fixed. If the total supply of an agent of production neither increases nor decreases no matter what price you pay for it then the payment made for the use of that agent is "rent." Outstanding examples of such agents are simple space or location and scarce natural resources. The type of income we are talking of was first noticed in connection with farming and land. Suppose that the demand for wheat becomes very great. At first only the best land will be cultivated and the price will have to be only high enough to get that land into production. But as the demand becomes greater, price will rise and less efficient land will be brought in at the "margin." As the marginal cost of the marginal farm rises the special return of the more fertile land will become greater and greater and this will be one source of rent. Furthermore, in some cases of fixed supply even the marginal enterprise will be earning a net return over all cost which, however, under the peculiar circumstances, will have no result in increasing supply and will merely serve to ration the fixed supply among would-be purchasers. This income, too, is called "rent" by the economic theorists.

The diagram which best shows the most usual case of rent is that of Figure 10(a), (b), (c), (d) (p. 113) and it will help us greatly if we first review that diagram. Figure 10 is important because it shows an industry in which no firm has any marginal profit incentive to expand. In other words, Figure 10 shows a condition of permanent (unless disturbed from outside), complete, and perfect adjustment. Yet from examining the separate sections of Figure

10 it is clear from the diagram that some very high net returns over costs are being received. Let us examine the Figure more closely. What it shows is that under the conditions assumed (pure competition, a stationary equilibrium, diminishing returns) price throughout the industry will be set by the "marginal cost of the marginal firm." What we mean is that the general market price will have to be high enough to cover the cost of the last unit produced by the least efficient firm in the industry, the firm which is just making out and which would be the first to drop out should there be a further price decline. Yet, as shown in Figure 10, there are several other firms in much more advantageous positions, and these other "intra-marginal firms," as we may call them, are doing very well at a price which merely enables their marginal competitor to break even. Their specially favorable position gives them a special return. It was from phenomena like these that economists worked out the idea of rent. Furthermore, by a small change in the diagram we could bring out the situation in which rent is earned even by the marginal firms. Suppose that for some reason the industry shown in Figure 10 could not have any more firms in it. It is impossible to increase output further. Suppose, next, that because of great demand for the product, price should rise. It will be seen that the equation of marginal cost and marginal revenue (in Figure 10 the same as price) would take place, even for the marginal firm, high above the minimum point on the cost curve. There would thus be returns all along the line over and above that which was needed as a minimum profit. All the analysis of Figure 10 can easily be translated into terms of equilibrium under monopolistic competition also.

### Economic Rent versus Contractual Rent

But let us define "rent" a bit more clearly. We have said that the phenomenon now called economic rent by the economists was first noticed in connection with land. David Ricardo, a stockbroker but also a landlord, noticed the wide variation in the rent paid him upon various farms on his estate, although the net returns to the farmers who rented them showed no such variation. He worked it out that the farmers (disregarding rent) had merely to cover their costs, and to make whatever was the needed amount of net profit to keep them in business, but that the rent paid upon the farm reflected the special fertility or advantages of each particular farm. Some were nearly marginal and some were not. Later economists, starting from his point of departure, carried the concept much further until now land rent is regarded as only a small part of a very general phenomenon.

"Rent" is nevertheless a confusing concept when first encountered, for the following reason. Not all the payments actually made in everyday life and called "rent" are in fact economic rent to the pure theorist. Still more complicated, not all the payment made in everyday life which a pure theorist would call "economic rent" goes by that name to everyday men. The first distinction to make is between contractual and economic rent. Contractual rent is the rent you agree to pay, say, to your landlady. This has to cover a host of out-of-pocket costs—heat, for example, and taxes, and repairs—which have nothing to do with pure economic rent. It is only that part of the payment which is due purely to location and space, aside from building costs, that could be called economic rent. On the other hand, contractual rent may be less than economic rent. The rent which you have contracted to pay may, for example, be set forth in a lease made ten years before. Because of inflation the rental payments may be far from adequate and so by an accident of contract and price change, part of the true economic rent is now going to someone other than the owner. Likewise, because of unsophisticated accounting, or simple difficulty of tracking costs, payments may be called profit or interest which are in fact economic rent.

### Unearned Income

Two final points must be mentioned before we leave the subject of rent. First, there are very few things whose supply is not capable of slight variation. For example, even the supply of land can be somewhat increased by draining, dyking, or irrigation. The economists do not consider these exceptions important enough to force a recasting of definitions. Our second point is more important. Rent almost from the beginning has had an association with unearned income. Thus, Ricardo pointed out that the great rental payments received by the English landlords at the time of the Napoleonic wars rewarded no effort and were merely a means of rationing a scarce commodity, land. However, one must remember that even if no present effort is being rewarded by rent, the right to receive it may have been paid for by very hard-earned dollars. To confiscate the income purchased would be highly unfair. Such considerations plus the extreme difficulty of disentangling the pure rental payment from a host of earned and necessary rewards make most economists very doubtful of an indiscriminate application of the "unearned" idea.

### Overall View and Summary

We have now reached a point at which we can put together the elementary theory of wages with the elementary theory of rent, to produce a first model of income distribution in a hypothetical stationary state, in complete adjustment. In such a supposed society, wages would be determined by the marginal productivity of labor, and labor's share would be set by the quantity of labor relative to the quantity of capital. We have seen that neither wages nor labor's share needs to be at a subsistence level. But what about capital's share? What about rent, interest, and profits? So far we have dealt only with rent.

Our model, however, as diagramed in Figure 10, indicates certain preliminary conclusions. Since there is supposed to be perfect adjustment and equilibrium all round, and since society is supposed to be completely stationary, it follows that there can be no "marginal efficiency of capital," no profits inducing expansion. Because of the differences in efficiency, location, and so forth, mentioned in connection with Figure 10, there may still be extra returns called "rent," but these do not serve in any way as incentives to increase output. Prices are set by the marginal cost of the marginal firms. And these only earn the "minimum" profit indicated in the cost curves, whatever that may be. Nor does one see offhand just where any interest would show up or why. Clearly we are in need of some much more detailed and probably more dynamic analysis. Let us proceed, therefore, to a more careful analysis of profits and interest.

# +++ XI +++

# The Full-employment Theory of Interest and Profit: The Stationary and the Growing World

With this chapter we will cross the final bridge into analysis of the dynamic world. Once basic profit and interest theory are grasped, we are in a position to move into the theory of unemployment, maladjustment, and economic problems generally. But before analyzing economic worlds that are fluctuating, it is important to understand what an economy would be like which was in a state of steady balance—either when growing or when standing still. That is our job in this chapter. For the moment we disregard the twin demons of inflation and unemployment. We disregard them not because they are unimportant but because their analysis is too complicated for one chapter. "One thing at a time" must be our motto.

## Profit versus the Marginal Efficiency of Capital

In Chapter IX, in explaining the theory of an industry, we made a sharp distinction between the types of profit called profit in a stationary industry, and the type of profit needed to induce growth. We saw that in a stationary society there can be a number of things people might call profit. For example, the man who owns his own business may think that he is earning a profit when he is merely earning the salary of the manager whom he would have to employ if he were not supervising the business himself. Or if he owns his own store, the rent might be confused with profit. We mentioned, further, that even in a stationary society there might be certain risks—hurricanes for example—not easily provided for, and industries subject to such special hazards might require a rather high prospect of profit to keep going. But none of these incomes needs to have anything to do with growth. As in Chapter IX, our main concern here will be the net expectation of profit from increasing output, and this, following Lord Keynes, we will call the "marginal efficiency of capital." We want to see what this is, and where it comes from, also what interest is and how the two are related. But we will still be studying all these questions in a world supposed to be free from unemployment and inflation.

## Essence of Profit, Investment and Interest

We may begin by stripping the process of growth, investment, profit, and interest to barest essentials. To do so, we omit many of the features usually thought to be essential. We will suppose that we are in a primitive society which uses no money and which is at a fixed level of customary technique and output. Say that we are dealing with a desert island whose inhabitants subsist by fishing, using a fish hook developed by their ancestors.

Suppose, next, that some ingenious member of our fixed society believes that he can make a better fish hook. He thinks that with the new-type fish hook he can catch twice as many fish. But first he needs time to whittle out the new-type hook and to experiment with its shape. Here will be the problem, for we may suppose that he has no spare food of his own. What to do? At this point we may say that the lender will appear. He is another islander, with some dried fish stored for the winter. Our experimenter persuades him to lend him some of the dried fish. Or perhaps our experimenter persuades another islander to lend him some of his daily catch, while he is experimenting, in return for a promise of a share in the expected doubled output. The arrangement is made and the experiment proves successful. We thus have here a perfect example of growth, profit, lending, investment, and interest.

The man persuaded to transfer his fish is, of course, the lender. The expected profit is created by our experimenter, who has increased output by using a new technological idea. The new hook constitutes investment. The amount of the investment, by the lender, is of course the number of fish lent. Finally the experimenter is able to offer the lender a special inducement because he expects an additional return (profit) through his new hook—a return of more fish than he lent. This we may call *interest*. What is left over for himself we call profit. And we have here all the basic essentials of the most highly sophisticated modern investment transaction.

## Some Objections

We cannot, however, stop our story at this point. One objection often made even to our primitive parable, especially in the case of dried fish, is that the dried fish are bound to rot sooner or later, and that the lender will be so delighted with the idea of getting fresh fish, in say six months when the new hook is completed, rather than having to eat half-rotted stores, that he will lend the dried fish "for free." In other words, he will ask for no extra fish to be returned to him. Conceivably such a thing might happen, though in view of the risk that the idea might prove a dud, it is not likely. Let us, however, suppose that there are several hopeful inventors, and that all of them meet with the possible lender of dried fish. One of them says, "I will return you two extra fish for the loan of ten." The next says, "No, I will return three." The third says, "Four." In short, they compete against one another, in the manner sketched in Chapter III, for the fish needed to support them during the time they are experimenting. The result will be that the one offering the highest return in extra fish (interest) will —supposing him to be as reliable as the others—get the loan of dried fish.

### Increased Output

But in bringing in many would-be borrowers, and competition, we also bring in the idea of market adjustment. Suppose the new type of hook catches on and many people imitate it. At first there will be high prospects of profit (in extra fish) from hook-making, but after a while the whole island economy will have adjusted to the new method. There will be enough hooks, and only the few needed to replace what is wearing out will continue to be made. Society will be in a new state of adjustment, although, thanks to the superior efficiency of the new method, total output will be higher than it was before.

Turn back now to Figure 9(c) (p. 106). Have we not really, in our little fish story, merely given the essence of the process shown in Figure 9(c), though without referring to money? A new technological possibility has created profit expectations. An increased prospect of profit has led to a desire to expand. In the fish story this leads to borrowing and to interest, but in both Figure 9(c), and in the fish story, the resulting expansion eliminates the special gain from increased hook-making. No longer will there be any special incentive to borrow, and so far as our particular story is concerned, the urge to borrow and to invest would disappear until some new idea came along to be experimented upon.

### Some Fundamental Questions

We have used our fish story to highlight the essentials of the interest profit transaction in the modern growing world. But does interest, profit, and investment always depend upon a stream of new inventions? Will progress ever come to an end? How does the process work in a monetary society? We will try to answer all these questions, and we begin in a modern, money-using society in which there is both the necessary mobility and the necessary enterprise, so that new methods are constantly being introduced, and society experiences constant pressure to expand. After we have carried through our analysis of interest under these conditions, we will then consider whether there is ever any necessary end to expansion.

## Interest and the Short-run Marginal Efficiency of Capital

We turn, therefore, to a modern, money-using society, and we ask our-selves: What is interest under these conditions? In the most immediate, down-to-earth meaning, "interest" is easy to define. It is the price paid for borrowed money. If you need $100, and you have no money or assets of your own, you will have to borrow from someone. Suppose that, in return for lending, he asks that you pay him at the end of three months not $100 but $110, your interest for that period will be $10 or 10 per cent.

Mere cash calculations, however, as we have pointed out several times, are not the fundamental thing. Most of the time money is borrowed to be used—that is, people borrow to buy consumer goods for themselves, or to meet the payroll of a new factory, or to build a new plant. Thus if, through high prices and inflation, the borrowed money is able to buy hardly anything, borrowing it becomes useless.

Again if, through inflation, the money which someone has borrowed from you at the beginning of a month is able to buy only half as much at the end of the month as it did at the beginning, then even though you will have received a 10 per cent interest payment in money you will in fact not have received any interest at all and, indeed, have lost a good deal of your capital. On the other hand, if money has become more valuable, in the sense of being able to buy more goods than when it was borrowed, then the borrower who returns a $100 loan, plus money interest in dollars which can now buy twice as much as those he originally received, will in fact be paying not 10 per cent interest but more nearly 100 per cent interest. Thus we see that the price for borrowed money, which is called interest, cannot be properly figured in money terms alone.

We will come back to problems like these later. The question we want to ask now is: How is the rate of interest ultimately determined in our growing, full-employment, noninflationary society? The method is shown in Figure 13.

In Figure 13 we assume that we are dealing with a society at a given level of full-employment output. The assumption of a given total output is vital and will not be relaxed until we get to business cycle and unemployment theory. But let us continue on the fixed assumption for the present. Along the horizontal axis of Figure 13 we mark off amounts, in dollars, of "planned saving" and "planned investment." We will see in a minute what these terms mean. On the vertical axis we mark off percentages of interest and expected profit. Parallel to the ver-tical axis we draw a line which we call the "savings line" and intersecting it is shown a curve labeled "marginal efficiency of capital."

"Planned saving" is the amount of money people will be planning to save from a given total output and income. In Chapter II and again in Chapter III, we saw that money put aside from current income "voted" to hold resources idle, which could then be used, when the money was borrowed, to construct new capital plant—that is, for "investment." The savings line of Figure 13 shows how much people are trying to save per period from the given current income. We show the savings line parallel to the vertical axis because most modern economists assume that in the short run the amount, or per cent, of planned saving is not affected by the rate of interest, but rather, other things being equal, by the amount of income. This assumption will be reconsidered in later chapters, but it will serve here.

Figure 13

THE SHORT-RUN MARGINAL EFFICIENCY OF CAPITAL

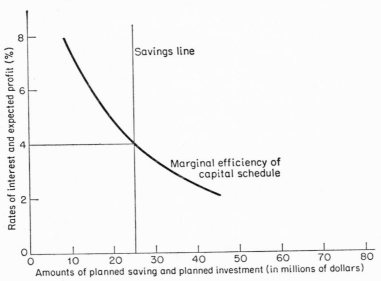

Source: David McCord Wright, *The Keynesian System;* Fordham University Press, © 1962 (p. 27)

We come next to "planned investment." By investment we mean the actual construction of new capital projects, instruments, training, or plant. This definition is different from that often heard in actual conversation. For example a man may say, "I invested $1,000 in General Motors." All that he will mean is that he has spent money on a piece of paper entitling him to a share in General Motors dividends. His purchase need not have anything to do with current construction. We use here, however, a narrower definition. "Investment" to us means money spent on actual current production investment activity, not the mere exchange of claims. But let us next go on to the short-run marginal efficiency of capital curve.

What will this curve measure? As shown in Figure 13, it will measure (1) the expected (2) per cent or rate of return over initial cost during a short period, say a year, for (3) various supposed alternative amounts of investment (4) assuming no inflation or change in output. But to make our curve at all realistic, we cannot assume that there are no changes in tastes, no inventions, no population changes. On the contrary since, in the real world, things are constantly changing, a short-run marginal efficiency of capital curve is a sort of "flashlight picture" of a rate of expected change in technique over a given short time. We do not, in other words, assume *no* change, but only that change is taking place in a certain expected way.

Why do we draw the short-run marginal efficiency of capital curve, in Figure 13, sloping downward? The truth is that it is not altogether clear that we are justified in doing so. For since the investment situation is constantly changing, some people feel that one might just as well draw the curve as a straight, horizontal line. This is particularly the case when we remember what a small part of the total capital stock of a nation is built in one year. Nevertheless, most economists feel intuitively that, over a year or six months, the attempt to increase total investment from, say, ten to twenty-five billion would make necessary a fall in the rate demanded. There might be, say, eight billion of 10 per cent projects available, but to jump to twenty-five billion we would have to take 4 per cent. Thus we draw our curve as a slope.

What is much more important to remember than the slope of any special curve is that since the curve represents a set of expectations, the whole curve can suddenly shift up or down as technique and other conditions change. But now let us go on to the determination of the rate of interest.

A very brief study of Figure 13 will show that the rate of interest, under the conditions we are assuming, must be set at the intersection of the short-run marginal efficiency of capital curve and the savings line. In Figure 13 this will be 4 per cent.

If the rate charged by lenders were higher than the intersection point in our Figure 13, then the amount people would be able to borrow and invest would be less than the amount they were planning to save from current income. Some money would be withdrawn from current income but not respent upon new investment. The act of saving would have kept some men and resources out of making consumption goods, but it would not be offset by any equivalent act of investment using the men thus left free. There would begin to be unemployment and a fall in prices.

On the other hand, if the rate charged by the banks were at less than the intersection point, then more people would be trying to invest than there was money being currently saved. Planned saving would be greater than planned investment. If more money were somehow put into circulation, either from cash hoards or by the "creation" of new deposits by the banks (we will see in later chapters how this works), the would-be investors would have more money, to be sure; but there would be no greater margin of resources available for investment than before. The price of this limited supply of investment resources would be bid up and there would be inflation. Thus the intersection point of Figure 13 is the only point of stable balance which avoids both unemployment and inflation. It must be remembered, however, that this ideal rate varies greatly over time. Every time the state of knowledge changes, every time cost or confidence conditions alter, we have to draw a new curve. And there will be a new intersection point and a new ideal interest rate.

## Summary on Dynamic Interest

We see that under the short-run, full employment, noninflationary conditions we are assuming, the rate of interest, in the dynamic world of continued change, will be set where the short-run marginal efficiency of capital curve crosses the savings line, and that it will alter back and forth as the curve changes. It must be remembered that we have here only a simplified first approximation of a total theory of interest. Development of a complete theory must wait until Chapter XIX. Yet even in an outline there are two questions still to be answered: First, is technical change the only possible source of an upward shift in the marginal efficiency of capital curve? Next, what happens if change stops?

The first question is easily answered. *Any* dynamic change which increases demand relative to supply, will tend, other things being equal, to create an inducement to expand. Thus, for example, an increase in population relative to capital will, under pure competition, lower wages and raise the short-run marginal efficiency of capital, and it should be pointed out that the mere drop in wage rates need not lower total payrolls. But we will develop such points in Chapter XVII. Again if someone thinks up a new product or discovers a new ore deposit, the marginal efficiency of capital may rise, and there are many other possibilities. But now we come to the second question: What if society runs out of ideas and feels no urge to expand?

## An End to Expansion? The Stationary State

Abstract mathematical analysts (and some others too) have often played with the notion of a society in which investment has reached a final limit. Such analyses usually assume a fixed set of wants, and a fixed set of productive ideas, population, and resources. It is then demonstrated that investors will start on the most profitable prospects, then the next best, and so on. A long-run marginal efficiency of capital curve is drawn, which, unlike our short-run dynamic curve of Figure 13, measures not the flow of current investment but the slow fall in marginal profit prospects as the total capital stock of a society increases in a *fixed* environment. We show this curve in Figure 14. As society accumulates equipment, the rate of expected profit and interest on new investment will fall.

Most economists, however, would deny that even in such a fixed environment the rate of interest would ever fall to zero. Cutting through a very complicated discussion, there are two practical reasons usually given for supposing that the rate cannot reach zero. It is said, first, that if men are not paid some interest, they will not only stop saving, but they will even use up the money and

**Figure 14**
**THE LONG-RUN MARGINAL EFFICIENCY OF CAPITAL**

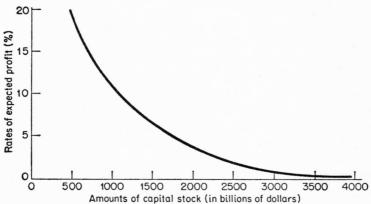

Source: David McCord Wright, *The Keynesian System;* Fordham University Press, © 1962 (p. 26)

resources needed to replace the machinery wearing out. It is said that people have a "time preference"—that present wants look bigger to them than future ones. A second reason for supposing that interest will never fall to zero is the idea that there will always be a certain number of distressed persons anxious to borrow. "Pawnshop" loans of this type will keep the rate of interest at a minimum.

### Theoretical Stationary States versus Actually Nongrowing Societies

We are steering the reader here around a most elaborate literature. Some people deny the problem we are talking about entirely. They say there cannot be any limit, or indeed any such long-run marginal efficiency of capital curve as we have shown in Figure 14. "Human wants are boundless." Fortunately, we do not have to take sides. Whether or not a state of complete saturation is possible, there can be no doubt that we are not in it now and are not likely to be. Anyone who considers the poverty of most of the modern world, the great explosion of population just getting under way, the number of new inventions and the tremendous change in the "expectations" of most people, must reach the conclusion that once we stop thinking only of small rich areas and consider the whole world, poverty is the rule and saturation is not in sight. Yet we are all familiar with the case of actual poor countries which are not growing. How can we explain them? Furthermore, we will soon find a paradox. In some of these poor but not growing societies, the rate of interest is extremely high, much higher than in the more developed nations. How can this be? Is it just the high interest rate that keeps them from growing?

Careful analysis of the problem will show that, while economic variables all interact, it is more often the failure to grow that produces the high interest rate than the high interest rate that produces the failure to grow. In most of the actually nongrowing nations of the world today it is not necessary to assume that it would be physically impossible to increase both output and profit at the same time, *if* the people wanted to do it, or the government would permit it. On the contrary, there may be many obvious profit opportunities which would be immediately available were the society reorganized in a more flexible manner, or were the people more energetic or more willing to permit change. But suppose we are dealing with a people who value serenity and routine more than anything else, and are more inclined to take a nap than to plan a new factory or to work in one. In such a case the existence of potential profit opportunities from introducing machinery or new methods is not very important. The people of this undeveloping country may even, in a vague, general way, want "growth," but they do not want the immediate disturbances which would be necessary to make growth possible. The mere fact that certain possibilities of profit through investment exist will not be enough in itself to induce growth, for the profit might not be big enough in itself to persuade people to go to the trouble of beating down all the obstacles and inertia that would have to be overcome to build the necessary plant. Or, again, imagine a country where the potential investor knows that all the additional income earned by a new plant is going to be confiscated immediately by the government; will he bother to do anything although numerous possibilities of adding to product and profit surround him? Probably not.

The inertia, instability, and risk of such nongrowing systems affect both sides of the loan market. Owners will demand a high interest return, even before replacing machinery that is wearing out, for without such an inducement they could turn their assets into cash and put their wealth into some liquid form, say a Swiss bank deposit, where their home government could not confiscate it. It might be safer also to have gold and jewelry than a factory which could be so easily nationalized. Thus in a lethargic country, full of political risks, the would-be investor is discouraged. Nevertheless, the possibility of using resources to increase output in ways that would be highly profitable—if it were not for fear of confiscation—plus the lack of any net saving, keeps the actual profit rate high. The society is at a high point on its long-run marginal efficiency of capital curve.

Lenders, however, are equally frightened in our supposed society; and despite the high potential rewards that are present, they will not do any net saving. Those few who do lend money will demand very high interest rates to compensate them for the high risks of loss. Thus, though the economy is poor, and there are many opportunities at hand, nobody makes any net saving, and though the society is stationary, the rate of interest may be tremendously high—15 or 25 per cent, or even a higher percentage. One of the familiar figures of the social pattern of the actually nongrowing society is, indeed, the money lender. He has accumulated a store of money and keeps lending and relending it. But the gold in the money lender's chests does not represent any net flow, for society as a whole, of current saving from current income. He lends the gold mostly to people who need funds for consumption. Either they are in distress—the old and the sick—or they are spendthrifts. Such loans are a million miles removed in nature from the investment process of a dynamic industrialism. They create no net resources. The saving of the money lender is balanced by the consumption of his clients, and his risk is great.

But the high rates of interest of the actually nonexpanding society are usually much higher than can be explained by simple risk. They—the 15 and 25 per cent rates we have talked of—are the result of a high *long-run* marginal efficiency of capital curve, balanced against a small, fixed stock of capital.

The basic reason for the existence of high interest rates, in the actual nongrowing world, is thus the presence of a great number of profit potentialities which the lack of net saving makes it impossible to develop. The rate of interest gets "stuck" at a high level and as this high interest shows up in the cost curve of the individual firm, no net profit *after* interest seems to be present. Well-meaning persons often say that if only the interest rate were reduced, in such a condition, all would be well. But what is needed is not so much a reduction in interest as an increase *in the flow of real saving*. Without net saving, a lower interest rate charged by lenders would only cause inflation.

## Modern, Dynamic, Industrial Interest

Very different is the case of modern, dynamic, industrial interest in a country like the United States. There the economy has been accumulating capital for so long that the society is far down on the long-run MEC curve of Figure 14. Some people have said the rate would be zero if it were not for technical change. This is probably wildly optimistic. Nevertheless, the average rate is much below that in the actual nongrowing minimum. Furthermore, the purposes of borrowing are different. In the actual nongrowing society, since there is no net investment, the only borrowing actually taking place is, on balance, mostly what we have called "pawnshop" loans—loans by the money lender to distressed and profligate people. This is the process often called "usury" and condemned by numerous writers, ancient and modern. Although the money lender—drawn vividly, for example, by Dickens in his novels—is not often an appealing type, much of the condemnation is unfair, for the money lender in the nongrowing society runs enormous risks both of default and of confiscation.

Very different is the modern bank which collects the net saving of a society and transfers it to the productive industrial borrower. In modern society it is the borrower who is often the strong party to the bargain. His strength lies in the productive power of the new technological combination which he is borrowing to put through. But the industrial borrower has to go through a marginal calculation for borrowing, as well as in all the other aspects we have seen. The profit expected on the last dollar borrowed must just equal the rate charged on that dollar. If the rate were less it would pay to borrow more. If it were more he would be reducing the total return just as in other calculations concerning marginal cost and marginal revenue.

### Liquidity

The present chapter does not deal with maladjustment. Nevertheless, we should mention at this point that the process we are describing does not always work smoothly, even in the modern world. Various forces, which we will describe in detail in the business cycle chapters, may force the short-run MEC curve very far down. But because of the desire for liquid cash the rate may not fall low enough to permit the full use of all planned net saving. Unemployment will begin. We will develop all this in the next part of this book, but let us now stop to summarize the ground so far covered.

### Summary

In the chapters on the firm, we first developed the demand curve, and next the supply curve, followed by the cost curve. Then we put the firm demand curve and cost curve together to show the "maximization" of short-run profit by the "equation" of marginal cost and marginal revenue. We switched next to the industry and external forces, and showed how "abnormal" profits would bring about expansion and so destroy themselves. But we saw that because of fundamental imperfections of adjustment, inherent in the real nature of things, and having nothing to do with "monopoly," certain basic differences of cost, and basic scarcities, were bound to survive in places and hence create "rent."

From rent we passed to the fundamental model of wages, which we saw had no *necessary* connection with subsistence, and from wages we passed to the problem of profits in the actually nongrowing society. We saw that the lack of growth in such a society was generally due to political instability and/or other social features. The poverty which resulted from lack of saving (brought on by the political maladjustment) showed itself as a high rate of interest, but the high rate was more a result than a cause.

And so finally we can summarize the case of distribution in the dynamic industrial society. We have seen how a flow of new ideas and changes in wants constantly increases output and creates new profit opportunities for net investment. We diagramed net investment profits in the short-run marginal efficiency of capital curve, and showed how it, together with the saving line, set the ideal rate of interest. It was also pointed out that were it not for imperfections or frictions of competition, which kept the expected rate of "abnormal" profit from being squeezed out too fast, there would be no expansion.

Behind the whole process of growth which raises total output and wages, and maintains profit and interest, is the creative power of the new idea embodied in the new capital instrument. Only one inevitable, unpleasant feature remains: to have rising wages, on average, and rising output, there must be continuing change. Thus the growing world can give almost everything *except* security in job routine. Here is a fundamental issue to which we must return. But now we must go ahead into new territory. That process of change which is, on balance, at the root of so much we like cannot always work smoothly. Why not? We answer this question in the next nine chapters of this book.

## Part IV

# OUTPUT, EMPLOYMENT, AND STABILIZATION

+ + + XII + + +

## Growth, Capital Formation, and National Income Measurement: Basic Concepts

Everything that we have done so far has been preliminary to the topics we are now beginning. The last few chapters have mostly been occupied with theories of adjustment and of stationary states. Now we begin upon theories of disturbance: Inflation, unemployment, instabilities and growth will be our main topics. But first we have to learn how to measure total output. Measurement is vital, for without it economics is often just a matter of opinion. Always, during economic fluctuations, *some* business or industry is expanding. Always *some* business or industry is declining. Without an approach to an objective measuring system, there will be no way of really judging what forces are in fact the operative ones at any given time. Therefore we learn the measures of output.

In this chapter we will not merely learn to measure. We will also try to analyze the reasoning behind the measures. In learning why they are what they are, we will also get a general plan of the economic system considered as one great operating machine. We will see, in much more detail than previously, how the flow of money relates prices to incomes, and how, in turn, the way in which those incomes are spent shapes the operations of the machine. Hidden in the technicalities of measurement is a general picture of the relation of the money and the productive structure, and once we get that picture clearly and simply in our minds we have a tool that we can use throughout the remainder of this book.

In beginning our analysis, to be sure, we still disregard the complications arising from foreign trade and from government action, but these gaps will soon be repaired.

## A Fundamental Model of Money Flows: Incomes, Prices, and Production

Let us begin by constructing a model which will show the essentials of any total economic system, considered as one great single mechanism for production and growth. As said, we will not include all the complications of real life. Nor will we even try to tie it down to any particular economic system, such as capitalism or socialism. Leaving aside problems of government and international trade and their difficulties, we will begin merely by specifying that the system uses money and is growing, and that there is neither unemployment nor inflation. Starting with these assumptions we ask ourselves what is the best way to form an idea of the general working of the system, looked at from the point of view of production. Perhaps one of the most useful over-all descriptions would be to think of the system as a vast "sausage machine." At one end some people would be putting "meat" (raw materials) into the "machine" (factories and equipment); others would be busy "turning the cranks" (processing the raw materials); and at the other end the finished "sausages" (final output) would be coming out to be distributed among all the workers on the machine and the population generally. Thus, in any economic system, we will find a body of workers, rewarded in various ways, a certain amount of durable equipment (the sausage machine), and finally a stock of raw materials and semifinished goods constantly being worked up into final output.

If our society were not growing, and if we could suppose for a minute that the machine lasted forever, then the picture of an economy as merely made up of men turning the crank of the machine, while feeding in raw materials, would be quite accurate. But everybody knows that in the real world few things last forever. Thus even if a society does not want to grow, but merely to stand still, that society will have to use part of its time and energy to replace and repair those parts of the sausage machine that are wearing out. In other words, all the energy of society cannot go into making "sausages," that is, "consumer goods" —things people eat, wear, and otherwise use to gratify their personal wants. Society also has to produce new parts for the machine. These new parts we call "investment goods."

Introducing investment goods makes the system a more complicated affair. It has to be thought of as having two parts and two outlets. The raw materials are being fed into it as before, the crank is being turned as before, but the flow of materials being processed emerges in two streams. First there are the sausages, the consumer goods, but next there are new pieces for the machine itself, pieces to replace what is wearing out. And these we have seen constitute investment goods.

Adding investment goods production, however, means not only that we have now two parts of the machine, and two outlets for final output, but also that we have two sets of laborers. In the example we first gave, everybody was busy, directly or indirectly, making sausages. Whether they fed in meat, or turned the crank which ground the meat, or passed the sausages around, they were all in the straight line of consumer goods production. But as soon as we begin to produce replacement parts and to talk about repair and maintenance of the machine, we add another group of workers. These men are not directly concerned in making sausages. They are concerned in keeping up the machine itself. We will call them investment goods makers. If they were to stop work, the flow of sausages would soon be a mere trickle, for the machine would begin to wear out and need new parts. Finally it would break down altogether.

But we do not want to talk just about a world that is standing still. Not only do nations want to keep production from falling, they want it to grow. Yet in order to increase production it is nearly always necessary to increase the size of the machine to some extent. Thus our system must now increase the size of its second sector. We need not merely to replace parts that are wearing out, but also to add to the total. Furthermore, in addition to making the machine bigger, some people will also be wanting to make it better—that is, more efficient. So the investment goods makers will have not two but three jobs. They will be making and installing parts to replace those worn out. They will be adding new parts to the total to make it bigger. And, finally, they will be making and installing different kinds of parts—new methods designed to make the machine more efficient.

Let us now look at the picture we have worked out of production in our growing world. First, there is the sausage machine itself and the people working on it. They put in the raw materials, turn the crank to grind the meat, and handle the finished sausages when they come out. All this we call consumer goods production. But next we have to add another part to the machine—this part being a machine for making machines. The new section stamps out new pieces of equipment to replace, enlarge, or to improve the existing machine. So the new machine-making section requires a set of workers of its own to feed material into *it,* turning its crank, and passing out its final product—new machinery—to those places where the new parts are needed. All this we call investment goods production. Adding a machine-making sector complicates our picture of our sausage economy considerably. But as long as investment goods production is only just enough to replace what is being worn out, the process as a whole can be smooth and even.

Now, however, we have to summarize our analysis in a still more disturbed and complicated picture: Imagine a sausage machine in full blast with people hard at work cranking out sausages. Yet imagine that, at the very time at which some men are trying to grind out sausages, other people are taking parts of the machine to pieces—adding to them, repairing them, changing them altogether. It does not take much imagination to see that there will probably be plenty of conflict and plenty of dislocation. People trying to turn the crank will find themselves interrupted by others who want to take out the old crank and put in a new one. Or just as things are going smoothly somebody will start trying to redesign the whole machine. Or some part will break down in the middle of the process and have to be replaced. Yet this picture of a machine being operated, being expanded, being repaired, being redesigned all at once is a true and faithful picture of any economic system which is trying to grow—not just capitalism, but any economic system. We need not therefore be surprised that things do not always go smoothly, and that they are hard to measure.

The task of economic measurement, indeed, is to try to bring some order out of this anthill-like activity. We need, first of all, to measure the straight flow of consumption and output of consumer goods. Then we want to measure the net additions to the total size of the machine. Then we want to consider something we have not so far mentioned—the changing size of the stocks, or inventories, of semifinished and completed goods passing through the machine. Finally, all these flows and stocks are in the real world mere changing collections of physical objects. In order to measure them against one another it is necessary to use money or some common value unit. Furthermore, we will discover that the flow of prices, the flow of money, and the flow of goods all link together in very special ways. It is time, therefore, to express our sausage-machine example in terms of money flows. It can be shown that the total value of income paid out, in a smoothly adjusted society, just equals the total money prices of output, and we will see, further, that the way incomes are spent, in a free-exchange society, affects the speed at which the machine can grow. Again, we will see the need for various money "balances" as output passes from stage to stage. All these are fundamental concepts for output measurement, for money and banking, and for the study of unemployment.

## The Money Flows

The basic diagram is shown in Figure 15, which represents the flow of money and the formation of prices in a drastically simplified system. The money flows presuppose certain production relationships, and we must therefore commence by describing the underlying production structure. In Figure 15 we assume that our system consists of only three industrial stages, whose products

Figure 15
INCOME, PRICE AND PRODUCTION FLOWS

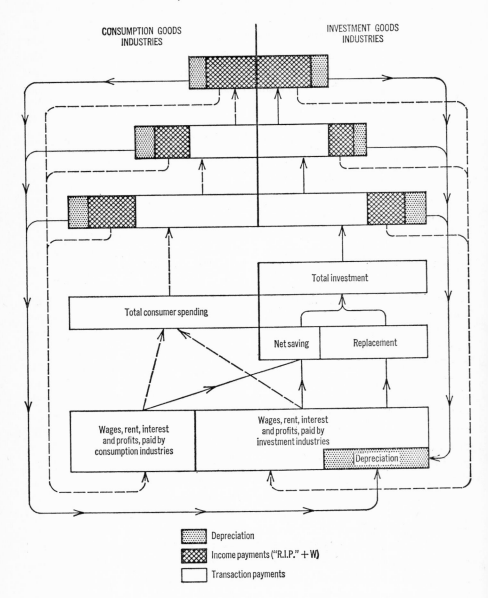

CONSUMPTION GOODS
INDUSTRIES

INVESTMENT GOODS
INDUSTRIES

Total investment

Total consumer spending

Net saving          Replacement

Wages, rent, interest
and profits, paid by
consumption industries

Wages, rent, interest
and profits, paid by
investment industries

Depreciation

Depreciation

Income payments ("R.I.P." + W)

Transaction payments

(and the payments for them) flow smoothly from one to another. These are indicated by the three horizontal bars, or "stages" shown at the top of the diagram.

In the first stage of output we suppose that raw materials—meat, say, and other things for sausages and tools—are merely being grown or mined. Drastically simplifying, we suppose that the firms in this first stage buy only two things: labor and equipment. They do not buy any half-finished goods or materials but, instead, using only labor and durable equipment, they grow or dig out their products directly from the soil. Having done so they then sell their product to Stage II.

Stage II, however, buys not two but three things. It buys labor, and it buys equipment, as does Stage I, but it also buys materials—the product of Stage I. The job of Stage II is to convert raw materials into semifinished goods.

Stage III is the stage of final output. Like Stage II it buys three things: labor, equipment, and the produce of Stage II or semifinished goods, and makes them up into the final product.

These three stages, we assume, feed smoothly into one another. While each stage is supposed to have a certain stock or pile of its goods on hand (what we have called "inventory") the stocks or piles are assumed to remain always of the same size. Since they never change in amount they are not shown in the diagram.

But there is a basic characteristic of the production side of the diagram. This feature is shown by the vertical bar dividing the three stages. What the vertical bar shows is that we are not just dealing with the sort of simple flow of sausages or consumer goods, through an everlasting machine, with which we began. No indeed. Following our previous description of the economic machine, we see that, in the last analysis, both production and the people producing can be grouped under two main heads: consumer goods production, on the one hand, and investment goods production, on the other. The producers of investment goods as distinguished from consumption goods, are those working with the machines that make the machines. The vertical bar marks off this investment group and shows the division—the left-hand, or longer side, indicating the stages of consumer goods production, and the right-hand, those of investment goods. Now let us examine more explicitly the flow of payments in the diagram.

The function of the diagram is, first, to show how money incomes are paid out in the process of production; and second, how the spending of these incomes is in turn related to the process of production in a market economy. In order to show the money–production relation, we make a distinction between those payments which individuals will consider as their *income* and feel free to spend or save, and those payments which are merely passed on to other organizations. To distinguish the different types effectively, we use blocks of three shadings. The small dotted blocks represent payments for depreciation—that is, payments for new machinery and equipment needed to replace worn-out machinery and keep the plant in condition. We omit obsolescence deductions (deduction for change), to keep our diagram simple, but they could be added in the same way, and we assume that depreciation allowances and the purchase of equipment for replacement coincide. In other words, as fast as money is put aside to take care of depreciation, it is immediately used to pay for a new machine part.

Again, spaces which are crosshatched indicate payments to individuals which they can consider as their personal income. In capitalist society these are wages, salaries, rents, interest, and profits. Finally, the white spaces are for intermediate payments—money taken in at one stage, but needed to pay for the products of an earlier stage.

Following our classification, it will be seen that Stage I has only dotted spaces and crosshatched ones. The reason is, as explained, that we are assuming, for simplicity's sake, that people in Stage I get all of their products out of the ground either by farming or digging in mines. The economic units (businesses or state trusts) at this first stage, therefore, have no outside payments to make save depreciation to cover replacement. All the money coming in will be used either for depreciation—to buy new machinery to replace that which is wearing out—or to pay wages, salaries, rent, interest, and profits. And remember we have assumed, again drastically simplifying, that depreciation allowances are spent on replacement as fast as they are earned.

Payments in Stage II are more complicated. Businesses in Stage II are obliged first to pay the people in Stage I for what Stage I has made. This is shown by a white space in the second bar exactly equal in size to the cost of the output of Stage I. But in addition Stage II has also to earn depreciation on its machines, and to pay the people working in it—that is, wages, salaries, etc. Thus Stage II also has a dotted and a crosshatched space. Stage III, again, is like Stage II. It first has to pay Stage II, as is shown by a white space equal to the cost of the output of Stage II; and next it has to make its own payments; that is, its own depreciation, wages, salaries, and so on. So again we add crosshatched and dotted spaces.

But when we get to Stage III we have reached the end of the process of production. Hence the total length of the bar in Stage III with both of the consumer and the investment goods sides added together, will give you the *total value of all the final output in the system*—consumer goods plus equipment. Economists have a name for this. They call it "gross national product." It means the total value of all final output during a given period, including depreciation.

## Prices and Incomes

We have a good deal of work left to do before we can apply our simplified figure to the classifications used in the real world. But let us first try to learn all that the Figure can teach us concerning the fundamental relationship as we see them in this simple form. One of the first and most important of these fundamentals is that the total value of all the incomes paid out in the various stages of production, plus depreciation, will in the Figure be *exactly equal* in value to the value of total final output. Remember we began by assuming that there was neither unemployment nor inflation. The diagram also assumes a perfectly smooth continuing flow. Under these assumptions we will find from the diagram that the price of the final output will have to be just equal to the incomes paid out in making it. Indeed, the one is merely the total of the other.

We can read this identity from the Figure. We draw a black line from each dotted (depreciation) space and carry it around to the bottom bar of the diagram. In the same way we draw dotted lines from all the crosshatched (income) spaces and bring them around together to the bottom bar. The total of all these incomes and depreciation allowances will just equal the total value of gross national product.

Note, however, one thing. The total value of *incomes* paid out in the consumer goods industries, taken by themselves, is shown as *less* than the total value of the consumer goods produced, or the total value of consumer spending. Why? The reason is easily explained. The difference is made up by the depreciation allowances of the consumer goods industries. Depreciation costs are "charged" in the final prices of consumer goods, it is true, but under our assumptions, the money collected is transferred to the investment side to pay for replacing old machines. In consequence the income relating to them is paid out to wage earners working in the investment goods industries or "machine-that-makes-the-machines," and is used by workers in this section to buy consumer goods or to invest. Also it should be noted that in the diagram the investment goods industries replace themselves. That is to say, *their* depreciation quotas are spent in *their own* section to pay for replacing their own machines. "Loops" like these, in the money flow, are in fact very important and numerous in the real world, but the diagram simplifies them as far as possible. Since we have assumed the whole process to be smoothly continuing, the fact that money is making subordinate circuits is not important, for from the point of view of the whole process, the subordinate circuits cancel out.

The real point of the diagram remains valid. Under the conditions assumed, prices and incomes will be exactly equal, and their equality justifies another important statement. We can, under our assumptions, figure gross national product almost equally well if we get the sum of the incomes and depreciation paid out in a system, *or* if we get the money value of total output. Some nations do it one way, some the other, but the end figure is much the same. This simplified diagram shows the basic relation clearly.

The diagram also enables us to understand the fundamentals of yet another economic measure often used by statisticians. This measure is called "national income." The idea here is that output for depreciation is not really "net" because all that the machines do, which are bought with depreciation funds, is to replace what is wearing out and to keep us where we are. In order to find out what the *net* output of society is, in a given period, it is therefore necessary to deduct depreciation expenditures (or the depreciation output) and consider only what is left. This we do in the bottom bar (just discussed) of the Figure. At one end is a space labeled "depreciation." The remainder of that bar is made up of total net investment and consumer receipts, and the sum of these we will call "national income." National income—in the analysis of this diagram—is equal to gross national product *minus depreciation,* but we must qualify the simplicity of these terms when we come down to real life.

### Saving, Production, and the Money Flows

So far we have learned the essentials of what is meant by gross national product and national income. We have also learned to understand the equality of prices and incomes in a balanced system. With these two ideas in mind, we can now answer more precisely the question: What, in a balanced, smoothly running system, determines the amount of investment output being produced? In order to understand why this question is so important you have to recall the requirements for economic growth outlined in Chapter II, and also Chapter XI on distribution. Remember that we saw there that the output of a society is very closely related to the amount of machinery and equipment such a society has managed to accumulate. We called this stock of machinery, equipment, etc., the stock of "capital." By capital we meant the total of durable goods used to make further goods. But if the output of a society is greatly influenced by how much capital (machinery, equipment, etc.) it has, then obviously the growth of output will also be greatly influenced by how much more capital we can manage to accumulate. Yet men and nations alike accumulate capital through investment— that is, the production of more capital. In other words, the rate of growth of a full-employment society will be very much influenced by the *percentage of final output going into investment goods.*

If only enough investment goods are turned out to replace what is being worn out—that is, only enough to cover depreciation—society will not usually grow at all, though sometimes technical change will make some growth possible. On the other hand, the greater the size of *net* investment output—that is, the more machinery, equipment, etc., that is being turned out in *excess* of depreciation requirements—the faster the stock of capital can usually grow, and other things being equal, the faster total output can increase.

We can now repeat the relation of all this to the way money income is handled. The bottom bar in Figure 15, minus depreciation, represented the total of all the money payments in the system which people felt able to call their personal income. Corporations in the diagram will have to be thought of as merely deducting depreciation and paying out all their profits to shareholders as dividends. Otherwise they would have to be considered in figuring income and saving. To continue, the bottom bar is made up of the net payments concerning which people are able to make the decision to spend or to save. Under pure capitalism, and in the type of full employment, smoothly flowing, noninflationary economy we have shown in Figure 15, the size of net investment goods output depends on the amount of current money income people choose to save and invest. As we saw in the chapters on growth and distribution, if people spend money (vote) to buy nothing but consumer goods, the existing equipment of society will not even be maintained and it will soon begin to wear out. If only enough money is saved to cover depreciation, and only enough investment goods of the same type are produced to replace those wearing out, the society will stand still. But if people save money out of their share of national income, and invest it, then they will be voting to increase the size of the consumer goods machine—the size of the total stock of capital. And so society will be enabled to grow.

All this is shown in Figure 15 by drawing solid lines from various points over to a short space labeled "net saving." The lines show that all the people receiving money income, no matter where they may be working, may nevertheless be able to save and by so doing to influence production. Next we join the net saving space to the depreciation–replacement space, and thus get a figure for total investment. Finally, and in the same way, we draw dotted lines from "national income" to "total consumer spending" to show the spending of all the people in our society.

Now it is clear that if production follows the direction of money flows, as it is supposed to do in a competitive, capitalist economy, an increase in the net saving bar will increase the size of the whole investment goods sector, and with it, if the investment is productive, the rate of economic growth. On the other hand, a decrease in net saving will tend to decrease investment and slow down growth. The relations we are sketching, furthermore, can also be expressed in a socialist state. Theoretically, all saving in such a state could be managed through government taxation. The government could hold down spending by taxation and use the funds thus collected to build new investment plant. Except that the size of the various flows, and with it of the various industrial groups, is set by government rather than by market decisions of individuals, precisely the same relations would hold between prices, output values, income, and the industrial structure.

## Summary

In this chapter by the use, first, of the sausage-machine example and, next, of the diagram of price and money flows, we explained in simplest form some of the most fundamental dynamic relations of society. We saw how, in a smoothly adjusted society, the total of payments to individuals just equals the value of the total flow of final output and, more important, we have seen how the flow of production and the rate of growth is shaped by the way individuals spend their payments. It will be necessary, in the next chapter, to add many complications from real life, but these do not affect the basic logic of our sausage machine and its flows. Furthermore, from the examples in this chapter, we have the key to most of the major disturbances of the dynamic world. If the money flows are interrupted, unemployment may ensue. If they are speeded up, there may be inflation. If the consumer side of the sausage machine grows too fast, peculiar twists will often develop in the shape of the investment side. And if investors, or the state, try to produce investment goods faster than consumers are willing to save or be taxed, great maladjustment becomes inevitable. Here then we have a fundamental analysis upon which we can build a large part of the rest of this book.

# Growth, Capital Formation, and National Income Measurement: Practical Problems

The three previous sections of Chapter XII outlined the fundamental analysis behind the measurement of national output and income in pure form, and free from complications of the real world. We there worked out two measures: gross national product—the total value of final output during a given period; and net national income, which was there defined as gross national product minus an allowance for the depreciation of capital during the same period. National income was intended to be a measure of what was really "net," allowing for the amount of output needed to replace the current wearing out of equipment. We reviewed these definitions, and we also showed how, under our ideal conditions, the proportion of private net saving deeply influenced the rate of increase in society's stock of tools and equipment, and hence of economic growth. But now our task is to bring the analysis down to real life. This job falls into two halves. First, we must discuss the changes in classification that need to be made and the additional measures that need to be taken. Next, we go on to the practical problem of collecting data to fit the analysis we have outlined.

## Effect of Government on Income Classifications:
## Personal Income and Disposable Personal Income

So far as pure theory is concerned, perhaps the main omission of Figure 15 (p. 148) was the lack of any space for government output. By "government" we mean all branches of government taken together. The trouble with government output is that authorities are divided as to whether it is "saving" or "consumption," or "gross" or "net," or generally what class to put it in. Again, we shall see later that government has certain powers regarding taxing, borrowing, and coining money which can deeply affect the flow of spending. Because of these problems—both the difficulty of classification and the importance of government action—the calculators of gross national product and allied measures have simply put government income and expenditure in a separate classification and not tried to label it further. They have also been obliged to alter slightly the definition of national income given in Figure 15 and to add three other measures: net national product, personal income, and disposable personal income. Let us see how these work.

### Gross and Net National Product

In Figure 16 we give a diagram which, while it reflects most of the same basic relations shown in Figure 15, introduces the role of government and shows clearly how the different income measures are related in the real world. The box sizes and flow sizes of this figure are not intended to reflect exact actual proportions, but merely to diagram the general nature of these classifications. We begin at the left side of Figure 16 with a gross national product figure as before. It consists of the sum of consumption expenditure, gross investment, and government expenditures. We next deduct from gross national product and show flowing off to the right an allowance for capital consumption just as in Figure 15; and, as in Figure 15, this is shown flowing into gross saving. The remaining amount we call not national income but *net national product*. From net national product, in turn, we deduct "indirect" business taxes and show them flowing off to the government box. It is only the remaining sum, net national product *minus* indirect business taxes, that we now call national income. The reasons for this deduction require explanation.

### National Income

Indirect business taxes—sales and similar taxes—are presumably included in the prices of goods sold on the market, but these taxes are not considered to represent product in private business, nor are they retained as income by private individuals. Instead, these amounts are drawn off to help pay for *government* purchases which in turn appear in gross national product. The experts in such matters consider that to include the sums collected by indirect business taxes in the value of national income would involve double-counting. Accordingly, national income is net product *minus* indirect business taxes.

### National Income and Personal Income

We, however, are more interested in the functional flows of payment in the economy than in delicate points of classification. And when we come to the deductions from national income we find two flows of great importance. First we show, flowing down into gross saving, a flow for corporate saving. This is done because while theoretically all corporate income goes to the stockholders, in fact we shall see later that the corporation does a great deal of net saving

Figure 16
## OUTPUT MEASURES AND MONEY FLOWS

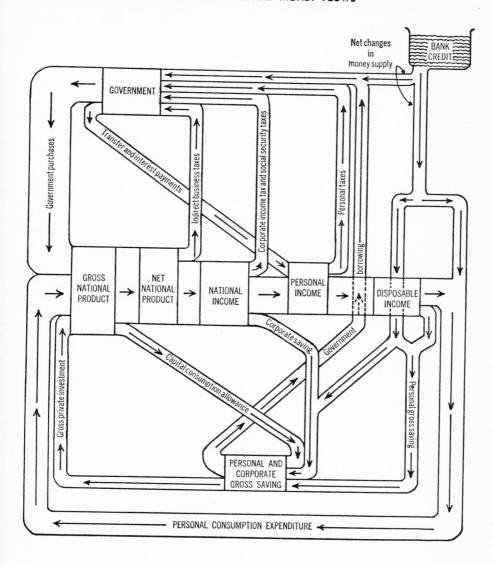

before the stockholders receive their payments. Corporations are thus among the most important "saving machines" in our society.

Flowing out of national income the other way from corporate saving are two more payments *into* government. These are corporate profit taxes and social security payments by corporations and contributions by individuals, both of which are used to finance government but which are included in national income. Only after all these have been deducted do we get a third and most important measure: personal income. Personal income represents that part of the national income which is *received* by *individuals* in the economy. We must realize that it is determined not merely by deducting from national income, as we have done so far, but by *adding* three flows *out* of government. They are *interest payments, transfer payments and subsidies*. We combine them in one stream.

### Transfer Payments, Subsidies and Disposable Income

Interest payments are, of course, interest payments made by government on its loans. To keep the Figure from becoming unbearably complicated they are shown as if they all went directly to individuals, though, of course, many come to individuals only *through* corporations. Transfer payments are more complicated. They are payments made by government to individuals but *not in payment for any current productive service*. Such payments are old-age pensions, pensions to retired soldiers or widows, unemployment benefits, and similar payments. The important word here is "current" services. Many such payments have been paid for in advance by all sorts of past services, including the sacrifice of life itself. But their one common feature is that they are in no way related to present production. The great significance of transfer payments is that, not being related to production, they move independently of it. Indeed, under modern institutions, they often move automatically in an opposite direction. For example, when production drops, unemployment benefits rise, transfer payments rise, and disposable income will not fall as the production drop would indicate. Greater stability in buying power results. Such a stabilizing effect may be of great importance.

### Subsidies Form a Hybrid Case

Subsidies of various sorts are often paid by government today both to individuals and to businesses. We may simplify, in this figure, as with interest, by showing them flowing only to individuals. They are paid to enable enterprises to operate which otherwise, it is felt, could not do so at the market price, or to persuade producers, usually farmers, not to produce what they otherwise would. The payments thus are made to induce action or non action and thus may be said to be for a "service", but they are not the usual type of production payment, and like transfer payments may vary independently of output.

## Disposable Personal Income

When we put together the share of national income received by individuals, plus the payments made to them by the government, either as interest, subsidies or as "transfer" payments, we have the total amount which individuals consider as their current income. Yet there are two more flows to be provided for. First of all, government takes as well as gives. The diagram shows it taking by indirect business taxes, by corporate profit taxes, and by social security taxes and contributions. But, before income really gets to the individual to be freely "disposed" of by him we must allow for just one more government "take": personal taxes, income and otherwise. Thus disposable income includes the addition of government interest and transfer payments, but it also must allow for the deduction of personal taxes, income and otherwise. Only after all these adjustments have been made do we reach a figure at which the individual feels free to decide whether to spend or to save.

## Personal Saving and Investment

Nevertheless, many individuals do save and so out of disposable personal income we show two flows, one into saving and gross investment, the other into personal consumption expenditures. Accordingly, we can bring around from right to left of our diagram three sets of expenditures: gross investment, personal consumption expenditures, and government purchase of goods and services. These three flows make up the gross national product with which we began. We have thus completed our survey.

## Summary

When one surveys Figure 16 it should be clear that, if the complications introduced by "government" could be omitted, Figure 16 would merely be another way of diagraming the same facts as Figure 15. There would be the same total expenditure bar (gross national product) and the same division of expenditure into depreciation, replacement, net saving, and personal consumption expenditure as in Figure 15. The introduction of government merely adds a second "whirlpool" of funds. Government "takes" from gross national product in five ways, one of which we have not yet mentioned. This fifth way (shown on the diagram in Figure 16) is *to borrow:* government borrows part of gross investment *funds,* although government borrowing is not shown in "gross investment" on the diagram. On the contrary, when government spends, it shows up either as government purchases of goods and services or as interest and transfer payments. (Of course we are skipping some difficult secondary problems of classification.) In addition to government borrowing we have seen four "takes": indirect business taxes, corporate profit taxes, social security taxes and contributions, and personal taxes. However, to get the full significance of "government," we must anticipate a bit and merely state as a fact something which sounds strange but which we will soon explain and prove. That fact is that government borrowing sometimes acts as a *net creation* of new money. Government also can coin money. Thus the government sector is capable of acting not merely as a passive agent in shifting money around, but also as a pump *injecting* additional money into the system. Obviously this role as "pump" can, for good and for bad, be a fact of overwhelming importance. We merely indicate the pump action by drawing, in Figure 16, a reservoir labeled "Bank Credit" in the upper right-hand corner. We will explain in detail in later chapters how this works.

Yet, leaving aside the difficulties introduced by "government" and the difficulty of classifying government outlay between investment and consumption, the fundamental fact expressed in Figure 15 reappears, albeit it in more complicated forms, in Figure 16. It is still the case that the rate of net investment, upon which largely depends the flow of growth, is to a great extent set by the amount of net saving made by individuals and other units. And from this fact we see yet more clearly what is perhaps the most valuable lesson of a study of these income flows: that the growing modern economy is constantly throwing itself forward into the unknown! Productive net saving means expansion, and expansion pushes beyond established knowledge. Growth comes through change and causes change. Thus the modern net-saving economy must be forever growing in order to stand still, forever changing in order to remain the same. Moreover, when something happens to stop the smooth flow of funds into change and growth, we get the problem of "unsuccessful" saving, to be developed in the chapter on unemployment. Here, in the pulse beats of the income flows, one finds the place at which most of the economic illnesses of society first manifest themselves.

### Some Practical Problems of Income Measurement

Although the last section finished the theoretical description of income measurements, we would get a most misleading impression if we stopped at this point. We would probably have the idea that the field of gross national product measurement was a clear and definite one, and that all one had to do was to go out and get easily ascertained facts and drop them into a computer. Unfortunately such a conclusion could not be more wrong and it is important that we know why. What may read as if it were an important shift in economic behavior will often, on examination, turn out to be some trick in the definitions. So in order to keep our feet on the ground we must spend a while running over these problems.

The first of these is that in the real world, production does not take place in the simple, symmetrical, straight-line process we have shown in Figure 15. Instead, production is full of "loops" and "whirlpools." The various industries feed in on each other and out again, as also do the money flows. A picture of an actual system therefore is likely to look much more like a bubble bath than the simple pyramid we have given. As long as there is a continuous and steady flow, the effects of all these loops and whirlpools cancel out. The *net* effect is the same as in our Figure.

Another complication which we omitted in Figure 15 concerns the problem of "inventory." Nearly every business keeps constantly on hand a certain stock of materials and goods. If the flow of production through the system is absolutely smooth we can forget about these stocks, for there will be no net change in their size. But in the real world, where the production flows are not always smooth and steady, the *net* size of inventories frequently fluctuates. This raises an important problem for gross national product and national income figures. Statisticians and economists settle it by treating *net* changes in inventory as a part of investment. Thus net increases in inventory are treated as increases in the investment total in gross product and national income figures, while net decreases decrease it.

A third important complication is related to monetary disturbances. The diagram is drawn on the assumption that there is neither inflation nor deflation. But in real life increases or decreases in the amount or value of money, or the intensity with which money is used, can upset all the price–income relationships. Thus if we read that gross national product is twice as large this year as it was last, we have to be careful what conclusions we draw. Not all the money income paid out in a society is related to someone's production. If the money figures go up there may not have been *any* increase in actual production at all. The whole thing can often be just a matter of higher prices. Problems like these will be discussed in the chapter on money.

So far the complications discussed, while difficult, are not overwhelming. We have now, however, to add three more which greatly affect the precision of statistical measurements of income and production and which have caused statisticians and economists more and more to shift from national income figures to gross national product ones.

The first of these complications relates to the problem of depreciation. In the real world any given factory takes *time* to wear out. How long the process will actually take is always a guess and frequently an arbitrary one. In modern America, indeed, a machine is more apt to be discarded because it is old-fashioned than because it is worn out. Accountants, we have seen, try to take care of these problems by taking deductions for depreciation (simple wearing out) and obsolescence (getting out of date). But since only a clairvoyant can tell what is actually going to happen, the deductions thus made are very much a matter of guesswork and personal judgment modified by government regulation. Furthermore, while depreciation deductions may be taken fairly steadily, the actual retirement and installation of machines may be extremely jerky. A great many may be installed in one or two years, but after that no more for several years following. Finally, while the actual deductions of accountants are arbitrary enough, there is an enormous amount of equipment for which nobody even tries to figure depreciation or obsolescence. The result is that the depreciation figure in a national income calculation is always a guess. Economists and statisticians therefore prefer to use the cruder gross national product figure, which at least is tied to more or less "actual" statistical records of production.

But GNP (the abbreviation for gross national product) still has its troubles. First, just what is "final" output? If you look at Figure 15 you can easily see that if we count all three bars at once we will get a much larger total than we really should. You should not count the wheat that has gone into the flour, the flour that has gone into the bread, and the bread itself all at once, as being alike final output. Only the bread is final. To try to include the flour, etc., involves double and triple counting.

Economic life, however, is always a circular process. There is never any clear-cut end or beginning. This can be shown to be true even in Figure 15. The various dotted and solid lines which we drew to show the flow of money incomes and payments toward the purchase of final output could just as well be followed backward to show the way final output is passed back to all stages of production and *then* used to help further production. In some problems, indeed, it is quite a puzzle as to whether a man works to eat or eats to work, though naturally we are generally right in saying the first rather than the second.

However, since the flow of goods and services *is* essentially circular, and since the process has no clear-cut stopping place, the designation of certain services as "final services" is often arbitrary. The choice we make frequently greatly affects the totals we publish. The statisticians have wrestled long and hard with such problems; nobody has yet found a complete, universal answer.

Next comes the problem of a distinction between consumption and investment. A house gives people a place to live and therefore is clearly a consumer good—one which satisfies men's personal wants. On the other hand, you can build a house to rent. In that case you can think of a house as a factory producing *house services.* If you do that, then it is an investment good. But what about a freak house built to gratify the extravagance or the queer tastes of someone? Let us suppose it is so inconvenient or so queer that nobody else would buy or rent it at any price. Can it be treated as an investment?

The truth of the matter is that if we follow our reasoning to the bitter end, the final national product is never anything *seen.* The ultimate aim of production is to produce not *goods* but feelings. And so the final national product is a set of feelings constantly going on in men's minds. Since we cannot measure feelings, we fall back on actual goods and services and hope that an increase in goods also means an increase or improvement in satisfactory feelings. This is a very doubtful assumption in many cases, but without such an assumption scientific economics would be almost impossible.

To return to the problem of defining consumption versus investment goods, statisticians and economists usually fall back on some sort of guess as to the general motives most people have when they buy certain things. Houses, are, as a matter of fact, usually bought with two ends in view—as consumption goods (to live in) and as possible investments through resale or renting.

Vacuum cleaners, on the other hand, are not usually bought as investments but merely to use. Jewelry, like vacuum cleaners, is also a durable good and may sometimes be bought with the idea of profitable resale. The estimators of national income and of GNP figures, following a sort of general customary prejudice, count houses as investment but treat jewelry as consumption. There is really no satisfactory line of distinction.

**Imputation**

We shift to some still more down-to-earth problems. One of the most important of these is the problem of "imputation." Actual GNP figures in the United States include many things that never see the market place. For example, an estimate for food grown on the farm but *consumed by the farmer* is included. Again, the estimated amount of rent which homeowners would have to pay if they did not own the houses they lived in is included. The "imputations," as they are called, are put in to make a more correct total of the goods and services finally produced.

Yet not all actual services are imputed or given an estimated figure in the GNP accounts. For example, the services of housewives are omitted. On the other hand, the value of the services of domestic servants is included. This leads to the often derided fact that if a bachelor marries his cook it reduces the gross national product figure! In times of international stress, exclusion of housewives from GNP leads to serious understatement of available resources. For example, during the last war the move of housewives into factories made a significant contribution to total output. Perhaps the GNP statisticians are just afraid to estimate what a wife is worth!

## International Trade and Investment

No modern economy is wholly self-sufficient. Some are deeply intermeshed with others : Canada, for instance, with both Europe and the United States. Even the United States is far from being as self-sufficient as many people suppose. Foreign trade, however, raises many complications in figuring gross national product and other income measures, which we have omitted in the diagrams. In the United States net foreign investment is made up by taking United States exports of goods and services, minus United States imports of goods and services and gifts to foreigners. The resulting net figure—plus or minus—is included in the investment figure for GNP. This procedure is open to many objections, but no perfect way of handling the problem seems possible.

## Summary

What are some of the practical problems which make GNP and other measures much less precise than theory would indicate? First, there are problems of determining what is truly "net" or "final" and what services to include or to "impute." Next, we saw that the flows of international trade, if fully spelled out, would introduce much more complication. Again, we saw that depreciation and obsolescence are almost impossible to figure objectively for the economy as a whole, and we saw that changes in inventory also pose a problem. However, the final thing which makes these problems of valuation particularly difficult is the constant changing of the value of money as prices go up and down. Such price fluctuations also affect the state of general business—aiding prosperity or depression. Therefore, before we go on to the full theory of business cycles and employment, for which we are now nearly ready, we must stop and consider in more detail the problems of money and banking.

# +++ XIV +++

# Money and Inflation

In the upper right-hand corner of the second gross national product diagram (p. 157), we showed a reservoir of "bank credit" with tubes running into the various flows of the economy like those of a pump. From the figure it is clear that the circulation of money could be greatly increased should more be added to the reservoir, and merely to look at the Figure is to see that one has here a major possible source of disturbance. The reservoir could have simply been labeled "Money" rather than "Bank Credit," but in modern economics direct inflation by issue of paper money is somewhat unusual. Generally shifts in the money supply are managed through the medium of bank loans. Nevertheless, changes in the money supply, though usually handled through bank credit, remain one of the most important sources of trouble in the economic system. Such changes are also one of the chief forces distorting societies' output measures. In Chapters XIV, XV and XVI, therefore, we must consider the monetary problem—the functioning of money and its regulation. We shall first discuss the general nature of inflation; next, the means by which inflation is most usually brought about in modern society; and, finally, the general mechanism of monetary control and its weaknesses.

## Changes in the Value of Money

In Chapter III on the organization of the market we described the basic nature, origins, and functions of money. We saw that it served as a medium of exchange, a store of value, and a standard of value. We learned that one of the greatest services given by money is that it enables us to compare various things which are physically quite different, and to estimate (or to "plan," if one wishes) the growth of society. But suppose that the money we use at one time differs in value from the money we use at another? It would be like trying to measure something with a foot rule that grew and shrank—a "foot" rule that was sometimes eight inches long and sometimes two feet! Yet money often behaves in exactly that way. Its value is constantly changing, and the measures which it gives are thus constantly being thrown out of line.

Yet, first of all, what do we mean by changes in the value of money? For most purposes the answer is simply that the value of money consists of its "purchasing power"—the number of other things it can buy. Thus, if a given sum of money in one year can buy two automobiles, but in another year can buy only one auto of the same kind as before, we may say that the value of money (so far as automobiles are concerned) has been cut in half, or that the value of autos (in terms of money) has doubled.

However, no one uses his money year after year to buy the same goods. In the first place, even those things which continue to have the same name, for instance automobiles, often become in fact so different over time in both design and materials, that a 1964 automobile can hardly be compared with a 1910 model. But even if we disregarded changes in design and manufacture, there would still be trouble. Here we come up against a problem which we have already mentioned in Chapter II in connection with pressure groups. Even when society as a whole is growing or shrinking, the output and the prices of particular articles will not necessarily all move in the same direction. Output and prices in some lines will be rising while in others they are falling, even though on average the total movement may be strongly in one direction. The output and prices of the various industries and goods that make up our total production never move in absolutely identical ways.

When, therefore, we begin to talk about, or to measure, changes in the purchasing power or "value" of money, we immediately run into the job of separating shifts in the general value of money from shifts in the prices of particular things. The prices of diamonds and brandy, for example, might be going down when the price of almost everything else was going up. Shall we allow a small shift in an unimportant line like that to throw our general estimate out of gear?

Measuring the value of money would be easy if all problems were as simple as our diamonds example. In fact, the questions raised are seldom so clear-cut. Perhaps the first problem to remember is that we nearly always want to measure changes in the value of money for some particular purpose—not just changes in money value in general. On the one hand, we may want to measure the change in the cost of living. In that case we will be especially interested in what is happening to the price of foods, of rents, of clothes, and of other things which people buy to fill personal wants. On the other hand, if we want to know the value of money regarding stock market prices, then the price of food will not be included in our figures at all and we can concentrate on stocks and bonds.

Economists and statisticians have worked out a number of different "indices" with which to measure changes in money values for various purposes. Since these indices are so important and often argued about, it is worth acquiring a general idea of how they are made up. And perhaps the most essential thing to know is that just as national income and gross national product figures are never precise or mechanical measures in the way that, say, the international meter stick is, so also price indices are never mechanical, impersonal things.

## Price Indices

In order to make up a price index we first must know for what it is going to be used. Is it a "cost-of-living" index, an "industrial-activity" index, a "stock-market" index, or what? Having decided on our general purpose, we then draw up a list of the products which are most important for that purpose and get their prices. A little thought will show that a good many borderline cases will be found that have to be settled in fairly rough-and-ready fashion. For example, does the price of new houses belong in a cost-of-living index, and do "cut-rate" or special sales lower the price of toothpaste?

When we have made up our list we have only begun the job. How much importance, how much "weight," are we going to give to each product? Since there are always some prices going down while others are going up, it would not be fair to allow the unimportant products to have the same effect on our measure as the important ones. Returning to diamonds, for example, a drop in the price of diamonds ought not to offset a rise in the price of bread in compiling a cost-of-living index. Economists and statisticians try to allow for problems like these by letting the price of some goods count, say, ten, fifteen or twenty times more than others in making up a final figure for each year, depending upon the importance they believe the indivdual products to have. But importance for whom? For example, which income group is to have its tastes most considered in making up a cost-of-living index?

We see how many headaches are involved in calculating a price index, and what a tremendous amount of room for argument there can be. By changing the products whose prices are to be included, and the importance given to each of them, it is quite possible to make any index rise, fall, or stand still, even though the original raw facts are the same in each case. What we have said is enough to give an idea of the difficulties involved. There are further complications connected with setting a beginning or "base" year, or in picking out the proper mathematical formula to be used in comparing totals.

We thus see that measuring the value of money is always a difficult job, and since all prices never move in the same direction, the value of money for some purposes may be going down just when its value for others is going up. Nor is there ever a wholly satisfying or completely impersonal solution for such difficulties. Let us, however, leave these problems of measurement to one side and concentrate on the general problem of why the value of money as a whole shifts from time to time, as compared with the value of goods.

The detailed forces which can distort the value of money are many and complicated to analyze. But to make a general catalogue we can group all the detailed forces under two main headings: (1) changes in the "velocity" or "speed" with which money is used, and (2) changes in the "quantity" of money as compared to output. Let us give some examples. First of all, as regards a simple increase in the quantity of money, if we enlarge the amount of money in use when there is no increase in the production of goods, people will usually start bidding against each other for the same goods as before, because they have more money in their pockets and want to buy more. The result of their increased spending is to push prices higher. "Controls," of course, can affect price changes, but we will talk about them later.

Even if the quantity of money were being increased while the quantity of goods being produced was still the same, prices would not always go up—at any rate not for a while. At first people might merely "hold" more money and not spend it. Economists describe such a process by saying that while the quantity of money has risen, its velocity has declined. In other words, though people have more money they are not using it as quickly, or as much as they did before.

### Cash Balances

Everybody is apt to keep a certain amount of money for unusual or emergency use. Likewise, most people with bank accounts try to keep some sort of average balance in the bank, depending upon the size of their income, their spending, and their other habits. In the same way, corporations have to maintain balances of various sorts to meet payrolls, change bills, and handle other claims. Finally, there will be some people or some businesses that have money which they could invest, but which for one reason or another they like to keep in "liquid" form. All these various stores of money are apt to have some more or less usual rate of turnover and to bear some relationship to the size of corporate or personal income. If all these usual habits and relationships regarding the holding of money do not change much, a good part of an increase in the quantity of money will soon find its way into more spending, either for investment or for consumption; and if output has not increased, or if some productive factors are fully employed, prices will rise. But if, for any reason, people's habits concerning the holding of money have changed, and they are prepared to hold a greater amount of money than before, for example in anticipation of lower prices, then the extra money may simply be absorbed and held without being spent at all.

Another type of change is also possible. People can decide to hold less money on average than they did before, and to spend part of the balances they have hitherto been in the habit of keeping. For example, during the German inflation which followed the World War I people suddenly woke up to the fact that prices were rising so fast (the value of money was falling so fast) that it was better to spend money, no matter for what, than to keep it for no matter how short a time. As a result, no one would keep money even for a day, and the velocity of money—the rate of spending—rose by leaps and bounds, production of goods lagged far behind, and soon not even the government could print money fast enough to keep pace. In Hungary in 1945, one United States dollar, in a few months, could buy eight octillion pengoes. When an inflation reaches this state, the old money is usually just wiped out and the government starts all over again. It is easy to see from such circumstances that if we want to understand the behavior of money and prices we cannot talk only about the amount of money or the amount of production. We have also to make allowances for changes in the desire of people to hold money and for changes in money's velocity. In the diagram, for example, in Figure 15 (p. 148), we disregarded all inventory and stocks of goods. But now it is important to realize that, in the same way, we paid no attention to balances of money or cash. We simply compared the flow of goods being produced with the flow of money income being spent—either for consumption or for investment—and left all problems of inventory and cash balances to one side. But in the real world such an analysis is too simple. For example, increased spending of money might not raise prices as expected because shopkeepers might for a while merely sell their accumulated inventory at the old prices. Pressure on prices might not start until after surplus inventory had been sold. In the same way an increased amount of money need not always raise prices at first, for people may merely be willing to hold a larger amount of cash. Finally, a drop in the amount of money need not reduce general income (or total spending) if, while the amount of money is declining, people stop holding as large balances as they did before and begin to use their money more actively.

### Inflation and Deflation

We have said enough now to be able to understand the basic outlines of the problem of inflation and deflation. Leaving aside for the moment the possible variations just referred to in the desire to hold money, the essence of the problem is most easily understood by thinking of it in terms of the comparison of two things: a stream of money-spending on the one hand, and a stream of goods being offered for sale on the other. As long as these two streams rise and fall at about the same rate, important changes in general prices will not be likely. If the stream of goods increases, but the stream of money-spending does not, then prices will tend to fall. If the stream of spending rises but the stream of goods rises about the same, then prices on average will be more or less undisturbed.

For example, during the first three terms of President Franklin D. Roosevelt the quantity of money in this country was very greatly increased (we will see later what methods were used to bring about the enlargement). Many old-fashioned economists prophesied immediate inflation. But the inflation did not immediately arrive. There were two reasons why it did not. In the first place, there was a great deal of unemployment, so that the output of goods for sale could be increased very quickly and easily as the stream of spending rose. Thus part of increased spending was absorbed in increased production. But, in addition, many people were so frightened because of the depression, and so unwilling to run risks, that they appeared to have become willing to hold an almost unlimited quantity of money, without spending it for either investment or consumption. Thus, although the money passed out for relief by the government was usually spent at once by those on relief rolls, it soon went from their hands to people somewhat better off who held increasing amounts of cash and made very little increase in their levels of consumption or investment. These people, at first in fact, frequently used the funds to "pay off" earlier debts, hence giving little immediate stimulus to the economy.

Economists have invented a convenient shorthand formula for showing these relationships of changes in production, in the amount of money, in the degree money is used, and in prices. This formula is called "the equation of exchange" and runs as follows:

$$MV = PT$$

Put into words, what it means is that all the money in a country (M) multiplied by its average speed of use, or velocity, (V) is equal to the average prices of everything sold (P) multiplied by the number of sales or "transactions" (T). There are many special complications and variations of such equations but we will not try to go into them here. The usefulness of this kind of shorthand notation can be seen by applying it to the New Deal experience just described.

What happened was that though M rose V fell, and T (sales, production) increased to some extent. P, therefore, did not show great change at first. We can indicate this as follows:

At first we can say the equation looked like this:              $MV = PT$
But next we can show it like this:                              $Mv = PT$
P (or prices) remains the same size in the second equation. But the size

of everything else has either grown or shrunk sufficiently to allow P to remain the same.

### Changes in Velocity

We must not, however, forget that if monetary forces can change in one direction they can also change in another. When this country went into World War II, many economists made the mistake of thinking that people were going to continue their depression habits and continue to be willing to hold money indefinitely. The administration economists relied on price controls to "hold the line" during the war, and most of them expected that increased production, plus a continued holding of money, would prevent inflation after the war was over. Many economists expected an immediate postwar depression and return to unemployment. But none of these expectations was realized. As soon as the war ended people stopped holding as much money as they had been doing and began to spend it more rapidly. Production could not keep pace with the increased spending. The machinery of control, deprived of public support, began to crumble. The law was repealed and thereafter prices rose rapidly. Thus, reversing depression experience, V rose faster than T. But would stronger controls have served to prevent the price rise? Before we can answer this question we have to ask a little more carefully just what inflation is.

### Defining Inflation

To many people inflation just means high prices, and deflation means low prices. But making the whole thing simply a matter of prices is unsatisfactory for many reasons. In the first place, the idea of inflation is strongly associated with the notion of something being "done to" money, or happening through a change in the money supply. But a little thought will show that prices could be forced up very high even though nothing had happened to money. A famine or a breakdown in production (say, because of a war) could create a scarcity which would cause prices to rise even though the amount of money had not changed at all. (Using our formula, such a process can be expressed as a reduction in T, MV being unchanged.) Although rising prices, brought about merely through famine or scarcity, are often referred to as inflation in some books, we will not use the term that way here. Our definition of inflation will be confined to rapidly rising prices resulting from (or coming through) increases either in the quantity of money or in its velocity. In other words, we keep the designation for high prices primarily resulting from changes in money. Where the price rise is primarily due to a drop in production, the resulting high prices should be referred to simply as "scarcity."

But how high does a price rise have to go to be called inflation? We will see later that almost any economic system, even socialist ones except in those countries which are under the most ironbound control, is sure to experience some price movements up and down. It follows that a useful definition of inflation has to allow some leeway for moderate price change. Shall we then call inflation a great rise in prices, very great rise in prices, or an extremely great rise in prices? We have here a question of judgment concerning which people will always differ somewhat. By and large, economists in defining inflation tend to hesitate somewhere between a very high and an extremely high rise in prices. Others dodge the problem by saying there are "degrees" of inflation.

Let us now summarize our steps toward a definition. We have excluded high prices resulting primarily from scarcity and production shortages. Also, though the point has not been mentioned in so many words, we have not adopted those definitions which describe inflation as merely a change in the quantity of money or its metal "base" (gold, silver, etc.); for a mere increase in the quantity of money need not change general prices though, of course, it can do so. An increase may be offset either by an increase in production or by a decline in velocity.

There are problems of business cycle theory raised here, but they have to be treated later. In the same way it is possible that a change in the metal "backing" of the money supply need not affect prices and expenditures at all. The argument for the gold standard is largely a matter of international trade theory, and a political one, and must be postponed for much later treatment. We therefore adopt for the remainder of this book the following definition of inflation: *Inflation is a rise of prices which seriously disturbs production and distribution relationships, and which is caused by, or accompanied by, an increase in the quantity of money or else in its velocity.*

### Explaining the Definition

Yet what do we mean by "seriously disturbs"? This brings us to the still more fundamental question: "What's wrong with inflation anyhow?" The first thing to remember about inflation is that if the price of everything changed in exactly the same degree, the changes would make no difference at all. Thus if you got twice as much money, but everybody got twice as much, and everything cost twice as much, you would be right where you were before. Incomes would change but prices would change also. In addition, though somehow people often find this a bit harder to see, if you got half as much money, but everybody else got only half as much, and everything cost only half as much, then, again, you would be no worse off than you were before. As long as all prices and all incomes changed alike, society would not be seriously disturbed. A drop in income would be offset by an exactly similar drop in prices.

The trouble with inflation and deflation, therefore, must be that all prices do not change just alike, and, in fact, disproportionate movements are just what do occur. Inflation and deflation operate as arbitrary and unfair methods of shifting around the wealth of individual people. On the inflation side the effect of a price rise is to confiscate part of the incomes of those people whose incomes do not change easily—fixed salaries, life insurance receipts, etc.— and to undermine and reduce the value of claims whose money value is fixed, such as mortgages, pensions, and so on. For example, the social security benefits originally set up are only about half as valuable now as they were intended to be and the rate has had to be increased. To be sure, before the labor union movement became as strong as it is now, inflation often benefited the receivers of profits and dividends while wages lagged behind price increases, and thus served for a while to stimulate business activity, though at a tremendous price in social dislocation.

Today, on the other hand, certain strong unions can manipulate prices and controls so as to raise wages faster than the general inflation, and hold profits down. The profits in such cases may still look big. But if we allow for price changes and the decline in the value of the dollar, such profits may even be less, in real terms, than they were before. There can thus be a so-called "profitless" inflation. Under such circumstances the struggle may become one in which certain strong pressure groups, farmers, for example, or unions of organized labor, are in effect, though indirectly, gaining a relative advantage over unorganized workers, salaried people, and people on pensions. We will come back to this problem later in this book.

## Inflation with Unemployment?

One additional point must be mentioned. It is often thought that inflation always operates as a stimulus to output—even as an "over" stimulus. But things do not always work out that way. Sometimes, as in Germany, Hungary, and China after World War II, inflation creates so much uncertainty about the future that nobody is willing to make any plans, and employment and production actually begin to drop. Without any stable unit in which to measure costs or calculate wages, businessmen are reluctant to make contracts. A man who believes that he has ample funds to build a factory may, for example, find that costs have risen so fast that half way through he is unable to complete it. Those who own valuable property or materials may not be willing to let them go under such circumstances. In such an atmosphere real production may decline though money is still being issued rapidly.

## Deflation

Turning now to falling prices or deflation, we find the same thing in reverse. There, too, and probably more promptly, the decline can sometimes create so much uncertainty as to cause a drop in production and employment. For the rest, we have merely to turn what we said about inflation inside out. Deflation unfairly increases the values of pensions, mortgages, and debts in general. Those bondholders whose bonds remain solvent during a deflation actually benefit in a higher real value of their interest. In other words, if the enterprises which issued the bonds stay solvent enough to pay interest on them, the interest will actually have more real purchasing power than before. But declining prices are likely to make many businesses insolvent, and unable to pay interest, because their prices are falling faster than their costs. The owners of bonds in such insolvent enterprises will lose. Again, though a fall in prices will benefit those who still have jobs and whose wages have not been cut (labor's share of total income rises in depression) this fact does not help the unemployed.

We are now able to say what is wrong with deflation and inflation. They generate arbitrary and unfair changes in the shares which individuals receive. Furthermore, by thus dislocating income and production relationships, they often create so much uncertainty and risk that they slow down growth, or even cause total output to drop. Society, to be sure, can take a certain amount of price movement and yet function fairly well. For that reason, in our definition of inflation, we mean by "seriously disturbs" an amount of price change that begins to slow down the efficiency and production of the system. Not all price changes do this, but the margin of tolerance either way is probably not as large as many people think. Lenin said that the easiest way to destroy capitalism is to debauch the currency and he was probably correct. But the record of modern socialist societies in controlling inflation is not too good either.

## Inflation, Prices, and Controls

It is time now to ask whether price controls make all we have said about money out-of-date. Specifically, we asked in the last section whether the post-World War II inflation could have been avoided had the Office of Price Administration not been abolished.

To understand the working of a control program it is important to remember that there is a case for price controls, a case grounded in one very important fact: Increased money does not always push up prices. Rising prices may sometimes push up the amount of money. In defining inflation we spoke of price increases resulting from, or accompanied by, a change in the quantity of money and its velocity. The fact is that the usual ideas of cause and effect can sometimes be exactly reversed here. For example, if people expect a price rise they may begin to spend more in order to take advantage of "low" prices while "things are still cheap." Individuals may draw down the balances they have been holding, while businessmen may make plans to increase output and borrow from the banks in order to do so. Such bank borrowing, we will soon see, may increase the quantity of money. So much spending, based on the expectation of a price rise, may send prices up. Thus, the expectation of rising prices will increase spending and the quantity of money, and so justify itself. But it must be remembered that without an increase either in the quantity or in the velocity of money, an expansion based on *mere* expectation would soon burst. Thus if the quantity of money cannot rise, an expansion based on mere expectation will find it much harder to continue. In any actual process, of course, the two forces of (1) price expectations plus (2) money changes may aggravate and reinforce each other.

Price controls, however, by cutting off the expectation of a price rise or a general wage increase, may have an important effect in stopping the spiral of inflationary expectations. But this service rendered by price controls, though it is valuable, never gets to the basic problem. One is never justified in feeling that price controls can safely be used as a permanent and complete substitute for taxation and restriction of the amount of money. To be sure "official" prices may always be nailed no matter how much money is released but the leak is the "black" or the "gray" market. The more money that is piled up, the greater will be the temptation to spend it. At first only more or less criminal elements of society will conclude shady deals at illegally high prices. But as evasions become more widespread, and public support for the control program declines, there will be more and more black marketing. In the final stages of collapse, in some countries, the black market becomes the *only* market. The official prices are maintained, and official minimum rations "guaranteed" but nothing can be bought at the official prices, or merely with official ration cards at any price.

We have thus several forces operating in any control program. On the one hand, there is the level of public enthusiasm and responsibility plus the administrative efficiency of the government. On the other, there is the growing volume of surplus cash. Just where the process of control will break down is therefore not a mechanical thing. An honest, patriotic people who believe that the control program is fair, and who have an efficient government, can obviously suppress a great deal more inflation than those who are less politically responsible or less convinced of the desirability of the program. But no matter how efficient the government and how patriotic the people, if money becomes sufficiently plentiful relative to goods, the control program will *always* fail. From the experiments of the Emperor Diocletian in the fourth century to those of the present day, controls have never restrained the effect on price of continued increase in the quantity of money.

Two final points must be made. First, the great argument for price and wage controls is that they stop the race for special advantages—for example, that of one union against another. But there will always be groups who will try to extort benefits *for themselves* while keeping controls on everybody else. A political-minded price administrator may avoid partial showdowns by giving in to these special groups. But each concession granted to one group makes all other groups dissatisfied. Soon the program will begin to lose the general public support without which it cannot function.

The second point concerns the general usefulness of such a program. Inflation, we have seen, is a very bad thing. But at least, during its early and middle stages, it does often serve as a powerful stimulus to production. However, a suppressed or controlled inflation does not usually have even this result, and the controls can come to cost more, and involve more friction, than the inflation itself.

### Summary on Money and Inflation

In this chapter we have surveyed what is meant by changes in the "value" of money and we have seen some of the problems involved in measuring it. We have further attempted to work out a definition of inflation, and finally concluded with the following definition: Inflation is a state of rising prices, brought about primarily through increases in the quantity of money, or its velocity, so high as to seriously disturb distribution and production relationships. A discussion of what was meant by "seriously" led us next to ask why inflation was bad, and we saw that the answer lay in the unfair exploitation of some groups by others. Finally, we asked if price and wage control could prevent inflation, if the quantity of money were being continually and rapidly increased, and we said that controls could not indefinitely hold back the flood. But there is one vital question that we have not yet answered: What, after all, is money in modern society, and how does it get increased? We take up this problem in the next chapter.

# +++ XV +++

# Money and the Nature of Bank Credit

The preceding chapter talked as if money were some definite substance which could be identified easily. In fact, however, this is far from true in modern society, and the nature of the things which can take on a monetary character is constantly shifting. Money, in essence, is anything that does money work. Almost anything durable and not too common can sometimes, and in some cases, be looked upon as a form of money. As a result yesterday's good definition may be almost entirely out of date tomorrow. All we can really say is that whatever article serves to some extent as a medium of exchange, a standard of value, and a store of value is to that extent a form of money. Where to draw the line, in any particular case, is largely a matter of judgment.

However, if we look closely at the American money supply, we will find three main classes of things commonly thought of today as money. The first type is ordinary small change: pennies, nickels, dimes, quarters, and half dollars. These coins are minted by the Treasury of the United States. They make up about 1.7 per cent of our total money supply and are chiefly used as a convenience for small purchases.

The next type of money is paper or "folding" money—the one, five, ten, and on up dollar bills. Paper money of this sort comes from two sources: the United States Treasury and the Federal Reserve Banks. There are many complicated regulations concerning the amount of such bills that can be issued, but we do not have to go into the matter in great detail here. For "folding" money or bills makes up only 20 per cent of the total money supply of our country.

But far and away the greatest part of American money is in the form of bank deposits. Yet we do not study about bank deposits only because they are the most usual form of money. Much more important is the fact that they are the part which is most changeable in amount. Thus it is mostly through changes in the amount of bank deposits that the great modern inflations have been engineered. For example, "demand" deposits in the United States stood at approximately thirty-five billion dollars in 1940, but by 1962 they had risen to over one hundred eighteen billion dollars. What we want to learn here is

*177*

the essential method by which our banking system makes possible such tremendous changes.

## Bank Credit Creation: How It Began

Many people think of a bank as being just a sort of warehouse for money. People who have this idea are apt to believe that certain individuals (the depositors) put their money into a bank, while certain other individuals (the borrowers) take it out again. The bank, they think, merely acts as a middleman or go-between. The fact that a bank can be a net "manufacturer" or "creator" of bank deposits is missed entirely.

A second important mistake about modern banking goes to the other extreme. Certain people who have learned in a vague general way that the banking system can create deposits jump to the notion that if ever there is a shortage of money, it is the fault of the bankers, and that all banks can easily lend from four to six times the money put into them. What we want to do now is to find our way between these extremes and get clear in our heads the basic principles of deposit creation. To understand the process, let us review something of its history.

In medieval times gold, silver, and gems were usually the most convenient things available as a store of value. But property was very unsafe, and the treasure a feudal lord kept in his castle was a ready target for people who wanted to loot. Within the cities, however, life and property were somewhat more secure, and so there developed the custom of depositing gold and other valuable objects with the goldsmiths of the cities. These smiths in turn gave various crude acknowledgments or certificates of their indebtedness to the people depositing the gold, as evidence of the amounts which they had received—in effect a sort of warehouse receipt. These receipts came to take many forms. They were the remote ancestors of our modern "negotiable instruments" —bank checks, bills of exchange, and so on. The important thing to remember is that men soon discovered that a bill of exchange or other acknowledgment of debt from a solvent goldsmith, merchant, or "banker" was a far easier and safer thing to carry about than a lot of coins or jewelry.

Because written claims were so much easier to handle than actual treasure, people came increasingly to exchange goldsmiths' acknowledgments or promises instead of the actual coin itself. Next, the goldsmiths in their turn began to discover that the treasure left with them was seldom called for. As a result the goldsmiths commenced little by little to issue or lend acknowledgments, or promises to pay, considerably greater in face value than the gold or other treasure which they actually had on hand. Overissue of goldsmiths' notes had the effect of pushing up prices, which started speculative bubbles, which in turn collapsed. Later on, as such fluctuations recurred, governments stepped in and sought to limit overexpansion by requiring certain minimum "reserves" or cash balances which had to be deposited in some specified place in proportion to various parts of the banker's business. At first these reserves were set only in relation to the bank notes issued by bankers, but later as more and more people began to use personal checks instead of bank notes, the reserve regulations were extended to cover bank deposits also.

What we have given is a sketch of about eleven hundred years of complicated history. It nevertheless furnishes the essential approach needed to understand our modern banking system. We have already said that many people who have not studied the subject think of a bank as a sort of warehouse into which some people put money while others take it out through loans. They have no idea that any net creation of new money may be involved. The reality is much more complicated. To a considerable extent the modern banking system can be thought of more as a creator of new deposits than a mere lender of the purchasing power of others—a creator of deposits, furthermore, whose activities are more limited (as far as legal machinery is concerned) by the size of certain balances called reserves than by anything else.

### What Is Meant by Deposit Creation

We must now discuss the way deposit creation takes place, and explain what we really mean when we talk about "creating" deposits or credit. The talk about credit creation often gives the impression that banks can grind out as much money or deposits as they wish. Many people, therefore, jump to the notion that if there is a shortage of money it must be the fault of the bankers. But the idea that the banking system can "create" as much money as it wishes is incorrect. One method of explaining what happens, a method which is considerably more than just a play on words, is to say that banks do not so much "create" credit as "recognize" it. By recognizing credit rather than creating it your banker is to some extent in the same position as a storekeeper. A storekeeper can advertise his goods. He can display them attractively, and he can lower their price. But he cannot run out on the sidewalks and *force* people to come in and buy from him. In the same way the ability of the banks to lend money and create credit is limited by the willingness of solvent and responsible *borrowers* to come to them. A banker cannot just *give* money away. He has to be reasonably sure of repayment, and if, for any reason, not many people who can be trusted or expected to repay are willing to borrow, then the banking system is helpless to get money into circulation even if the price of loans is drastically reduced. As we will see later, there is often a considerable range in which a banker can exercise his discretion. But unless he is totally irresponsible there are always limits to what he can do.

## Methods of Deposit Creation: A Single Bank

Let us now try to understand the basic mechanism by which the banking system, acting as a whole, can create credit or deposits. Let us begin with a bank that is just being established and see how it goes about setting up its business.

Banks for generations have been recognized as semipublic utilities or businesses "affected with a public interest," and strictly regulated. You cannot, therefore, start a bank in the way in which you start a grocery store. You have first to get a charter, either from your state or from the federal government, and these charters are granted only after careful investigations to see whether your locality is big enough for another bank and whether your project is a reasonably responsible one.

After receiving a charter, your bank must next sell stock and receive the payments of its stockholders. This process, too, is much more carefully supervised than in ordinary business. All stock, for example, has to be fully paid for and a "surplus" obtained before the bank can open its doors. But now let us suppose that the bank has both received its charter and collected all its stock payments. It is, therefore, about to start business.

The first thing our new bank will have to do will be to obtain some reserves. Reserves are of two kinds: those required by law, and those which bankers have found it wise to keep available to meet various calls that they think are bound to come up from time to time in the course of business.

The reserves required by law, or "legal reserves," are a very complicated subject in themselves, and we will discuss some of the problems connected with them in the next chapter. The legal reserves of a bank must be held in the form of deposits in some other bank or banks, or in cash in vault. For the present all that we need to know about them is that the major part of legal reserves of virtually all the important banks of the United States have to be held in the accounts of what are called Federal Reserve Banks. These Federal Reserve Banks are semipublic organizations, closely supervised by a board set up by the federal government. Here too we will save details for the next chapter. What is important to grasp now, however, is that our new bank will find that the necessary size of the minimum legal reserves which it must keep with a Federal Reserve Bank will be set in some definite proportion to the deposits which our new bank will soon be receiving. Furthermore, in order initially to buy or to increase a legal reserve deposit account, our new bank can give only two things in payment: actual cash, or checks (or similar claims) on other banks.

Since our bank is just being started, it does not yet know what the size of its deposits is going to be. On the other hand, it has just received from its stockholders a quantity of cash, or checks on other banks. So we may suppose that to get the ball rolling, our bank takes a guess as to what its volume of business will be, and hence what size its necessary legal reserves will probably have to be, and uses that amount to buy reserves with the Federal Reserve Bank.

But the needed legal reserve balances will take up only part of the money our new bank has received from its stockholders. Nor are such balances the only balances or reserves which our bank will need. In addition to the legal reserves deposited with the Federal Reserve Bank, our new bank will know that as soon as it opens for business, it will also need some actual money with which to cash checks and so on. Such sums of money are called "vault cash." How much vault cash a bank will need depends upon the circumstances of its business, but some vault cash is always required and, since 1960, such vault cash can be counted as a part of reserves.

Finally, the new bank will want to have a certain amount of leeway in its business. It wants to make money to be sure, but it also wants enough slack to be able to expand or contract a little when unexpected calls are made upon it. To take care of this problem, some of the remaining money taken in from stockholders will probably be used to buy what are called "secondary" reserves. These are bonds or "portfolio" reserves which are highly "liquid"—that is, which can usually be sold very quickly and without much risk of loss, producing cash or currency, but which also pay a certain amount of income in interest.

Let us now stop and look at our new bank. It has not as yet received a dollar in deposits or made a loan. But it has reached a point at which it is ready to start operations. It has spent some of its money on the purchase of bonds as secondary reserves. It has turned some of its money into vault cash, and it has used some of its funds to purchase reserves with the Federal Reserve Bank of its district. Finally, just at the beginning, it will probably have a further amount kept on hand to meet the unexpected emergencies of a new venture. Now it can begin to receive deposits. But as soon as we begin to talk about deposits, we reach the heart of our problem. Just how will the new bank's deposits come into being?

Of course, one obvious way that a new bank will begin to have deposits is that the people will begin to walk in from outside and make deposits. However, deposits from outside are not the most important thing to remember at this stage of our explanation. Let us take an extreme case and suppose that no outside deposits are made at first. It might seem to you that in that case our new bank would never be able to get started. But you would be quite wrong. While it is unlikely that a new bank would receive no deposits from outside, it could nevertheless be quite possible for such a bank to start business, begin operation, and create deposits though at first no one came in to make any deposits at all! The reason is quite simple. When a man borrows money from a bank, he does not usually take out his money in dollar bills or coin. Instead the bank merely sets up a deposit for him and gives him a checkbook. Suppose at the beginning of the opening day Mr. Jones, a sound borrower, appears. The bank will probably say, "Certainly, Mr. Jones, we will lend you the money. Just sign this note and we will set up an account for you." In terms of accounting, the essence of the transaction would be as follows: On the liability side of its ledgers the bank will enter Mr. Jones's deposit. His deposit will be entered as a liability because Mr. Jones does have the legal power to draw it all out right away. On the asset side, however, they will put his note. The books will balance and Mr. Jones will have his account.

Now we come to the key point. Will the bank actually have to pay out all the money they have lent Mr. Jones and allotted him in his new deposit? The chances are the bank will not. For when Jones begins to spend his money, how will he do it? Not usually by drawing out coin or folding money and carrying large sums in his pockets. More probably he will write checks on his new account. But, again, you may think that writing checks will only postpone the difficulty. The people who get the checks will want to use them in some way. Even that, strange as it might sound, does not mean that money will necessarily be drawn out of our new bank. Here we meet a basic fact: Many of the people who receive Mr. Jones's checks will themselves be or become depositors in our new bank. Of course, some funds will be drawn out at first, and a wise banker will have forseen that fact and allowed for it. But as the bank becomes established, it is probable, other things being equal, that a larger and larger proportion of the checks drawn on our new bank will be redeposited in that very same bank. Let us say that that happens with Mr. Jones's checks. He gives checks to Mr. Brown; and Mr. Brown deposits them to his own account but in Mr. Jones's bank—our new bank.

Now when checks drawn on a deposit in one bank are merely redeposited by somebody else in that same bank, all that the bank has to do is to shift claims away from one depositor and over to another. If Jones has borrowed $1,000, and given a check for that amount to Brown, and Brown has deposited the check in the same bank Jones borrowed from, all that the lending bank will have to do is deduct $1,000 from Jones's account and increase Brown's by the same amount. Not a cent will the bank have to pay out.

Furthermore, as long as all the banks in the system are expanding loans at about the same speed, much the same sort of thing could happen as between all of them. Thus, even if Jones's checks are not deposited in our new bank but in some other, this still need not call for a withdrawal of funds from our new bank, if at the same time that Jones's checks are redeposited elsewhere, somebody else's checks, to approximately the same amount, are deposited in our new bank. Once our bank has established itself, this sort of offsetting probably will occur, on average, if all the banks in a system are expanding at about the same rate. Very little actual currency, bills and coins, need be called for.

At the end of each business day, each bank in a town may send one of its men to what is called a "clearing house." In a clearing house each bank calls out the amount of the checks which it has due from other banks, while the other banks call out the amount they have due from it. Bank A will find it owes Bank B $5,000. But Bank B may find it owes Bank A $5,000. The two sets of checks are merely offset against each other. We do not mean to say that this is what always happens. But as long as the various banks are closely in step with each other, the process will be similar. Furthermore, if all the various towns and cities are expanding more or less in step, there will again be little need for actual cash. True, there will be some net movements one way or the other, but what the system can rely on with some confidence is the law of averages.

## Methods of Deposit Creation: Multiple Expansion

In order to take the next step in our explanation we have to go back to what we said in the last section about legal reserves. Remember we said there that the necessary legal reserves which the banks had to keep in vault cash and with the Federal Reserve Banks were set at a fixed proportion of the deposits of those banks. Let us for the moment say that the ratio is 5 to 1. Thus, if the banks, as a group, happen to have an extra million dollars available to put into legal reserves, they could legally and theoretically create new deposits through loans to the amount of five million. And as long as all the banks were keeping more or less in step there would seem to be nothing to stop them from doing so. Very little money would be needed to settle up between them.

Some people have the idea that because the system might expand fivefold, any single bank with an unused reserve deposit in the Federal Reserve Bank of, say, $1,000 could immediately and without difficulty lend (create new deposits) to the amount of $5,000. For example, they might think that if the new bank we were talking about in the last section had, say, $20,000 available in legal reserves on the day it opened for business, it could thereupon and without more ado make loans (create deposits) to the tune of $100,000! This is too simple.

The trouble is that the president of our new bank could not be sure that all the money lent (deposits created) by his individual bank would stay in his bank. True, on average, things might even out, but he could not trust the law of averages too far, particularly in a new enterprise. Therefore, he would at first lend (set up deposits) not more than an amount equal to the size of his new reserve deposit in the Federal Reserve Bank, with perhaps a bit more if there were idle funds which he might at first happen to have on hand and which he thought would not be needed either for vault cash or for secondary reserves. In other words, he would lend not $100,000, but at most only about $20,000. The reason is that if he lent only that much, he would probably have allowed himself ample margin in case of a sudden unexpected withdrawal of funds from his bank. If necessary, he would turn some of his reserve deposit or other assets into cash to meet the demands being made on him.

And yet it remains true that on average, and for the system as a whole, the banks do much of the time expand their deposits to something like the number of times their legal reserve balances that the law permits—in our example, 5 to 1. How can it be that, although no single banker may be conscious of lending more than his bank has on hand, the system as a whole can somehow (if there are solvent borrowers) lend out to, say, five times the amount of its reserves depending on what the legal ratio happens to be?

Let us suppose that we are dealing with a banking system or set of banks which already allowed their deposits to expand to the full limit permitted by law. They now have some vault cash, some secondary reserves, and legal reserves equal in amount to exactly one-fifth of their deposits. Say that 5 to 1 is the legal ratio. We can then say that, within the limits set by law and prudence, they have expanded as far as they can go.

Now let us suppose that someone comes in and deposits a check drawn on banks in another group than the one we are discussing. Let us say, merely for example, that the check is drawn on a foreign bank. So far as the particular banking system, or group of banks, we are dealing with now is concerned, this $1,000 is a net increase. Let us call the bank which receives the deposit Bank A. The effect of the new deposit on Bank A will be twofold. First, Bank A's deposits will have gone up by $1,000. But, in addition, Bank A will also find itself in possession of the check drawn upon another bank which its new depositor has used in making his deposit.

Since the depositor's check used in setting up his deposit is a check on another bank, and not merely Bank A's own check, Bank A can send the depositor's check to the Federal Reserve Bank to increase Bank A's legal reserve deposit. Thus, Bank A could increase its legal reserves by $1,000. And this extra $1,000 could legally support an increase in A's loans of $5,000. One thousand of this is already taken up by the new depositor's deposit. But many people would jump to the conclusion that Bank A would without more ado make loans (create new deposits) to the extent of the remaining possible $4,000.

In fact, however, Bank A is likely to act much more conservatively. Bank A may increase its loans by less than $1,000, if anything, but the extra funds will gradually trickle through from one bank to another, with the system, adding to the total of deposits at each step, until finally the maximum expansion is reached. What Bank A will probably do is to set aside for legal reserves not $1,000 but $200, and lend the remaining $800. Suppose that this new loan deposit of $800 is all drawn out at once and put in some other bank, B. Bank B will find its deposits have increased by $800, and that it now has an outside check available for possible reserve purposes of $800. But Bank B, in turn, will go through the same calculation as Bank A. Bank B will put aside for reserves not $800 but $160 (one-fifth of $800) and lend the remaining $640. This $640 we may next suppose is drawn out and goes to Bank C, which again makes a deduction for reserves and lends the remainder, and so on. Thus, gradually the total of deposits for the system rises although each individual bank is lending much less than its theoretical legal potential.

We may show all this in the following way:

## BANK DEPOSITS AND THE MONEY SUPPLY

Bank A has added $1,000 to its deposits.

Bank A gets a new deposit and check for $1,000.

Bank A puts aside $200 for reserves and lends out $800, which is deposited in Bank B.

Bank B has added $800 to its deposits.

Bank B puts $160 aside for reserves and lends out $640, which is deposited in Bank C.

Bank C has added $640 to its deposits.

Bank C puts $128 aside for reserves and lends out $512, which is deposited in Bank D.

Bank D has added $512 to its deposits.

Bank D puts $103 aside for reserves and lends out $409.

The process may be supposed to continue until, adding the left-hand column, we get:

$5,000 total additional deposits.

In this way we see that it is possible for the system as a whole to lend out five times an addition to its legal reserve—though no individual bank is lending (creating deposits) in anything like that ratio.

## Summary

In this chapter we have tried to show something of the main modern source of increase in the money supply. We have sought to explain how it is that the banking system, acting as a whole (and if there are enough solvent borrowers), can create new deposits. But, next, we have explained the curious fact that the multiple expansion of deposits can take place without any single bank's being conscious of lending anything more than the funds coming into it. Thus, we are now able to see that both of the views which we mentioned at the beginning of this chapter are wrong. It is not true that banks are merely go-betweens—only lending the money their depositors entrust to them. But neither is it true that a bank which happens to find itself with $1,000 of excess reserves will thereupon be likely to lend, say, $5,000 in new deposits. As we say, multiple expansion of deposits will probably occur in a much more complicated way as funds trickle through from bank to bank.

To see how well we have grasped the essentials of the problem, let us use the following test sentence: "A bank's lending ability can sometimes be reduced by an increase in its deposits." At first the sentence may seem to be nonsense. If a bank has more deposits, won't it be receiving more money to lend out? That would certainly be the case if banks were just go-betweens for the lender and the borrower. In fact, however—and here we have the key point—the main determinant of the legal lending power of a bank is not so much the amount of its deposits as the size of its legal reserves relative to those deposits. So whether or not an increase in deposits will mean an increase in the bank's lending power will depend on the way those deposits come into being. If the deposits are made by new depositors, depositors drawing checks on a different banking system, then the bank's lending power will be increased. For the new depositor must bring with him to set up his deposit either cash or checks on other banks. These sums can, as we saw, be used to increase the individual bank's reserves and lending power. On the other hand, if the increase in deposits merely comes about through an increase in loans by the individual bank—that is to say, if the new deposits are created by the bank's own act— then, in the first instance anyway, no addition has been made to the bank's reserve balances. And since on the contrary the ratio of deposits to reserves has now increased, the potential lending power of the bank—its surplus reserves— must have been reduced. More reserves will now have to be earmarked to support the additional deposits which have resulted from the new loans.

# Introducing the Business Cycle:
# The Mechanism of Credit Control

Our preceding two chapters have been something of a detour. In Chapters XII and XIII we laid the foundations for a study of business cycles, stabilization, and unemployment by outlining the various measurements of output and income, their relation to one another, and to the flow of savings. But we saw that these measures could be greatly distorted by variations in the money supply and in prices—especially when bank credit got out of line. Accordingly we were obliged to stop in Chapter XIV and study the nature of inflation. Finally in Chapter XV we studied the mechanism by which bank credit could be expanded or "created." We are now almost ready to go back to the problem of the business cycle.

Industrial fluctuations of some sort have been noticed for at least the past 250 years. Adam Smith in *Wealth of Nations,* published in 1775, noticed a phenomenon which he called "overtrading," and there are earlier discussions. But industrial fluctuations were not at first recognized as the deeply seated behavior pattern that the modern economist considers them. Instead, attention was focused primarily upon the monetary disturbances that usually accompanied such upheavals. It was thought that if only the quantity of money and credit could be kept from overexpanding there would be no important economic disturbances. Few modern economists entirely accept so optimistic a view; nevertheless it will help us to get a clear understanding of the fundamental problem if we begin with the money side and with "too much" purchasing power. In this chapter we want to ask two questions: First, what are the institutions which transfer funds and create credit? Second, by what mechanism and on what principles do we seek to stabilize these flows? Only after we have cleared away these preliminary problems can we reach the cycle itself.

## The Types of Credit Institutions

For purposes of our present analysis, we may divide credit institutions into two main types: those which, in theory, merely transfer funds, and those which not only transfer funds but also (as we saw in the last chapter) create them. Among the most important lending institutions which merely transfer funds are the following:

*Investment Banks.* As we saw in Chapter IV, investment bankers or investment houses have historically performed the function of marketers of corporate securities. Corporations wishing to raise capital, whether by means of bonds or stocks, do not usually possess the sales organization required to sell securities to the general public. Instead, they sell them to middlemen—investment bankers—who then sell them to the public at a slightly higher price, the difference being payment for marketing services. Some business firms depend on the reinvestment or "plowing back" of earnings as a source of capital for expansion. In this case, the savings and investment functions are combined into one.

*Life Insurance Companies.* Insurance companies are playing an increasingly important role in the savings and investment functions process. A large percentage of the nation's total personal saving takes the form of insurance. For millions of people the purchase of insurance constitutes virtually their only saving. At the end of 1961 life insurance in force totaled 586 billion dollars and total assets of life insurance companies were over 126.8 billion. During the same year policyholders paid in 12.5 billion in life insurance premiums. (Source: Stat. Abstr. of U.S.)

Insurance companies invest in a number of ways. The most important items in their portfolio are corporation bonds, government bonds, and loans on real estate. As yet, insurance companies are not heavy investors in corporate stocks. (In most states they are prohibited by law from investing in common stocks, or at the very least, stringent restrictions are placed on their stock holdings.)

*Special Agencies.* In addition to banks there are numerous special agencies for extending credit to consumers, such as personal finance companies, sales finance companies, cooperative credit unions, installment sales plans. While in theory they cannot create credit, in fact their influence may be considerable.

*Savings Banks.* Savings banks are banks which take deposits only for fairly specific lengths of time and with, theoretically, rather tight restrictions upon the right of withdrawal. They do not create credit on any large scale but invest their funds mostly in long-term securities. Their investment policies are not unlike those of the insurance companies. They are a relatively small part of the total credit picture.

*Federal Savings and Loan.* This form of credit institution has been growing rapidly. From the point of view of credit creation they are not unlike savings banks but their volume of business is large and growing.

*The State and Federal Governments.* People are increasingly realizing the role of government as a credit and an investment institution. Government, both state and federal, influences investment and credit decisions in two ways. In the first place both the state and federal governments can tax individuals and corporations directly and use the money thus collected to finance government investment projects. It is often a very difficult job, as we saw in Chapter XIII, to decide whether a given state or federal project is investment or consumption, but it is certain that the importance of government investment has greatly increased over the last 30 years and appears to be growing.

The second way in which state governments and the federal government influence investment and credit decisions is through directly operating state or federally owned credit institutions making loans to individuals or corporations. Among these have been the Home Owners Loan Corporation, the Reconstruction Finance Corporation, and various farm credit institutions. At present there are the Federal Savings and Loan banks above mentioned.

Finally, we will see later that both state and federal governments, particularly the latter, can greatly influence investment activity and the money supply by the way they tax and the way they borrow. These effects will be shown in detail when we come to the problem of stabilization.

*Corporations and Other Businesses.* An ordinary business far removed from banking—say, "Smith's Grow-Well"—is not usually thought of as a credit or investment institution. Yet even such a business can have important credit and investment angles. The first way in which an ordinary business can influence investment and credit decisions is through its depreciation and obsolescence funds, and its "plowed-back" earnings. We have seen that the accountants of any well-run business will take care that, before net income is computed, deductions are made to provide for the replacement of that part of the machinery thought to be wearing out during the year, and also of that part thought to be getting out of date. We mentioned in Chapter XIII some of the problems that arise in connection with these deductions. Nevertheless, they form a very important part of the total gross savings of our system.

Many corporations and other businesses, however, are not content merely with depreciation and obsolescence requirements. They "plow back" some of their profits and thus, as we pointed out earlier in connection with investment banking, they save and invest at one and the same time. "Smith's Grow-Well," for example, would use some of its profits to build a new plant. Reinvestment of profits for expansion is, again, one of the most important sources of net savings in the United States.

There is another way in which ordinary corporations, finance institutions, and businesses influence spending and saving, though it is often a bit harder to see. That way is by means of the corporation's credit policy. If a corporation becomes more generous in the terms it gives its buyers—in other words, if buyers are given a longer time in which to pay and are allowed to run-up charge accounts more than formerly—those buyers will have their purchasing power, at least for that moment, greatly increased. Likewise, if all businesses become more lenient as to the dates and amounts of payments, if there is, for example, a greater amount of installment buying permitted, the whole system can feel, for a while at the least, an inflationary stimulus.

*Commercial Banks.* When we talk of the inflationary effects of more generous installment terms we have gone beyond the mere transference of savings and begun to talk of credit creation. And we have seen that overwhelmingly the most important form of credit creation today is the creation of deposits by the commercial banks. Indeed, the main earmark of a commercial bank, compared with savings banks and other merely transferring institutions, is that it lets its depositors draw out and transfer their funds by check in a less restricted way. From this process, as we saw in Chapter XV, comes the major creation of deposits. But we must not forget that commercial banks are important not merely as creators of money (deposits) but also as transferrers of money. While we have spent a great deal of time showing that commercial banks are not *only* go-betweens, lending the money of their depositors, we must not forget that they also *are* go-betweens, though not exclusively so. Thus the commercial banks both transfer resources through their operations and bring about new increases in the amount of deposits. The greater part of their business normally belongs more under the first head than the second. Since the commercial banks are so numerous and so important we will concentrate most of our attention upon them for the rest of this chapter.

### The Mechanism of Credit Control

*The Federal Reserve System.* The Federal Reserve System is patterned after the central banking organizations of Europe, though adapted to the customs and economic practices of this country. Instead of having a single bank, the System includes twelve Federal Reserve banks and at least twenty-four branches in various sections of the country. Thus there is considerable decentralization. On the other hand, major problems of credit are largely in the hands of a central board.

All national banks are required to belong to the Federal Reserve System and state banks may join. While only half of the 13,500 banks in the United States belong to the Reserve System, these member banks hold about three-fourths of the total deposits and roughly 85 per cent of demand deposits (those which can be withdrawn without notice). The Federal Reserve banks are owned by the member banks. However, the Reserve banks are strictly regulated and dividends on their stock are limited to 6 per cent.

The Federal Reserve banks perform two basic roles. One is to carry on certain service functions for the banks of the country, the national government, and the general public. The most important service functions are holding member bank reserves, furnishing currency for circulation, clearing and collecting checks, acting as fiscal agent for the national government, and exercising supervision over operations of member banks. Most of the employees of Federal Reserve banks are engaged in performing these service functions.

The second major function is to maintain a sound money and credit base for business activity. In terms of influence on prices, employment, and the level of economic activity, this is the key role of the Federal Reserve. We will discuss it in more detail shortly.

Basically, the organization of the Federal Reserve System consists of the following: (1) the Board of Governors, (2) the twelve Federal Reserve banks, (3) the Federal Open Market Committee, (4) the Federal Advisory Council, (5) the member banks, with their branches.

*Board of Governors.* The Board of Governors consists of seven members appointed by the President and confirmed by the Senate. It makes most of the major policy decisions of the Federal Reserve System.

*Federal Reserve Banks.* Each of the twelve Federal Reserve banks serves a different region of the country. They are located in Atlanta, Boston, Chicago, Cleveland, Dallas, Kansas City, Minneapolis, New York, Philadelphia, Richmond, St. Louis, and San Francisco. Their influence on general Federal Reserve policy is not so great as it once was, although each bank does give representation to the views and interests of its own region through its local Board of Directors.

*Federal Open Market Committee.* The Federal Open Market Committee is composed of the seven members of the Board of Governors, plus five other members chosen by the regional Federal Reserve banks from among their presidents. One of these is always the President of the New York Federal Reserve Bank. As its name shows, this Committee determines the policy of the twelve Federal Reserve banks in regard to buying and selling United States government securities in the public market. The Committee's investment policy has a powerful influence in determining the cost and availability of credit.

*Federal Advisory Council.* It is made up of twelve private commercial bankers, one selected annually by each of the twelve Federal Reserve banks. This group meets with the Board of Governors at least four times a year to discuss and make recommendations for Federal Reserve policy.

*Other Regulatory Agencies.* While the Federal Reserve System is the most important regulatory body for the commercial banking system, there are several others. In the first place, those state banks which are not members of the

Federal Reserve are under the sole supervision of the state banking authorities. And those authorities do, of course, retain some control over state banks which are members of the Federal Reserve.

Next, the national banks, though all must join the Federal Reserve System, are also under the supervision of the Comptroller of the Currency, a federal official.

Nearly all the state banks and all the national ones are insured by the Federal Deposit Insurance Corporation (F.D.I.C.), a federally chartered and operated institution. This corporation was set up after the crash of 1929 and the bank holiday of 1933, to avoid the suffering entailed by bank failures. It operates on the general lines of a regular insurance company but has considerable supervisory power over the insured banks. Finally, while the Secretary of the Treasury, a federal official, theoretically has no control over the money supply, we will see later that by his decisions regarding government borrowing and related matters he has in fact considerable influence on bank policy. Likewise the taxes and appropriations voted by Congress may greatly influence the banking system.

*Summary on Regulatory Authorities.* It will be seen that there are at least five major sets of regulatory authority in the American banking system. First, there is the Federal Reserve System with the regional banks and central Board and committees. Second, there are the various banking commissions of the fifty states and the territories. Third, comes the Comptroller of the Currency. Fourth is the Federal Deposit Insurance Corporation. Fifth, there are the very great, though usually indirect, influences of the Secretary of the Treasury and the Congress. Thus, though we shall concentrate on the Federal Reserve System in the rest of this chapter, it will be easy to see that there must be many matters of detail which will not be elaborated in this book.

### Principles of Credit Control

Let us now briefly discuss some of the general principles of credit control. Why do we bother to control the banking system? There are two main aims: First, we wish to have a sound and solvent banking system. Second, we want as much as possible to prevent inflation and deflation. We will concentrate here on the inflation–deflation problem.

*Why Do We Permit Credit Creation?* Some readers of the description of deposit creation in Chapter XV will undoubtedly have wondered why such a process should be permitted at all. Why should we want to have an "elastic" money supply—one that expands and contracts? There are several reasons.

In the first place, the demand for cash and for loans is "seasonal." There are some times of the year in which various industries are more active than at others, or in which people are more apt to buy (for example, the Christmas season). A flexible banking system which permits the credit and currency supply to expand and contract with these swings is therefore highly desirable.

*The Price Level Problem.* The second reason for permitting bank credit creation is more complicated, and to understand it we must refer back to Figure 15 (p. 148). In that Figure we diagramed the flow of money and production, and we showed how the proportions of saving and spending affected the rate of growth. We know that more analysis is needed on these lines and we will come back to the problem in the next chapter.

The essential point for present purposes is that Figure 15 is a "snapshot" picture. That is, it shows the economic system as of a single moment, and does not allow for the disturbances introduced by growth. Yet Figure 15 also shows that, in the society it represents, a certain part of GNP is being set aside for *net new investment*. But if a society is having net investment, that society will almost certainly be constantly increasing both its equipment and its output of consumer goods. And we will see that this constant growth involves serious monetary problems.

We learned in Chapters XIV and XV that one of the most useful ways of thinking about money is in terms of a stream of money *being spent* (both for consumption and for investment goods) constantly meeting a stream of goods (of all sorts) *being offered for sale*. The trouble about growth is that, when it is taking place, the stream of goods offered for sale is constantly increasing. But unless some special action is taken, the stream of money spent will not usually be increasing. In terms of Figure 15 this means that, if output is growing and if prices are at first unchanged, we will be obliged in each period to show each bar in Figure 15 constantly increasing in length. For since production of goods will be increasing while prices remain unchanged, the total money value of output in each stage will be increasing.

Yet on the other hand, if the money supply has *not* increased, the amount of actual money income and spending will not be likely to grow at first. Consequently, either some goods will have to go unsold or else prices will have to be reduced. This need for price reduction will be avoided only if by pure blind luck people happen to start holding, on average, less and less money. In other words, an increase in V could serve to maintain prices, even though M were fixed. But while velocity does change from time to time we cannot expect it always to be exactly offsetting in the way we need. Since, therefore, we cannot usually rely on velocity changes, we are obliged to increase the quantity of money slowly as output grows if we want to keep prices on average from falling. Credit creation by the banking system is extremely well fitted to the task of increasing the money supply.

There are, to be sure, a certain number of economists who feel that prices *should* be allowed to fall. They argue that since increases in output are usually accompanied by cost-reducing improvements, businesses and society generally will be able to adjust themselves to a price fall without too much difficulty. And they further maintain that the attempt to stabilize prices will cause certain "distortions" in the "structure of production," which will have the effect of inducing booms followed by depressions. We will mention this problem in the next chapter.

The majority of American economists, however, incline toward a policy of relative price stabilization. They feel that a slow fall in prices has the effect of somewhat discouraging investment; that it sometimes forces unnecessary reductions in money wages which, though they do not affect real living standards, still cause friction; and that the price fall increases the burden of the national debt. For all these and other reasons most of them favor either a more or less stable price level, or in some cases a slowly rising one. But such a policy means that if the national income is growing the money supply must be allowed to grow also. We will further see, in the chapters on international trade, that the stable price-level policy is not always consistent with international monetary stability.

## Methods of Credit Control

*Rediscounting.* The Federal Reserve System, as originally established, sought to bring about the adjustment of output and the money supply through an *automatic* mechanism. It was hoped that an automatic system would avoid criticism since it would not involve anyone's personal discretion. The fundamental problem is, of course, to find some way of keeping the supply of money in step with changes in production. The framers of the system thought that if they could keep credit creation somehow closely tied to increases in output all would go well, and so they worked out the following scheme: They supposed that most banks would usually have very little slack—that is, that most bankers would lend about as much as their legal and other reserves permitted. If, therefore, a bank wanted to increase its loans it would usually have to increase its reserves. To meet this problem the Federal Reserve Act provided that the bank could take some of the notes which its borrowers had given it in connection with their loans, and "rediscount" them. That means that if, say, Joe Brown had borrowed from the X bank and given a note for, let us suppose, $1,000, due in 60 days, the X bank could then take Joe's note to the Federal Reserve bank and sell it for a certain amount. The X bank could either use the proceeds of the sale to get dollar bills and coins from the Federal Reserve bank (to use for vault cash), or it could have the amount of the sale added to its *reserve* account with the Federal Reserve bank. Now if the bank had the money added to its reserve account and increased its reserves by $950, then under a 20 per cent reserve system it could *legally,* not practically, increase its loans (that is, the new deposits set up in favor of borrowers) by five times that much. Thus, it would have $950 in reserves supporting $4,750 in deposits. But we have already seen that as a practical matter a bank would be very unlikely to make such fivefold expansion.

Let us, however, continue explaining the original basic Federal Reserve idea. The notion was that if the banks were allowed to rediscount only certain types of loans—in other words, if they could get extra reserves only by selling certain types of borrowers' notes, etc., to the Federal Reserve banks—then the banks would be so afraid of being caught without the right kind of loans, when they wanted to get more reserves, that they would come automatically to confine themselves to certain special types of business. More specifically, it was hoped by this method to persuade the ordinary commercial banks—the only ones which created credit—to stick to very short-term loans, closely tied to production. If a man wanted to build a factory, paying off his loan very slowly over the years, the framers of the Federal Reserve Act thought that he ought to sell bonds or stocks, or to borrow from some savings bank which did not create credit. For as he borrowed from a bank which set up new deposits or created credit, as described in Chapter XV, he might be adding immediately to the money supply, but it would be some time before production would be increased. Thus the price of goods might be forced up and there would be tendencies to inflation. On the other hand, if a man borrowed to buy, say, shoes to offer for sale, the increase in goods and the increase in money would happen virtually at the same time, and there would be much less danger of price disturbance.

But rediscounting under the Federal Reserve Act was not intended merely to influence the type of loan. It was also set up as a weapon for both stimulating and discouraging credit expansion. When a bank sells or rediscounts one of its borrower's notes, it has to pay the Federal Reserve bank for this privilege of getting cash or reserves. Now if the Reserve bank thinks *too much* credit is outstanding, it could raise the price which it charged—"the rediscount rate," it is called—and thus make it very expensive for a bank to get extra reserves or cash. On the other hand, however, if the Reserve banks want to stimulate credit expansion, they would make the rate very low and hope that that would lead the banks to get more reserves and to expand loans.

There were many weaknesses in this original Federal Reserve idea. In the first place it is based upon the notion that the commercial banks are always "lent up" to the limit of their various reserves. In a time of reasonable prosperity and stability this is a very plausible assumption. Of course a bank has to have enough reserves to satisfy legal requirements and common prudence. But on the other hand, if a banker is not lending as much as he otherwise could he is not taking full advantage of his profit opportunities. Thus no small part of the art of banking consists in estimating and steering a reasonable course between precaution, on one hand, and profits, on the other. This means that the banker will not want to have idle reserves if he can help it. But during the years following the Great Depression of 1929 the surviving banks found themselves in possession of reserves permitting a much larger expansion of loans than the low economic activity of the 1930s permitted. The chief outlet for banks was purchasing government bonds. Later on when things became more active, it was much easier and less expensive to sell government bonds than to bother to rediscount as a way to get additional reserve.

Yet another reason for the collapse of the original Federal Reserve idea lies in the fact which we pointed out earlier: the commercial banks are not merely creators of deposits but also transferrers of money received from their depositors. They are now, in fact, in control of such immense sums received from the public that it would be very difficult to invest all that money in the very narrow field of short-term "inventory" credit allowed for in the original plan of the Federal Reserve System. Thus, for good or bad, American commercial banks are increasingly becoming investment institutions, and the whole idea of rediscounting and automatic control has largely been pushed to one side. We must therefore consider some of the other and more modern methods of controlling the money supply.

*Reserve Requirements.* It has already been pointed out that member banks are required by law to keep a certain percentage of their deposits on reserve at the Federal Reserve banks. We have also seen how fractional reserves provide the basis for loan expansion on the part of the commercial banks. Through increasing or decreasing the size of required reserves, the Federal Reserve can, therefore, exert control over credit creation and the size of the money supply.

Two classes of banks are designated for reserve requirement purposes: *Reserve city banks* are member banks in cities; and the remaining member banks are called *country banks*. Actually, the distinction between the two classes of banks is more a matter of the kind of business done than it is a matter of geography any more, but old labels stick. Under existing legislation, the legal reserve requirement for country banks can be varied by Federal Reserve authority between 7 per cent and 14 per cent of demand deposits and between 10 per cent and 20 per cent for reserve city banks. The legal reserve requirements for time deposits for all member banks can be varied between 3 per cent and 6 per cent. Only Congress can change these brackets.

*Increasing* reserve requirements tends to *restrict* the expansion of credit and hence of the money supply on the part of commercial banks. This means they have less excess reserves and as a result cannot do as much lending. *Decreasing* reserve requirements may tend to stimulate the expansion of credit and the money supply. In this case the commercial banks find themselves with increased excess reserves, and as a result they can expand credit and the money supply if they so desire and if there is a demand for loans.

*Open Market Operations.* This term refers to Federal Reserve purchases *and* sales of United States government securities in the open market. When the Federal Reserve *purchases* government securities from a dealer, commercial bank reserves are *expanded.* The expansion happens because the dealer selling the securities will undoubtedly deposit the check that he receives in his bank. His deposit leads to an increase of demand deposits on the liability side of his bank's balance sheet and of its deposits at the Federal Reserve bank (reserve balances) on the asset side. Thus, the excess reserves of the commercial bank have been increased.

For example, if a dealer sells a thousand-dollar government bond to the Federal Reserve and deposits the receipts in his bank, with a reserve ratio of 20 per cent, the amount of required reserves is increased by $200 and the amount of excess reserves by $800. The bank then can, if it so desires, lend out the $800, thereby expanding credit and the money supply.

Similarly, if the Federal Reserve believes that credit is being created and the money supply expanding at too rapid a rate for the good health of the economy, it can sell some of its holdings of government securities. This means that the excess reserves of commercial banks will be reduced, and credit and money supply expansion can be curbed. In extreme cases where the commercial banks have no excess reserves, the sale of government bonds by the Federal Reserve can force the commercial banks actually to call in loans and thereby reduce the money supply. Open market operations and changing the reserve requirements of member banks are usually considered to be the two most important controls over general monetary and credit conditions possessed by the Federal Reserve. Many would rate open market operations as being the more important of these two.

*"Moral Suasion."* This refers to the pressures which the Federal Reserve authorities may bring to bear upon member banks to restrict or to expand credit creation. For example, Reserve officials may make public statements warning against making loans for speculative purposes, or they may send out warning letters to member banks. Similarly, they may bring pressure to encourage an expansion of loans and investments when economic conditions are depressed.

*Selective or Direct Credit Controls.* By the Securities and Exchange Act of 1934, the Board of Governors of the Federal Reserve System was given the power to set minimum margin requirements in the stock market. However, the

Board has never been given power to regulate margin requirements on the commodities exchanges. Buying securities on margin means the practice of having the customer arrange with his broker to make a down payment for his stock and borrow the rest of the purchase price from the broker, using the securities as collateral. The aim of margin requirements is to curb stock market speculation. The Federal Reserve has increased minimum margin requirements on several occasions. During the stock market upsurge of 1963, margin requirements were raised to 70 per cent; in other words, the stock market was put more nearly on an all-cash basis.

We saw earlier in this chapter that the type of credit granted by individual businesses affects the money supply. Increasingly, the Federal Reserve is entering this field. Consumer credit controls were first utilized during and after World War II. After the outbreak of the Korean conflict they were reactivated. The Federal Reserve Board regulated installment credit by setting minimum downpayment requirements and limiting the length of the period over which payments could be spread. The Federal Reserve also set terms for mortgage credit on new houses. Both installment and real estate credit controls were suspended in 1952 as inflationary pressures eased.

Congress has never granted the Federal Reserve Board the power to regulate installment credit and mortgage credit on a permanent basis. These powers have been granted only as a temporary basis during periods of national emergency. Selective credit controls restrict the use of credit for the purchase of goods whose output must be curtailed, in order to divert scarce materials to the production of military goods. Such a policy helps to keep demand more nearly in balance with reduced supplies in these lines. The net result is that selective price increases are curbed and the necessity of rationing these goods may also be avoided.

*Treasury Controls over the Money Supply.* In addition to the various methods of influencing the size of the money supply possessed by the Federal Reserve, the U. S. Treasury, as we have already mentioned, also possesses several powers which influence it. The Federal Reserve System, for example, is required to have a 25 per cent "gold certificate" reserve against its liabilities. The actual gold is held by the Treasury. Yet in 1934 the President increased the price of gold from $20.67 to $35 per ounce. This decrease of 41 per cent in the theoretical gold content of the dollar increased the gold holdings of the Treasury from four billion dollars to 6.8 billion. This also meant that the gold certificate holdings of the Federal Reserve were increased by roughly the same amount; which meant that the Federal Reserve could, if it so desired, greatly increase member banks' reserves or Federal Reserve notes in circulation by buying government securities in the open market.

Under the Silver Purchase Act of 1934, Congress declared it to be government policy that the monetary reserves of the nation should be made up of one-quarter silver and three-quarters gold. The price at which the Treasury was required to buy silver was set far above the then world market level, though it has since risen, and the Treasury was also required to issue silver certificates against all silver purchased. As a result the quantities of silver which the Treasury purchases directly influence the size of the money supply.

The amount of Treasury cash and deposits also influences money and credit conditions. The money which the Treasury collects from the taxpayers is kept either in the form of cash in the Treasury or in the form of deposits in the Federal Reserve banks or in "tax and loan" accounts with commercial banks. Until World War II no funds were held in commercial banks until spent for goods and services or used to repay debt. When taxes were paid, private deposits in commercial banks were decreased. By increasing or decreasing the size of its cash holdings and deposits, the Treasury influenced money and credit conditions. To reduce such swings government "tax and loan" accounts with commercial banks were invented.

## Private Debt, Public Debt, and Credit Control: A Summary

The foregoing ways in which the Treasury can affect the money supply are relatively unimportant compared to the government's influence through borrowing. Hidden behind our treatment of control methods and control organizations there is one fundamental fact which can easily be forgotten: In our society all increases in the money supply except actual imports of gold come through the creation of debt. Indeed, since the government seizes the gold and gives the banks gold certificates in return—which are a special sort of debts—even an increase in the gold supply involves an increase in debt. Thus, in any case, to increase the money supply means to increase debts of various sorts. And if any large amounts of old debts are repaid, there must be an offsetting creation of new debts or the money supply will shrink. Of course all sorts of foolish conclusions can be drawn from the perfectly matter-of-fact, common-sense statement we have just made. Our statement does *not,* for example, mean that the size of the national debt is never something to worry about. Nor can we jump from the fact that an increase in production means an increase in debt to the idea that any increase in debt increases production. The fact remains that it is through increased credit (debt) that money is usually increased. Therefore, to control money is to a great extent to control debt creation.

# ✦✦✦ XVII ✦✦✦

## The Business Cycle: Too Much Purchasing Power

In the preceding chapter we began upon the problem of economic instability. We saw how the monetary mechanism from time to time got out of gear, and we learned some of the methods which have been tried to regulate debt creation and changes in the value of money. Now we can put the tools together and discuss the business cycle as such. Many economists feel that the word "cycle" is in itself misleading. It suggests a mechanical rhythm like the cycle of a steam engine. But the fact is that attempts to prove that industrial fluctuations have a definite rhythm have not been very successful. Furthermore, it is quite certain that recurrent periods of prosperity and depression can spring from many different sources. So far as causation goes, a depression is like a broken leg. No single theory will do. The most that can be accomplished is to prepare a catalogue of the usual sources of the trouble. In this chapter we will discuss the case of a depression due to "overinvestment" and "too much" purchasing power. Modern popular literature in the United States has almost entirely concentrated upon the opposite case of depression due to "too little" purchasing power. But in terms of history the depression from "too much" is far older. It is also the characteristic maladjustment of the underdeveloped nations that make up most of the world today. Finally it is a convenient bridge between bank credit control and more comprehensive theories. Accordingly, the case of "too much" purchasing power will be our starting point.

### Basic Diagrams of Stable Growth

The fundamental figures for our analysis are shown in Figure 17. Figure 17(a) is a greatly simplified GNP diagram. It is assumed that some omniscient statistician has managed to sort government outlay into the appropriate consumption, replacement, and investment divisions so that there is no need to distinguish between private and public sectors. Also all the usual loops and whirlpools of the money flow are neglected. The result is as if the complicated output and income measures of Figure 16, over a number of years, had been

Figure 17
STABLE GROWTH AND "FORCED" INVESTMENT

(a)

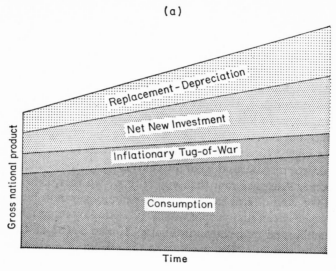

(b)

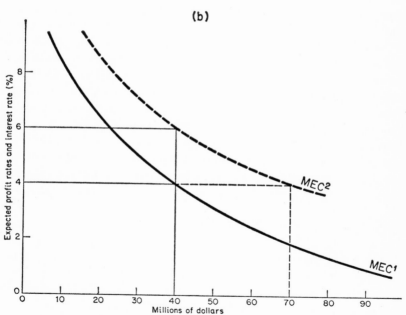

Source: David McCord Wright, *The Keynesian System;* Fordham University Press, © 1962 (pp. 11, 31)

resolved into the simple bottom bar of Figure 15 and then stood on end, side by side, for a long period. The Figure represents an economy which is in a state of balanced growth without either inflation or unemployment. The bottom band shows consumer outlay, the next band represents net new investment, and the top strip shows replacement. The dotted areas will be explained shortly. Figure 17(b), on the other hand, is simply a repetition of Figure 13, the basic interest diagram, except that more than one marginal efficiency of capital schedule is shown. The MEC schedule is very changeable, as we pointed out in Chapter XI.

The next question is, How are (a) and (b) related? The answer can be readily given. Later in this study we will present a very refined theory of the rate of interest, but at present only the very simple theory presented in Figure 13 is needed. In Figure 13 we saw how the rate of interest could keep the flow of real saving or free resources equal to the value of the flow of money saving from current income. A higher rate than equilibrium, we there saw, would mean that not all the flow of real saving, or free resources, would be employed. A lower rate would mean that people would try to employ more than were available. The equilibrium rate, shown in Figures 13 and 17(b) at 4 per cent, just balances off the stream of real saving and the stream of money saving out of current income. This flow, shown in (b), is exactly equal to the middle or "investment" flow of (a). As long as the going rate of interest, the saving line, and the required flow of real and money savings are in harmony there will be no difficulty. But suppose something happens to make people want to invest more than they have been doing, but there is no increased desire to save—what then? Let us say that the dotted strip shown in Figure 17(a) represents the amount that investors would *like* to encroach upon consumption if only consumers would let them. What will happen?

The problem will affect the diagram in (b) also. Investors are wanting to spend more on investment, if they could, because the marginal efficiency of capital schedule has shifted upward. There is a generally more favorable state of expectation. As we saw in Chapter XI, if we want to prevent inflation, the controllers of credit under such conditions will have to permit, or force, a rise of the rate of interest. This is shown in (b) at 6 per cent. If, however, they do not do so serious maladjustment will occur.

### The Problem Stated Practically: Socialism and Capitalism

We said in the discussion in Chapter XII that the problem of saving and investment could be handled under socialism by means of taxes and state outlay rather than by private saving and private investment, but that the essential relationships would be much the same. This similarity is strikingly evident in the type of disturbance we are about to describe. The essential difficulty is that either private investors or the government want to build new projects faster than consumers want to release resources to them. If a socialist government wishes to avoid inflation it can impose heavier taxes and use the proceeds for construction. But taxes are never popular, even under socialism, and the lowering of the standard of living which they cause may be more than even a socialist population would tolerate—if they knew the real source of the trouble. In the same way a capitalist central bank—in the United States the Federal Reserve System—which wanted to prevent inflation could raise the rate of interest. But it, too, would encounter political difficulties. It would be accused of raising the "price of government," of "holding back growth," and so on. The temptation to allow a little inflation would be great under both systems. But as we are assuming full employment it will not be physically possible to expand without squeezing consumption somehow. Here we have to stop to examine a very important and confusing bit of terminology—the "equality" of saving and investment.

## The Equality of Saving and Investment

Under the full-employment assumptions we have used so far, we have set up the rate of interest problem in terms of balancing two streams—a stream of investment goods, or what may be called "technologically unappropriated resources," on the one hand, and a stream of money savings from current income on the other. To the "classical" or orthodox economists of the early nineteenth century these streams were always and necessarily equal. They meant that if a man saved—that is, did not spend a dollar on consumption—he necessarily and promptly invested—that is, spent the same dollar on investment goods. Later on Lord Keynes and many others pointed out that the two streams did not always coincide so neatly. Sometimes, as we have seen, the dollar put aside was not spent at all, and there were tendencies toward depression. Sometimes the banks permitted more credit to be created, or unspent cash was put into circulation and there were tendencies toward inflation. But no sooner had economic analysis settled down to this second account, which recognized possible discrepancies between the two streams, than Lord Keynes turned around and again announced that "saving" and "investment" were "necessarily equal." Yet, after much discussion this third version implying necessary "equality" was also accepted. Hence great confusion.

The problem is easily solved once we realize that the "equality" of saving and investment spoken of by the modern economist is an entirely different thing from the "equality" supposed by the orthodox economists of a hundred and fifty years ago. We can explain the difficulty in two ways—with reference to flows of money accompanied by changes in prices, or with reference to actual production, general prices remaining unchanged. Let us begin with actual production. What the orthodox economists were talking of, so far as actual production goes, was a stream of equipment and plant actually in process of being made. They thought that changes in the rate of interest kept the value of this stream of goods (general prices remaining unchanged) in line with a parallel stream of money savings. But when the modern economist talks of saving and investment as "equal," he is, in terms of actual production, thinking not of goods being manufactured, but of whatever pile of goods happens to be *left over* from consumption at the end of whatever given time interval he is talking of. Saving, he says, means unconsumed output at the end of some interval. Investment means unconsumed output at the end of the same interval. Since they are the same pile of goods left over, they are the same thing. Yet clearly to talk of a net pile of goods *remaining* over and above what has been consumed during a time interval, is not the same as talking about a stream of goods *being made* during that time interval, and its relation to the money flows during that time interval.

It will help if we state the practical problem that makes this discussion necessary. Various economists in various undeveloped countries, wishing to increase their country's actual store of physical equipment, have found that their country did not have the flow of money saving needed to set aside a large enough flow of free resources to build the projects they desired. In terms of Figure 17(a) the top two bands are not large enough. But some of these economists have heard that saving and investment are equal or the "same thing," and they have jumped to the conclusion that if they went ahead and tried to construct the projects they wanted, using newly created money to pay the bill, somehow the needed physical resources would magically appear, and with them the needed "saving." The argument usually runs that the increase in "investment" will raise income and so make possible the needed "saving."

Unfortunately the argument could not be more unreliable. It is true that if investment is productive it may, some day, after it is completed (or *if* it is completed) raise actual production and make possible a larger stream of "technologically unappropriated resources." But eventual increase in production takes time. What is more likely to happen in the short run is that the increased investment spending will only raise the *money value* of physical output. It need not raise real output at all. The next effect of the program we will shortly see is often famine, inflation, and the abandonment of uncompleted projects half way through, because the consumers are unwilling to stand further deprivation.

To be sure many economists have shown that if we rearrange the national accounts at the end of a period, just as we talk of the heap of goods remaining at the end of a period, we can show an accounting "equality." Some people will have increased cash balances, for example, and we can balance these against the money value of "investment." But this is a mere juggling of accounts. It is far removed from the stream of actual production set by the "votes" of a stream of actual current money saving, of which the orthodox economists were talking. Fortunately the student does not have to go any deeper into the intricacies of the subject for there is a perfectly plain and easy way of clearing up the entire confusion:

### "Planned" Saving and "Planned" Investment

Everyone admits that during any given period of time a certain number of people will be planning to save a certain amount of money from current money income. Everyone further admits that during the same period a certain number of people, but not necessarily the same ones, will be planning to borrow or to spend a certain amount of money on the current construction of new plant and equipment. All economists further agree that these two sets of plans do not have to agree at any given period. "Planned" saving, therefore, and "planned" investment do not have to be equal. But if investment and saving *plans* do not agree, then any number of things can happen. Prices may go up or down, national income may go up or down, or the rate of interest may go up or down. We will see a great deal more about these movements in the chapters on unemployment. It is enough to realize that under conditions of full-employment growth, such as we suppose in this chapter, if we want to prevent inflation, the method to be used in reconciling divergent saving and investment plans is appropriate changes in the interest rate. Having made our terms clear, we can now go on to discuss what will happen if people are *planning* to invest more than they (or others) are *planning* to save, and if the controllers of credit are not allowed to raise the rate of interest.

### The Tug of War

We suppose that we are in a democratic capitalist state in which profit prospects have suddenly increased, and that the money authorities, either because they have miscalculated the extent to which the MEC schedule has risen or because of political pressure, have failed to raise the rate of interest. Say it is left at 4 per cent. This will mean, as shown by Figure 17(b), that the amount of planned net investment will be nearly doubled. What will happen?

Let us suppose that the new project is a mine or a commercial space rocket. Because of government subsidies or new discoveries, glowing prospects of profits are held out. The rate of interest has been kept low. The banks have plenty of reserves and are eager to lend. How will the new industry behave? Since there is full employment (though this is an elastic and ambiguous concept, as we will see in the next chapter) we assume here that they can get more labor only by "raiding" other businesses. What we mean by this is that they obtain labor and raw materials from other businesses, especially those making consumer goods, by offering higher prices and higher wages. The expanding investment industry can afford to do this because the banks are behind them and will lend to them. If they are a government bureau they can do it because the government is issuing them the money to pay for the higher wage scale. Suppose, in either case, that by thus offering higher wages and prices the rate of investment *is*—for the moment—nearly doubled and consumption is lowered by the tug-of-war space of Figure 17(a). It looks as if everything were doing well.

But wait a minute. Two simultaneous actions have occurred which are bound to cause trouble. First, the real output of consumer goods has been cut. Second, the total money incomes of workers have risen. Nobody is likely to have increased his desire to save very much. On the contrary, those who have just shifted over to the mines or rocket bases in response to higher wages have more money in their pockets and are anxious to spend it. So spending for consumption increases just when the supply of consumer goods has been cut. There can be only one result: a "secondary" or derived inflation in the consumer goods industries. Government may try to control prices, but even then black markets will soon begin to appear.

Suppose, however, that government does not try to control prices. Consumer goods industries will be making inflationary profits, and they in their turn will try to expand. They try to lure back some of their former labor from the mine by raising their bids on wages. The mine finds it is beginning to lose labor. What will it do? It will borrow some more money from the banks or get some more money from the government, and raise wages and prices again. A tug of war over labor and materials, or an "inflationary spiral," is now well started. It can continue for some little time, first one side and then the other raising wages and payrolls to hold scarce labor.

A good example of the sort of thing we are imagining is given by the development of Brazil in recent years. The Brazilian government launched a series of grandiose investment projects, notably the great and enormously costly new capital at Brasilia, far in the interior and almost inaccessible save by airplane. No one pretended that Brazilian tax collections, or saving, could possibly cover the cost of these enterprises. The money was produced by outright inflation; the work went ahead and labor was attracted by the identical process of competitive bidding through inflation which we have just been describing. Meanwhile prices rose at the rate of 50 per cent a *month*. Foreign exchange difficulties increased. There was general chaos and in this case revolution.

Similar behavior (economically speaking) has been frequently observed in Russia since the Soviet regime began. There, too, the government has tried to use inflation as a substitute for voluntary planned saving by individuals, and there, too, the sort of tug of war we have been describing has taken place. More typical capitalist examples can be found in nineteenth-century booms. In all cases the one thing in common is the attempt to expand equipment faster than the people, left to themselves, would permit. But what brings the boom to a close?

## The Crisis

It would seem that with endless inflation and omnipotent government, the various totalitarian inflations would be unbreakable. However, history teaches us differently. The force ending the totalitarian inflationary boom is called the "collapse of the currency."

Collapse of the currency can come in several forms. In the famous German inflation after World War I, the inflation came to an end only when no one could be found to hold money for any length of time however short. The velocity of the money supply increased so fast that prices were rising faster than the government found it practicable to print money. At this stage the process is near its end. The essence of the process we are describing is that the government is keeping men at work on its favored project by continuously outbidding the rest of the economy. The outbidding is managed by offering continuously higher wages and prices, financed by new money. Once prices are rising faster than new money can be issued by government, or once the people refuse to hold the money on any terms, the method no longer works.

A more modern type of collapse comes when prices are nominally controlled by the government, but such large amounts of cash money are in the hands of the public and so little can be bought at the legal price at the official stores that the black market flourishes and the general political structure of controls begins to fail. Under such circumstances the old currency becomes a "nuisance" to the planners. It is time to wipe the slate clean (wipe out the cash holdings of the public) and start again. The Russian economy, for example, has thus exhibited a perfectly clearly marked succession of overexpansions, inflations, and devaluations, and overexpansions again, quite like a capitalist business cycle and from causes rather similar to many capitalist cycles—a desire for rapid expansion, a lack of sufficient real saving.

The second limit on ruthless inflation is the failure of foreign claims or foreign exchange. If a country is obliged to import large quantities of foreign goods and if its currency becomes worthless, and it has used up its gold reserves and other foreign means of payment, it must reorganize the money system or starve.

Let us now, however, leave these extreme cases and discuss the crisis in a capitalist free exchange society in which, to be sure, there will have been some rise in prices but less than the drastic distortions we have been discussing. How does the crisis develop in these more moderate surroundings? Two immediate possible sources are obvious and simple. First, the banks may exhaust their reserves and be unable to create more deposits. Second, the special project starting the boom may be completed. Let us commence with the banks. If an overexpansion is solely the work of profit-motivated private business, financed by too easy money, it will be evident that, as the process of bidding and counterbidding for resources goes on, the banks will find their reserves becoming exhausted. They will have to raise their interest rates or reduce their credit extensions. Either way, they cannot continue a boundless increase in loans and the boom will be ended. Of course, if the matter concerned merely one nation, government could always change the laws regarding the currency backing. But when a country is experiencing a boom it often begins to run into foreign exchange difficulties. It begins to import more than it exports and, unless loans are forthcoming from abroad, its depreciating currency will buy less and less abroad and external pressure will end the expansion.

The next difficulty may come from the investment side. Either the new project sparking the inflationary boom may be physically completed or businessmen may revise their expectations concerning profit and abandon the expansion when it is half done. Let us begin with the completion of the project. Clearly if the inflationary method of squeezing consumption for saving has worked and the great new project has been completed there will be no need to continue the inflation. A crisis ensues which we will describe shortly. In the words of Albert Aftalion, a noted French economist, "The bucket is full." However, we meet here for the first time an idea of the greatest importance in cycle analysis: It is not so much the amount of expansion that counts in cycle analysis as the rate of expansion. Often the boom becomes geared to a given rate of *increase* of output and even though a very great deal of investment is still continuing, the mere fact that it is no longer speeding up may serve to start a crisis.

Before we discuss the problem of rate of expansion let us discuss the problem of business expectations. The essential motivation for business activity and investment, bearing in mind all the qualifications expressed in Chapter IV, is what may be called the "perspective" of profit. We illustrate this in Figure 18(a) and (b). In Figure 18(a) we show a diagram reflecting a businessman's estimate of future profit prospects on a given project. When referring to a possible future investment, the diagram becomes simply part of a more detailed analysis of the marginal efficiency of capital for a single firm. It is not the same thing, however, as the marginal efficiency of capital schedule or curve shown in Figure 17(b), because that refers to profit expectations for alternative flows of investment for the whole of society, during a given interval. But Figure 18(a) refers to one business only. Returning to Figure 18(a), we show there a sort of pennant-shaped area between two lines marked "Cost Expectations" and "Price Expectations." The area represents the net expectation of profit for that project for the foreseeable future. We need not suppose the businessman thinks that prices are in fact going to fall, and costs to rise, in the way we show in Figure 18(a). What these lines indicate is that the businessman thinks, "Well, next year I can be sure of getting at least that much, and my costs are not likely to be any higher than the figure I have put down." Then he will think, "Year after next I should reduce the amount I am sure of by a little to allow for the unexpected. Also I should suppose costs will go up a bit. Who knows? There may be a strike." In other words, the area between the lines represents the diminishing perspective of what he thinks he can be reasonably sure of in the way of profit margin as he peers into the future. In Figure 18(b) we complete the analysis by showing a three-dimensional diagram with a dimension added for expected sales volume. The volume of the pyramid shown will constitute the total profit expectation—that is, as much as the businessman feels he can be sure of. It is this perspective of profit which furnishes the real incentive for business action and for investment.

We now apply Figure 18 to the crisis resulting from too much purchasing power. Remember that, in the capitalist case, the investment boom was started by a rise of the marginal efficiency of capital (perspective of profit) in some one industry. We will explain, in Chapter XX, that this need not be directly related to consumption or to the consumption level. The expanding industry we assume has a peculiarly favorable perspective of profit because of government subsidies, or because some new invention is expected to make costs very low, or merely because (some academic theorists argue) the rate of interest has been lowered to keep prices stable. However that may be, the tug of war we have been describing will begin. And as the tug of war goes on, costs will start rising. In terms of Figure 18(a) the lower line shows a rise in the level of expected costs which is faster than the rise in expected prices. Or both lines may rise, but expected prices will not rise as fast as expected costs. It must be remembered, in this connection, that businessmen are fluctuation-conscious. They know that what goes up often comes down. Thus even though present prices may be rising as fast as costs, this does not mean that the business community will think the prices will stay that high. On the other hand, the debts they are now incurring will have to be paid even when prices have fallen. Thus they may think that future profit margins are not adequately guaranteed. Increasing uneasiness over the future may develop. Either the businessmen lose confidence in the future

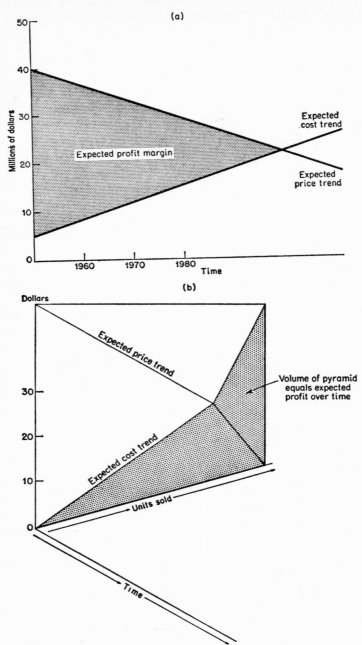

Figure 18
THE PERSPECTIVE OF PROFIT

(a)

Expected cost trend

Expected profit margin

Expected price trend

Millions of dollars

1960    1970    1980    Time

(b)

Dollars

Expected price trend

Expected cost trend

Volume of pyramid equals expected profit over time

Units sold

Time

Source: David McCord Wright, *The Keynesian System;* Fordham University Press, © 1962 (p. 57)

and cease to borrow, or the banks lose confidence in the future and cease to lend. Either way the industry will cease expanding or will slow down, and a downswing is likely to occur.

## The Downswing

Why should stopping the special project that was "sparking" the boom cause trouble? Are we not in a state of inflation? Are we not bothered by too much purchasing power? Why then a slump? The answer lies in the problems of foresight, adjustment, and rates of change. In order for planned saving to be constantly equal to planned investment, which we have seen is a first requirement for a state of balanced growth, the total number of resources employed in the expanding industries must be just sufficient to absorb those being released in the declining ones. There is never such a condition that all lines are prosperous or equally prosperous together. The most we can hope for is that the differences balance each other. But if one line falls or declines faster than others are rising, a *net* shortage of purchasing power will develop and society will be forced into a decline. The sudden shift from inflation to collapse, often seen at the upper turning point of a boom, is due to this failure of balance. An important number of industries have begun to decline *faster* than others are still rising, and the resulting initial shortage of purchasing power, or drop in income, drags down the rest of the economy.

## The Banks and the Downswing

It is just at this point that theories of credit control become least satisfactory. A central bank can always stop a boom or an inflation, if it is permitted to act, by raising the rate of interest and reducing the amount of excess bank reserves. But powers of stimulation are much more limited. All that credit authorities can do is to act negatively. They can lower the rate of interest, they can reduce reserve requirements, they can reduce margin requirements for stock purchases, and, if they have the authority, they can permit more generous installment-buying terms. There is an old proverb that you can lead a horse to water but you can't make him drink. As we saw in our description of credit creation in Chapter XV, the bankers cannot force people to invest and to borrow. The result is that credit control, while enormously powerful in restricting credit, is quite weak in inducing expansion. As far as the business cycle is concerned a central bank is an automobile with brakes but no starter.

The writer has often used the following analogy to explain the problem of credit control. Imagine an auto out of gasoline at the top of a hill. The driver wants to slide down the hill fast enough to be able to surmount the next hill by momentum only. But as he starts down he finds himself going dangerously fast

If he puts on the brakes he can keep from running off the road, but he may slow himself down so much that he won't be able to get up the next hill. If he does not put on the brakes he may wreck himself. So it is with credit policy. If expansion is restrained too abruptly and severely it may not be possible to get the economy going again, for the banks can only act permissively. On the other hand, if inflation is not stopped soon enough the situation may get out of hand. Thus banking and credit policy, taken alone, are seldom able to carry the full load of economic stabilization.

# The Business Cycle: Rates of Movement

In the preceding chapter we analyzed one of the most usual types of economic fluctuation—the overinvestment cycle—and its connection with the problem of credit policy. But we have much more ground to cover before we work out a complete theory of the cycle. In the ultimate sense, indeed, no theory of business cycles gets much beyond what we have had to say earlier concerning the forecasting and adjustment problem. The cycle is a problem of growth, change, and friction. We cannot always expect the advance into novelty to work smoothly, and that is the essence of our problem. However, it is possible to analyze the matter a little more closely. We can say that the business cycle occurs when the economy generally, or a large part of it, is advancing at a faster rate than can be maintained; or else when a leveling off in the expansion of existing industries is not matched by an upsurge in the development of new ones. In this chapter we will concentrate upon some of the forces causing expansion at a faster rate than can be maintained.

## The Simple Speculative Boom

One of the classic types of industrial disturbance is the simple speculative boom. Suppose people think that great profits can be made in a particular line and they begin to purchase the stock of corporations engaged in it. A small speculative flurry is possible, without over-all credit expansion, if purchasing power is diverted from other lines, but a really serious maladjustment requires some inflation. Yet only a very little net credit expansion can start the ball rolling. The feature which distinguishes the speculative boom from a genuine expansion is that in the speculative boom people no longer buy because of long-range income prospects but simply because they hope to *resell* at a quick profit. The price of the stock today, or of the town lot, or even of the tulip bulb, to give some historic examples, depends upon the expectation that it is going to be higher tomorrow. Such a boom cannot level off. The boom only continues as long as new waves of buyers are attracted, and they are attracted by the hope that prices will *keep rising*. As soon as the expectation of a further price rise is ended new buyers cease to come in and the entire boom collapses.

Speculative behavior like this can accompany and reinforce many different types of more fundamental disturbance—for example, the investment tug of war outlined in the previous chapter. One especially important field in modern economic life is in labor relations. Often a company will grant wage concessions quite readily if the situation is inflationary and the concessions are easily passed on to the public. But once the expectation of easy price rise ends, a very different psychology reigns and companies caught with wage contracts which they had made in the expectation of raising prices will be left holding the bag. If such companies are an important part of the economy their difficulties can help to bring on a slump.

## The Wage Lag

A similar phenomenon is conceivable in the wage-lag theory. It has often been argued that during the upswing of a boom, wages lag behind prices because there is at first a good deal of unemployment which lowers the bargaining power of labor and keeps wages down. As a result of low wages people get a false idea of the marginal efficiency of capital, and investment is encouraged to surge ahead. But as the boom goes on and unemployment declines, wages begin to rise faster than prices. Profit prospects are revised downward and investment begins to decline.

There is considerable logic in this theory but it does not appear to be significant in practice. If that were all there was to the business cycle, the cycle would long ago have been ended. Indeed, in modern society a large part of the wage level is often lifted by collective bargaining before prices have risen. We will consider the consequences of such behavior later.

## The Shift to Profit

An alternative, and factually contradictory, possibility of slump is raised by what is called the shift to profit. Here it is expected that profits will continue to rise in the boom. Receivers of profits, it is supposed, do not spend as fast as the rest of society. Consumption fails to keep up with investment, and a crisis follows. Like the wage-lag theory this explanation is a logical possibility but cannot possibly be a complete theory in itself. It is also unlikely to occur under modern conditions.

## The Consumption Lag

A shift to profit, however, is only one of the conditions which might bring on a much more general state of affairs called the consumption lag. Lord Keynes spoke of what he called the "normal psychological law of consumers' behavior." According to this "law," and disregarding all changes in prices and phenomena like the shift to profit, consumption rises as output rises but not as fast. A gap develops between the trend of output and the level of consumption. Since it is presumed that investment is made only when increased consumption is expected, we find ourselves, so runs the theory, compelled to invest faster and faster just when consumption is rising more and more slowly. "Something will have to break." Here is another possible source of trouble. But again a reference to the facts shows the theory to be much less universal than it might appear. In the first place investment, we will see later on, does not always depend upon an increase in consumption. In the second place it is now well known that consumption does not always conform to the normal law but often rises, unexpectedly, as fast as output or faster. We will come back to the problem when we reach the general theory of unemployment.

## Physical Relationships and Rates of Change

Thus far we have dealt with price changes, changes in psychology, that sort of thing. But one set of distortions in the rate of advance is supposed to be primarily the result of physical fact. It is the situation which sometimes results when the demand for investment comes to depend, physically, upon the rate of increase in consumption. Economists call this the "acceleration principle," or the "relation." Let us give the usual explanation.

In regard to our fertilizer industry let us suppose that the technical conditions are such that in order to turn out 1,000 bags a month 100 machines are needed. We assume further that each of these machines lasts exactly 10 years, and that they have been installed at the rate of 10 each year. Since 10 were installed in each year, and since they all last exactly 10 years, it follows that, once all 100 machines have been put in, there will be a regular need to replace 10 of them every year. So long as 1,000 bags are wanted, neither more nor less, the replacement demand for fertilizer machinery will be 10 a year, neither more nor less.

But now let us suppose that the demand for fertilizer goes up. 1,100 bags are wanted instead of 1,000. In that case, if the ratio of machinery to output is unchanged, we will need 10 additional machines, in addition to the 10 required for replacement. The result is that the demand for machinery ordered by our fertilizer plant will suddenly shoot up from ten to twenty. A 10 per cent increase in consumption will have produced in that year a 100 per cent increase in the need for machinery. This is what is meant by "acceleration" and it can easily be seen that magnifications of this sort, multiplied again and again, can produce tremendous bottlenecks and shortages.

Proceeding on the same simplified and mechanical basis we can find some still more surprising things. Suppose that in the period following that in which demand had risen to 1,100 bags, demand continued to rise but that the rise this time was to 1,150. It would seem that with the market continuing to increase, investment prospects would continue profitable. But under our simple assumptions this would not be true. Since the increase this time was 50 instead of the previous 100, only five new machines in addition to replacement would be needed. Thus investment demand, instead of increasing or standing still, would *fall* to 15 machines. A "decrease in the rate of increase" would lead to an absolute fall in the demand for machinery from our plant. Once an expansion has begun, it will be necessary not only that demand should grow but also that it should grow by an unchanged amount in each period. If it does not—if, though it keeps on growing it does not grow as fast, then the total demand for machinery will fall. Although we will see later on that our example can seldom be applied to the real world with mechanical exactness, nevertheless, the fact that investment can sometimes come to depend not on the level of demand but on its rate of change, is undeniable. Furthermore, it will be seen that were we to attempt to fit together in advance, to produce a smooth total, all the various rates of change, and accelerations of them, we would have a tremendous job on our hands.

### Backlogs, Frontlogs, and Echoes

One of the trickiest of these problems of stabilization and rates of expansion is called the "backlog." Let us take housing as an example. Suppose that the population is increasing fairly evenly. The chances would be that about the same number of additional houses would be needed every year. If we wanted a stable housing industry, we should have to gear it to this steady demand, and fluctuations in either direction would be most undesirable. Say that the normal output for a given general situation and distribution of wealth would be 10,000 units per year. But now suppose that for four of five years—during a war, for instance—no houses are built, and a backlog of accumulated demand piles up. In our example, this comes to about 50,000 houses. Could even a planning board, using careful advance planning alone, satisfy this backlog promptly— and still stabilize the private industry? Unfortunately it could not. Under the conditions described the task would be impossible no matter what the form of government.

Suppose we decide to satisfy this housing demand right away. Thousands of young architects, foremen, and skilled workers are trained. A huge increase in plant is undertaken. The industry suddenly raises its capacity from 10,000 units a year to 50,000 units. The backlog is satisfied. But then will come a crisis: We shall not want 50,000 new houses every year. We want 50,000 houses only now. Once the backlog is satisfied, demand drops to the old level of 10,000 and about four-fifths of the men who have gone into the housing business are out of jobs. Yet there has been no overproduction. Not one house too many has been built. It is simply that (from the point of view of stability) we have built them too fast.

The dilemma, as we have stated it, has been put in a very rigid way, and while it is true that there can never be an absolutely perfect solution, the student must not suppose that some sort of workable compromise is impossible. Let us for the moment, however, continue to analyze some of the problems of the rate of change. Perhaps the most important idea to get in connection with the backlog problem is that it does not necessarily depend upon unexpected interruptions of production, imposed from outside, as was the case in the example we have given. On the contrary, there is also something which might be called the "frontlog" problem. By this we mean the similar difficulty raised by a great *new* invention. It works in exactly the same way. Instead of supposing that house construction has been interrupted, let us instead imagine that somebody invents some particularly attractive and convenient new type of house. The results will be much the same. Many people will *all at once* want to build the new type of house and there will be a construction boomlet. But after a while, when demand for that kind of house is more or less satisfied, the boom will slump off. Similar jerks and rushes can occur in the case of new types of turbines, machinery, factories—any sort of product. Finally, even the stocks of inventory held in stores and factories can accelerate. Essentially, the problem is one of the *durability* of equipment and the *changeability* of wants. And it is in no way confined to capitalism.

### The Echo

As long as one sticks to fairly mechanical examples such as we have been using a further complication can be worked out called the "echo." In the echo if a great deal of machinery has been installed at approximately the same time, and with the same service life, other things being equal there will be a tendency for it to wear out at the same time. Thus if there is a hump or bump of capital installation, due say to the backlog, that bump might have an echo years later when it became necessary to replace the wornout machinery. Obviously the problem of planning investment to allow for the echo as well as for backlogs and acceleration would be well-nigh insuperable.

### A Sample Cycle Model

Mathematicians have had a wonderful time working on the type of complication we have been describing. Merely to give one example, among many, of the type of difficulty they have described, let us explain one of the most famous models. Suppose we are to start expanding. As there is unemployment, we will say that the expansion will not encounter any bottlenecks as it progresses. First there will come an increase in investment, but the increase in investment will start a more than proportional increase in consumption. This is due to changes in confidence and to something called the "multiplier," which we will explain in Chapter XX.

But an increased rate of consumption, it is supposed, will call for still more investment, more investment will multiply again and call for more consumption. The whole process surges merrily forward, until it reaches what is called the "ceiling." By ceiling is meant the full-employment level of output. Either because there really is full employment or because some important bottleneck in production has been encountered, it is no longer possible to keep expanding at as fast a rate as before. Here a curious situation develops: To have a continued demand for investment, consumption must keep rising (acceleration principle). But to have consumption keep rising, there often must be more investment (the multiplier). Thus in the very mechanical model we are describing, both components of output come to depend upon continued expansion of each other. As soon as it becomes physically impossible to expand any *one* of them, the incentive for the expansion of the other disappears and the entire process collapses.

The student must not suppose that the sort of situation we have sketched is likely to occur with such precision in real life. The mathematical model leaves out all problems of price expectations and confidence. Further, it is seldom that machine demand is related to physical increases in consumption in the exact way we are assuming. There is nearly always some slack in the system. Machines can be worked overtime, for example, and methods can be changed. But, particularly in new industries, some approach to these physical rate-of-change problems can be found and we must add them to our list of possible complications which may develop during growth, and cause a downswing.

### Concluding Statement on Business Cycles

We come now to the task of putting together a general statement of the problem of economic fluctuations. First, last, and all the time, we have seen that it is necessary to remember the connection between economic fluctuations and economic growth. Possibly there could be an organized society in which wanton change and disturbance occurred without any concomitant growth. But this is quite unlikely. On the other hand, there cannot be a growing society which is not being disturbed. Thus change does not always cause growth, but growth *always* causes change. If an economy is not growing it is likely to settle into an equilibrium. Wars, to be sure, can disturb things, as can plagues, famines, and so on, and these can cause increasing poverty. But the apparently built-in instability of our society, its constant shifting of men and techniques, are the result not merely of outside forces but of the dynamism inherent in our technique and in our relative freedom from the dead hand of custom. It is the growth process, then, that underlies our problem. Let us try, therefore, to put together a sort of global picture of what changes necessarily go on during an expansion. We can outline the problem as follows: (1) The pattern in which consumers spend their money must change, and change asymmetrically. (2) The over-all rates of total consumption will rise and fall—likewise the short-run "propensity to consume" schedules. (3) The way various materials are put together in the process of production and the types of machinery used will necessarily change as output grows, even if there are no new inventions. (4) New inventions and new products will almost surely be introduced. (5) Introduction of new types of durable equipment, plus interruptions of durable goods production or rapid shifts in demand, will create frontlog and backlog difficulties, or simple accelerations in the demand for equipment. (6) Expectations of businessmen and of bureaucrats as to the future will be constantly changing. (7) The lumps and bumps in capital installation may result in inflationary conditions or, alternatively, in deflation. (8) In the course of such disturbances general wage rates and cost–price relations will probably shift. (9) Men must in any case be moved from old to new industries. (10) Some shifts in relative prices, wages, and profits will therefore be virtually certain to occur.

This whole process over the long pull may exhibit certain stabilities. Thus over the long pull, consumption parallels output. There appears some long-run tendency toward a degree of uniformity in the ratio of the stock of equipment to total output. But in the short run no such easy uniformities of movement are apparent. And it is clear that it would be almost miraculous if the totality of these manifold inherent changes, which we have if anything understated, always balanced out. To the man who really studies the growth process, the amazing thing is not that the system sometimes does not work but that it manages on the whole to do as well as it does.

We must not get the idea that the essential problem is necessarily an offspring of capitalism. On the contrary, almost all the items in our list of disturbances would be apparent to some extent in a socialist state. For both capitalism and socialism therefore, the problem is what to do about the inherent instabilities of growth. But before we come to stabilization policy we have another disease to consider: prolonged unemployment.

# +++ XIX +++

## Introducing the Theory of Employment and Unemployment

So far we have written as if there were two clearly demarked conditions called "full employment" and "unemployment." We have also often appeared to imply that the economy would get into trouble only when the full-employment limit was reached. Neither of these ideas is correct. An economic downswing can be caused by bottlenecks or by lack of demand long before expansion has arrived at full-employment level. Furthermore, it is possible to have a situation in which the economy is showing continued upward and downward movements without ever reaching a satisfactory state of general employment. Also the line between full employment and unemployment will be found upon examination to be extremely vague. We are obliged here, therefore, to examine in detail the theory of employment and unemployment. We will be particularly interested in the analysis of long-range unemployment, and when we have given a full account of employment theory we will be ready, in the next chapter, to give a first discussion of the problem of economic stabilization.

### What Is Full Employment?

Most people would probably say that we have full employment when everybody has a job. But what kind of a job? Almost at once we find ourselves involved in problems of social values, and of what is "reasonable." Let us give an example. An employer says he can offer 40 jobs. That sounds promising. Then you ask him how much he is willing to pay and he says $5.00 a week and a 15-hour day. Next you find a man who says he is anxious for a job. But then you ask him how much he wants and he says $500 an hour and a guaranteed 40-hour week. Obviously neither of these gentlemen would be taken seriously in computing unemployment statistics—yet where does one draw the line? Let us outline the way actual full-employment estimates are made—for example by various government bureaus.

The first thing the estimator has to do is to estimate the "size of the labor force." Partly this is a matter of simple census figures. But there is much more to the job than that. For the estimator has to decide how many people ought to have jobs. Or at least he has to decide how many people most people think ought to have jobs. In other words, the estimator has to decide some of the following questions: How many women should we expect to have jobs? How many seventeen-year-old boys should we expect to have jobs? How many sixty-three-year-old men do we expect to have jobs? All these questions are important in determining how many jobs make up full employment, and none has a simple, easy answer.

But not only do we have to decide how many and what types of people we are going to allow for. We next have to ask how many hours we want them to work. For, of course, the number of hours of work considered customary will greatly affect our estimate of full-employment output. Finally, we must allow for the fact that in even the best-organized society there will be a certain amount of movement from one job to another, and a certain amount of re-organization constantly in process. This will mean that there will always be a certain number of people frictionally unemployed—that is, people in process of shifting from one job to another. Only after we have decided how many and what types of people to include in the labor force, what hours they will work, and how much frictional unemployment to allow for, can we go ahead with our estimate. It is clear that there is an enormous range here in which no clear-cut answers are possible.

After we have somehow determined what size labor force and what hours to allow for, the job becomes somewhat easier. We next get statistics of "productivity" for our society, and guess from them how much the type and number of people we have allowed for would produce during the hours we have allowed for. Finally, we try to figure out what the price level would be—how much, in other words, the money value of our estimated output would be. Only then would we have our estimated full-employment gross national product.

Many explanations of the theory of employment skip all these preliminary calculations. The problem is treated as if we somehow knew from the beginning exactly what full employment and unemployment were. This is quite wrong, and it is important today for the citizens to know that it is wrong. Just as a price index is not an impersonal, mechanical thing, just as gross national product figures are not impersonal, mechanical things, so also full employment is not an impersonal, mechanical thing. Rather the idea of full employment is the reflection of a combination of social and political standards—a shorthand statement that by and large we are satisfied with the performance of our economic system, that about everybody has a job we think ought to have a job, at wages and hours we think they ought to have. If we do not understand the haziness of the idea, we will be confused either by those, on the one hand, who try to hide unemployment by too narrow a definition of the labor force or by those, on the other hand, who seek, by means of too broad definition, to exaggerate the shortcomings of our economy.

In the remainder of this chapter we will overlook the problems of definition and write as if there were a precise number of jobs and a precise size of gross national product which would be called full employment. The student must not forget, however, that this is only a convenient way of speaking. Nor should he be surprised if we sometimes, later in this book, talk of "more than full" employment. All that more than full employment will mean is that sometimes— for instance during a war—a nation may be working at more than normal intensity. Hours may be longer and many classes of people at work who would not normally be so. Even in peacetime there is nearly always a good deal of slack in the system. For example, men may be willing to work overtime for a short period.

### The Basic Theory of Full Employment

Having learned what the concept of full employment means in general, we can now go on to discuss the basic theory. We shall follow in this book the terminology of the late Lord Keynes, since that has now become standard throughout the profession. According to Keynes, we have full employment when the "inducement to invest" and the "propensity to consume," taken together, add up to full employment. We must explain what these terms mean. But before getting into problems of detailed definition, one thing must be stressed. The requirements for full employment just stated do not say that we have full employment only when there is high consumption, *or* when there is high investment for that matter. All that is said is that the inducement to invest and the propensity to consume taken together add up to full employment. If the inducement to invest is high, the propensity to consume can be low, and vice versa. In other words, a state of full employment is a reciprocal relationship and bears no necessary universal connection with either high consumption or high investment as such. But let us now go on to see what the terms "inducement to invest" and "propensity to consume" mean.

*The Inducement to Invest.* We have already explained the basic meaning of the inducement to invest, although we have not referred to it by that name. The inducement to invest means that flow of investment which one would get by comparing the marginal efficiency of capital and the rate of interest, as shown in Figure 17(b), (p. 201), under the usual restrictive or *ceteris paribus* assumptions. Since we have already obtained an introductory idea of the relation of interest, the marginal efficiency of capital, and the investment flow, let us go on for the moment to the propensity to consume.

*The Propensity to Consume.* We begin by asking what are the forces shaping consumption in our society. Obviously, there must be a great many. One is religion. People of one sect or faith may save more money or goods than another, and it so happens that the United States and northern Europe have mostly been under the influence of religions which valued saving. Also, there are manners and customs which, even when particular individuals are not themselves conscious of being influenced by any ideal standards, often trace back to religious influences. Again, there are attitudes toward the family —the desire to provide for one's dependents, etc. All these forces together strongly influence a society's general attitude toward consumption.

Another set of influences, often overlooked, center around social organizations and political guarantees. A country in which ownership of property is insecure, and it is likely to be confiscated by the state, will not be apt to have a great volume of private productive saving and investment. If money is saved at all, it is likely to be hidden or hoarded; or people will buy jewelry and other portable stores of value.

Economists in recent years have sometimes considered only "economic" forces—particularly the distribution of wealth—and left basic cultural questions to one side. Thus, it has been an observed fact that the larger a man's income the larger the average amount he saves. But there is nothing mechanical about this. The facts are that our manners and customs do not encourage the rich to spend on the lavish scale of ancient civilizations. It is not the capitalist distribution of wealth, but the distribution of wealth plus certain manners, customs, and political institutions, that gives us our savings habits. And as manners change, and economic and political organization changes, quite different behavior can begin to show itself.

Another economic influence affecting the amount people save from their incomes is the quantity of money. When a man has a large store of liquid cash, he is, other things being equal, more apt to spend, or indeed to invest, than when he has not. So the size of cash balances must also be allowed for.

The brief mention of influences upon consumption habits just given is not intended to be complete. We are trying to impress upon the student that saving and consuming are not mechanical things, easily predicted through fixed statistical ratios. Sometimes, it is true, statistics do help. But one must never forget that the statistics are only the *record* of the results of many social forces, and that the *forces* shaping these results can themselves change. When manners, customs, and politics begin to change, the statistical ratios will change too.

When, however, we remember that statistical measures are measures or labels for results, and not independent forces in themselves, then they furnish a convenient shorthand way to describe how the community reacts under given circumstances. And of such measures or statistical concepts, one of the most useful is something called the "propensity to consume." In order to understand what this is, let us imagine the following set of circumstances:

Manners, customs, etc., are not changing very much. We are able to find out how much of their income people will spend on consumption at each possible level of gross national product. We then put the figures together and get a schedule as follows:

Figure 19
**THE PROPENSITY TO CONSUME**

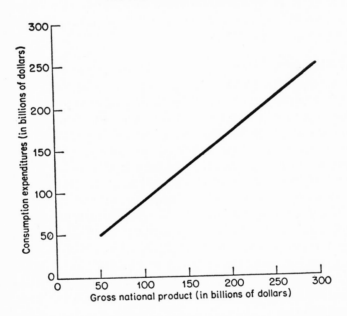

Or we might draw a similar chart showing the per cent consumed, instead of the amount, for each GNP level. In either case we could call the chart (following Lord Keynes) the "propensity to consume schedule." It would be a shorthand graph of the effect of a given set of savings habits upon consumption at all relevant levels of GNP. In other words, like a demand curve it is drawn under a *ceteris paribus* assumption.

The importance of a chart of this sort is that it enables us to separate the effects of a *mere* rise in gross national product from the effects of a basic shift in savings habits. This was a problem which bothered earlier writers on business cycles a good deal. Just because people are saving more, or less, than they did before, we cannot jump to the conclusion that fundamental saving habits have changed. It may be only that gross national product has risen or fallen. By the use of the propensity to consume schedule we clearly distinguish the effect of output change from a change in habits. And if our schedule is correct, it will enable us to read off, at once, exactly how much will be saved (GNP-consumption) at any given level of gross national product.

But we must never forget that any actual statistical consumption schedule is a mere shorthand description of the results of many complicated forces over a *short* period. If these forces change, the schedule will change and the statistics will be out of date. So far, the record shows that saving habits, and the resulting schedules, tend to shift upward over the long pull. Recent experience, furthermore, indicates that even in the short run they are considerably less stable than was at first supposed.

## Predicting Employment Levels

We can now apply our rudimentary concepts to the problem of predicting the likely level of employment. First, by the method outlined in the introductory section of this chapter (pp. 220-1), we decide what figure we are going to call full employment—what goal we are aiming for, in other words. Next, having decided upon our GNP level, we consult our propensity to consume schedule and find the likely level of consumption and the amount people will be planning to save. The final step will be to analyze the marginal efficiency of capital. Given the GNP level and the level of consumption, what will be the profit expectations on new investment, and also what will be the rate of interest? If investment plans so calculated (the inducement to invest) appear to be capable of absorbing planned saving, one forecasts full employment. If they seem to indicate an excess of investment plans over planned saving, one forecasts "more" than full employment and inflation. If less than planned saving, one forecasts unemployment. The problem is never as simple as we have made it sound. Nevertheless, the analytical skeleton we have given is used today by all schools of economists as a first approach to the forecasting problem.

## The Rate of Interest and the Full-employment Problem

We are a long way yet from the full complexities of forecasting in the actual world, but before we go further we have to develop one final tool of analysis in our basic framework. It is necessary to work out a full theory of the rate of interest. Up to now we have dealt with the rate of interest as if it were a simple matter of the intersection, at full employment or more than full employment levels, of the marginal efficiency of capital with the "savings line." In other words, we assumed for simplicity's sake that there was only one possible flow of planned saving, given the level of output. But orthodox or classical interest theory was much more sophisticated than that. It will help greatly if we review it.

The basic point of much of our previous chapters on the business cycle is that investment outlets and plans are highly variable. In other words, because of bottlenecks, new inventions, changes in prices and so on, the marginal efficiency of capital is liable to keep shifting. What mechanism did the orthodox economists think was available to equate savings plans and investment plans? In part they thought that changes in the rate of interest would do the job. But they added something more. They thought, though they did not use modern labels, that the rate of interest and the propensity to consume schedule were so related that a fall in the rate of interest would mean a rise in the propensity to consume, and vice versa. That is to say, they thought that saving money was like growing potatoes. The higher the price of potatoes, other things being equal, the more potatoes are grown, and the lower the fewer. So it was, they thought, with interest. The savings line would shift as the rate of interest shifted. One could draw a supply curve or savings just as for any other commodity.

The orthodox theory of adjustment, then, ran as follows: If a great new discovery comes and the MEC rises, that would increase demand for loans. This (barring changes in bank credit, or credit rationing) would raise the rate of interest. A higher rate of interest would increase the amount of planned saving people would undertake, and make more men available for investment in the new project. On the other hand, as the new project sparking the boom neared completion, the MEC would begin to fall, the rate of interest would fall (for demand for loans would slacken) and planned saving would decline (consumption would rise). Thus, supply and demand forces, working through the rate of interest, would bring about all needed adjustments. Labor and resources might, it is true, be shifted back and forth to some extent between consumption and investment; there might be a certain amount of short-run frictional unemployment, but no serious or prolonged maladjustment.

There are three main criticisms often made of the orthodox theory of adjustment. The first is the idea that if consumption changes, the marginal efficiency of capital will change with it. In other words, it is assumed that investment depends upon consumption in a very rigid mechanical way. We will have to discuss this problem in detail in the next chapter. All we need to say now is that the perspective of profit may in the short run be quite unrelated to the level of consumption. A great new invention, for example, may be so profitable that it will pay to introduce it even though consumption generally is falling. For example, in a country like Canada, if many new ore fields were discovered and being opened, a drop in the level of Canadian consumption would not discourage investment at all, or cause any fall in GNP. Reduced consumption might even help to open up the new mines by making more labor available. So as to whether a fall in the consumption level (or vice versa) discourages (or encourages) investment, the answer is sometimes Yes, sometimes No— depending on the nature of a particular expansion. We will discuss this problem in much more detail in the next chapter.

But we must now go on to two more criticisms which are unfortunately entirely true. They are: (1) the rate of interest need not change fast enough, or even respond at all, to prevent unemployment; (2) even if the rate of interest changes, this does not often, in the short run, directly affect the amount of planned saving, or the propensity to consume. It is true that over the long pull, and other things remaining unchanged, a low rate of interest may discourage planned saving and vice versa. Also, at times a rise in the rate of interest may be accompanied by a quick increase in the amount of planned saving. The United Kingdom in 1952 was one example. But many special factors were at work in that instance, and the most usual and reliable expectation is that in the short run planned saving is highly interest-inelastic—i.e., not much affected by changes in the interest rate. It follows that the orthodox theory of automatic short-run full-employment adjustment cannot be relied upon because (1) the rate may not change, (2) even if it did it might not affect consumption. But now we must ask why the rate would not change.

## "Liquidity Preference": The Modern Theory of Maladjustment

It is time to supplement the simple supply and demand theory of the interest rate we have been using so far with a more complicated and realistic version. Unfortunately, planned saving and the MEC schedule together do not alone give us a complete theory of interest. To cover the field, we must consider in detail Lord Keynes's theory of "liquidity preference." Keynes's theory is built on the well-known fact, only briefly mentioned so far, that people do not always want money to invest or to spend. Sometimes people want cash balances or bank deposits just to hold. Keynes calls this the "desire for liquidity" or "liquidity preference." At times, he writes as if variations in liquidity preference and in the quantity of money available were enough by themselves to give us a *complete* theory of interest. We do not accept so extreme an interpretation, as will be seen later on. But let us for the moment proceed on the lines of Keynes's general analysis, that in the end we may produce a complete theory combining both Keynesian and orthodox analysis.

In the chapters on money we mentioned that what exactly is meant by "money" is often debatable. Lord Keynes, however, in discussing money meant cash and bank deposits, but he admitted that there were many difficult problems of classification and various types of "near" money or "liquidity substitutes."

For present purposes we may use Keynes's definition. He divided the total money supply into two parts, $m_1$ and $m_2$. The formula for the total money supply thus is: $M = m_1 + m_2$. The symbol $m_1$ means money held to satisfy the "transactions and precautionary" motive; $m_2$ means money held to satisfy the "speculative" motive. Keynes defines these two labels broadly enough to cover the entire field of money holdings. In the same way he termed all the motives that might lead a man to want to hold money, taken together, "liquidity preference," which he symbolized by L. He divided this into $l_1$ and $l_2$; so $L = l_1 + l_2$. By $l_1$ he meant the "transactions and precautionary" motive for holding money, and by $l_2$ the "speculative" motive.

By transaction and precautionary motive is meant the demand for business, personal, and household balances. Everybody likes to keep a certain amount of purchasing power—cash or bank deposits—on hand to meet emergencies, pay bus fares, and generally carry on the routine of life. In the same way every business also needs petty cash and bank deposits to meet payrolls, pay for materials, and so on. These two motives very broadly interpreted comprise what Keynes refers to as $l_1$.

"The speculative motive," $l_2$, is much more complicated. It consists of money to provide against special risks and to "out-guess" the market. One special risk is, of course, the risk of failure of an enterprise. A man may hold money, rather than invest or spend it, because he is afraid any business in which he invests may go bankrupt. Simple panic-hoarding of this sort is an important feature of many downswings of the business cycle. Again, at the beginning of a crash, say a stock-market panic, there may come what is called a "liquidity panic." Everybody may be so scared they may all start calling in all their debts at once. Since we have seen that the total of credit is generally much greater than the total of cash, and also that bank deposits are usually created via the incurring of debt by someone, it will be seen that if a liquidity panic of this sort starts, the whole population of a country can bankrupt one another. Dynamic special panics of this sort are a little difficult to fit into Keynes's abstract scheme. But let us call them part of $l_2$. However, we have not yet reached the special feature in which Keynes was most interested.

The essence of Keynes's speculative motive refers not to solvency but to something more complicated.

Under some circumstances a man may hold cash rather than invest it, not because he has any fear of the solvency of the available companies, not because he is afraid he will fail to get his interest or his dividends, but because he fears that the capital values of the stocks or bonds may slump. In order to understand this reasoning, we require more technical analysis than in the case of simple precaution or fright.

When you buy a stock or a bond, what you are buying, from one point of view at least, is simply the right to receive an income in the future. To be sure, in the case of a bond we have seen that this income is fixed in advance, and that there are certain penalties which the bondholder can invoke if he is not paid his interest. In the case of stock, on the other hand, we saw that the dividends are not fixed in advance and that the stockholder has a different set of legal rights. We also mentioned various hybrid cases which need not concern us here. The important thing to remember for present purposes is that in deciding upon the value of an expected income stream, major use will generally be made of the rate of interest. For example, if the rate of interest is 4 per cent and the expected income is $4 a year, then, other things being equal, the capital value of that income will be $100—that is, $100 will be the sum which, invested at 4 per cent, would give an income of $4 a year. But suppose the rate of interest becomes 5 per cent. The capital value in that case, other things being equal, would then drop to $80. For at 5 per cent only $80 is needed to give $4 a year, whereas at 4 per cent $100 was needed.

Calculations of this sort are not, of course, always made in so mechanical a fashion in the real world. The valuation has to be adjusted so as to take into account both the degree of risk involved and the length of life of the loan. However, the basic principle is the same. The rate of interest is used to compute the capital value of the expected income stream. And the student will notice that if the amount of the income stream is unchanged the higher the rate of interest, the lower the capital value of that income stream. Thus $2 a year at 2 per cent will be worth $100, but at 4 per cent it will be worth only $50.

It follows from all this that fluctuations in the rate of interest will be likely to induce important changes in the capital value of stocks and bonds. From the potential fact of change, we find a concluding and very important reason for holding cash. Even if one is not worried about solvency, still, if the rate of interest has fallen to a level so low nobody believes it can stay there, then it will seem wise not to invest or lend at low interest rates, but to hold cash. For if the interest rates go up, we have seen that the value of investments made when they were low must go down. Still worse, however, from the point of view of employment, the lower the rate of interest gets to be, the stronger the expectation will probably become that it will rise again. And thus the lower the interest rate the greater, other things being equal, the liquidity preference or desire to hold money rather than to invest it. Thus, Keynes thought that most people would refuse to lend at rates lower than about 2 per cent, and would rather hold money.

There are several variables at work here during boom and slump. One is simple stock speculation. Suppose dividends actually being declared are $2 a share and the stock is selling in the market at $50 a share. The "yield" on the stock is thus 4 per cent. Suppose that dividends remain for the moment at $2 a share, but people feel the market is going up. They begin to spend some of their money balances ($m_2$) on stocks—in other words, $l_2$ has declined. The price of the stock rises, say, to $100. The yield is now 2 per cent. On the other hand, suppose the price of the stock is $50 a share and the dividends $2 as before. We are back at a 4 per cent yield. But suppose the dividend shoots up to $4 a share. Either stock prices will rise or the yield has now risen to 8 per cent.

The important point to remember is that these various yields, rates, and capital values are constantly being compared one with another by investors. For example, if a bank has money to lend and finds it can get 8 per cent on sound investments, it will hardly continue lending at 4 per cent. It will put the money in the more profitable lines and begin to charge more. For one thing, if there is so big a spread between bank charges and profit prospects, there will be a rush of borrowers to the banks (increased $l_1$), soon pushing interest on bank loans up to something like a comparable rate. By transfers and cross purchases like these markets for bonds, loans, and stocks are kept more or less tied together, and wide discrepancies are rare save where great differences in expectation about the future exist. Prices of first-rate stocks, for example, ought to bear some relation to the capital value that would be obtained by using the rate of interest on loans to capitalize the expected flow of dividends. However, if there is some special force operating, say a "discounting of inflation," this rule may not hold.

Returning, then, to the theory of employment, if the MEC schedule falls but the propensity to consume does not rise—that is, planned saving continues unchanged—and if the speculative motive is so high that the rate of interest does not fall, we may get a situation in which planned investment exceeds planned saving—in Keynesian language the propensity to consume and the inducement to invest taken together no longer add up to full employment. Under these circumstances a general decline may ensue until society has become so poor that there is no longer any net attempt at planned saving greater than planned investment. On one side will be a block of idle men. On the other will be a block of idle money. This, in a nutshell, is the most usual form of employment equilibrium.

### Interest Theory: A Final Synthesis

Our summary diagram of interest rate theory appears in Figure 20. Figure 20 shows the saving line cut by three alternate MEC schedules. $MEC^1$ is the usual 4 per cent equilibrium schedule. $MEC^3$ is the 6 per cent one—though we shall have to reinterpret it in special Keynesian language. $MEC^2$ is the important one for the special Keynesian case. Here the MEC has fallen so low that at no point short of ¼ of 1 per cent does planned investment cut the saving line. But because of liquidity preference—the speculative motive—the rate of interest has stuck at 2 per cent. Planned saving is far in excess of planned investment and GNP will clearly start to fall.

## The "Marginal Efficiency of Capital"

Now we are obliged to turn to another side of the problem. Keynes was at times guilty of saying that the rate of interest was a "purely monetary" phenomenon—that it was "solely" determined by liquidity preference and the quantity of money. How can this statement be reconciled with our MEC and planned-saving analysis? Despite much dispute by some of the narrower

Figure 20

**THE MEC SCHEDULE AND THE SAVINGS LINE**

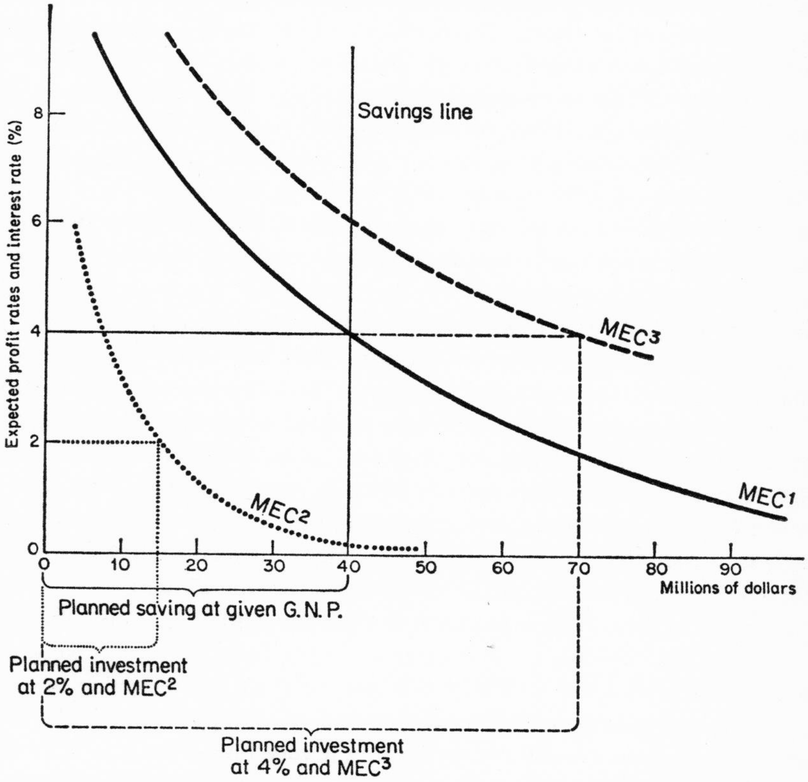

Source: David McCord Wright, *The Keynesian System;* Fordham University Press, © 1962 (p. 31)

Keynesians, the two lines of thought and modes of language can be fitted together quite easily. Let us first take the unemployment case.

We have seen that with $MEC^2$, only a preposterously low rate of interest would equate planned saving and planned investment. Indeed, some economists deny that any rate of interest would do the job, and some have even proposed negative rates of interest (government subsidies to borrowing) to offset the risks of deep depression. But Keynes pointed out that people have known interest rates to fall in the past and then rise once more. And if one takes the point of view of the present volume, one can, in fact, be sure, barring special social forces, that the MEC and the rate of interest will in fact rise once more—some day. Should a rise occur, loans made at 2 per cent or less will suffer serious capital declines for the reasons given in the last section. Accordingly, Keynes taught—and correctly as far as the immediate circumstances were concerned—that as the rate of interest fell toward 2 per cent, people would have greater and greater liquidity preference ($l_2$) and so the rate could not go much below 2 per cent. It is at this point, if we consider only the circumstances of that moment, that interest becomes purely monetary.

The orthodox theory taught that interest was really the price paid, as we saw, for free resources, or "capital disposal" as they sometimes called it, which was a scarce commodity with a price (interest). But one can hardly say that free resources are scarce when there are unemployed workers, idle plants, and unsold materials. So taking a very short-run view, the rate of interest does then stick at 2 per cent because of "monetary" forces, and a "purely monetary" idea is correct. On the other hand, a longer-run view does not support this idea. For if we assume that the maladjustment is temporary, then the various saving and lending institutions will soon once more be needed. Likewise, the habits of thrift and saving will again be useful. So it would be most unwise to liquidate them because of temporary slump. During the Great Depression of the 1930s, arguments like these were ridiculed. Yet, we did have a recovery, and the low interest rates and lack of desire to save left over from the depression did make the inflation much worse. But mention of inflation leads to the other side of the problem: maladjustments which occur when the MEC is high. Is the rate of interest "purely monetary" then?

To answer this question we consider once more $MEC^3$. It cuts the saving line at 6 per cent, which is clearly the equilibrium rate of interest if we want to prevent inflation in a free exchange economy. But at the beginning of an upswing there will often be a great many loans financed at low interest rates and sometimes a large government debt bearing a very low interest rate. Government will not be anxious to have the rate of interest go up. For either the capital value of government bonds will then go down—which will shake the credit of government—or the interest on the national debt will have to be raised, which will mean a need for more taxes—always an unpopular idea. It is, therefore, at this point that the notion of interest as "purely monetary" can be brought in and misapplied with seriously disturbing results. Yet in fact Keynes's language can be stretched to cover this "orthodox" case also.

The answer to the paradox and seeming confusion lies in the $l_1$ function, the transactions and precautionary motive. Keynes sometimes wrote as if $l_1$ were a simple function of income levels. In other words, transactions and precautionary or $l_1$ demand was *solely* set by the size of *today's* income. But this is quite wrong. Suppose, as already suggested, a great new discovery has been made, a great new ore deposit found, or something of that sort. We have now our MEC[3] case. What then? Clearly people will want to expand their output. They will start today to prepare for a greater output (income, GNP) tomorrow. But this means a greater need for money. The expectation of *future* expansion raises the *present* demand for money. Why? Because transactions, payrolls, material purchases, etc. are expected to increase, and businessmen want to be ready. That is to say, $l_1$, the transactions and precautionary demand for money or liquidity preference rises today because people want to try to raise output tomorrow. But if the supply of money is not increased and there is no interference with the market, the rate of interest will, indeed must, rise and for a good Keynesian reason: liquidity preference has increased relative to the money supply. Of course the real force operating here is the rise in the MEC. But if one wishes to pick up the story in the middle and start with the consequent rise in $l_1$, there is nothing formally wrong with doing so—if one remembers what is really going on!

Two footnotes, however, must be added at this point. At the beginning of a boom there may be large $l_2$ or speculative balances lying idle. If these are transferred to satisfy the $l_1$ demand, the rate of interest on loans will not at first go up. Planned investment will exceed planned saving. But such a process merely operates as an increase in MV (velocity times the money stock) and hence in the money supply. If output can be readily increased, neither interest nor prices need rise. But once the $l_2$ balances are absorbed we are back in the higher interest rate case.

The second footnote concerns governments which sometimes refuse to let the interest rate rise, but instead seize control of credit and ration bank loans to prevent inflation. This method may or may not work—depending on political forces—but it in no way affects our analysis of the market economy; it belongs in the literature of planning. Such schemes will be discussed later in this book in the general section on capitalism versus socialism and controls versus the free market.

## Thrift

So far we have considered the effects of a shift in the marginal efficiency of capital schedule. Comprehensive coverage requires us now to touch on an opposite possibility: an increase in thrift or, in Keynesian language, a fall in the propensity to consume. Most Keynesian writers assume that a fall in current consumption must mean a fall in the MEC schedule. Does not investment depend upon consumption? We will see in the next chapter, however, that strange as it may seem investment at any one point of time does not necessarily depend upon the level of consumption at that time. In the next chapter we will learn that there is a type of investment called "autonomous" investment. Autonomous investment does not depend upon the general level of consumption, rather it is induced by profit expectations growing from some special individual new idea or technique. We will elaborate all this in the next chapter.

But suppose we find ourselves in a situation in which investment is "autonomous"—say a new vein of ore for some rare, badly needed metal has been discovered. In such a case profit prospects—the MEC schedule—will scarcely be affected at all by a drop in consumption say of food, for the current demand for investment and prospects of profit come from developing the new mine—not from sales of consumer goods. In terms of Figure 20, what one will have is a shift "to the right" of the savings line, the MEC curve being unchanged. Many economists would then say that since the line and curve, in the new position, would intersect at a lower point, interest would fall and investment increase.

Literal Keynesian language raises a new difficulty however. To a literal Keynesian the interest rate cannot fall unless "liquidity preference" has fallen relative to the quantity of money, just as they say that interest cannot rise unless "liquidity preference" has risen relative to the quantity of money. But, as in the previous section, a little further refinement of terms avoids the difficulty. This time we will split $l_1$ into two classes "household" balances for personal spending, and "business" balances.

Now a fall in the rate of spending (increase in saving) will mean that people do not need as many "household" balances, because they are not spending as much. On the other hand the general set of conditions shaping liquidity preference for business balances, and $l_2$ balances has not changed—so surplus cash released by the fall in "liquidity preference for household balances" can be used to help satisfy an unchanged set of liquidity preferences for business balances and $l_2$. General liquidity preference, therefore, has fallen relative to the quantity of money and thus the interest rate will fall.

## Figure 21
### ALTERNATIVE WAYS OF EQUATING PLANNED SAVING AND INVESTMENT

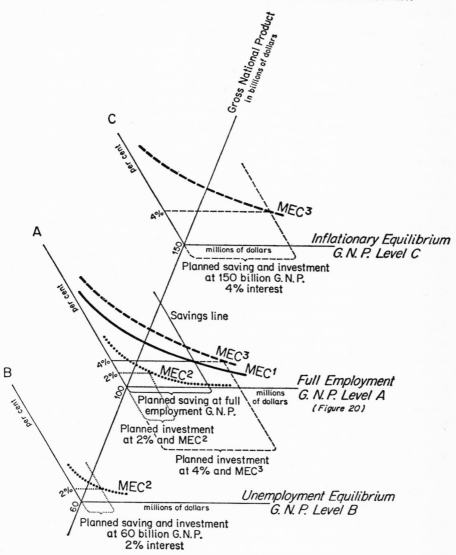

Gross National Product
In billions of dollars

C

Per cent

4% - - - - - - - - - - - - - - MEC3

*Inflationary Equilibrium*
*G. N. P. Level C*

150    millions of dollars

Planned saving and investment
at 150 billion G. N. P.
4% interest

A

Per cent

Savings line

MEC3
MEC1

4%    MEC2
2%

*Full Employment*
*G. N. P. Level A*
*( Figure 20 )*

B

Per cent

100    millions
of dollars

Planned saving at full
employment G. N. P.

Planned investment
at 2% and MEC2

Planned investment
at 4% and MEC3

2%    MEC2

*Unemployment Equilibrium*
*G. N. P. Level B*

60    millions of dollars

Planned saving and investment
at 60 billion G.N.P.
2% interest

Source: David McCord Wright, *The Keynesian System;* Fordham University Press, © 1962 (p. 41)

We cannot, it is true, in this second section, be as sure that the rate will fall to precisely the correct figure, as we would be that it would rise to the correct figure, in the previous section. Nevertheless with a high MEC curve for autonomous investment and no basic change in $l_2$ a new full employment equilibrium, with increased investment, is highly likely.

### Summary on Interest

We thus see, again, that over the long pull and in a growing free market without inflation or unemployment, interest is the price paid for borrowing and is in the last analysis the result of the intersection of the marginal efficiency of capital and the flow of planned saving. In the short run, however, interest is *also* the price paid for parting with liquidity. To have full employment, the rate must equate both liquidity preference and the money stock, on the one hand, and the MEC and planned saving on the other. Since there is no special reason why these three forces need always concur, we may find ourselves in conditions of either unemployment or inflation. In time of unemployment, furthermore, a very short-run look at the system might call the rate of interest purely monetary. But this case in no way denies that in time of full employment and high MEC the prospects of profit also affect the rate of interest. To call the rate purely monetary under boom circumstances is to fall victim to a misguiding definition.

We can summarize Keynesian interest and employment theory in Figure 21. Figure 21 is a three-dimensional diagram. Along the diagonal line are measured various levels of gross national product. This line is cut by vertical planes A, B, C. Plane A is simply Figure 20 turned sideways. The gross national product figure for Plane A is set, just by way of example, at one hundred billion dollars. Let us suppose, now, that the marginal efficiency of capital curve on Plane A drops to $MEC^2$. The rate of interest, however, remains at 2 per cent because of liquidity preference, just as in Figure 20. Planned investment is, therefore, less than planned saving, but adjustment via the interest rate is prevented by liquidity preference. What forces, then, can be called in to bring about a new equality of planned saving and investment and a new equilibrium?

Let us rule out for the moment all question of a change in prices. If price change is ruled out the answer to our question must be that the new equilibrium will come about by means of a decline in gross national product. Such a new equilibrium is shown in Plane B. Because of the excess of planned saving, gross national product has fallen. When the level shown for B has been reached, planned saving will be so much reduced by the increasing poverty of society that it will drop to the same figure as what is left of planned investment. Output has declined and there will be, on the one hand, the block of idle money; on the other, the block of idle men we have already spoken of. But remember we reach this conclusion on the assumption that prices are not allowed to fall. The much more complicated case of price decline will be treated in Chapter XX.

Let us, however, discuss one form of price change here: price increase. Suppose we go back to Plane A and assume this time that the MEC schedule has risen to MEC³. Yet, let us say that for some reason the rate of interest is not allowed to rise. Either the banks create more money or unspent balances of cash are released. In this second case, essentially that of Chapter XVIII, planned investment will exceed planned saving. If Plane A represents a less-than-full employment position, a smooth general expansion of real output can be started up to Plane C. The increased income will produce the needed increase in real saving. This is the seductive possibility that has produced so many disastrous mistakes in government finance in the underdeveloped nations— and not only in them. For if Plane A represents not unemployment but a state of full employment or a condition in which serious bottlenecks will be encountered as expansion begins, then physical output will not rise, or not rise greatly, and the new equilibrium of Plane C will represent, for the most part, merely an inflationary change in money values.

Our three planes summarize, however, the three possibilities inherent in discrepancies between planned saving and planned investment. They are changes in the interest rate, changes in output, changes in prices. Some combination of these three movements is, of course, also a fourth possibility. Figure 21, nevertheless, summarizes almost completely the modern theory of unemployment. The next question to discuss is what can be done to obtain full employment. We begin on this task in the next chapter.

# The Problem of Recovery and Stabilization

We come now to the concluding chapter of the part on output. In the preceding chapters we have seen that while the marginal efficiency of capital schedule was highly variable there did not exist any mechanism immediately and automatically varying the propensity to consume in an offsetting manner. The result is that from time to time we are confronted with shortages of effective demand, and in some cases these shortages are more than short run—lasting for several years. The question is: What can be done about them?

Here we must revert to the principle, laid down at the beginning of Chapter XIX, that there was nothing sacred about either high consumption or high investment as such. Which variable we want to influence depends upon the circumstances of the particular case. Nevertheless, it remains true that one can only influence the unemployment problem through *either* the propensity to consume or the inducement to invest, or both together. We will follow current analysis and begin with consumption, then we will take up investment, and finally we will attempt a rounded treatment.

## The Propensity to Consume and the Multiplier

One of the most seductive ideas in the armory of employment theory is something called "the multiplier." The multiplier is based upon a concept, the marginal propensity to consume, derived from the propensity to consume schedule which we already know. By "marginal propensity to consume" we mean not how much a man consumes of his entire income but of an increase in his income. In other words, the idea refers not to consumption from one's total paycheck, but to how much one consumes from a raise. This proportion of consumption from an increase, the marginal propensity to consume, we will abbreviate to MPTC. The MPTC is important because from it we can calculate the multiplier and from the multiplier it is often thought we can tell how much a government deficit will increase employment and prosperity. The formula for the multiplier is as follows:

$$K \ (or \ the \ multiplier) = \frac{1}{1 - the \ marginal \ propensity \ to \ consume}$$

Thus, if the marginal propensity to consume is ½, K or the multiplier will be 2. The long-run logic of the idea is that in order for people to save and to invest, they have to have consumption increased by a more than proportional amount. Thus, if investment flow is increased, consumption volume will rise even more. From this principle people often jump to the idea that if the government increases its deficit and the multiplier is, say, 2, then we can be sure that consumption (and employment) will rise by twice the amount of the deficit. Naturally, if this were really true, it would be a very important idea. Unfortunately, there may be many slips in application to reality. It is necessary for us to understand the pitfalls of the concept.

We assume we are in a state of unemployment and begin with the condition shown in Figure 22.

**Figure 22**
**THE MULTIPLIER**

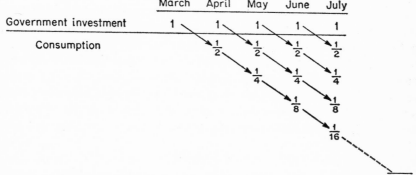

Source: David McCord Wright, *The Keynesian System;* Fordham University Press, © 1962 (p. 19)

We label the spaces at the top "March," "April," "May," etc., to show the passage of time. We could just as well call them "Monday," "Tuesday," and "Wednesday." In fact, this problem of how long the process takes is one of the major headaches. But let us skip that for the time being.

The top row shows a series of "shots," or injections of government investment into the economy—that is, a sustained increase in income flow of one billion per period. From each of these injections we have drawn a line of arrows. Let us see what they mean.

The money invested by the government in March (or on Monday) becomes somebody's income. That is to say, there is a rise in income of one billion dollars. This, of course, cannot be spent instantaneously, but will be spent in the next period in an amount set by the MPTC formula. Since we are assuming an MPTC of ½, this means that half a billion dollars will be spent in April (or on Tuesday). But again, this half billion spent is someone's income, so in May (or on Wednesday) one-half of one-half, or one-fourth, of a billion dollars is spent. In June it is one-eighth, in July one-sixteenth, and so on. It is easy to see that the series is approaching 2 in value.

But the government is making a series of injections and each of these is sprouting its line of consumption expenditures; so that soon, as shown by our figure, we have a continuous government flow of one billion supporting another billion in current income. Thus, everything has worked according to the formula and everything looks fine. But in fact there are many problems.

In the first place, we have assumed our spending was net. But if money used by the government to pay for increased investment comes from taxes collected from income that would be spent or invested anyway, then there will have been no increase in outlay for the economy as a whole, and no net stimulus. The government investment would merely have been at the expense of private consumption or investment and no multiplier will occur.

Of course, however, if the government taxes fell only on hoarded money or on money that was going to be hoarded, then the process would operate as an increase in velocity and a net stimulus. The same thing would be true of borrowing from individuals or corporations. But these cases, while clear enough theoretically, are not so important in practice. In practice, if we wanted to be sure of a net increase in money outlay, the best thing to do would be to borrow from the banks. In a depression this would almost surely operate as an increase in the amount of money.

But even if the money used to finance the government investment is a net increase, this still does not ensure that the flow of government investment will be net for the economy as a whole. For if the government investment takes a form which scares off or prevents an equal amount of private investment that was going to be made—and this sometimes happens—then again the government investment will have been at the expense of private investment.

Let us suppose, however, that the government investment is in all respects a genuine net flow and let us ask what happens after that. First, even if the government outlay is genuinely net, and demand increases, there will not be an increase in real consumption or employment unless (1) pressure groups of labor and business do not absorb the higher outlay by higher prices and costs, and (2) the increased spending leads to an increased prospect of profit upon additional production. We will come back to these problems later. Let us assume that at first all goes as supposed. What then? We will find that there are in fact four different multipliers, or rather four different things sometimes spoken of as the multiplier. They are: (1) the multiplier "by definition"; (2) the short-run multiplier; (3) the ideal multiplier; (4) the actual results of an expansion of government investment.

The multiplier by definition need not keep us very long. It suited certain economists to define the multiplier as being instantaneously effective. But obviously the process, in reality, must take time. For the sake of theoretical consistency such economists would give a different value to the MPTC for each period in order to get the required results. All you need to know is that the process is not in fact instantaneously effective.

The second type of multiplier is the short run. Everything is going as expected, but the process has not yet had time to become fully effective. That would be the case, say, in the period we labeled May.

The third type of multiplier, the ideal, is what most people think of when they speak of the process at all. In the ideal multiplier everything is working as expected and there has been time enough for the full expansion to take place. By July, in the diagram, this condition would have been substantially reached.

The fourth multiplier, what actually happens, is of course the only really important one, and unfortunately is almost wholly unpredictable, for the following reasons:

First: There is no reason why, in the real world, the value of the MPTC should remain unchanged. It might rise or it might fall. Either way one would get a different value for the multiplier.

Second: Offsetting, independent changes might occur in private or government investment.

Third: The increase in spending might be absorbed (as in full employment or where there are militant pressure groups) merely in higher costs and prices, without any increase in real output or employment.

Fourth: On the favorable side, we have not explained what happens to the other half of the income rise which is not consumed. The rise in consumer spending could induce a general improvement in confidence. The money not being consumed might then be invested. This would have the following effects: The shift in the MEC schedule might merely lead the government to curtail its spending. In that case the new private investment would simply take its place. But in other cases the government might continue spending as before and the new investment would be net. In that case a new multiplier would begin to operate on top of the old one.

Fifth: The time periods are unpredictable. Increased optimism would generate new orders and anticipations. On the other hand, the stimulus might have to be dragged out indefinitely.

The one thing we can be sure of is that while there may be some general stimulus from increased government or private investment this cannot be precisely calculated and under some conditions it may be nil, or merely inflation.

## Consumption and Investment

We encounter here one of the most basic of relationships, that between consumption and investment, or between consumption, investment, and increased output. If an increase in spending is to result in more jobs (not including those directly furnished by government) it can only do so if someone thinks it is profitable to increase production, and not only profitable to increase, but profitable to do so by hiring more labor. Much of the literature reads as if an increased outlay automatically led to increased sales, increased profits, increased output, and to more men being hired. But none of this has to happen. We do not want to be like the man earlier referred to in this book who bought shoes for $12 a pair and sold them for $6 a pair. When they said, "You won't get rich that way," he said, "Oh, but think of the turnover!" In fact, if expected costs are rising faster than prices there may be *no* stimulus to increased jobs, although spending is rising rapidly.

We will return to these issues shortly. At the moment we need to discuss the opposite side of the same confusion. It may be maintained that though more consumption will not of itself give us investment, still, *without* consumption or increases in consumption there can be no investment incentive. Investment is treated as depending simply and mechanically upon consumption. No one, for example, is presumed to build a new textile plant unless the money value of textile sales is rising. It is assumed that there is a single fixed technological relation between consumption and investment such as we talked of in the chapter on rates of movement and the acceleration principle. Clearly, this is a very important point and we must discuss it in detail.

The fact is, however, that in the short run there is no necessary relation between the level of current consumption and the level of current investment. We say "short run" because if one follows any single project to its end the notion of satisfying consumer wants will usually appear at some point. But the fact still remains that in no interval of historical time is there a necessary relation between total consumption movements and total investment movements. The inducement to invest may rise just when the propensity to consume has fallen and vice versa. There are four reasons why this apparently perverse behavior can be found. First, there is the better product. Even though demand for textiles in general may be falling, still a new and brilliant pattern might catch public fancy and result in profit for its maker although cloth in general was not selling well. Second, there is the cheaper product. Even if total sales and prices are falling, invention of a new kind of loom might cut costs so drastically that it would be worthwhile building the new plant despite the falling market. Thus in 1963, for example, the Bethlehem Steel Corporation began the construction of the largest single steel plant in history though demand was far below capacity for its existing structures. Third, there is the determined industrialist. A man may feel that the market is wrong. He may think that prices are bound to go up or sales to increase, and he may go ahead and build on that assumption though his hunch may not have enough data behind it for certainty. Strangely enough it is possible for the hunch to be self-verifying. The outlay on plant construction—however indefensible on objective grounds at the time it was made—may yet induce a rise in confidence that will start things going again. As Lord Keynes put it, "Only a little more than an expedition to the South Pole is 'investment' dependent on an exact calculation of benefits to come."

The fourth reason for increasing investment when consumption is falling concerns projects based on long-range population forecasts—municipal subways, for example. Unemployment will actually stimulate such projects. Since they are based on the long-run trend, the existing lack of demand will not affect their usefulness and low costs in depression will even make them more attractive. For example, the Hutchinson Parkway near New York City, built in the 1930s and now nearly obsolete, was denounced as a piece of useless extravagance that would never be utilized, but it was undertaken because of low costs and to give jobs. Summing up, then, we have four cases: The better product, the cheaper method, the determined industrialist, the industry geared to the long-run trend. None of these cases requires a stable or rising current consumption level as a prerequisite for investment. The situation is even more complicated by the fact that the industrial structure does not consist merely of machines that make consumer goods, but of machines that make machines, and of machines that make machines that make machines, and so on. Anywhere in the system the better product, the cheaper product, the determined industrialist, and the long-run project can occur without warning. Furthermore, the fact that consumption is declining several stages down will have almost no relevance to the introduction of a new product or method several stages up. Thus it is quite possible for investment to rise just as consumption is falling, and vice versa. Objective economic reality includes at any period a brooding mass of new technical patterns trembling on the verge of discovery and utilization. And whether such patterns are to be utilized depends primarily upon the perspective of profit described and diagramed in Figure 18 (a) and (b), after the prospective investor compares it with the rate of interest. Nor does the consumption level play an overwhelming role in shaping such perspectives.

### Wage and Price Reduction and Full Employment

A true understanding of the relation of consumption to investment was necessary before we could discuss the fundamental question of the relation of price and wage reduction to increases in employment. Many people today follow Lord Keynes (in his more extreme statements) and assume that price and wage reduction will be useless in stimulating employment. They argue tacitly upon an assumption of universal pure and nearly perfect competition and assume that wages and prices must move together and with little net effect. Indeed, Lord Keynes has argued at times that unions could not reduce their own real wages even if they tried because the wage cuts would be immediately translated into lower prices.

Modern economic theorists do not follow so simplified an approach. They may still debate which is the most convenient method of getting full employment, or the most quickly effective, but that wage and price reduction alone *could* give full employment, if persisted in long enough, is not often denied today. There are three main reasons. The first or Keynesian reason is somewhat elaborate and not too relevant. The argument runs that a fall in wages and prices may release cash balances from payrolls to the satisfaction of liquidity preference, which may lower the interest rate and raise the inducement to invest. Lord Keynes mentions this possibility but does not assign much importance to it. More practical are the next two effects of price and wage reduction, namely, the effect on spending and the stimulus to investment.

The crucial fact to remember here is that men have expectations and feelings about long-range or normal values. Nearly everybody knows that if the economy is sometimes down it also is sometimes up, that if prices occasionally fall they also occasionally rise. As prices fall, those people who have cash balances left will find them getting progressively more valuable in terms of real purchasing power. To give an extreme example, if you have a million dollars cash, have been refusing to spend, and can buy the *Mona Lisa* for a dime you would be tempted to do so. A continued fall in prices will at some point begin to raise the propensity to consume. Economists usually call this the Pigou effect, after Professor A. C. Pigou who explained it. Still more important, a similar effect is observable with investment. As prices and wages fall it becomes possible to build new plant at a fraction of its usual cost, and those with courage enough to build in the depression will enjoy a great advantage over their higher priced competitors when prosperity returns.

Curiously enough Keynes himself has indicated these possibilities. He said in part:

"So it is indeed not unlikely that the individual [businessman] seeing his own costs reduced, will overlook at the outset the repercussions on the demand for his product. . . . Since a special reduction of money wages is always advantageous to an *individual* industry, a general reduction . . . may also produce an optimistic tone in the *minds* of entrepreneurs which may break through a vicious circle of unduly pessimistic estimates of the marginal efficiency of capital and set things moving again on a more normal basis of expectation. . . . When we enter on a period of weakening effective demand, a sudden large *reduction* of money wages to a level so low that no one believes in its indefinite continuance would be the event most favorable to a strengthening of effective demand." [1]

We can thus see that investment and consumption do not necessarily depend upon one another, and further that Lord Keynes himself admitted price and wage reduction could sometimes give full employment. It is time therefore to consider the problem more practically and comprehensively.

## The Problem Broadly Considered: Alternative Unemployment Possibilities

Those who take what might be called a mechanical approach to the problem of unemployment and of the business cycle are apt to note merely that planned saving is too high for full employment. They seldom stop to ask why planned *investment* is insufficient. Yet we have already said that one can equally well think of the problem in terms of the inducement to invest rather than the propensity to consume. Why is the marginal efficiency of capital low? That is at least as important a question as "What is the consumption level?" Indeed in underdeveloped countries, obstacles to investment are usually considerably more important than consumption. Here we come to a vitally important question often overlooked.

Once it is granted that wage and price reduction might at some point bring about full employment of a sort, it is easy for the ultra-orthodox economist to say that unemployment is always the result of too high a wage rate, and one can always define the term in such a way as to make this statement true. Some idea of normal or reasonable wages is almost inseparable from practical applications of the unemployment concept. But granting this much, it is important to realize that there are *two* quite different sources of unemployment in the modern world. The first type, and the one we have been expounding so far,

[1] Italics added. J. M. Keynes, *General Theory of Employment, Interest and Money,* Chap. 19, pp. 261, 264–5. Reprinted by permission of Harcourt, Brace and World, Inc., and also of Macmillan & Co. Ltd., and of the Trustees of the Estate of the late Lord Keynes.

is that appropriate to developed industrial states. Plant exists which *could* give jobs but for some reason it is not being utilized. This is the so-called "poverty in the midst of plenty" often spoken of in the literature. Quite a different type of unemployment may exist in the underdeveloped nations. There may not be *any* plant in existence to employ the population, at any living wage—even the crudest subsistence. Such unemployment, sometimes called "classical," is the result of too small a stock of capital, unlike the unemployment of the developed nations which springs from a "maladjusted" or "excessive" capital stock, or from cost-price maladjustment.

If unemployment is the result of a lack of real construction sufficient to employ the growing population at any tolerable wage, the remedy obviously is to stimulate *investment*. But many economists of the underdeveloped countries, trained in modern Western thought—which seldom mentions this possibility—make the tragic mistake of trying to cure unemployment by increasing *consumption* in a country which does not have the physical means of subsistence! The result is unavoidable—famine and inflation. The mistake is allied to the one spoken of in Chapter XV where the definitional "identity" of saving and investment is confused with an increase in real output, and extravagant projects are undertaken with no real saving to support them. The Keynesian underconsumption analysis, even on its own terms, is suitable only for developed nations.

But can we be sure that lack of consumption is always the source of unemployment even in modern industrial nations—say, the United States? The answer is No. For example, if the population or labor force jumps suddenly, as is happening in the mid-sixties, there will not be enough jobs at existing wages to absorb the present (1964) wave of teen-age labor—unless a great increase in plant and in investment takes place. Accordingly we should be thinking now of the stimulation of investment. And we must remember that a mere rise in spending does not mean any necessary increase in the perspective of profit or the inducement to invest. In other words, what we need to do is to inquire into forces retarding the marginal efficiency of capital. Here we need a much deeper analysis.

Remember our explanation of the basic problem of stability in a growing nation. We saw that a flow of planned saving required a flow of novel ideas and expansions to absorb labor set free for investment uses by the saving act. We have now seen, further, that the motive for this investment was the perspective of profit. But it follows from our analysis, and that of Chapter II, that if entrenched groups resist or suppress the technical changes needed to increase productivity, yet at the same time demand higher money wages, the cost–price relationship will be such that no adequate net inducement to invest will survive.

Once the marginal efficiency of capital has been forced into collapse by pressure groups and investment cut off, then an apparent "shortage" of purchasing power will be found; for the multiplier works negatively as well as positively and a drop in total investment, not offset by consumption change, will cause a more than proportional drop in current consumption. Popular agitation, however, will usually miss the fact of investment prospects and concentrate only upon "lack of consumption."

Here we meet for the first time a problem of the greatest importance. Suppose that for some reason the collapse of the marginal efficiency of capital is due to international trade considerations. The crucial flow of investment needed to give full employment is in the form of exports, and the exports of some nations are being hampered by too high a level of costs relative to other nations. In such a situation the only helpful policy is one designed to lower costs. But if we approach the matter in mechanical fashion we may only make the situation worse. Thus if we lower the interest rate to stimulate the inducement to invest we will probably encourage people to move money out of our country, and hence we will begin to lose gold. If we leave the problem of costs untouched and merely try to stimulate demand this will, if anything, make our foreign competitive position worse. In short, by thinking only of consumption we have made things worse. Thus we find that when we discuss the inducement to invest, we bring up a host of new problems, especially international ones, which must be grasped before a full theory of economic stabilization can be evolved. Let us therefore move on to the basic theory of international trade and to the problems of pressure groups before we attempt a final synthesis.

# Part V
# PROBLEMS

## ✦✦✦ XXI ✦✦✦

## A First Introduction to International Trade

In the preceding chapter we saw that international trade is often one of the major problems of employment policy. In a growing society, we have learned, the economy constantly moves forward into a partially unknown future. Because the future is not fully known people make mistakes, and there are maladjustments. Some economists—for example, Lord Beveridge—have sought to get rid of uncertainty by imposing tight planning of the direction of investment. But as soon as there is important international trade these plans can never be fully reliable. Foreigners may suddenly stop buying a nation's goods, or a foreign nation may invent a cheaper way of making a country's principal export. Domestic planners cannot always anticipate these changes, and certainly not always offset them. Large-scale reliance on international trade makes it impossible to eliminate the unexpected, even with the tightest planning.

Stabilization policies are similarly limited when we discuss wages and the rate of interest in relation to international trade. An isolated country may play with its money wage level and its interest rate as it chooses without fear of outside disturbances. Not so the country involved in international trade. We will see later that a low rate of interest to stimulate investment within a country may have the effect of aggravating an outflow of gold and thus causing much maladjustment. Likewise the internal wage rate that makes a country's unions happy may cripple it in its international dealings.

Finally any country that lets its living standard become dependent upon a large flow of imports is thereby almost obliged to keep up with the rate of technical change of the rest of the world. If it does not keep up, it will have to be sending more and more of the output of its economy abroad to buy the same amount of goods in return. But modernization and the "security" of particular groups frequently conflict. All these statements being perfectly true, the question is, Why have international trade at all?

## Why Have International Trade?

If one looks at the trade statistics of the United States one will find that international trade makes up about 5 per cent of total United States trade. This does not seem a great deal. Many people therefore argue that it would be well worth while to take a cut of only about 5 per cent in our living standards if that gave us the independence of policy and freedom from risk that they think would follow from isolation. Unfortunately this line of reasoning wholly understates the costs of isolating an economy. Leaving out all question of the political commitment of a nation, and considering only economic analysis, it remains true that foreign trade is a far more important part of the economic welfare of a society than the crude percentage figure we have given would seem to show.

There are two reasons why the percentage figure is inadequate. First, the goods imported, while small in quantity, may be vitally important so far as the quality of our own products go. A specific example is the alloys used in making fine steel. They may not cost much in terms of the total but without them the product would hardly be worth buying. Second, international trade is more important than it looks because of the importance of the "margin" to total prices and sales. The chapters on value theory showed us that a cutback of 5 per cent in sales could wipe out a firm's profits. Likewise the cutting off of a 5 per cent margin of investment would be "multiplied" several times over in unemployment. International trade is thus a much bigger thing than we first think it is.

## Comparative Cost

The most easily understood reason for international trade is simply the old established principle of the division of labor. Total output, we saw in the beginning of this book, is increased if everybody concentrates on the things he does best, and this is as true for nations as for people. Furthermore, natural resources are not evenly distributed over the earth's surface, and neither are populations. Some people prefer to be poor in their own country or region than to move to another (if they could). By dealing with one another in international trade many of the advantages of specialization are secured without everyone's moving around; and a country does not have to have all needed products within its borders in order to benefit from the most improved industrial methods.

The simple division of labor argument is an easy one to see, but international trade theory does not stop with the merely obvious cases. Suppose, instead, you have two countries—one of which does *everything* better than other countries, while the other does *nothing* better than any other country. The scenery of this second, unfortunate nation is only fair. Its people are not especially skillful. And such natural resources as it possesses are of such inferior quality that all of them can be developed more easily elsewhere. What will happen to these two remarkable nations? Will one of them make everything while the citizens of the other simply curl up and die? Not at all. International trade theory has developed a principle for such cases called "the law of comparative cost." It may be briefly, though trickily, stated as follows: ". . . the greatest world output results when each nation or region concentrates upon those things which it makes *most* best, or *least* worst." Let us try to understand what this formula means.

The basic point is best explained by an example. Suppose a businessman employs a stenographer. The businessman, we may suppose, learned to type while he was in college and can now do it much faster than anyone else in town. The stenographer on the other hand may be only fair as a typist, and, just to make our case extreme, we may say that she cannot do anything else very well either. Yet it will pay them to pursue their respective jobs. The businessman will not spend his time typing, even though he is good at it, because he could make more money running his business. An hour's work, say, as executive might yield him $50 while the stenographer might only cost $5 an hour, and the value of the extra typing that his superior speed would permit might be only $5. So he manages and she types, and both are better off. The same analysis can be applied to nations.

Let us say that the United States could make "better" (imitation) Oriental rugs and cheaper ones than can be made in the Orient. Would it pay us to build expensive factories to do so? Not at all. Our comparative advantage in the field of machine tools might be so great that it would be far more profitable and sensible to put our money into machinery-making than to use it for light consumer goods. On the other hand, the nation with no advantages will still be able to find something that other countries do not want to do, because they can make more money in other lines. The disadvantaged nation can go into these comparatively unprofitable fields, and though its standard of living may never be very high, it can nevertheless make out.

We see, therefore, that one of the major reasons for international trade is the fact that resources and skills vary greatly, yet one of the most curious facts which a study of actual markets brings out is that the greatest volume of trade is not between countries widely differing in resources and specialties, as one would expect, but between very similar countries. Thus industrial countries do not trade most with primitive countries, as one might think, but with each other. To explain such odd behavior economists very early in our science gave a further elaboration to the theory of comparative cost. Their further elaboration concerns not the absolute costs or absolute scarcities between two countries, but the relationships *between costs* of various articles *inside* each country. Let us take a simple example.

## Relative Cost Ratios

We begin by taking some unit for measuring cost of production inside each country. As our concern will be proportions, this unit can be dollars, labor, or some composite package as long as it is consistent between commodities. Let us now assume that in the United States wheat takes one cost unit per bushel to produce and ball-bearings take one cost unit per 100. Then one bushel of wheat will, in equilibrium, exchange for 100 ball-bearings. Move next to a foreign country. Here we may say that a different cost unit is being used, but again all that is needed is consistency between commodities, for again our main concern is proportions. In the foreign country we will say that wheat again takes one cost unit (of *their* measure) per bushel, and ball-bearings *two* cost units per 100. In the foreign country therefore one bushel of wheat will exchange for only 50 ball-bearings. Note that this example says nothing about absolute costs. Everything in the United States might be more expensive or cheaper; all that matters, once more, is proportions.

Now let us see why it would pay to have foreign trade. Look at it from the American point of view. The United States will gain if for 100 ball-bearings it gets anything more than one bushel of wheat (the original exchange price *inside* the United States). The foreigner will gain if for one bushel of wheat he can get anything more than 50 ball-bearings (the original price inside his country). By trading together a new international equilibrium can be established with an exchange ratio of wheat for ball-bearings somewhere between 1 wheat for 50-plus ball-bearings and 1 wheat for minimum 100 ball-bearings. Anywhere in that range both parties will be better off from the deal, for their total production will be greater. Furthermore, as the two markets become more and more merged each country will become increasingly specialized. The United States will concentrate more on ball-bearings, the foreign country more on wheat. Exactly where the ratio of exchange will come to rest, just how far specialization will be pushed, cannot be calculated precisely from the data we have given. We do not know, for example, the relative demands for the two goods, the way costs might change during the adjustment, or the size and variation of the national incomes of the two countries. What does emerge clearly, however, is that mere differences in relative costs within the different countries engaging in international trade are in themselves sufficient to make international exchanges desirable. The statistics, in fact, prove that incredibly small proportional differences within and between highly industrialized nations can account for a vast volume of international trading.

### International Lending

The next phenomenon to which the law of comparative advantage quickly leads is international lending. If one country does a lot of saving and has a fine machine tool and equipment industry, the rate of interest in that country will start to fall as its factories are expanded. In other countries, however, where there may be much labor and many natural resources, but few factories and little equipment, the demand for capital may be great and the rate of interest high. Under such circumstances it does not need elaborate analysis to see that both nations will gain if the one with capital lends to the one without. Many problems, however, both of policy and of politics are raised by international loans and we will return to them when we discuss the specifically monetary side of international trade.

### Reasons for International Trade : Summary

What we have said so far boils down to the fact that we have international trade because it makes possible a higher real standard of living than would otherwise be the case. We have shown how this operates through the simple division-of-labor argument, through comparative cost, and cost ratios, and through the mutual benefits of international lending. Another point may be mentioned, though it is not strictly part of economic theory: the relation of relatively unrestricted international trade to world peace. When the nations of the world attempt to isolate themselves economically from one another, or when they each attempt to extort greater amounts from others than they give themselves, the temptations to get access to needed materials by conquest rather than trade is very great. To this fact may be added all the sources of political friction that a program of attempted mutual extortion can create. Bastiat, the nineteenth-century French economist, summed up this side of the problem in one pithy sentence: "When goods cannot cross borders, soldiers will." His observation is as true today as it was in 1848.

### Some Cases for Isolation and Protection

Considering all the arguments for international trade that we have outlined, it may seem remarkable that there should still be so much pressure for a policy of relative economic isolation. Few people in modern Western nations, to be sure, wish completely to cut off foreign trade, but there are many who wish to restrict it greatly or to hamper it by comprehensive schemes of protection for home industry. Let us see what some of the principal arguments are which are used to justify this outlook.

*Low Wages.* It is often said that America ought to have a tariff against foreign goods in order to protect the "high United States wage level" against foreign competition from low-wage labor. The argument sounds plausible but it does not in itself make a case for protection. What matters in this world is not wage rates but costs. If the capital equipment of a country is sufficiently plentiful and productive and its labor is sufficiently skilled, the net unit cost of a good made by high-wage labor may yet be much less than the unit cost of a good made by low-wage hand labor. For example, a Chinese might get ten cents a day and an American $10 a day, but if the American turned out two hundred goods in the same time in which the Chinese turned out one good, the American good would be cheaper. Thus, it is not true that high wages necessarily serve as an insurmountable disadvantage.

*Particular Industries.* Another way in which people argue for protection is by appealing to cases in which individual industries have been crowded out by foreign competition. What we have here, however, is the universal fact that growth does not necessarily make all lines profitable at once. The policy which underwrites the most rapid rate of over-all growth may involve abandoning particular industries which are no longer efficient. If there is full employment the people employed in the obsolete lines will move over into other, more productive ones. Total production will be greater and the fact that some goods are now being made abroad rather than at home will not matter at all.

*Infant Industries.* We switch now to a case which has been recognized for over a century by economists as being more or less valid. That case is the infant industry argument. When a country begins to compete in a given line it may lack the requisite know-how, or its market may not be big enough to enable its producers to hold their own against established foreign producers. In such cases a tariff may give the infant industry time to get on its feet and to develop to the point where it can stand alone. The real objection to this policy is a practical one. The industrial infant is seldom willing to admit that it has reached maturity. The tariff may linger on long after the need for it has passed. Economists are inclined to think that in such cases a subsidy is preferable. Consumers can buy at the world price, while the infant industry is subsidized for its initial losses. Here too the infant is likely to want to remain in the subsidized class but, politically speaking, subsidies are usually easier to terminate because they have to be voted on and are more visible to the average man.

## The Real Reason Why People Advocate Protection and/or Isolation

The truth of the matter is that the real reason for much of the opposition to international trade, and to free international trade, is not to be found in any of the usual stationary arguments. The real objection is the one mentioned in the first paragraph of this chapter: dislike of the insecurities of growth. We already know that such insecurities are universal but when they cut across national borders they are more easily seen. As long as we speak of a world which is settling down at some given equilibrium, it is not hard to show that the general standard of living of all countries would be greatest under universal free trade. Under such circumstances, it is easy to show that most of the clamor for protection from "foreign competition" is based largely upon selfishness of various sorts (if the other fellow cannot sell in my country I can put my price higher). And indeed we will see shortly that selfishness is, by and large, the basic motive even in a dynamic world. Nevertheless, introducing the idea of growth makes the problem much more complicated.

The trouble is that while specializing in the things one does best (relative to other things) will make for the greater total output, it will also make each individual economic unit more open to shock when there is change. Yet change, we have seen, is an essential part of growth. And the change which raises the average living standard of a country may nevertheless depress the economic standard, or power, of obsolete or nearly obsolete groups within that country. So also it is with the changes which benefit the average living standards of the world as a whole, compared with the power or living standards of countries within that world. The economy of a country as well as a single industry, may become "obsolete," and this can happen whether all nations are socialistic or capitalistic.

The obsolescence of a country's economy may be due to two main sets of forces. In the first place it may result from entirely impersonal, outside pressures. We have already seen that as output grows the pattern of wants will change, and likewise that the methods of production must change. But what this means is that regions or countries whose industry is geared to the demand for one or two main products may suddenly find that those products are no longer in demand. For example, if nylon supplants cotton, or if synthetic rubber takes the place of real rubber, there will be large areas of the world which are bound to experience a drop in importance, and (barring charity or subsidy) in income, quite independently of how they are socially organized. The only way such a threatened region or nation can avoid this drop is if its inhabitants are sufficiently resourceful to make a quick change to some other product still in demand. The reaction of Denmark in the 1870s to the cheap food and grain of Australia and the Americas is an outstanding example of a constructive response. The Danes concentrated on highly specialized and cultivated products which could hold their own against the change.

Unfortunately, however, not every nation has always been so intelligent. Sometimes, furthermore, it has not been possible to make such a response. But modern ideology has produced a new type of obsolescence. There may be nothing wrong with the resources or manpower of a nation so far as mere well-being is concerned. But the nation may become so "routinist" in its attitudes, so impregnated with the love of security and serenity, that it ceases to keep up with its neighbors and gradually lets its plant and methods go out of date. If such a country is still able to feed itself, it can, to be sure, lapse quickly into poverty and stagnation without causing a major disturbance. But if such a country is not able to feed its population from its own resources, a great problem is presented. Either it must try to live forever on the charity of its neighbors, or it will have to seek to coerce and cajole weaker neighbors into supporting it by buying the high-priced or obsolete goods which it produces—always a difficult thing to do.

From this discussion we see that while general free trade will, on average, raise the living standards of the world, it nevertheless implies certain penalties. First, a nation must be prepared to find some of its products out of date and stand ready to transfer to new lines. Next, a nation must be willing to maintain a competitive industrial pace if it wishes to retain its living standard. Finally, as we will see in more detail shortly, the planners of a nation will always have to keep on watch for disturbances and insecurities coming from outside. For all these reasons the temptation is to control and cut down foreign trade.

## Summary

In this chapter we have given the essentials of the standard academic theory of international trade and why it is carried on. We have seen that men and resources are not evenly distributed over the earth and for that reason, if no other, it pays various regions and nations to specialize and to trade with one another. But we have seen a further reason. Where differences exist in the *relative* or proportional costs within nations, opportunities for profitable international trade may be created. The analysis behind this we called the law of comparative advantage: Let each country concentrate upon what it makes most best, or least worst and the greatest total benefit will be gained by all.

In the second half of the chapter, however, we considered the other side of the argument. We found that as soon as the factor of dynamic growth and change enters, the arguments pro and con for free trade become much more complicated. These problems will merge, in our later analysis, with the problems of unemployment and stability generally to form a much more comprehensive, if less tidy picture. So far, we have done no more than lay the foundations. It is time to go on to the monetary aspects of the problem.

# The Monetary Side of International Trade

International trade analysis developed from money difficulties, and indeed it is Adam Smith's exploration of the "real" forces underlying money upsets in international exchanges which gave rise not merely to international trade theory but to the whole body of modern economics. When Smith began to write the dominant school of economic analysis was what is called the Mercantilist School. As the ideas of the mercantilists were primarily monetary we can use them as a convenient beginning for our monetary explanation.

### Gold and International Trade: The Mercantilists

Mercantilism is a school of economic analysis running far back into the history of thought but coming to a peak about the seventeenth century. Because of later criticism, the intelligence of many mercantilists has been much underrated; but if we set out to understand what they were trying to do, we will find that many of them make considerable sense on their own terms. The truth of the matter is that mercantilism, with its emphasis on gold and silver, is essentially *war* economics.

At the beginning of the late medieval period many European countries were nearly as far advanced on the road to parliamentary democracy as England. In what is now Germany, for example, we find various governing assemblies, "estates," etc., all actively participating in government and more or less democratic. The introduction of the professional and *paid* army, marching under orders from central authority, ended that European development. Such armies could be hurled against the cumbersome feudal consultative bodies and militia long before they could organize for defense. Only where natural obstacles—the English Channel, the Swiss mountains, and the floods of the Netherlands, for example—could prevent immediate blitzing, could a true parliamentary regime survive.

The result of the use of paid armies for profitable conquest was that as a general rule the countries with the most money could have the biggest armies, conquer the most territory, and take the most plunder. But when we come to money a special difficulty appears. Nobody was willing to trust the fluctuating special coins of individual countries. The only thing that would be generally accepted was gold, and to a less extent silver. This was particularly the case once an army had left its own territory. So we can revise our formula to say that the country with the most gold or silver could have the biggest regular army and conquer the most territory. Of course, like most formulae, there were exceptions but on the whole it was reliable. The importance of gold and silver was fine for countries like Spain with access to the mines of America, but what could the rest do?

The mercantilists had an answer. Sell more than you buy, they said, and other people will have to pay you gold or silver to make up the difference. Thus if a country could manage to restrict its imports and increase its exports, the resulting "favorable" balance of trade would bring in gold just as much as if that country possessed mines of its own. When the theory was evolved the elaborate international means of payment we now know had not yet spread over the earth and to reason in terms of gold and silver was the logical thing to do. Once the "treasure" came in they thought it could be used for military equipment, or hoarded in the royal treasury until needed.

## Adam Smith and the Gold Standard

It is customary to date the rise of scientific economics from the refutation of mercantilism by Adam Smith and his friend David Hume, both of them Scottish philosophers with French training. But it should be realized that their refutation does not so much reduce the mercantilists to nonsense as represent a shift in fundamental political values. Adam Smith's economics is appropriate to a cosmopolitan, peace-loving point of view, in which there is free and open dealing between all countries, and wealth is to be obtained by production rather than plunder. Mercantilist economics makes sense of a sort if one assumes a world of perpetual war and plunder. But Smith showed that more wealth could be obtained in other ways. Once one's values switch from plunder to production there is no difficulty, Smith proved, in showing that the real "wealth of nations" lies in their power to produce, not in their store of gold, which is in itself mostly useless. Thus he made fun of the various plans for a favorable balance of trade to obtain gold, but he went further and laid the foundations of modern analysis by saying that not only was it a mistaken aim to try to pile up gold, but also, under his assumptions, it was futile to try to do so.

The analysis used by Smith and more explicitly by Hume is as follows: Suppose that by putting on high tariffs and otherwise hampering imports, you succeed in getting a favorable balance of trade. Gold then flows in, let us say. But what happens? People, he said, will spend the gold. When the gold is spent, it will increase the money supply at home. Production, however, has not increased. The chapters on money in this book have already told us what happens in such circumstances. There will be an inflation. Home prices will rise and as they rise domestic goods will become more and more expensive in the world market. Sooner or later, in spite of tariffs and other restrictions, foreign goods will be so cheap, relatively, and domestic goods so expensive that the balance will swing the other way. The home country will buy more abroad than it sells and gold will once more flow out. Smith thought that with any reasonable freedom of trade an equilibrium would come about naturally in which each country would automatically receive its fair share of the gold supply.

## The Basic Logic of the Gold Standard

Smith's demonstration can be criticized in several ways, but as it forms the basic logic of the international gold standard we must explain that concept before we add qualifications. The aim of the international gold standard, which flourished from about 1840 to 1914, was to foster international trade and capital movements by keeping the money of all countries on a common base and freely convertible. In effect the whole world was made part of a single money system. Exchange rates were set in terms of gold. By this we mean that if the standard English pound had five times as much gold in it as the standard United States dollar, then one pound would be equal to five American dollars. Similarly, if a standard United States gold dollar had five times as much gold in it as a gold franc, five French francs would equal one gold dollar, and by simple arithmetic twenty-five Franch francs would equal one pound.

Almost more important, for an understanding of how the system worked, was the fact that the *price levels* of all the countries of the world were supposed to be tied together. Indeed, it was just on this point that the system met its downfall. Many people feel that the international gold standard was intended to give "sound money" in the sense of an unchanged or "stable" price level. Unfortunately that is a mistake. The gold standard was intended to give a stable rate of exchange between countries— £1 equal to $5—that sort of thing, but the stability of exchange *rates* was to be maintained by changes in home price levels. Let us see how this works.

The mechanism is essentially that sketched by Smith and Hume. Barring minor adjustments, which we will outline later, a country which consistently bought more than it sold, and which did not have offsetting credit payments, would begin to lose gold. As a result, under the gold standard, the banks of that country would begin to restrict credit and reduce loans. With a reduced money supply, it was thought, prices would fall in the country losing gold. On the other hand, the country receiving gold was supposed to act the other way. Credit would be expanded and prices would rise. It will be seen that with inflation in the receiving country and deflation in the losing one a price adjustment would eventually occur which would stop the gold movement and bring about a new equilibrium. Such is the logic of the true gold standard.

There is nothing wrong with the theory on its own terms, but for it to work there must be a flexible pricing system both upward *and* downward. In modern society, however, with embattled pressure groups willing indeed to take a raise but never a cut, the system works with more and more difficulty since it specifically depends not on stable prices but on price changes. Countries receiving gold, the United States for example, have been afraid to permit the credit expansion which the gold standard called for on the ground that the later deflation would be extremely difficult to manage. They have therefore hoarded the incoming gold—which spoils Smith's mechanism. Countries losing gold have found it difficult, if not impossible, to persuade their pressure groups to accept the reduced prices and wages that were needed for adjustment. In consequence an unemployment deadlock may occur, as it did in England in the twenties. Yet the need for finding a way of keeping the economies of the world in some relation to one another remains as great as before. Indeed, in the light of the modern population explosion and the clamor for economic growth, the need for coordination is even greater. Many problems result, but to understand them we must analyze the mechanism of international payments in more detail.

### The Pattern of International Payments

Before going into the elaborate theory of international adjustments it will help to see specifically, and practically, how individual payments are brought about. Suppose I am Bill Smith in America, and I want to buy an English sports car. The English manufacturer has no use of my dollars in England. On the other hand, I have no pounds. What do I do? Fortunately for me, problems like this turn up every day. I go to my local bank which may or may not deal directly in foreign exchange. It will, nevertheless, sell me a draft "on London" for the value in pounds which I need. How many dollars I will have to pay will depend on the rate of exchange—that is, how many dollars it currently takes to buy one pound (or the other way round).

But where did my local bank get the draft for pounds which it sold me? It may be that in the first instance the local bank merely bought the draft in pounds from some big city bank regularly in the foreign exchange business; let us say it is a New York bank. However, that only moves the problem back a step. Where did the New York bank get the means to sell a draft in pounds in the United States? To answer that we have only to turn the matter around. Suppose you are Joe Brown in England who wishes to buy an American optical instrument. You, in turn, have pounds but no dollars. You therefore want to buy a draft on New York, so you take your pounds to your local English bank. It, in turn, might either deal directly with a New York branch or go to the London branch of the New York bank offering pounds for a draft "on New York" in dollars. If the student possessed an all-seeing eye that could follow through the thousands of transactions that take place daily he might find that it was precisely Joe Brown's pounds that went to Bill Smith to buy the English car, just as it was Bill Smith's dollars that Joe Brown got to buy the American instrument.

It will be clear that transactions are not, in fact, usually matched up in this individual way. What occurs is that banks which regularly deal in foreign exchange keep balances in the various foreign countries in the currencies of those countries, just as they keep balances in dollars. The foreign balances may be held by them in foreign branches or the banks may merely carry accounts with various foreign banks. However that may be, it is clear that there will be held at all times in the financial centers of the world, a mass of balances in all the currencies of the world, and that individual buyers and sellers are constantly adding and subtracting to the total of these balances.

## Determination of the Exchange Rate

We must now go one step further. If you think a bit you will see that when a number of people having dollars want, say, Swiss francs to pay people in Switzerland (or perhaps to deposit in Swiss banks) the effect will be to raise the price of Swiss francs. That is to say, the people with dollars will have to pay more and more of them for the same number of Swiss francs. This ratio between the two currencies is what we mean by the exchange rate, and in the case we are imagining, one would say that "dollars" had fallen, or depreciated. Furthermore, it is never a matter of two currencies alone. Exchange dealers are constantly on the watch for profitable opportunities for what is called "arbitrage." Arbitrage occurs when there is a gap or discrepancy between exchange rates of several countries. When a gap appears, it will be possible to change, say, from pounds to dollars to francs and back to pounds and have *more* pounds left than when you started. As the world's exchanges are so sharply watched for this kind of thing discrepancies between rates, in a free market, are apt to be eliminated almost instantaneously but can sometimes briefly occur.

As with most commodities, it is possible to speculate in foreign exchange. By this we mean that one can buy "forward" exchange—that is, exchange for future payment. Also, there may be all the apparatus of "bulls" and "bears" familiar to students of the stock market.

## The Exchange Rate and the Gold Standard

Are there no limits to fluctuations in the exchange rate? Under the full international gold standard, certainly. Only within a narrow range called the "gold points" could exchange rates fluctuate. These points were set by the cost of shipping gold. As long as it costs you less to take a slight cut in the value of your dollar than to ship gold you will take the cut. But as soon as variations in the exchange rate become serious and threaten to exceed these limits, gold will be shipped.

Under modern conditions of "freely flexible" or semicontrolled exchange an almost endless variety of combinations can occur, but again one must ask: Are there *no* more fundamental forces at work under all this superficial chaos? Again, the answer is Yes. But before we can thoroughly appreciate the fundamental forces we must take a more general view of the over-all factors shaping international trade in the modern world. Such a view requires familiarity with a few more tools of economic analysis.

## The Balance of Payments and the Balance of Trade

One of the most important bits of terminology and analysis used in international trade theory is the distinction between "the balance of trade" and "the balance of payments." By the balance of trade we mean a comparison of the value of the total flow of goods between two countries, or between one country and the rest of the world. For example, if we are talking merely of France and the United States, and if France sells 20 million dollars' worth of goods to the United States and the United States sells 20 million dollars' worth of goods to France, the balance of *trade* would be even. We should keep in mind that the goods the United States buys do not need to be imported physically into the country. For example, if an American tours France, sailing on a French Line boat and living in France for several months, he might be said to be importing French goods even if he brings nothing back with him.[1]

In addition to the balance of trade there is another balance, the balance of payments. Suppose one country buys 10 million dollars' worth of goods and services from another but sells only 5 million in return. Clearly the balance of trade between these two countries is out of line. The country buying more than it sells has an adverse balance with the other. But need this be disastrous? Not at all. What really matters is the balance of payments. By balance of payments is meant the total of all payments between each country and the world. The

---

[1] There are many terminological disputes on these problems. Some economists do not include "services" in the balance of trade, but label them separately. As long as the general principle is understood, the name used seems largely a matter of choice.

case we have given may be a case of "triangular" trade. Country X may be buying 10 million from Y, and only selling 5 in return. But X may be simultaneously selling 10 million to Z and buying 5 million in return. The student will find, from a little figuring, that in the world exchange markets these various demands will cancel out. Nor need we stop at triangular exchange. "Multilateral" balancing of four-, five-, or more sided exchanges is possible.

There is yet another way among many in which the balance of payments can balance, when the balance of trade does not. Suppose that in the past a country has lent a great deal to other countries, and as a result has large sums due it in interest payments. One way in which the interest on past loans can be paid is by having the citizens of the creditor country import consumer goods from the debtor country and pay for them with the sum sent in by the debtor.

We can get statistical pictures of the balance of payments for the United States and for most industrialized countries. The Table in Appendix C (p. 384), gives the balance of payments for the United States for the years 1961, 1962 and 1963.

You will observe that the balance balances. They all balance. Apparently there *are* no foreign trade difficulties!

Questions like these are the result of a definitional or accounting illusion. In a mere accounting sense the balance of payments, for a given period, always balances. Just as the asset and liability sides of a corporation's accounts always balance (assuming the accountants and company officials are competent and honest). But it would be as foolish to suppose that a corporation was solvent just because its books balanced as to suppose that a country had no foreign trade difficulties just because its balance of payments, for a given period, balanced. The balance of payments always balances because something must always occur to bridge any gap—an international loan let us say, a gold outflow, or a fall in national income. But the mere definitional equality tells nothing about real equilibrium.

Now that we know the difference between the balance of payments and the balance of trade, and understand that the eternal balance of the balance of payments is mere accounting, we can consider the more fundamental relation between currencies—gold standard or no gold standard.

## Purchasing Power Parity

The fundamental principle underlying the economic theory of exchange rates has been given the somewhat formidable name of purchasing power parity. This means that in equilibrium in a free international pricing system, the prices of similar goods, allowing for exchange rates and the cost of transport should, on average and on balance, be the same. A more sophisticated version would have it that changes in the relative price *levels* of two countries trading together would either have to be reversed or reflected, in equilibrium, by a change in the exchange rate. Purely by way of illustration, and an oversimplified one at that, if a bolt of cloth costs \$5 in the United States and a bolt of similar cloth costs £1 in England, the rate of exchange, in equilibrium, between the two countries should be £1 equals \$5, or else the price of cloth must change in one country or the other, or in both.

We have stated the principle tentatively because it is no more than a general tendency and subject to many qualifications. For example, the international comparison of price indexes is always difficult; some goods are so heavy and expensive to move that they are practically never shipped. Nevertheless, the constant pressure of international trade is toward keeping world prices in relationship either by changing the prices or by changing the exchange rate, and two-thirds of the pressure toward international trade control and exchange manipulation, which we will study in the next chapter, is derived from attempts to evade this fact. Somehow, over the long pull, and in spite of extraordinary obstacles, the fundamental purchasing power parity relationships have a habit of reasserting themselves. One special factor, however, can in the short run pull them far out of line even in a free system. That factor is : capital movements. Funds will be used to pay for imports, or to pay the salaries of foreign experts or teachers, or to pay the bills of their own students in foreign countries. *If the borrowed capital could not be used for these purchases it would be useless.* Thus money is not the essence of the transaction.

Now let us look at things from the point of view of the lending country. If the borrowing country spends all the funds borrowed upon products produced by the lender there will be no exchange difficulties. Indeed, there need be no specifically foreign-exchange transactions at all. The lending country, or its banks, will set up accounts in its home banks, as in the case of any other borrower, and as the funds are spent, checks will be cleared at home between the account of the borrowing government and those of the home firms from whom it is buying. We saw in the chapter on bank credit (p. 182) that this may often involve no more than a shifting of the balances allotted to different depositors within one bank.

Yet suppose the borrowing government discovers that it can buy the goods it wants more cheaply in some *other* nation? Here is where the purchasing power parity price relationships begin to be felt. Under the true gold standard, free trade, and unrestricted lending, there is nothing to compel the borrower to buy in the lender's country. We should not, however, jump to the conclusion that trouble is bound to begin if the borrower does not buy from the lender.

Once more, as we saw earlier, we may have a case of triangular or multilateral trade. Ghana, let us say, might borrow money from the United States and spend it in Britain, but if Britain, in turn, used the proceeds of her sales in Ghana to buy in the United States, the exchanges would cancel out. The trouble will begin if there is no such balancing out of demands. In that case, under the gold standard, the lending country will find itself losing gold with all the disturbing consequences to domestic short-run equilibrium which this may imply.

## Off the Gold Standard

We are straying from the problem of capital movements as such, and before we discuss the problem of stabilization let us take up capital movements where exchange rates are not fixed and where the gold standard is not followed. It might appear at first that there could be no capital transfers under such a system, since there is no common form of money. But this would be a mistake. As before, if credits in the lending country are spent on goods of the lending country no foreign exchange difficulties need arise. However, much more important and more complicated cases are found when matters are not handled so directly.

## The Canadian Case

To give an example of the intermeshing of the problems we have been discussing, let us take the case of Canada after World War II, when Canada found herself a major producer of uranium and other desired elements and minerals, for example iron. In addition, Canada's reputation of responsible government and sound finance as well as her rapid growth and need for capital made her appear a very attractive field for foreign investment—United States and European. Either by loans or by the purchase of subsidiaries, quantities of foreign capital were attracted. At the same time Canada was on a "freely fluctuating" exchange basis—that is, her dollar was allowed to exchange in the markets of the world for what it would bring. Because so many foreigners wanted to obtain Canadian money to buy shares in Canadian enterprises or property in Canada, the Canadian dollar sold at a premium. Thus at one point it took $1.07 United States money to buy $1.00 Canadian. How was the capital actually moved into Canada?

In the last analysis foreigners wanting to obtain Canadian dollars could only do so if there were Canadians available who wanted foreign goods of some sort. If one could find a Canadian, for example, who wanted to buy a share of General Motors he might be willing to sell Canadian dollars in return for a check on a United States bank in United States dollars which he could use to buy the stock. There were also, of course, instances similar to those already mentioned, of a Canadian company using a German loan to buy German machinery direct, etc. But the great part of the capital movement took a different form.

The scarcity of Canadian money in the world markets relative to the demand, and the resulting premium on the Canadian dollar, upset the price relationships. Canadian products, costing $1 at home to make, now cost $1.07 in the United States. Naturally, United States purchases of many such goods stopped rising, and even declined. On the other hand, a Canadian with his $1.07 dollar found the United States and other countries wonderful places in which to take a vacation or to buy. The result was an enormous increase in Canadian imports of consumer goods and a highly adverse balance of trade. In effect the great capital transfers into Canada were being managed by the big increase in Canadian imports which, in turn, was enabling Canadians to live much better than they otherwise would. Yet though the balance of trade was adverse, the balance of current payments was in equilibrium. The flow of foreign capital into Canada—that is to say, the number of foreigners willing to exchange their money (which Canadians could use to buy their goods) for Canadian dollars to buy property in Canada—kept the process going.

It is important to realize that things were *pro tem.* contradictory to what the purchasing power parity theory would have called for in equilibrium. For the cost of living was higher in Canada, just when the Canadian dollar was also at a premium. A $1.07 dollar was imposed on top of a 5 per cent or so higher living cost. Yet, as long as the movement of capital into Canada lasted, the discrepancy could remain. Canada's investment surplus and trade deficit served as opposite sides of the same movement.

### Summary

In this chapter we have tried to outline the fundamental logic of the money mechanism of international trade. We have shown how individual exchange payments are actually made, and the forces pulling them together. We have shown the essential logic of the relation of national price levels to one another and how these relations can be distorted in the short run by capital movements. Most important, we began with the essential functioning of the gold standard and with Adam Smith's and Hume's refutation of the mercantilists.

But there is, in the short run anyway, one important flaw in Smith's and Hume's apparatus. They do not consider the possible effect of gold "sterilization" or hoarding by a receiving country which wants to stabilize prices. One ancient and spectacular example of gold hoarding is India. For thousands of years Hindu families have accumulated treasure and never spent it. The result has been that India has traditionally served as the sponge of the world's gold supply. But the modern gold standard creates parallel temptations. The true gold standard works not through price stability but through price changes. Modern nations have often been unwilling to allow these price changes to occur. Gold is once more hoarded to prevent inflation, prices artificially held up to fight deflation. All these forces create basic questions of international organization to which we now turn our attention.

# +++ XXIII +++

## Foreign Trade Policy and Problems

We have now reached a point at which we can summarize the problems of international trade and the policies which have been urged to meet them. We have maintained there can be no question that, on balance and on average, international trade and international lending raise total world output, and benefit most of the participating nations. Indeed, under stationary assumptions it can be shown to benefit all of them. But like many other stationary economic analyses, when the conditions of a dynamic world are intruded the theory loses a good deal of its optimism and precision. The trouble is that growth comes through change, and causes change, and as we have already hinted, regions and countries can become "obsolete"—the goods they produce, in other words, being no longer wanted, or no longer wanted so intensely. Just as there is never any guarantee that the growth which benefits a nation as a whole will benefit all the individual industries of that nation, so also there is no guarantee that the growth which benefits the world as a whole will benefit every nation of that world. International trade policy has, therefore, two dimensions: long-run growth, and short-run stabilization and adjustment for special regions and nations. We begin with long-run growth.

### Long-run International Economic Policy

As explained in Chapter XXI, there can be no doubt that considering the long-run interests of the world as a whole the best policy is free trade. The argument is not merely economic but political, especially with references to world peace. Nevertheless, we also saw in Chapter XXI that economists have always recognized certain exceptions, of which the infant industry is the most usually conceded.

There are, however, other arguments; military necessity is perhaps the most cogent of them. For example, the island of Great Britain can never be wholly self-sufficient in food, but there is an obvious military advantage in maintaining a good deal of agriculture. The method used for many years has been to allow most foods to be freely imported into Great Britain and to sell at the world price. This gives the city dwellers the advantage of cheap food. But on the other hand, the government enables the farmer to stay in business by paying him a subsidy, or deficit payment to make up for the difference between his costs and the world price. There are, of course, conditions attached to such aid. Unless the farmer meets government standards of efficiency, he receives no payment. While the taxes levied to meet these deficiency payments are considerable, they are much less than the cost to the consumer in higher food prices if tariffs were used instead.

### Adjustment

How heavy a bill a nation wants to pay for "self-sufficiency" of this sort, how much the fostering of new enterprises is worth to a people are questions involving the country's political standards. The economist, as such, can point out the price but he cannot make the choice. The same problem arises concerning the degree to which a nation should adapt its home economic policy to international changes. Some adaptation clearly has to be made, if there is any international trade at all, but how much weight is to be given international considerations and what methods are to be used are again questions of fundamental policy. Once more the economist can point out the price but not make the choice. Nevertheless, it is important that we understand the basic mechanics of the problem. We turn now, therefore, to the second half of our inquiry: not long-run general aims, but the day-to-day functioning and adjustment of international economic life.

What free trade is to the question of long-run aims, the gold standard is to the problem of adjustment: the counsel of perfection. If it be true that the world as a whole benefits most from free trade, that the total of world growth is best fostered by a free flow of capital, that the losses of individual industries and states are compensated for by the increased total expansion, and that inflation is a poor way to organize society, then it follows that some international mechanism of coordination is highly desirable. And no method so far discovered worked as well as the gold standard—when nations were willing to abide by the rules and permit the needed adjustments. But like all roses it has its thorns. These, we have seen, center around its great reliance on price flexibility. Two sample problems may be mentioned as a beginning : the transfer problem, and business cycles. Let us glance briefly at business cycles.

### Business Cycles

The essential difficulty which international trade raises for business cycle and stabilization policy is that often the policy needed for international trade adjustment is in exact contradiction to that which domestic full-employment and cycle policy would call for. Take the case of the United States in 1963: In order to stimulate the United States economy and get men back to work, many people felt that America should lower its interest rate and unbalance its budget. Regardless of one's view of the essential merits of this policy, one vital point stopped its full adoption. At the same time that United States business was lethargic, European business was booming. Interest rates were high in Europe because of genuine capital scarcity, and on the other hand, wages and other costs were relatively low compared to the United States. If the United States adopted a low interest policy, the foreign holders of U. S. balances would be tempted to shift them into European currencies where higher interest rates could be earned. Such a policy would aggravate the gold outflow from the United States and put increased pressure on bank reserves. Unbalancing the budget produced similar difficulties. For more spending in the United States would, if anything, keep that country's prices up, whereas the root cause of the gold outflow was that United States prices were too high relative to the prices of competing nations. Thus, domestic and international economic policies were in head-on conflict.

Let us shift now to an opposite case. In the 1920s the flow of gold was away from Europe to the United States. Under the logic of the gold standard we have seen that the country receiving gold permits a monetary expansion which, after a while, reverses the flow. But in the 1920s the dominant school of economic thought in the United States held that a stabilization of U. S. prices would also stabilize the business cycle and prevent depressions. Thus, they were unwilling to permit the rise in United States prices, which international gold standard logic called for, because they felt that that would cause an eventual downturn. Evidently acceptance of international trade and the gold standard severely limits a country's freedom of action, where cycle policy is concerned.

### The Transfer Problem

Reference to the 1920s brings us to one of the most difficult questions, that of the transfer problem. By "transfer problem" is meant the mechanism of loan repayment, or of intergovernment reparations and indemnities. One of the important requirements of the gold standard is that transfers between countries should not be so sudden and so large that they break down the system. Let us first give a peacetime example.

Americans are apt to forget that it was from Europe, especially England, that the crucial share of capital came to build up our country. At first we anticipated the Canadian case by running a very adverse balance of trade, compensated by net long-term loans which furnished the needed payments on current account. From 1873 to 1914 our balance of trade seems to have become slightly favorable, but the interest payments on past debts made up the difference. Note, however, that no large-scale net effort was made by our creditors to collect the principle. They were on balance satisfied to take their interest out in purchases of our goods.

How long this stage would have lasted it is impossible to say. World War I brought an end to the period. The Allies, to pay for war supplies, sold back to us most of their American securities. No problem of transfer was involved in this case since the demand for United States munitions and supplies was virtually insatiable. However, there was trouble ahead. To understand why, we must consider the dreary history of war reparations.

When Germany defeated France in 1870, an indemnity of one billion francs was imposed on the French, and it was stipulated that the German army should not withdraw until the indemnity was paid. Everyone thought that France would be occupied for years, yet in a very short time the indemnity was paid in full. How was this managed? The answer is not difficult. The French were the owners of a quantity of *foreign* securities derived from their past lending throughout the world. By selling these securities in the exchanges of the countries from which they came, the French were able to obtain enough gold to make the indemnity payments.

Successful payment of the French indemnity of 1870 led to exaggerated ideas as to how much strain the international mechanism could handle. Accordingly, after World War I, enormous reparations were charged to Germany. At the same time the United States tried to collect the huge loans which it had made to the Allies in the latter part of the war. But the situation was very different in 1918 from what it had been in 1870. The 1870 war had been short, and France had a great store of foreign securities. In 1918 all participants except the United States were economically exhausted, and the Allies were left with few and the Germans with almost no foreign securities. Lord Keynes in *Economic Consequences of the Peace* (1919) argued that Germany could only make the reparations by running an immense export balance with the Allies and the United States ("favorable balance of trade") and that to collect its reparations, the United States would have to make Germany the most powerful industrial nation in the world. He doubted if the world demand for German exports would be elastic enough to permit such a development without a catastrophic price reduction for German goods. On the other hand, Professor Bertil Ohlin, of Sweden, thought that the first installment, if somehow paid, would so raise the total *income* of the receiving nations that they could increase their purchases of German goods. A sort of revolving fund could then be created. Germans would pay an installment on their reparations, the money would be spent on German goods, and then the Germans could use that money again to make another installment payment.

The question at issue between Keynes and Ohlin was obviously a factual one. What was the actual elasticity of demand in England and the United States for German goods? If the Germans managed to scrape together the means for a few payments, would this result in a real increase in the demand for German goods? The factual question is still hotly debated, but we shall never know the answer because, in fact, no real attempt was made to manage German reparations through actual increases in German exports. Let us see what was done. It could scarcely have been stranger. Individual United States citizens, acting through banks and investment houses, bought the bonds of German municipalities and industries. The American balances thus raised were transferred to the German government by loans and taxes. By means of these funds the Germans were able to pay their reparation installments to the Allies. The Allies turned the money back to the United States to pay interallied war debt installments, and the Germans borrowed the next round of payments by more bond issues!

Our account streamlines a complicated process. However, not just with reparations, but in foreign loans generally, the United States played the part of a young—some would say ingenuous—creditor nation. We lent our debtors enough on Tuesday to pay back what they owed on Monday's borrowing plus what they wanted on Tuesday. On Wednesday we lent them enough to cover what was due on Monday's *and* Tuesday's borrowing, plus what was needed by them for Wednesday. On Thursday the same delightful process was repeated, and so on *ad infinitum*. As long as the United States continued willing to lend, all went well.

Unfortunately, such a method of handling international transfers is bound to be somewhat fragile. It depends upon an unbounded optimism and prosperity of the lending country. When in fact the United States suffered what might have been otherwise a mild depression, the fragility of the international debt and payment structure turned the domestic depression into a major collapse. The financial merry-go-round ceased to function and the problem worrying Keynes and Ohlin was presented in full force, and for the first time the Germans were confronted with the necessity of really financing reparations by exports. Whether they could have done it or not under "normal" conditions remains debated, but the conditions of the 1930s were not normal. First the United States national income, and with it the capacity to buy from foreigners, dropped disastrously. Next, reverting to the habits of former generations, America imposed a high tariff which, in effect, ruined not just Germany, but another of our trading partners, Japan. Japan was buying great quantities of our raw materials, particularly cotton, and unless she could sell or borrow back from the United States, she was not likely to have the means of payment. The gold standard mechanism was totally unable to bear the strain imposed and for a while economic collaboration collapsed. There was an epidemic of exchange and other controls.

Two conclusions emerge from our discussion so far. First, under normal peacetime conditions it is practically impossible for a large-scale creditor nation to expect a sudden, prompt repayment of the principal of its loans. Slow piecemeal retirement extending over generations is the best that can be expected. The most likely case indeed is that net repayment will never occur, but that the principal will be re-lent as it is repaid. The creditor nation will content itself with taking the interest out in imports of goods. But this leads to a second conclusion: Unless willing to lend today for what was borrowed yesterday, *forever*, a creditor nation must be prepared to import at least enough from its debtors to enable them to pay the interest on their loans.

A majority of Americans in the twenties were quite unconscious of any such obligation. During our long tutelage as a borrower from abroad, we had applied tariffs repeatedly to foster infant industries. Many southerners to this day, indeed, maintain that the real cause of the Civil War was the desire of northern industrialists to impose higher tariffs. Southern writing in the 1850s is full of references to the Tariff–Abolition combine. Yet it cannot be denied that in United States experience the infant-industry argument did work out (which is not to say that the same job could not have been done in better ways), and in the peculiar circumstances of the United States at that time no very serious payments problem was presented to the world. But all this changes when the United States is a creditor nation. Eternal relending, world bankruptcy, or substantially free trade remain the alternatives open to a great creditor nation.

## Exchange Controls

In view of the number of difficult choices raised by the international financial market it is not surprising that nations should have made strenuous efforts to insulate themselves from its full impact. Such efforts practically always take the form of one system or another of exchange controls. One of the favorite methods is devaluation.

## Devaluation

Setting aside transfer crises of the abnormal type we have been sketching, exchange controls are practically always the result of an attempt by a nation to avoid bringing its price movements into line with those of the rest of the world. The student will remember that under the purchasing power parity theory, explained in Chapter XXII, the prices of similar goods, allowing for the exchange rate, should be roughly the same in any countries on a comparatively free international trade basis. There are exceptions to this rule, of course, especially with commodities which are extremely expensive and heavy to ship, but purchasing power parity remains a good basic rule of thumb. If the prices of one country get out of line so that its exports are notably more expensive than those of its competitors and if it is politically difficult to bring the particular pressure groups involved into line, the cry is always raised: "Why not devaluation?"

A numerical example will show how devaluation works. Let us take an exchange rate of £1 equals $5 and let us say that for some reason a bolt of cloth, which we take merely as a sample, now costs £1/10 (one and one-half pounds) to make in the United Kingdom but that equivalent cloth can be made in the U.S. for $5. We leave out tariffs and transportation costs. It will be evident that the purchasing power parity relations are out of line. United Kingdom cloth will now cost $7.50 in the United States as against a $5 United States product. Clearly United Kingdom exports will be hurt.

There are three possible ways out. Cut wages in the United Kingdom (we assume prices have already been cut to the bone), introduce new and cheaper methods of making cloth in the United Kingdom, or devaluate. To cut wages will involve stiff union or employee resistance. To use new methods may be almost as difficult, since it will probably involve disturbing established job categories. But if the value of the pound is cut so that one pound equals only $3.32, then, without directly disturbing United Kingdom wage relationships, United Kingdom exports could once more be made competitive with the rest of the world—cloth, for example, selling in the United States for $5 again. It is clear how great a temptation devaluation is, politically speaking. But before we yield, let us compare alternatives.

The first great objection to devaluation is that everybody can play at that game. By picking an arbitrarily low exchange value for one's currency, one can make one's exports temptingly cheap, *and* undercut the producers in other countries. Good for you but rough on them! This sort of devaluation policy has been aptly called the "beggar thy neighbor" method. Obviously other countries are not going to sit still and let this sort of thing go on. They will retaliate by devaluing their own money or by other methods of reducing your exports (putting on a quota for example), which would set a limit to the quantity of goods you can ship into their country. We see that devaluation runs a serious risk of setting off a chain reaction or reprisal and *re*-reprisal.

Even on its own terms, however, devaluation is not all peaches and cream. If exports are made cheaper, equally, imports are made more expensive. Suppose a metal could be imported into the United Kingdom before devaluation at a cost of £1. After devaluation (in the example we have given) it might cost £1/10, a 50 per cent rise in costs! Note, however, that we have said "might" rise. It could be that the devaluing country was so large a part of the market for that metal that the mining country would not be able to raise its prices to compensate for the devaluation. In that case the devaluing country would be able to shift part of the cost of devaluation on to its weaker suppliers. When the United Kingdom left the gold standard in the 1930s, for example, food prices were in a worldwide slump and devaluation cheapened United Kingdom products without raising the cost of imported United Kingdom food. But those were special circumstances, and the risk of retaliation, plus higher import costs, make the practice a highly dubious one.

There is one final objection to devaluation which goes beyond pure economics but is nevertheless vital. Devaluation even when successful is a sort of economic aspirin. It is a short-run cure for the immediate pain, but does nothing about the fundamental fault. By apparently relieving the difficulty it may encourage a country to continue the mistaken policies that made it necessary in the first place. For example, a country encountering payment difficulties may be tempted to devalue when the crux of the matter is lagging productivity resulting from inability to discipline lethargic pressure groups. Reliance on devaluation, instead of on efficiency, may relieve the immediate difficulty for a few years, but foreign competitors will continue to get further out of line and the eventual adjustment job will be even more difficult.

## Other Types of Exchange Control

Because of the danger of retaliation and of higher import costs, a whole battery of other, and most ingenious, methods of control have been worked out. One of the most widely used of these is "blocked currency." A country in transfer difficulties—for example, Germany under Hitler—might continue to pay interest on its foreign debts to a special set of accounts in its *own* banks. The accounts might be absolutely blocked—i.e., merely held in trust for eventual payment—or more often they or some part might be spent within a country for the goods of that country.

A variant of the blocked account is the "tied loan" now being used by the United States in its foreign-aid program. As condition for receiving a loan or gift, the foreign country or borrower is required to spend all or a certain amount of the funds received upon United States products. Often the commodity to be bought is specified in the transaction, as well as its price. In the United Kingdom at one time the tied-loan mechanism was in effect extended to private lending. A Foreign Issues Committee was set up to pass upon loan applications from foreigners approving only those that would involve sufficient purchases of United Kingdom goods to prevent exchange difficulties.

Yet another ingenious scheme is the multiple exchange rate. In some countries—for example, in some South American ones—all foreign balances received by private citizens must be transferred to the government, which then sells foreign exchange for various prices depending upon what the foreign balance is wanted for. If a person wishes to import a fur coat, say, or rare perfume, he might have to pay 50 pesos on the dollar, whereas if he wants to import a vital machine part for his factory he might have to pay only 10. Schemes of this sort obviously make possible large-scale control of foreign trade, and through it of the economy generally.

Another control is the requirement of export and import licenses. A much milder form of control, and one practiced by virtually all countries today, is the establishment of special funds to be used to buy and sell foreign exchange, to tide over short-run difficulties and to curb speculation. Often such funds are operated secretly, since their aim is to keep the speculator guessing.

## The Attempted Re-establishment of International Cooperation: The International Monetary Fund

By the end of World War II it was apparent that some substitute would be necessary for the gold standard, at least for some time to come, if any international cooperation and trade was to be re-established. The mechanism decided upon was the International Monetary Fund, outlined at the Bretton Woods Conference in 1944. The Fund attempted to work out a reasonable compromise between the unrestricted gold standard and complete chaos of the exchanges. The basic mechanism consists of a fund of foreign currencies for all the countries of the world, made up by contributions in their respective currencies from all the participating nations. Exchange rates were fixed for the different currencies, and the participating nations were allowed to draw on the fund, to meet their deficits in particular currencies, when encountering *short-run* difficulties. A permissible range of devaluation was specified, and in case of more fundamental disequilibria, a special agreement might be obtained for more drastic changes.

The fund did not at first live up to the rosy expectations entertained for it. Basic disequilibria between the "key countries" called for far more drastic changes than had been expected. Nevertheless, complete monetary disorder was prevented. In the meantime, however, many experts have begun to question the whole approach upon which it was based.

Behind the search for stable exchange rates lies a much more fundamental aim—the re-establishment of free lending and trading relations between nations. In particular, greater capital movements were desired. But it was felt by many economists that the control and licensing schemes often needed to maintain fixed exchange rates were a greater obstacle to international relations and international lending than the *impersonal* risks of a freely fluctuating rate system. It was argued that while both were bad, a businessman had rather take his chances with outguessing a fluctuating market than with the possible red tape, bribery, and obstruction of a control system. We will return to these problems of policy in a later chapter.

## Basic Outlook

Behind all problems of mechanism lies the matter of fundamental outlook. There cannot be a real re-establishment of the international market without two basic things: First, a belief by the nations of the world that the disturbances inevitable from international trade are worth their cost. Second, some willingness to discard extreme nationalism and the tendency to identify foreign lending with exploitation. These two forces are the real obstacles to that free flow of capital which on balance is so much needed in the underdeveloped nations of the world. Lenders are not willing to part with their capital if it is likely to be confiscated or "blocked" as exploitation. Even in so stable a country as Canada in the 1960s the forces of nationalism deeply disturbed the international market and the development of the nation. Seizure of foreign utilities without neutral valuation shook the confidence of foreign lenders, while attacks upon the Canadian trade deficit, which we have seen was the necessary means of transferring the capital being borrowed, shook the economic base of the nation until wiser counsels began to prevail. If such manifestations were found in a stable member of the British Commonwealth, it is not surprising that the lot of the investors in more volatile or newly created nations has been even more difficult. Here are the fundamental problems of ideology which transcend economics, and yet which form so important an element in what actually occurs.

Behind all such social prejudices one is likely nearly always to find, in one form or another, the conflict of individual or group security with general welfare. Accordingly, before returning to the final problem of national and international stabilization we must study some of the major pressure-group problems within a nation.

# +++ XXIV +++

## Government and the Economic System: The Competitive Ideal

In the three preceding chapters on international trade we have seen how important it is that an economic system retain the qualities of energy and adaptability. Nations cannot afford to live entirely by themselves, and yet as soon as they commence to deal with others they must be able to adjust to the disturbances which are bound to flow in from outside. In this matter of adaptability no greater problem is raised than how wide a zone of market power is to be tolerated. The question comes up in connection with two principal forces. First, the question of business power; next, the question of unions. A modern political state finds here one of its major problems and we shall give four chapters to this question of power blocks as it exists in modern society.

The method we will use in dealing with the problem is, first, to present a chapter reviewing the general theory of the subject and then to follow that with a chapter describing the actual machinery of regulation. These chapters deal with the problem of business power. Then will follow two chapters dealing with the problem of labor power. And with both topics we first deal with the general principles and then with specific machinery. Let us begin with the business problem.

### The Case against Monopoly : What Is Monopoly?

Here we must make an appraisal of that elusive type of modern competition which we sketched at the end of Chapter IX. We saw that while pure competition was rare, pure monopoly, in the sense of the business absolutely free from any outside competition, was impossible. An absolutely pure monopolist would have to control everything. As long as there are independent substitutes—tea for coffee, corn for wheat, and so on—the power of a single producer is somewhat limited. And so what we find in reality is varying zones and degrees of market power, some large and some small but with very few clear-cut lines.

## Monopoly and Other Types of Market Power

Economists have found it useful, however, to classify the types of market power under several heads. First is the single large seller of a clearly marked commodity which has few close substitutes, and which operates in a field that for one reason or another competitors find difficult to enter. This is what most people have in mind when they think of *monopoly*. But even limited monopoly of such a type is extremely rare or nonexistent in the United States.

The second type of market occurs when there are a few sellers of about equal size. If there are only two sellers, this is called *duopoly*. If there are several large sellers of about equal size, say three or four, sharing the field, this is called *oligopoly*. The distinguishing feature of oligopoly and duopoly is that the fewness of the competitors forces each of them to take account of the others' policies and creates elaborate problems of strategy.

The third type of market power, *monopolistic* competition, exists when there are many competitors but each has a group of attached buyers who prefer them to other sellers. Since each seller is relatively small, however, and the acts of any one do not greatly affect the general situation, sales policies can be set more or less independently. That is to say that the action of one man does not necessarily provoke immediate retaliation from others in the field. Nevertheless, a market of this sort, as we saw in detail in Chapter IX, is not pure competition, since there is in each case a small zone of special control. Finally, there is the case of *pure competition* which we have explained earlier.

The labels just given refer to types of market power among sellers, but a similar situation can exist regarding buyers. A single large buyer, for example, can sometimes force the sellers to make his a specially low price. This is called *monopsony*. Similarly, with a few buyers one may have *oligopsony*, and so on. But returning to the case of sellers, there is one condition frequently found in the United States. In it there is a single, large seller controlling a substantial proportion of the field, say 40 per cent, but surrounded by many smaller firms. Such a case may be called *megapoly*. It is not monopoly nor yet oligopoly. But the large seller may play the role of price leader by a mixture of moral influence and perhaps, in some cases, fear of reprisal. The large company may have a strong influence over the policies of the others in the field.

## Strategic Expectations versus the Fixed Curve

Such a complicated listing as we have given may not at first seem helpful. But as one analyzes the elements that make up the definitions of monopoly and competition, an important line of distinction emerges which will be employed in our final conclusion. That is the line between the company which is trying to form strategic expectations in an uncertain market and the company which is merely setting the most profitable price against a known demand curve. The first type of company is combating the largely unknown and cannot be said to be in equilibrium. The second type is merely adjusting to one set of known circumstances. It is this second type, and its adjustment to the known fixed demand curve, which is usually used as the basis of most monopolistic theory and of the case against monopoly. The fixed demand curve diagram for the single firm is given in the maximization diagram of Figure 8(c). The diagrams showing the contrast between pure competition and monopolistic competition for an industry, under fixed equilibrium conditions, are shown in Figures 9(c) and 11(c). In these three diagrams the static case against monopoly clearly appears. On the basis of the analysis there presented it will be said that the existence of zones of market power leads to higher prices and smaller output than if there were pure competition.

Before we can compare the analysis needed for a state of strategic uncertainty, however, we have much more work to do. We must, in particular, discuss the stationary case for "good" monopoly. Strangely enough, especially in Europe, there is a strong school of economics which believes that private monopoly is frequently a good thing—provided only that it be "reasonable." It is said that diagrams based on a mere blind search for profits do not explain actual behavior. What is the analysis behind this point of view?

## The Stationary Case for Monopoly

The case for good monopoly and for monopolistic agreements is essentially the same case as that often presented for an administratively controlled state. The values which are appealed to are the values of short-run efficiency and smooth performance. It is argued that the market cannot adjust itself accurately and smoothly and that in order to ensure smooth performance it is necessary to have the market directed by government or by groups of particular private industries. It is further argued that a reasonable monopoly will not charge an unreasonable price but, on the contrary, will concentrate upon earning a fair profit in a smoothly efficient manner. The more frequent policy in Europe is to have not one business but several, but to have them fix prices by agreement among themselves under the direct or indirect supervision or "indication" of the government.

It is argued that such a system of cooperative, directed planning by private business can introduce new inventions in a "rational" way, can subsidize research, and, by over-all direction of national effort, yield a smoother and at the same time more efficiently progressive society than the competitive one.

There has always been a minority school in American life which favored this outlook.

Although its proponents would repudiate the parallel, close analysis will show that the ideal of cooperating, good monopoly is closely akin to the ideal of directed socialism. In both cases it is assumed that society should be governed by a coordinated ruling group trained in standards of *noblesse oblige* and intelligent administration, and in both cases it is felt that the individual efforts of individual units cannot be relied upon to coordinate the working of society as a whole. Indeed, it sometimes seems that the only dispute left between the good monopolist, and the socialist, concern who shall constitute the directing class. We will return to this problem of socialism in Chapter XXVIII on comparative economic systems. We have, to be sure, somewhat overstated the parallel here in order to show fundamentals.

## The Political and Social Case against Monopoly and Monopolistic Agreement

So far the only argument we have listed against monopoly and monopolistic agreement is the purely economic one that prices would be higher and output less than under pure competition. We have seen it is maintained that under certain régimes of good monopoly with high social conscience, the purely economic argument does not hold. Indeed, any fair-minded person who studies the problem must admit that, in fact, the single seller and the business cartel do not necessarily behave like Ebenezer Scrooges, and do not necessarily squeeze the public for everything that can be extracted from it. It will be found that the case against monopoly and monopolistic agreement must be much wider than the simple case of monopoly price setting under fixed conditions. Canada and the United States repudiated the idea of good monopoly some seventy-five years ago for reasons far wider than economic theory. The two lines of argument are (1) the limitation of power and (2) the fostering of mobility and inventiveness. Let us see how these arguments work.

Those who favor government action to limit monopoly and monopolistic agreement usually argue as follows: A cooperating bureaucracy, whether it be called business or government, tends to create a self-perpetuating group. In determining which industry shall expand, and which shall not, we also determine who shall have power and authority. There is no chance to rise on independent terms since all society is under the same over-all direction. Furthermore, when such a group makes a mistake, the mistake can be disastrous since it embraces the whole social system.

It is argued, on the other hand, that in the competitive society individual decisions do not have the same all-embracing scope and, therefore, particular errors have a chance to cancel out. It is further argued that if society is not merged into one coordinating institution, there will be more scope for experiment and for the emergence of new men, new factories, and new ideas.

The good monopolist, it is said, and the good monopoly group, do not *stay* good. No implied decline in morality or intelligence need be inferred here. But what is meant is a decline in adaptability and insight. Those who argue for competition maintain that the constant flow of change in modern society can only be understood by a continuing revision of ideas and methods. But when all promotion is in the hands of a particular group there is a tendency to promote clever disciples of the existing technological and business outlook rather than men with the needed new approach to the changing problem. The difficulty has been referred to at times as the "Ben Hur" dilemma. It will be recalled that Ben Hur, when he was a galley slave, noticed that those men who continually rowed on one side of the ship became misshapen, one arm becoming much stronger than the other. He asked permission to be shifted from side to side so that his body would not become twisted. When the ship was sunk, Ben was able to swim because he had had the foresight not to be misshapen. The others drowned.

The parable applies to industrial efficiency. A business too efficiently geared to one set of conditions may lose the power of adaptation, and since the one thing we can be sure of is that external conditions are bound to change sooner or later, it is argued that the society which in the short run seems inefficient because it is under many managements and many directions, may, in the long run, prove to be the most efficient, since, precisely because it is not over-committed to one set of methods and one set of policies, it can adapt more easily to change. Whatever one may, personally, think of this argument it is the basic argument of the Canadian and the American policy toward monopoly and monopolistic agreement. The ideal of good monopoly has never as yet received widespread popular endorsement in the United States.

### The Competitive Ideal: Pure Competition

If we repudiate good monopoly are we thereby bound to support an all-out enforcement of pure competition? Unfortunately, here too, careful consideration of the problem does not lead to a simple solution. We will find that we must reject all-out pure competition, and that we are brought back to the type of competition which consists of the formation of strategic expectations under uncertain conditions. Before we can work out a final competitive ideal, however, we have to discuss the case against pure competition, and examine the inadequacies frequently found in pure competition in the world of change, disturbance, risk, and lack of perfect knowledge.

## Equilibrium versus Balanced Growth

We have first to ask under what circumstances the competitive ideal must be expected to operate. From the earlier chapters of this book we can see that, in a growing society, competition can, at most, on average, hope to operate only in a world of balanced growth. Equilibrium in such a society, we have repeatedly seen, is a precarious situation for small parts of the economy, or during short intervals. It is true that the word "equilibrium" is sometimes used in connection with full employment. Economists, we have seen, frequently say, for example, that there is full-employment equilibrium when planned saving is equal to planned investment. But such a mode of expression is really a misuse. By "equilibrium" one should mean a condition which, if not disturbed from outside, will continue indefinitely. But the equilibrium, so called, of planned saving and planned investment is never anything more than a short-run or an almost instantaneous affair. The fact that there are enough new projects, or investment outlets available, in the year 1964, let us say, to absorb all current planned saving does not mean that there will also, necessarily, be a number of new projects capable of absorbing all planned saving in 1965. The balance is instantaneous, and does not prolong itself. Over-all balanced growth depends, in our society, upon the continual appearance of a margin of unforeseen unpredictable novelty. There is never any guarantee in the short run that such novelty will be found.

It follows that the best we can hope for, in a state of balanced growth, is a condition of constant but offsetting change. Furthermore, if this state of balanced growth is to continue, it will do so only if people can forecast the future with reasonable accuracy or at least have the self-confidence to launch enough new ventures to absorb the margin of planned saving. In other words, full employment and growth alike depend upon the creation of a social atmosphere in which enough people are willing to launch enough new projects, requiring enough men and materials to start them, to give continuing full employment and continuing expansion. We do not need to prove this proposition here because we have already analyzed the full-employment problem in earlier chapters. What we need to ask now, however, is: Would pure competition, universally and strictly applied, give such a necessary environment?

## Pure Competition, Risk, and the Forecasting Problem

In approaching pure competition it is important to remember that pure competition and a world of small businesses are not the same thing. It may be that a world of small businesses of the cottage type would be desirable by certain standards of political value, but such a world is not the world necessarily implied by the economic definition of pure competition. All that pure competition means, we remember, is that the individual producer *thinks* that, acting alone, he has no influence upon price. We diagramed this state of affairs by a perfectly elastic individual demand curve (p. 91).

We refer here to the analysis at the end of Chapter IX in which it was pointed out that there was no necessary connection between the size of business and whether it is or is not purely competitive. A purely competitive producer can be a very wealthy and sophisticated individual with a staff of economists— not just a peasant or subsistence farmer. The important point is that although a purely competitive producer may fully realize he himself cannot change market price, this does not mean that he thinks market price will remain un- changed! No American citizen can elect a president of the United States by his single act and yet all of us know that there will be a presidential election every four years and probably a change fairly often. So it is with the purely competitive producer. Let us take a practical example.

Suppose, for instance, that you are a cotton planter. Even though you may be a very wealthy individual, operating a large enterprise, you still will not be able to change the price of cotton, acting alone. Regardless of how many acres you plant or do not plant, the price of cotton will be much the same. But, on the other hand, if you are not a moron you must know from experience that the actual price of cotton is continually changing, and for a variety of reasons. The result is that while in a given market you are supposed to think that your demand curve is a perfectly elastic one at the market price, your idea of the behavior of price in the real world may be quite different. For you know that the market is continually being disturbed. You set your output, then, with regard, not to the price as it is today, but to the price as you *expect* it to be or hope it will be when the crop is picked. Your production plans will be based not on present prices but on expected prices.

Not only are you guided by expected prices in making your decision, but also you are guided by expected costs. You know that the cost of your material and labor has changed in the past and that it will change in the future. Conse- quently, both for cost relations and demand relations you, the purely competi- tive producer, are dealing not with the known and the certain but with the expected and the uncertain. Nor is there anything in pure competition which would give you any greater ability to read the future than if you had been a monopolistic competitor.

The important point is that, for a society to be eternally sure of a state of balanced growth, each producer would have to have "perfect" knowledge. To have perfect knowledge, each producer would have to be equipped with an X-ray eye enabling him to penetrate the consumer's skull and read the future pattern of his wants about six months before the consumer had them. Next, the producer would have to be able to adjust his production and build his plant so quickly and accurately that the vision seen by his X-ray eye could be implemented by virtually immediate new construction, and immediate changes in the direction of output. The combination of such perfect knowledge with perfect adjustability is what we called "perfect competition" in Chapter IX, and it will be seen that such competition is an impossibility.

Now comes the real point: Would the presence of pure competition automatically give us perfect competition? In other words, would the mere fact that industry was organized in a crowd of small producers, all making identical products, automatically give them that perfect knowledge and perfect adjustability required for perfect competition? The answer, obviously, is No. Clearly the "Smith's Grow-Well" Company is not going to be able to predict future changes in its market any better just because it is no longer allowed to put its name on its product, and instead merely turns out identical cans marked FERTILIZER in a market shared with many other people. Nor will the management of Grow-Well be any better able to adjust production, quickly, to changes in wants just because it no longer knows its customers and its customers no longer know it. In summary, we can have pure competition sometimes, but perfect competition is an impossibility in any market. The best that we can have, best in the sense of most competitive, is a state of pure but imperfect competition. Yet it often follows that hordes of small producers with limited resources will misread the future much more than a group of producers who have some resources and some control over their market. We will discuss, shortly, the implications of this fact for the competitive ideal but, first, let us discuss certain shortcomings of pure competition which have no reference to the forecasting problem.

## Natural Resources and Cut-throat Competition under Pure Competition

Although the purely competitive producer may make some effort to adjust output to expected price, he has no control over the price itself. He has simply the choice of withholding what he has produced, or else of taking what is being given in the market. Because of this lack of control the purely competitive market is especially subject to what is called "cut-throat competition." Cut-throat competition, to the businessman, frequently means merely that someone is selling below his costs. We mean by this, not the cost of the low-cost seller, but the cost of the man who complains of cut-throat competition. The term is thus often used as a means of preventing the person with the better idea and lower cost from giving the public the benefit of his invention. However, there is another meaning of cut-throat competition which is more acceptable to the economist. We have spoken many times of long-run, or fixed costs such as depreciation, interest, and forces like that. Over the long pull these are real costs of production which must be covered, but in the short run, especially when a great deal of equipment has been installed at about the same time and when there is a decline in general demand, prices are often carried down by purely competitive producers to the very minimum of short-run costs—far below the necessary long-run level. To be sure, the long-run real costs will make themselves felt after a while by an actual need to rebuild as the plant wears out. But such a situation may not be felt for some time. In the short run the purely competitive producer may dump goods far below real cost. Although the term "cut-throat competition" is capable of great misuse, the fact remains that the sort of situation we have talked about is real and constitutes a real disadvantage of pure competition.

## Natural Resources and Other Real Costs

There are numerous other costs which, for one reason or another, do not show up in the business balance sheet, even under competition, but yet must be borne by the community. In a world regulated only by pure competition, for example, individual producers are able to pour smoke and soot into the air, polluting the homes and destroying the health of an entire community. Yet this cost, which should be borne by those who are really at fault, or should at least be deliberately apportioned by the community, is shifted over to the budgets of hundreds of innocent people, most of whom have no direct contact with the industry and many of whom, furthermore, are unable to meet it. The existence of pure competition, taken by itself, cannot overcome this evil and, as in the case of the Los Angeles smog, social action is necessary to deal with a social cost which escapes private market calculations.

Again, in the case of many natural resources, such as commercial fishing, unregulated pure competition gives great encouragement to complete destruction. If our descendants are to eat, say, salmon, the salmon must be allowed to spawn sufficiently. But a small producer, alone among thousands, has no motive for self-restraint. Suppose he thinks the rivers are being fished out and decides not to catch as many fish. Will he help the fish or only make an unnecessary present to his competitors? Conditions being what they are, there is nothing for him to do but go on fishing, whether he thinks it unwise or not. For withholding his catch will not remedy the situation at all. He is too small a part of it.

Thus we see that the state has to step in to enforce certain costs which would otherwise be lost sight of under pure competition. In the same way, only the state has the power to preserve natural resources on a large scale such as national parks, wilderness areas, and that sort of thing.

### Profits and the Marginal Efficiency of Capital

In Chapter IX we saw that without abnormal profit incentive there would not be enough people willing to expand—to take the risk of launching new inventions, new industries. And we saw how one source of such abnormal profits were the mere frictions of imperfect competition. But would the expensive research projects undertaken in modern society be profitable if the discoverer of a new idea or method could rely for a special reward merely upon the short interval between the launching of his project and the time in which his competitors could imitate it? The answer is No. Without the protection given by patents, copyrights, trade names, and advertising it is probable that the rate of expected profit on new enterprises would not be adequate to cover the risks of launching them.

The reader should ask himself just how much research would be done in particular fields if, instead of labeling his product, each producer were required merely to write "FERTILIZER," or "ELECTRICITY," or "RAZOR BLADES," or something of that sort on the container.

### Summary on Monopoly and Pure Competition

In the preceding sections we have reviewed some of the deficiencies of monopoly, on the one side, and pure competition, on the other, as ideals for industrial organization. We have seen that the argument against good monopoly is in effect that the good monopolist does not stay good. That is to say, there is a tendency, in the organization which has no competition, to settle down into routine and to cease to develop. In this connection it should be pointed out that the mere existence of other units in the same field is not the same thing as independent competition. Unless there is true independence in setting policy, prices, and method, the mere fact of plural ownership will not, in itself, suffice to give the needed industrial activity.

On the other side, pure competition is open to a number of criticisms. The mere fact of pure competition will not of itself give any better ability to forecast the future than existed under monopoly. Indeed, it may provide less. While price reduction can sometimes help to stimulate the economy, as we will see in Chapter XXIX, nevertheless there is also a possibility of cut-throat competition under any purely competitive market, which can have extremely unstabilizing effects. Natural resources and certain real costs are not necessarily reflected in a purely competitive market, and the state must step in to find ways of making them felt and of preserving them. Finally, the purely competitive system need not give adequate profit to induce a sufficient flow of research and development. Thus, if we value change, adaptability, and growth it is probable that a world of compulsory pure competition, once it is realized how drastic the requirements of such a world must be, would be even worse than a world of good monopoly.

## The Competitive Ideal

It is time now to attempt to formulate certain general principles of monopoly regulation. Clearly, we do not want perfect competition, for that is impossible. Nor do we want pure but imperfect competition, for that is frequently undesirable. Nor do we want monopoly or monopolistic agreement of the cartel type, for that also is undesirable. What, then, have we left? Obviously, our task must be to work out a series of compromise standards which will balance the various problems already mentioned. It will help to list some of the standards which must be borne in mind.

## Standards for Antitrust Action

From our long discussion it will be seen that the problem of industrial organization is not to be solved by mechanically applying certain sweeping rules. The most that can be done is to set up guide posts which will have some reference to particular situations. We can, nevertheless, indicate some of the major standards.

## Political Standards

One of the basic reasons urged for the maintenance of competition in the United States and Canada is to preserve opportunity for new ideas, new families, and new businesses to come to the fore and to maintain a plurality in the social structure. What this standard calls for is a fair chance for new enterprises and new ideas. Competition is advocated to prevent the development of a tightly knit, cooperating, self-perpetuating power group. What this standard calls for is a society in which efficient small business has a chance to become big on independent terms and inefficient large business has a chance to become small if it fails to meet the competitive test.

## Economic Standards

Economic standards for industrial organization fall under two heads. First, there is the need for incentive, a fair reward for extra risk and the extra cost of research and the launching of new enterprise. Second, there must exist a sufficient number of alternative sources of supply and sources of policy to give the consumer a fair choice in making his selection. But the emphasis upon equilibrium and mere numbers often leads the theorist to forget that frequently the real source of the competition which we want is *uncertainty* rather than large numbers. If there are enough producers in the field for the given industrialist to be unsure, uncertain when he may be faced by a new and better product, this may be far more effective in maintaining industrial vigor and growth than merely to be one of a swarm of producers of a standard article. In other words an oligopolistic industry of independent, technologically progressive, producers may be much more progressive, and with greater output, on average, than a purely competitive one. This is the competition of "strategic expectations" spoken of earlier (pp. 279-80).

There is however, emphasis on the word "independent." If the oligopolists are allowed to become, in the European term "rationalized"—if, in other words, they cooperatively set prices, standards, and the rate of technical change—the uncertainty, which is the real source of competition "among the few," will be absent. It is true that entire uncertainty will paralyze effort, but comfortable certainty will put people to sleep. Thus the aim of the market should be enough order to permit action, enough disorder to keep producers active.

### Practical Applications and Questions

We will discuss the problem of machinery in detail in the next chapter. However, there are two points which should be mentioned here. First, there is the matter of size. The standards outlined in this chapter do not involve any necessary attack on size as such. It is not the absolute size of the business so much as the proportion of control which it holds. Second comes the question of efficiency. It is sometimes argued that the size of individual plant which is most efficient is much less than anything in the nature of modern, large-scale business. However, efficiency is a great deal more than just production. It must not be forgotten that a coordination of the flows of materials through a business, the planning of its output, and the attempt to forecast conditions are all also parts of efficiency and all must be considered.

A more complicated question arises in the nature of advertising and of the labeling of particular products. We have already seen in Chapter IX that if one takes a perfectly stationary equilibrium point of view then pure competition will give the best results. This would mean the entire destruction of all forms of advertising. Such a conclusion does not seem sensible. A certain amount of advertising is undoubtedly wasteful; nevertheless, if the inventor of a new method or product had no means of making the public aware of his discovery the invention would be useless. Again, if a man had no way of letting people know that he was the maker of a particular good there would be no incentive for him to try to make his good, or product, better than others of the same type. Nobody would know who the maker was and the temptation would be, if anything, to produce shoddy goods at a cheap price.

Finally, it must be realized that a certain amount of market power, a certain number of attached buyers, will give the business a degree of leeway in planning output which is almost indispensable in facing what Professor Joseph Schumpeter has called the "gale of creative destruction." We are in fact caught here in the problem of the golden mean. Too much security, protection, and power will lead to lethargy; too little will also paralyze energy and initiative. Much of the impatience shown by pure economic theorists with legal decisions springs from the unwillingness, or inability, of the pure theorist to realize that the problem is not a purely mechanical one. Let us therefore go on to a discussion of the specific means of regulation which have been adopted.

# Government and the Economic System: Maintaining Competition and Regulating Business

We saw in Chapter XXIV that working out an ideal of competitive organization was not always a simple task and that our discussion left us with the problem of balancing a number of standards which were always to some extent in conflict. We shall find all the problems outlined in our theoretical discussion reappearing in the legislation enacted to solve the monopoly problem. But before we can discuss the legislative machinery, we must first realize that not all government intervention is designed to "maintain competition"—even allowing for all the manifold interpretations of which that phrase is capable.

## Public Utility Regulation

From very early times it has been found necessary for the government to exercise special supervision over certain areas of the economic system. For example, Adam Smith points out that government usually has to build light-houses since it is seldom to the interest of any one individual to do so. But quite aside from direct government ownership, there is a large class of businesses in which competition has been found to be unworkable or needlessly wasteful. In these cases, even when the government does not step in directly to operate a business, it does supervise the policies of the private firms allowed to work in the field. Sample public utilities are telephones, water companies, electric light and power, and so on. It would not be practical to have half the telephones in a city on one system, and the other half on another, with no connection between them. Yet in fact when the telephone was first invented, attempts were made to do just that. In the same way, to have two electric power systems in one town with no communication, or two water systems, would involve much inefficiency and needless duplication. Industries like these are usually called "public utilities." The government, either state or federal, sets the rates at which the company can sell its services and regulates the type of product. Some people, of course, have always advocated that the government should go further and operate these utilities themselves. Is there a real difference between a privately operated public utility and a publicly owned one? Proponents of private operation name two: First, promotion policy can be more flexible, second, private business cannot use tax revenues to cover loss.

Not all public utilities are equally minutely regulated. Railroad and trucking companies are supervised by the Interstate Commerce Commission in rather a different way from the manner in which power companies are supervised by power commissions. But the one thing common to the field is that no longer is the competitive mechanism solely relied upon to bring about adjustment. Consequently the problem of maintaining competition is a secondary one.

### Maintaining Competition: Historical Background

We turn now to the task of maintaining competition. Prior to 1889 in Canada and 1890 in the United States there was no positive law to force competition. However, the common law, the customary law of the English-speaking world, was hostile to the notion of monopolistic agreement. Contracts "in restraint of trade," as they were called, were unenforceable; and these contracts covered a large field of operations, particularly where attempts were made to buy up supplies in advance, or to fix prices. One must not, however, suppose that there was ever a world of pure competition. As we have already remarked several times, the village economy, not merely of the medieval period but much later, was much more a matter of custom than competition. Nevertheless, with the Industrial Revolution and the spread of modern methods of communication and finance, the area of real competition enormously increased—both economically and geographically—particularly in the first two-thirds of the nineteenth century.

With the panic of 1873, which is still regarded by some economic historians as the most disastrous in modern capitalist history, a long period of dull times and deflation was ushered in. As always in such periods, attempts were made by businessmen to maintain prices by monopolistic agreement, and the period of the 1880s saw the rise of many huge combinations. Ruthless and underhanded methods were sometimes used, although the literature of the subject has exaggerated them. However, it did look for awhile as if almost every major industry would be brought under the control of a single combination.

In Europe the effect of the merger movement was generally to modify legal prejudice against combination. In Britain the House of Lords, for example, held that a price-fixing agreement would be all right provided the prices were "reasonable." But the United States took a different approach. In 1890 the Sherman Anti-Trust Act was passed and it became a definite American policy to restrain attempts at monopoly and monopolistic agreement. The principle sections of the Sherman Anti-Trust Act are extremely broad. They run as follows:

SECTION I. Every contract combination in the form of a trust or otherwise or conspiracy in restraint of trade or commerce among the several states or with foreign nations is hereby declared to be illegal.

SECTION II. Every person who shall monopolize or attempt to monopolize or combine or conspire with any other person or persons to monopolize any part of the trade or commerce among the several states or with foreign nations shall be deemed guilty of a misdemeanor.

Stiff penalties were provided, which have been rendered even more drastic with the passage of time.

## The Sherman Anti-Trust Act: Enforcement and Interpretation

At first no great effort was made to enforce the Sherman Anti-Trust Act, and those attempts that were made came to grief against a series of court decisions which, in effect, drew all the teeth of the law. It was not until the Standard Oil and American Tobacco cases of around 1911 that the law first came into its own. In these cases the Supreme Court held that combinations and monopolies must be broken up, and both Standard Oil and American Tobacco were obliged to divide, or to divest themselves of a large share of their holdings. The court, however, refused to render a blanket condemnation of all monopolistic power. Instead, the court held that it was only an "unreasonable" combination in restraint of trade that was illegal.

This "rule of reason," as it is called, has been much criticized by economists; and yet, in the light of the discussion of Chapter XXIV, it is difficult to see how the Court could have ruled any other way. We see this even more clearly, now, than was the case fifty years ago. The increasing refinement of our theories of competition have made us realize more and more how ferocious would be the task of transforming industrial life into anything like pure competition. We also saw in Chapter XXIV that it is by no means necessarily certain that pure competition would be desirable even if we could get it.

Nevertheless, the court took a hostile attitude toward single sellers in a large field and explicitly condemned many of the so-called "predatory" practices which had been indulged in by some of the larger businesses.

There has always been a school which felt that the anti-trust laws were designed more to stop dishonest or predatory practices than to break up size as such; and in the United States Steel decision rendered in 1920 the Supreme Court refused to dissolve the company, although at that time it had come close to absorbing most of the field. The main reason for sparing U. S. Steel was that its formation had not been attended by any of the practices which the Court had condemned in connection with Standard Oil. Nevertheless, the company escaped dissolution by an extremely narrow margin; and, from 1920 on, it has steadily declined in the percentage of the total market which it holds, though of course it has increased tremendously in absolute size.

The depression of 1929, and the "lamentable thirties" which followed it, had the same effect as the panic of 1873. In both cases, businessmen attempted to get together to fix prices. Only this time, under the leadership of the New Deal, the government itself set about trying to organize cartels of various sorts. Anti-trust activity, however, took on renewed vigor with the Alcoa decision in 1945 and the passage of the Celler Amendment in 1950. Let us discuss these for a moment.

### The Celler Amendment

The Celler Amendment is an amendment to one of the supplementry acts passed by Congress in strengthening the Sherman Anti-Trust Act. We will discuss these supplementary acts later. The Celler Amendment forbids the purchase of the assets of another corporation where the effect of the merger would be "substantially to lessen competition." The logic of the amendment is as follows: The Sherman Anti-Trust Act, it is said, was not intended to stop the development of large businesses through superior efficiency; but the Celler Amendment is designed to prevent the amalgamation of businesses into a large unit simply by purchase. If it were not for the amendment, it is said, anybody with enough money, no matter how inefficient a manager he might be, could buy up so large a portion of the field as to threaten monopoly; and proponents of the amendment contend that, once the near-monopoly has been formed, it is always difficult to unscramble the egg.

On the other hand, many people maintain that since the aim of the Sherman Anti-Trust Act is to maintain competition, and since one of the principal valuable features of competition is *independent* opportunity, the Celler Amendment, forcing almost every merger to receive the approval of the federal government, in effect makes the federal government an arbiter of industrial expansion. However that may be, the Celler Amendment has been used to prevent the merger of Bethlehem Steel and Youngstown Sheet and Tube, and in a number of other cases.

### Alcoa and Cellophane

In earlier chapters we talked of the difficulty of defining a product and defining an industry. The Aluminum Company of America (popularly known as Alcoa) case brings these issues into sharp relief. The Aluminum Company of America unquestionably controlled 90 per cent of the production of virgin aluminum in the United States, though the remelting of aluminum already produced formed a substantial supplementary supply. Alcoa had not been guilty of any of the predatory practices frowned upon by the Court, and the only thing that could be cited as evidence of any attempt to control the field was that the company had had enough confidence in its own potential expansion to buy up, in advance of demand, most available bauxite deposits from which aluminum is made. During World War II the company built several plants for the government. But after the war the federal government refused to return the plants to Alcoa, and the Supreme Court, or rather the Circuit Court of Appeals acting for the Supreme Court, decided that Alcoa was a "monopoly" and that even though it had not been guilty of any illegal or predatory policies it should be provided with competitors. Accordingly, the Court forced the sale by Alcoa of its shares in Aluminium Limited (Canada) and other companies and also allowed the federal government to set up Reynolds Metals as an alternative manufacturer of aluminum, using the plants which Alcoa had built.

The real issue of the aluminum case is: What is an industry? There seems to be little doubt that Alcoa did have substantial control of the production of virgin aluminum. But can we take a production standard alone as the index of an industry? Many economists think not, for aluminum has many rivals. There are stainless steel, copper, tin, and numerous other substitutes. However that may be, the Court in the Alcoa case took a technological production view of what constitutes an industry.

In the DuPont and Cellophane case (1956), however, the Supreme Court took the opposite position in holding that DuPont did not have a monopoly in its cellophane production. There was no question but that DuPont produced almost 75 per cent of all cellophane. But cellophane, said the Court, constituted less than 20 per cent of all "flexible packaging material" sales. Thus the Court, in the Cellophane case, took a market approach and considered substitutes in the market rather than the technical control of the production of a particular commodity.

Anti-trust action has also been vigorous in the case of "basing points" and "patent licensing." A basing-point system is an agreement among producers that all prices shall be quoted as if the good were being shipped from a particular town, called the "basing point." The classical case has been that of "Pittsburgh plus" pricing of steel. Rates on steel were quoted as if the steel had been sent from Pittsburgh, although in fact it may have come from a much closer, or from a more distant, source. Patent licensing refers to the right of the holder of a patent to set conditions upon its use. Holders of patents often used them as means of building up effective control of an industry. This was particularly the case with the United Shoe Machinery Company, which in effect by the use of patents not only controlled the making of shoe machinery, but also to a large extent the operation of the shoe industry. However, in the Shoe Machinery case, and in the matter of Pittsburgh plus, the Supreme Court has greatly weakened restrictions of this sort.

Another drastic holding of the Supreme Court in recent years has been to force the ouster of the DuPont family from control of General Motors. It was held that since the DuPont family had control both of the DuPont concern and of General Motors this constituted too large a single block of industrial power. The DuPonts were forced to sell their holdings, but in order to avoid inflicting a needless sacrifice of capital values, a special tax act was passed to limit liability for capital gains involved in the sale, and the sale of stock was permitted to be spread over a considerable interval of time so as to provide for orderly marketing.

### The Electrical Case

The paradoxes of anti-trust action have perhaps been most strongly seen in the recent Electrical case. In the Electrical case it was found that many of the executives of Westinghouse, General Electric, and other companies had conspired to fix prices on electrical equipment. For the first time in the history of the act the criminal penalties were invoked and there were not only fines but some jail sentences. The evidence does not leave much doubt that a price-fixing agreement had been formed. On the other hand, within a comparatively short time after the prosecution of the companies for making the agreement, the government was again protesting that the larger companies were cutting their prices too far. In other words, having first prosecuted the companies for setting a price which would protect all members of the industry, the government next protested the use by the larger companies of their lower-cost plants to bring down prices. In this objection we find one of the principal paradoxes of anti-trust enforcement, and we are brought up with it against a second and parallel stream of development and regulation which has quite a different basis from that which we have been exploring so far.

### The Confusion of Size and Competition

We have spoken many times, in the preceding chapter and in this one, concerning the confusion of "competition," or pure competition with "small business." It is easy to confuse the maintaining of a world of small business with the maintaining of competition. And yet, if we think about it, we can see that these two may be quite different. Competition involves independent action, and independent price setting. But the attempt to maintain a world of small businesses may involve ending just the independent action which was originally the aim of the competitive system. For if the independent policy, say, of the more efficient man begins to make him "too big," he may be stopped. One aim of competition is to get as low prices as possible for the consumer. But suppose it is the large business which has the lower price? Again, another aim of competition is to enable the more efficient new idea to come in. But suppose that the more efficient new idea puts certain small businesses out of operation. Thus, the standard of protecting small business, and the standard of obtaining dynamic competition and continued independent growth are in serious conflict. We find these problems particularly important when we consider the various supplementary statutes which have been drawn up in connection with the antitrust laws.

### Supplementary Anti-Trust Legislation

The first of the most important supplementary legislation was passed in 1914. It consists of two acts, the Clayton Act and the Federal Trade Commission Act. The idea was to clarify and make more definite the meaning of monopoly and competition. The Clayton Act listed a number of practices as unfair and illegal. They were: (1) discriminatory price cutting, (2) tying contracts, (3) the acquisition of stock in other companies to obtain monopoly power, (4) interlocking directorates. But these practices were prohibited only where "the effect may be to substantially lessen competition or tend to create a monopoly." And since the power of interpretation has remained in the courts, the Act has not been as sweeping as it sounds.

Parallel with the Clayton Act was a Federal Trade Commission Act which created a commission to prevent unfair competitive prices. This commission has been most useful in the matter of fraud and mislabeling. It issues each year a large number of cease and desist orders. For example, electro plate cannot be stamped "sterling," and that sort of thing.

Supplementing the Clayton Act is the Robinson–Patman Act of 1936 which was aimed at chain stores that undersold independents in their area. The philosophy here is the assumption that a large business can drive out the independents by selling below cost, in one area, and recouping by charging higher costs in another area. The charge, frequently made, is that sales "below cost" can be used to form a monopoly which thereafter can raise prices above the competitive level. The Robinson–Patman Act was aimed to prevent transactions of this sort, and also favoritism.

Finally there come resale price maintenance acts, the Miller–Tydings Act of

1937 and the "Fair Trade" and McGuire Acts of 1952. The problem here is that when a manufacturer has spent a great deal of money on advertising, building up the good will of a particular line, he does not like to see the good sold at a bargain by a retailer. Tactics of this sort are called "loss leader" sales. The customer is enticed into the shop with the idea of buying at a bargain something which would be more expensive elsewhere. Once in the shop it is hoped that he will buy other things. But, in the meantime, the product used as bait, to entice him in, will have lost something of that "prestige" or snob value which it formerly had.

In order to protect the good will of the manufacturer, the Miller–Tydings Act provided that resale price maintenance contracts—that is, contracts by the manufacturer and the retailer stipulating the price at which the retailer would sell the good—would be permitted whenever state statutes made them legal. But soon a further development appeared. The so-called "fair trade" laws were enacted by some states. These provide that when a manufacturer has made a contract with any single given retailer within a state, the manufacturer can then forbid any third party from selling the good at a lower price than that stipulated in his contract with some other retailer. In 1951 a federal court decided that "nonsigner" clauses of this type were invalid. Shortly thereafterwards the McGuire Act was passed permitting nonsigner legislation if the state chose to enact it. There has been much debate, and while a majority of the states do have nonsigner fair trade clauses, there are still a great number which do not.

### The Robinson–Patman Act

We have seen that the Robinson–Patman Act was passed to prevent discrimination between purchasers and to bring about uniformity of price. However, opponents of the Act have charged that in effect it puts a dealer into a straitjacket in which he is not able to have adequate flexibility of policy. One case is of particular interest and that is the problem of the "time dimension" in deciding whether a price does or does not cover costs. Suppose, for example, that a new branch of a chain is opened and that prices are set on a basis which the company knows will almost certainly, eventually, yield a profit—once the volume reaches the usual figure. These decisions are often not mere guesses but are based on a very considerable amount of experience. But, in such a case, is a company to set its prices on the basis of its volume as of the first month of opening, or can it be allowed a reasonable time to see whether the marketing method will take hold and reach an appropriate volume? This is one of the many questions which come up in dealing with the problem of sales below cost and of alleged favoritism.

It will be seen that in the case of the fair trade acts, resale price mainte-nance, and the Robinson–Patman Act there are many possibilities in which the law can be so construed as to cut down on that experimental independence which is the essence of true competition. In addition, it has become increasingly customary to exempt certain groups from the requirements of anti-trust policy —farm cooperatives, miners, storekeepers, and so on. And thus it becomes somewhat difficult to see whether the government really believes in true competi-tion or not. In the light of these developments we must ask ourselves, How competitive is the American market?

## How Competitive Is the United States?

If the aim of anti-trust legislation was to bring about universal pure com-petition, then, clearly, such legislation has failed. If the aim was merely to bring about a world of small businesses, then, equally, the legislation has failed. But we have seen that neither of these aims is really rational or desirable. What the anti-trust laws have succeeded in doing is to prevent the existence of monopoly in the usual meaning of the word; that is to say, to prevent the existence of a single entrenched seller in a large, well-defined field. Next, the law has to a very large extent prevented industrial cartels in this country except under the explicit sanction of the government—for example, during the brief New Deal interlude. The law has achieved an organization of American busi-ness largely in terms of oligopoly and megapoly and in most cases with a fringe of smaller independents around the big firms. While this picture may not fit that of any abstract theory, it is submitted that it has not worked too badly.

In the first place, there does not seem to be any conclusive evidence of increase in the concentration of American business since 1900. Again, as of 1948, there is important evidence to show that the American industrial system had displayed a great deal of turnover and mobility. Dr. A. D. H. Kaplan of the Brookings Institution found that of those corporations which were the 100 largest in 1909, only 36 were still in the top 100 in 1948. In other words, 64 of the top corporations in 1909 were no longer in the top group by 1948. In addition, Dr. Kaplan's figures show a tremendous shift in the type of industry at the top, a relative decline in steel and coal mining, for example, and a tremendous expansion in petroleum. Finally, his figures show that the share of national income earned by the 100 largest corporations before taxes had, if anything, declined between 1909 and 1948.

It must not be supposed, of course, that there have been no further develop-ments since that time. Some recent studies have attempted to show that the 100 largest corporations now have a slightly larger percentage control of the total economy than they did before. But these debates turn on matters of 3 or 4 per cent and in a field like this where so much depends upon matters of definition, one cannot put much faith in alleged changes within so small a range.

Perhaps the most important point to remember is that much of the drive toward cartelization and monopoly comes today not from business so much as from other forces. For example, the revenue laws bear with particular weight against new, small business. Again, the urge for security and stability on the part of individual pressure groups leads to movements to weaken competition. We see this in the case of some of the fair trade acts for example. Finally, the attitude of the labor unions toward the monopoly problem is ambiguous. To obtain a rounded picture of the situation it is important, therefore, to consider wage setting, wage determining, and the regulation of unions.

# Dynamic Wage Theory and Union Action

From the problem of fostering competition we now turn to an opposite set of government activities, the at least partial discouragement of competition in the labor field. As with business market power we shall begin with a chapter on the general economics of the subject and follow that with a chapter on labor history and present regulation. But, before discussing general economics, there are two important factual trends which must be briefly mentioned. They are: (1) wages have on average risen *no faster* since the union movement became strong than before, and (2) the share of total income going to wages has remained stable in spite of the rise of unions. We must not conclude from these trends that unions are unimportant, but the factual record should be stated at the beginning, since so many people feel that a union movement is essential to a wage increase. Let us next, therefore, go on to examine dynamic wage theory and see, first, why wages rise and change even without unions and, next, the effect of union movement upon wages and growth.

## How Can Wages Rise without Unions?

As a start to understanding how wages can rise, even without unions, it will help if we turn back to what we have learned about economic growth. You will recall that in Chapter II we said that the formation of capital was one of the major intermediate aspects of economic growth. Living standards, we said, were, in the last analysis, a race between the inventor and investor, on the one hand, and the stork on the other.

The same principle applies to wage levels. Suppose something happens to make businessmen want to expand—to hire more men or to build additional plant. They will want more labor. If most qualified workers are already employed, businessmen will start bidding against one another for men. Wages will go up. As a rather grim example, the Black Death in England in the fourteenth century killed nearly a third of the population. Labor was scarce. Feudal lords started bidding against one another for laborers. They encouraged serfs bound to the soil to run away from other masters and work as free men for them. Wages soared. Solemnly in Parliament the Lords condemned such practices. Solemnly they all swore not to "steal" each other's labor. Unanimously they all went home and kept on doing it!

But modern industrialism does not play the role of a "black death." Instead a new invention, embodying a new technological possibility, may induce industrial expansion. Such inventions, it must be remembered, need not imply unemployment. Furthermore, the productive power of the new idea may be such that the real income of everybody may go up together. Even after paying higher wages there may still be a comfortable profit left for the businessman and the investor—from the increased total output. All that is fundamentally required is a willingness to learn new skills and to move into new lines. The process will at one and the same time raise the level of wages and provide the physical equipment needed to pay those wages. Some people will, of course, say that this description is mere fancy theory. But the facts are impressive. Thus Professor John T. Dunlop writes:

> The level of average hourly earning in industry as a whole increased approximately thirteen times in the period 1820–1945. From less than 8 cents an hour the average wage during these 125 years increased to over $1.00 an hour. At the same time the prices entering into the budget of wage-earner families doubled. As a consequence what an hour of work would buy increased over six times in this period. . . . From 1919 to date the level of money wages has more than doubled, while the cost of living is approximately the same. These are striking figures. The first simple fact about the wage level then is that it is an inclined plane. Alexis de Tocqueville, that shrewd observer of American democracy, asserted over a hundred years ago "that a slow and gradual rise of wages is one of the general laws of democratic communities." [1]

We have, to be sure, seen that this process of expansion does not always proceed smoothly, and that the economy must pass through temporary conditions of "semiglut." But the fact of a long-run upward trend cannot be denied. Thus a competitive (though never purely competitive) society, without unions, did raise real wages. Again to quote Professor Dunlop:

> The role of trade union influence on this rising wage rate level was probably relatively minor in the 125 year period as a whole. No question is more fundamental to the economy of the next generation than whether the historical relation of wages and prices is to be continued under strong unions. [2]

### Wage Increases with Unions: Stationary Theory

But now we have to ask whether the presence of labor unions hastens the process of raising living standards to any important degree. We want first to

[1] *Wage Determination and the Economics of Liberalism*. Reprinted by permission of the Chamber of Commerce of the United States.
[2] Ibid.

see whether union action can operate to raise the living standard of a *given* group of workers, and next whether it can operate equally well for *all* workers.

As long as we stick to pure equilibrium theory, the answer is clear and rather adverse to the union. Union action *can* (for a time) raise the wages and living standards of those members *who still have jobs* above what the purely competitive market wage would have been. But except in very special conditions some workers will lose jobs, and the total output of society will be somewhat reduced.

Why would employment and output be reduced? In the chapter on the pure theory of wages we saw that in purely competitive equilibrium adjustment, additional men are employed until the value of the amount added to total output by the last man (marginal product) hired just equals his wage. According to pure equilibrium theory, therefore, when the wage is raised, and if no other conditions have changed, employment will generally be cut back until a new equilibrium adjustment is reached.

So far as the mere fact of some cutback in jobs is concerned, it would make little difference whether or not the business being forced to pay higher wages was monopolistically competitive or not. For theoretically, in any case, though the exact equilibrium would be different, the business would have been producing at the intersection of the MR and MC curves. A wage rise would shift the cost of labor upward and so a cutback would be in order. Thus the gain in living standards of those who retained jobs would be at the expense of those who lost them.

It is conceivable, however, that a very strong union in a stationary state might in rare cases be able to force an employer to continue employing the men he would like to dismiss. Let us see how this works. First of all, the action of the union in raising wages would disturb the general equilibrium. If we are considering an industry with many competitors, the gain would be temporary. Employers finding themselves earning less than minimum profit (or no profit, or making losses) could either shut down at once, or else fail to keep up the plant. That is, as depreciation allowances were collected they might be diverted into more profitable investment elsewhere and the original plant allowed to decay.

But in the case of an employer with a high monopoly return, enough might still be left, after wage rates were raised, to persuade the employer to keep up the plant and to continue to employ more men than he wished. But in this case all that the union would have done would be to cut itself in as a partner with the employer in the *exploitation of the public*—often including other labor groups. The gain in justice or equity is not clear. Finally, however, in a dynamic world many other forces would be started which would tend to undermine the monopoly position.

## Wage Increases with Unions: Dynamic Theory

Let us therefore now turn to the dynamic growing world and disregarding the possibility of a sudden catastrophic change in technique and farming conditions, such as occurred in England in the eighteenth century, consider the case of a growing economy in which new methods and capital expansion are operating on balance to raise the average standard of living. In such a world, although the decisions of businessmen to expand are raising average wages and output (by process described in the preceding section) this does not mean that each individual wage group will be growing more prosperous. For those in obsolete lines will be bound to feel a declining demand for their services in that field. Just as businesses are constantly moving, sometimes rapidly, sometimes slowly, out of old fields and into new ones, so also workers are doing the same thing. From this fact we get a theory of differences in wages even under pure competition. A very scarce and valuable skill will at first command a high wage. If, however, men are easily trained for the field and there is pure competition more and more workers will come in and wages will fall. On the other hand, if training is long and expensive, even though there is pure competition throughout the economy, then despite the purity of the competition the supply of workers will increase more slowly and wage rates will never fall as far as in the first case. Applying these simple ideas to the real world, an elaborate theory of wage differentials can be worked out. Of course, as already implied, such shifts are not instantaneous. Sometimes adjustments takes a full generation or even more. But still no question of monopoly *need* be involved. There need be only simple ignorance, habit, and inertia.

Marginal ratios and combinations, in such a growing changing world, will not necessarily be matched up with the perfect precision called for in pure theory, and the general wage level need not be, at any one time, as high (or as low) as it would be if the process of growth were stopped and a perfect purely competitive adjustment carried through. Some wage groups will be getting more and some less than an ideal calculator would determine, but such divergences need not be the result of any monopoly forces. Competition could be entirely pure, but it will not be perfect. Because of the unavoidable imperfections of space, time, and knowledge, adjustment might be lagging either for or against labor.

It would seem undeniable, under these conditions, that unions might from time to time *hurry up* the increase in wages which the competitive process would eventually have given, and do it without damage to the economy or to employment. On the other hand there is always the danger that they will overdo the job. The main danger is that, once we get very far from the idea of wages, market-determined, attention becomes concentrated upon a *particular* group of men relative to a *particular* set of plants. The opportunities, the interests, and the welfare of society as a whole can be forgotten. A fair wage, for example, is not just what *one* plant can pay *one* group, but the wage which gives a reasonable chance for a job to all who are qualified to work, and which does not cut off the expansion of the industry. A new invention, for instance, might create incentive for expansion that would benefit all concerned. But if the union strikes prematurely for too high a wage rate it can destroy the marginal profit incentive, or marginal efficiency of capital, and stop the expansion before any great increase in output has occurred. Thus at a low wage, a great number of primitive farmers, in an undeveloped country, might find employment. On the other hand if a small group, already hired, strike for high wages they may cut off general expansion and leave the surplus labor on the farm and create a growing split in the level of development.

The complicated relationship between union action and *general* inflation and unemployment will be considered in Chapter XXIX. What we are interested in here is merely the question of *when* union action can be considered successful. We may begin with two of the most usual cases. Suppose we have a plant in a given town. The plant is relatively new and represents a very large fixed investment. Let us next suppose that a union, either by collective bargaining or an actual strike, pushes up the amount of dollars per hour paid to each worker employed. What will be the results? Many different cases can be imagined. The plant may be a part of an industry which is booming and which draws upon a relatively limited group of trained men. In such a case wages may have been due to go up, and the union, if it has affected the result at all, will merely, as already explained, have hastened the process which competition would eventually have carried through anyway. Again, there may be a general inflation. The plant may thus be able to raise its prices to offset the effect of the wage increase, and here too the union may merely have hurried up a process which would have occurred anyway. Economists call this the "chanticleer" case after the rooster who thought he made the sun rise by crowing! An inflationary price and wage rise may have been due in any case. In the first example the increase in *real* buying power would be permanent (as long as there was no change in fundamental conditions). But in the second case, any increase in real purchasing power for the workers would be temporary. Unless the union could keep insisting upon yet *further* increases, faster than those given in the rest of the economy, real gains would be temporary and would soon be eaten up by a higher cost of living.

Let us turn now to some of the other possibilities and, as before, let us distinguish between the standard of living of those who *still have jobs* and the standard of living of labor as a whole, or of a given labor group as a whole. Suppose we take the case of a plant in an industry that is no more than moderately prosperous, and assume the union succeeds in imposing a higher level of money wages. Or suppose we take the case of an industry that is declining, but in which the union succeeds in maintaining the rate of wages paid. What will happen? Clearly, in either case those workers who still have jobs may well be better off because of union action than they would otherwise have been. But if we are to argue from the point of view of the *general* welfare, the possibly better position of those who still have jobs cannot be treated as *net* gain until we balance against it the condition of others who have lost jobs altogether or been forced into some lower-paid work.

But our analysis so far has overlooked what is likely to be the most important aspect of the problem. What a wage increase usually does, in practice, in a dynamic world is to encourage the introduction of new methods and of labor-saving machinery. When labor is made more expensive, the economic principle of "substitution" comes in, a special stimulus is given to installing new tools and new methods that will cut down on the number of men hired and thus reduce the total wage bill. As earlier pointed out, the men who *still* have jobs will not be hurt. But those who lose them will suffer. To be sure a special demand will be created for machine tools, and it might seem that this expansion would offset the bad effect of layoffs elsewhere. But there is no guarantee that the increase in labor income and opportunity in machine-making will always, in the short run, offset the losses in other work opportunities. Our analysis shows that the *new idea* introduces a "break" in the so-called normal process of competitive valuation. The labor income displaced may, in the short run, be more than the income added. Of course, as the unions become stronger and more routine-minded in the machine tool industry *also*, this break becomes more difficult and less effective, but the power of the new idea remains very great.

But even assuming that incomes balance out, the total social effects are not necessarily desirable. A class of semidepressed unemployables may be created —handicapped people who otherwise might have earned a decent, though not rich, livelihood, but who cannot earn the high wage rate imposed by the union. Technological unemployment, in other words, may be greatly increased beyond what would spontaneously occur. Much of the outcry concerning automation stems from forces of this sort.

As unions become more mature and stronger, they often begin to fight the tendency to modernize, and to adopt work rules designed to restrict technological change and prevent new methods. Without going into the rights and wrongs of this, it might seem that if the introduction of new-type methods and machines were prevented, and if the laying off of men were made expensive because of high separation pay, then the increase in wages might be made to stick for all members of the union. Often, too, the adjustments we have been talking about do not come all at once, and it then will look at first as if the analysis we have given was false.

But it is a mistake to look just at a given plant, or at a given plant for a short time. Other businesses and other and newer plants must be considered. Keeping up the wage rate, and preventing or hampering the modernization of an industry that is in trouble, may only serve to make that industry go under all the faster. The railroad industry, for example, would probably have been much better able to hold its own against trucks and planes had it been less deeply embedded in the union red tape from which it is now trying to escape.

Again, even if a given plant cannot be modernized, that still does not mean that the union will not eventually suffer. The depreciation allowances, as we saw in our discussion of equilibrium theory, may be diverted to building a new plant elsewhere. Finally, if the attempt is made to make high wage rates stick throughout the industry or throughout the country, the marginal incentive for new investment *can* be cut off and general unemployment started, and the general growth of output retarded.

## Featherbedding

Judge Thurman Arnold, former Assistant Attorney General of the United States, in *Bottlenecks of Business,* gives the following examples of union practice. Although Arnold's specific examples date from some time back, similar conduct can still occur even when technically illegal. They give a brief outline of the seamy side of union activities.

Let me give you an example. The Anheuser-Busch Brewing Company has always been fair to organized labor. It attempted to construct a million-dollar addition to its brewery in St. Louis. The whole project was stopped because "Big Bill" Hutcheson, president of the carpenters' union, got into a dispute over whether carpenters or mill hands should do a small portion of the job. The company was helpless. It was willing to pay any reasonable wages or insure any reasonable working conditions. It had entered into a contract with a recognized union. But it could not build its building. Construction was stopped in the middle of the winter when the men needed the work most. It was stopped against the vote of the Central Trades Council composed of labor unions of St. Louis. Such is often the plight of the well-meaning friend of labor who finds himself a victim of the use of collective bargaining by a labor dictator to destroy another union.

And how about the consumer? Let me give another example. In the city of Chicago, Carrozzo, another labor dictator, prevented the use of ready-mixed concrete.

The obsolete puddle-method had to be used, or buildings would not go up. Consumers all knew of this outrageous extortion, yet they were helpless.

Another example—a contractor was building a long row of houses. Teamsters drove up with bathroom fixtures which they left on the curb in front of each house. The contractor asked the teamsters to help carry the fixtures in. They answered that it was against the union rules for them to work behind the curb and drove off. He asked the plumbers and carpenters to give him a hand. Then everyone on the job picked up his tools and walked off in protest.

The contractor finally went to a union business agent. Money changed hands. Everyone started to work again. But the bitterness and resentment of that contractor have made him a foe of organized labor for the rest of his life. No legislation is going to change that attitude. And when that attitude is multiplied in the hearts of thousands, labor legislation is not going to work.

One more illustration from small business. A small hatter in Washington was struggling to survive against heavy competition. He took pride in his shop. After a struggle between pride and thrift he put his savings into a new coat of paint for his shelves and walls. He got it done by a CIO union. Immediately the AF of L union put a picket line in front of his store. He began to lose business. The union told him that before the picket line would be removed he would have to have the painting done all over again with AF of L labor. This is a true story, and similar things happen and will continue to happen all over the country so long as small groups are permitted to use the privileges of collective bargaining for illegal purposes. [3]

Recent acts of Congress have attempted to curb such union action, but the problem is still very much a live one, as may be seen in railroad union disputes.

From all that has been said it is easy to see that the question whether the unions can hasten the rise of the wage level in a dynamic society is not a simple one to answer. Sometimes they undoubtedly can do so, and without serious harm to the economy. On the other hand, we have also seen that numerous undesirable results can be entailed. Though some groups have extorted spectacular gains from the economy, for a while anyway, it is not at all clear that such cases have raised wages *as a whole* above what they would have been. Even if the size of the money paycheck has been increased, accompanying inflation has often eaten up the gains. Perhaps the most surprising thing of all is the factual trend with which we began: The statistics strongly indicate that though the unions may have greatly speeded up technical change in some lines and retarded it in others, they do not appear to have had any important net effect upon labor's total average *percentage* share. The *proportion of total output* going to labor appears to have remained remarkably stable. This does not mean that labor unions have had no effects, or no ill effects upon the size of total output, or that their influence could not become still more important. But it does indicate that

[3] From *Bottlenecks of Business,* pp. 242–244, by Thurman Arnold, copyright, 1940, by Reynal and Hitchcock, Inc. Reprinted by permission of Harcourt, Brace and World, Inc.

their direct influence in bringing about proportionate redistribution in favor of labor has been much less than would have been expected.

### Nonwage Economic Aims: Fringe Benefits

As unions have become more conscious of the limits of wage action they have tended to place more emphasis upon what are called "fringe benefits"— pensions, vacations, and so on. Here one can certainly see a number of definite and beneficial results. But even these are not all net. For example, increased vacations may cut down output, and pension plans may divert so large a share of the funds which would have gone into corporate saving as seriously to impair noninflationary industrial progress. Thus two well-known liberal economists, Professor Paul Samuelson and Professor Kenneth Boulding, have even said that "private pension plan increases are more pernicious than straight wage demands."

One special feature of the private pension plan is that it helps to immobilize labor. If the pension is of the type often used for American college professors, whereby a man can move from one employer to another without losing his pension rights, the case is not so bad. But a pension which is lost by shifting tends to tie a man down. A middle-aged man may want to shift, but may not dare risk losing his pension. He may feel trapped and become embittered. This transfer angle is brought out in a circular of the Bureau of Labor Statistics (U. S. Department of Labor), dated February, 1951, in which is said: "The great extension of pension plans, seniority, and similar job rights raises special problems in the transfer of workers from non-defense to defense jobs."

Perhaps the most discussed measure now is the "guaranteed annual wage." The proposal is that each worker be guaranteed a definite minimum annual wage, regardless of how many days he may or may not have worked. In effect, the basic risks of unemployment are thrown upon the employer. This kind of guarantee has worked quite well by smoothing out the flow of income to workers in industries suffering from seasonal variations. Carried further, however, it involves great disadvantages. The trouble is that the individual business, no matter how large, cannot foresee the movement of the business cycle, or even (with entire confidence) shifts in the demand for its own products. But once it has hired a man it will owe him his annual wage no matter what happens. A great increase in business risks is involved. Still more important is the burden on risky new investment. The small, new, expanding firm is apt to be both without adequate means to furnish the guarantees and especially unable to predict its market. The measure will thus fall heavily on new investment and greatly favor monopoly by discouraging new business. It overlooks the dynamic nature of growth.

## The Noneconomic Aims of Unionism

So far we have been talking in terms of the usual capitalist–competitive society, and as if the sole aim of unions were merely to raise wages and living standards. But we have already seen that unions often have numerous other aims besides increasing wages, and also that some unionists, at the least, are not so much interested in repairing the defects of the competitive economy, or adding to its performance, as in supplanting it by various quite different forms of social organization. We are obliged therefore to consider these noneconomic aims, and also the alternative types of society often advocated.

We can begin by discussing those standards which are frequently spoken of as merely supplementing the usual competitive economy. Perhaps the one most often referred to is the role of the unions in helping to overcome what is called "sociological anonie." This impressive term refers to the feeling of aloneness that a man may often have in a large organization. It is frequently said that being a member of a union gives a man a sense of "belonging" which he could not otherwise get and thus fills an important social need.

There can be no doubt that unions can make a contribution in this respect, but it is also often true that they are frequently no more able to do so than many other agencies, including the employer. The basic problem of anonie is one of *size,* and in a tremendous union, for example the United Mine Workers, the individual member can be quite as much lost as in a big corporation. Furthermore —as David Krech and Richard S. Crutchfield point out in *Theory and Problems of Social Psychology*—unions sometimes deepen the "depersonalization" of labor–management relations. This problem of communication and morale within large units is one which far transcends mere unionism or mere capitalism.

Evaluation of the communication problem, however, leads us into a discussion of the alternative forms of economic organization sometimes advocated by unionists. The special union ideology often centers around what is called "industrial democracy." In its most extreme form this means the self-management of each plant by representatives elected by the men in the plant. It is often said that a society so organized would largely avoid pressure groups, insecurity, and conflict, release the instinct of workmanship, and give a greater sense of participation to the worker than the capitalist industrial organization can do.

To see this idea of industrial democracy in proportion it is necessary briefly once more to review the problem of growth. Growth, it will be remembered, comes through change and causes change. The mere fact of expansion in and of itself must shift the pattern of things people buy, and also the way they are made. There must be a constant reorganization of the means of production. Furthermore, change comes through independent minds, and will not long continue in a society which does not allow risk, independent thought, and experimentation. All these points have been explained in earlier chapters.

The weakness of the ideal of industrial self-government or industrial democracy is precisely that it overlooks this growth problem. Whether consciously or not, the ideal of a number of self-governing, industrial communities with security for all is obliged to be a static one, and this for several reasons.

The mere fact of technical change may upset the worker. As Krech and Crutchfield put it:

> Technological changes in and of themselves . . . frequently operate so as to balk the expression of many important needs of the worker on the job. . . . The worker whose painfully acquired skill has suddenly become useless and meaningless by some new invention or improvement in production methods finds himself facing very serious psychological problems. Not only must he learn new skills and routines in work, but his feeling of personal worth and self-esteem, based in many instances on his mastery of now obsolescent skill, is threatened. Technological development has resulted in the frustration of strong needs formerly expressed upon the job and *best expressed* on the job.[4]

Thus, as we saw in Chapter II, love of one's work or the instinct of workmanship is not always a constructive force. Sometimes it leads a man to fight socially desirable change and more efficient methods. Again, if the security-in-routine of each *individual* industrial unit is to be the highest value, then there can be no continuing reorganization of production such as growth requires and the competitive market permits. Finally, if the attempt is being made to plan the *over-all* growth of society, this cannot be reconciled with complete industrial self-government of the *individual* plant.

One very friendly critic, Lord Lindsay of Birker, a former Oxford University teacher who was given his title by the English Labour government, has contributed a further observation. He writes:

> One of the most persistent ideals of early trade unionism was that of the "self governing work-shop," in which the distinction between the management and the managed had entirely disappeared. Unfortunately experiments made of setting up such work shops have always, or nearly always, been inefficient. It is interesting to note that the Russians started with the same idea—that the worker, the ordinary simple worker at the bottom, should run the business—and they have had in the interest of efficiency, progressively to give up any such notion.

Again, on the question of the combination of industrial democracy with general planning, Lord Lindsay writes:

[4] David Krech and Richard S. Crutchfield, *Theory and Problems of Social Psychology,* New York, copyright 1948, McGraw Hill Book Co., Inc. p. 539.

What I am concerned to point out is that the making a business in itself demo-cratic is not the same problem as making the management of an industry responsible to the community as a whole. Either of these problems could be solved without solv-ing the other. . . . Discussion *for* us is not the same thing as discussion *by* us.[5]

In conclusion, we may again ask whether management of the plant by elected union officials would really give a greater sense of participation. The trouble is that the union leadership may become just as remote as the employer, or even more so. In this connection the *London Economist,* commenting in 1949 on the dock strikes of that year, said: "This union has the worst record of unofficial strikes because its enormous size, wealth, and power place its leaders in a position so exalted that only an exceptional man can keep in close touch with the rank and file. Consequently the Union has, in the minds of its members, become an entity as remote as the government or the employer." In other words it is only in the small union, if then, that the sense of participation might be in-creased. The ideal of the self-governing workshop or industrial democracy, therefore, is not so much a reaction to capitalism as a revolt against the indus-trial revolution itself. It is one more example of that routinist versus adventurist struggle which we have already spoken of.

## Unions and Technical Change

The fact of the matter is that even on a simple reform basis, and without reference to more drastic reorganization, the union movement contains within itself a tremendous drive toward the sabotage of technical change. This may seem a strange conclusion in view of the fact pointed out in an earlier section that one of the first effects of union-initiated wage increases (or any wage in-creases) is to stimulate the introduction of labor-saving machinery (p. 306). It might appear from this that the union movement gave a special *stimulus* to tech-nical change, and many unionists and other people have so argued.

The truth is, however, that when a union is just getting strong enough to begin to raise the wages of those of its members who still keep their jobs, but is not yet strong enough to lay down ironclad work rules, it does operate to stimu-late technical change. But once a union has become fully matured and really powerful, there are tremendous forces pushing it toward a policy of routine and technical stagnation. This drive takes time to work itself out. It cannot be judged on the basis of a few years; and always, of course, there are exceptions. But there is nevertheless always a very strong tendency to develop toward stagna-tion. Why is this?

Essentially the problem lies in one of the most fundamental aspects of de-

[5] Lord Lindsay of Birker, "Philosophy of the British Labor Government," *Theological Differences and World Order,* F. S. C. Northrop, ed.; Yale University Press, 1949.

mocracy—the problem of equality. As the union gets more and more powerful, it begins to take on more and more responsibilities of the employer. Especially is this true of the job of deciding, in the lower ranks of the business, who shall be promoted. But as the union begins to take over the responsibilities of the employer it also inherits the problems of the employer, and one of the most important of those is the age-old conflict between "equality" and "efficiency," in the sense of the recognition of the exceptional man. There is the problem of balancing the gain from allowing the best man to go up quickly against the possible loss entailed by the resentment of those of his workmates who have not been promoted.

Unfortunately one of the most universal as well as one of the least admirable traits of the human race seems to be jealousy—of the man who is going ahead faster than you. True democracy which, in Thomas Jefferson's case, is a gospel of democracy of *opportunity,* becomes confused with literal equality. Nothing can be harder than to tell a man that Joe Brown is going ahead faster than he, because Joe is *better* at the job. This immediately puts the other man on the defensive. As Professor Frank Knight has put it, "Freedom of opportunity implies the possibility of being defeated—yet perhaps not being defeated is one of the most important human wants." Yet some differences have to be recognized. Even Mr. R. H. Tawney admitted that.

What a mature union is always tempted to do, and what it generally ends up doing, is to keep the peace by adopting some sort of "objective" method of selection—usually seniority. Tom Jones is thirty-five years old and has been in the plant ten years—therefore he rates such and such a position. Really inefficient men may usually (but not always, or always easily) be laid off. But there is a great mass of mediocrity that is protected. It may be argued that for simple work one man is just about as good as another. But it is easy to exaggerate uniformity. Still more important, not only is the exceptional man held down, but there is little or no incentive to excel. For no one, save in the most special circumstances, can move any faster than seniority will take him. We are speaking now of the mature, deeply entrenched union such as the railroad unions and those in the building trades. As Mrs. Honor Croome puts it, "Excellence is suspect; he who excels might constitute himself a pace-maker . . . all must travel in convoy at the pace of the slowest; whoever follows a privately charted course is almost by definition a pirate."

For the same reasons the established union drifts into opposition to technical change; technical change upsets the work classifications and introduces an element of uncertainty which disturbs routine seniority. The work rules of the railroad unions were probably more or less reasonable when they began. They are now based on an almost totally obsolete technique, but they are important in slowing down modernization. It should be stressed that this drift toward stagnation is something over and above the intention of individual labor leaders. Nor can the relative tolerance sometimes found in still-young unions be taken to refute it. The problem inheres in the nature of the institution itself, and given time will nearly always appear.

**Summary**

From the considerations sketched in this chapter it will be seen that the general problem of labor market power is very much like that of business power. Neither can be condemned offhand or entirely. As some degree of market control helps a business to reduce risk, so also a degree of market control may help a union to eliminate sweatshops and underpayment. But just as we cannot let business zones of market power become too strong, so also we cannot let labor zones grow too strong either. The union movement, once it matures, contains within itself a tremendous bias toward technological stagnation. Breaking the market up into independent self-governing and secure industrial units means the stoppage of growth. If we cannot, on the one hand, say to the workmen, "Take what the market gives you," we are still obliged, on the other, to say, "If you try to get very far away from market-determined wages, you will end economic growth and the opportunity to better yourself. Furthermore, you may find yourself almost bound for life to a given plant." These things have not fully come to pass thus far only because our economic life is not yet made up merely of a series of security-conscious pressure groups.

One final point must be made. We have dealt with market power—business and labor—in terms of rational economic ends. But this is somewhat innocent. The megalomania of the old-fashioned industrial tycoon is often balanced today by the megalomania of the modern industrial unionist. Neither monopoly nor unions can always be treated as the result of simple economic calculations. There is also the ruthless will to power. And this can be just as much present though the particular institution bear an avowedly unselfish label.

# +++ XXVII +++

# History, Organization, and Regulation of Union Power

From a discussion of economic theory we turn to the actual organization, regulation, and history of the union movement. We will find that just as in the case of corporations the increasing power of the individual unit, and the serious consequences of its policies, has led to more and more regulation. The general approach has been different to be sure, but in neither case does the modern state tolerate unlimited freedom of action. Let us begin with history.

## History of American Labor Unions

It is quite difficult to say accurately when the American labor movement started. Its roots might be traced back to the benevolent societies of pre-Revolutionary War days. These societies consisted of skilled artisans who joined together to provide themselves and their families with financial aid when serious illness, debt, or death struck a wage-earner. Yet these benevolent societies were hardly the "higher-wages–better-working-conditions" unions we know today.

We might also want to trace the origins of American labor unions back to the guilds of medieval Europe. But that would not be wholly accurate because the guilds became more like combinations of businessmen to control competition than employee combinations.

Probably the safest thing to say is that the first *bona-fide* American unions of the kind and purpose we know today were those started at the close of the eighteenth century. They were organized in New York, Boston, and Philadelphia among such craftsmen as carpenters, shoemakers, and printers. They were "craft" unions, that is, their memberships were made up of people doing some particular type of work rather than of all the workers of a given business. Generally, the few unions of that time were confined to local areas and lasted only for a short time. They were concerned with higher wages, shorter hours, and union security among other things—along with welfare activities such as those performed by the benevolent societies mentioned above. The bargaining technique of those early unions often differed radically from the modern procedures.

*315*

The union simply announced the wages and working conditions it wanted and if the employer did not agree—boom!—they had a strike. A compromise might be worked out later. This differs from modern practice in that nowadays the direct action of a strike occurs only after negotiations between the employer and the union representatives have broken down.

As the embryonic union movement took on speed and strength, employers reacted. They fought back at the unions through blacklisting (refusing to hire) union members and through the courts. In one of the more famous cases, the members of the Philadelphia cordwainers' union (the term "cordwainers" means "shoemakers," and originated when they worked on cordovan leather) were found guilty in 1806 of a criminal conspiracy to raise wages. The case and the decision were based on old English common law which made combinations in restraint of trade illegal. In this case the mere combination with the purpose of bettering the members' condition was taken to be illegal. Later, judicial attention was directed toward the means used to obtain the goals of the union rather than toward the existence of the union itself. As the judicial attitude shifted, it was the strike and the boycott which became subject to legal action.

Partly because of the unfavorable court decision mentioned above and other similar decisions, and partly because of the business recession following the Napoleonic Wars, union membership dropped to a low point in 1820. But from that low the union movement sprang with new life, spreading itself over more workers, over more crafts, and even beginning to include some factory workers.

Between 1827 and 1832, the American labor movement made a brief venture into the world of politics. For example, in Philadelphia some of the craft unions joined together to nominate candidates for political office who would represent the interests of the working class. Workingmen's parties were formed in many cities.

The political programs of these politically conscious unions included such things as the ten-hour day (frequently people were working from sunup to sunset); restrictions on child labor; free public education; abolition of imprisonment for debt, of competitive convict labor, of seizure of tools and wages for debts not paid, of sweat shops, and so on.

While these politically motivated organizations did elect some public officials, little came directly as a result of their activities. Nevertheless, by affecting the legislative programs of the other parties, this short excursion into politics did change or speed up the course of law in regard to the reforms desired.

In the early 1830s the worker's interest in union political activity declined, and in its place came a renewed interest in organizing workers. In addition to a surge in numbers, there was a strong tendency toward federation. By the late 1830s the union movement encompassed about 300,000 workers—a figure not reached again until a decade or so after the Civil War. Indeed, it was not until the late 1930s that as large a *proportion* of the individuals who were potential union members actually were in unions.

But with the financial panic of 1837, the union movement in the United States went into reverse. Membership declined and unions collapsed as unemployment spread, as union treasuries were depleted, as employers became poor pickings for wage demands. The effect of the events of 1837 and the aftermath was to turn the worker's attention away from simple "business unionism," that is, unions whose goals are merely the practical ones of higher wages and better working conditions. The worker became interested instead in more philosophic ideas of consumer and producer cooperatives, and in impractical ideas of cooperative communities with community ownership of tools and land. This was the period when the worker became a political and economic theorist rather than a bread-and-butter union man.

After the panic of 1837, as business improved, as the price level rose, as better transportation between localities made competition more intense, as technological change began to force workers into other occupations, as immigrants began to pour in and swell the labor force, the union movement became conservative. It became conservative in the sense that the unions dropped philosophic social reform and visionary social schemes to concentrate once more on business unionism with demands for higher wages and better working conditions. The decline of utopianism was also followed by several attempts at national federation of individual crafts. The growth of union membership and the federation movement which came with the return to business unionism continued through and after the Civil War, though it was reversed by business recessions from time to time.

The period after the Civil War was marked by industrial strife and by attempts to form national unions encompassing more than one craft. An unsuccessful attempt was made at national organization by the National Labor Union, which brought together local unions, national craft unions, citywide labor organizations, and various social reform organizations. But it fell to pieces when it became less concerned with the workers' immediate interests of higher wages and better working conditions and more concerned with politics—the latter to the point of nominating a presidential ticket (which then declined the nomination).

## The Knights of Labor

Not long after the formation of the National Labor Union, the Noble Order of the Knights of Labor was organized. Starting first as a secret organization out of fear of employer blacklisting, the Knights were in an extremely strong position in the 1880s, and it appeared that it would weld American labor together. Membership was open to virtually anybody, skilled or unskilled, of any race—except bankers, stockbrokers, gamblers, those who made or sold intoxicants, and a few others. The "brotherhood of man" was the central theme of the organization, and even employers could be admitted.

In effect, the Knights wanted to substitute a cooperative society for the competitive enterprise system. In theory, strikes and similar collective bargaining and fighting techniques were secondary devices to the Knights; education and political activity were the chief tools. However, business union ideas did dominate for a short period; the strikes which ensued gave the Knights some great victories for its members and later some painful losses. Several unsuccessful strikes, and internal dissension over whether to use the business union approach or to rely on political action, led to the decline of the Knights.

In the remainder of the century following the Civil War, much blood was spilled over union matters. There were, for example, the Molly Maguires—a secret society—in the Pennsylvania anthracite coal region. Its actions were directed mostly at particular mineowners and operators. Murders were committed. When it was all over with, 19 leaders of the Molly Maguires had been hanged and many others imprisoned. There was the Homestead (Pennsylvania) strike in 1892, when pitched battles between striking steelworkers and company-imported Pinkerton men left 10 dead. There was the Pullman Car strike, which resulted in 25 dead and 60 injured.

**Enter the AFL**

But returning to the Knights of Labor, as they declined the AFL (American Federation of Labor) grew. It was organized in 1881 under a different name, which was changed to the present one in 1886, and consisted primarily of craft unions. In effect, the AFL was a reaction to the Knights—to its admission of unskilled workers, to its interest in politics and in broad and indirect social change. The AFL faithfully illustrated business unionism. The goals were higher wages and better working conditions, and they were to be gained directly from the employers. No reliance was to be placed on the government (for many years the AFL was opposed to social security) and nonpartisan tactics was the watchword in the AFL in regard to politics. In elections the AFL rewarded its friends and punished its enemies, and that was as far as the AFL would go in politics. Following the lead of its president, Samuel Gompers, the AFL accepted the capitalist system as the environment in which it would work.

The AFL grew slowly at first but nevertheless it grew; especially quick growth occurred during World War I when prosperity, labor shortages, and favorable government attitudes articulated through wartime control boards aided the movement. For many years the AFL dominated the American labor scene. From 1900 until the defection of the CIO (Congress of Industrial Organizations) unions in the middle 1930s, the AFL contained some 70 to 80 per cent of all union members. Its competition was small. There were the railroad brotherhoods which were independent of the AFL, but they maintained friendly relations with the AFL. The only significant opposition to the AFL's dominance came from the IWW (Industrial Workers of the World). This was a militant union made up of unskilled miners, migratory farm workers, and some factory workers, which was formed in 1905. The IWW called for direct seizure of the economic order, to the end that the workers should run the industries as self-governing units. The roles of employers and even of the government were to be negligible. But the IWW's record of industrial sabotage and violence, even during World War I, brought public opinion against it and its membership dwindled in the 1920s.

During the 1920s union membership remained quite stable. Perhaps the failure of the union movement to grow might be explained by the high level of employment and relatively high real wages throughout most of the period, which made unions less attractive to workers. Part of the stagnation of the movement during the 1920s can be attributed to strengthened employer opposition. The employers put on a strong public relations campaign, to convince the American public of the justness of the "open shop," that is, of not restricting employment to union members only. In addition, employers' associations blacklisted the trouble-making workers and obtained financial assistance for employers during strikes. The courts handed down an unprecedented number of injunctions against labor unions. Company welfare plans and stock-sharing techniques reduced the apparent advantages of union membership to the worker.

With the depression of the 1930s, union membership declined seriously. The decade of the 1930s was a turbulent period for the American labor movement. It saw the split-up of the AFL, which will be described in the following sections. It saw the government and the courts assert their weight behind the labor movement. It saw the sit-down strikes in which the workers, in effect, took over the property of the employer. It saw bloodshed, as in the Memorial Day, 1937, battle in Chicago where 10 people were killed and 80 wounded when massed demonstrators, police, and armed guards clashed. But above all, it saw a tremendous growth in the numbers of union members.

What was virtually nothing in Revolutionary War days grew to 3 per cent of the labor force around 1900, became 8 to 9 per cent in the 1920s, 15 per cent in the late 1930s, and 24 per cent of the labor force in the postwar period. What started soon after the American Revolution has not been a slow process of social change. It has been an undulating movement—spurting in prosperity, declining in recession, frustrated by the dilemma of business unionism versus utopian–political–radical unionism, split also and slowed by the conflict between those who wished to organize all the workers of an industry (whatever their job) into a single union, and those who wished to organize the unions along craft lines—that is, according to particular types of work.

## Organization of the American Labor Movement

Although the majority of trade unionists in this country since 1955 belong to the loose federation called AFL–CIO, it must not be supposed that the movement is really a tightly coordinated institution. In the first place there are some fourteen independent unions including the largest union of them all, James Hoffa's teamsters with 1,400,000 members. But in addition there are all sorts of overlaps, latent differences of interest, and parallelisms within the AFL–CIO. The main source of disagreement is still exactly the question of industrial versus craft unionism which explained until 1955 the existence of two major union federations—the AFL and the CIO. In the early 1930s there was a growing desire on the part of some of the leaders in the AFL to expand the AFL by organizing the large, highly mechanized industries. Up to that time the AFL had been rather unsuccessful in getting these industries unionized, partly at least because of its craft union organization. The AFL convention of 1934 agreed to permit the organization of these new industries, but with the proviso that the jurisdictional rights of existing unions should be preserved. This resulted in grants of AFL charters to the rubber and auto industries, but the jurisdiction of the newly created unions was limited to exclude certain skilled craftsmen and maintenance workers from coming under the jurisdiction of other AFL unions. After complaining that the new industrial unions were being mistreated in regard to jurisdiction, and finding themselves defeated at the next AFL convention, the leaders believing in industrial unionism pulled out of the AFL and set up the CIO. More precisely, the 10 unions participating in what was called the Committee for Industrial Organization (operating within the AFL) were told by the AFL to disband their efforts to organize the mass-production industries. The Committee rejected the request, and not too promptly the AFL suspended all 10 unions. The CIO was thus set up as a separate federation, but since 1955 the two federations have been "reunited."

Structurally, the AFL–CIO works as follows: locals are affiliated with the AFL–CIO. There are a scattering of local unions without any national affiliations who are associated directly with AFL–CIO. There are also six departments within the AFL–CIO which settle problems of jurisdiction, collective bargaining, the use of the union label, and see to the interests of broadly related union groups. These departments are: Building Trades, Industrial Union, Maritime

Trades, Metal Trades, Railway Employees, and Union Label Departments. Of these, the Industrial Union department is the most significant, being the stronghold of Walter Reuther and all the unions that used to be members of the CIO. Finally, there are various state bodies related directly to the AFL–CIO whose constituent parts are local unions within the city and state union organizations.

Organizationally, then, the federation would appear as shown in simplified form in Figure 23.

**Figure 23**
**ORGANIZATION OF AFL-CIO**

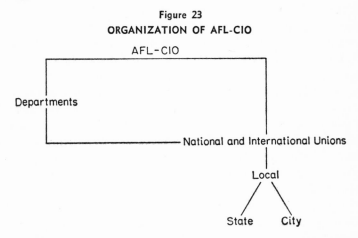

The national union holds most of the power *vis-à-vis* the federation. The federation can expel unions for violations of rules or policy, but prefers persuasion to self-destruction. The federation is mainly a service organization, with most of the financial power resting at the national level. The federation involves itself with international affairs, problems of organization, legislation, research, publicity, lobbying, ethical practices, civil rights, publications, community service, worker education, and political action. Many of these same functions are also conducted independently by the large national unions.

Controlling policy for the AFL–CIO is determined in biannual conventions which have many of the aspects of a political convention. Union representation at the convention is based on membership, and voting power is allocated among the nationals by membership size. Thus the large unions have the dominant voice in policy determination. Between conventions, an Executive Council consisting of president, secretary–treasurer, and a host of vice presidents administers the affairs of the AFL–CIO, with the help of an Executive Committee and a General Board.

In the union movement, it is usually the presidents of the two major federations and perhaps the presidents of the national unions who are most mentioned in the newspapers. While one should not underestimate the importance of these individuals in making policy, we should not allow their publicity to overshadow the shop steward or the business agent—the union representatives who make the day-to-day contacts with the representatives of management.

The shop steward is paid by management, and he spends most of his time working on the job for which he was hired. But in addition to this, the shop steward represents the union members in his section of the plant in regard to their grievances. If one of the members in his department of the plant feels that he is not getting a fair deal from the company, the shop steward will make a complaint to the foreman. If the problem can be solved on that level, that ends it. If not, the grievance proceeds up through the higher echelons of both the union and the management. This job of the shop steward is a tricky one. Sometimes the steward knows the worker's grievance is not justified, in which case he will try to convince the complainant to desist. If the complaint is justified, then it is his job to get results from the foreman. Unless this personal contact is smoothly carried out, relations between labor and management on the plant floor can be so bad as to offset any amicability which exists on top. The grievance procedure can be very helpful to management by increasing the communication between employees and the employer. In this manner, small and not-so-small problems can be solved quickly—before they blossom into serious sources of dissatisfaction on the plant floor, with consequent bad effects on production.

In addition to carrying out on-the-spot dealings with management, the shop steward may perform functions for the union with respect to the members in his department of the plant. He may collect dues, or enforce union rules, or even attempt to induce nonmembers of the union in his department to join.

The business agent is only slightly different from the shop steward. He carries on many of the same functions. However, the business agent is a fulltime union officer, paid by the union. Furthermore, unlike the shop steward, he plays an important role in the negotiations of new contracts with management. In some industries, particularly the construction industry, the business agent wields a great deal of power. For example, in some cases he can call a strike without any notice, though in most other industries the members must vote for a strike; since labor–management contracts in the construction industry are very complex and detailed, it is not difficult to find some minor violation on which to pull the men off the job. In the event of a strike, the contractor can lose a great deal of money because frequently he posts a bond which is forfeited unless the job is completed by a certain date. An unscrupulous business agent can use these circumstances to extort money from the contractor, sometimes by the rather subtle technique of setting up his own building supply firm and then requesting the victimized contractor to limit his purchases to the business agent's firm.

## The Taft–Hartley Act of 1947

The power of organized labor came increasingly into question after the war and the thought was expressed that the pendulum of legislation and court decision had swung too far in the favor of labor. A court decision in 1941, for example, upheld the right of a union to impose a boycott that drove a company out of business. Also, the Employment Act of 1946 committed the federal government to all practicable measures to promote maximum employment, production, and purchasing power.

The early postwar years were marked by a rise in industrial strife. Then the economy reverted to peace, wages and prices were decontrolled. The work week was reduced. Unions fought to maintain their wartime high weekly earnings. Many grievances built up during the war had not really been settled so much as postponed. A consequence of these factors was a series of strikes in the major mass-production industries resulting in a pattern of wage increases of $18\frac{1}{2}$ cents an hour in 1946. This first-round settlement was followed by others with fringe benefits—paid holidays, health and welfare benefits, and so on—continuing to play an important role in the bargaining.

The percentage of work time lost to industrial disputes reached 1.43 in 1946, the highest to date. Even in 1937, a year particularly noted for labor unrest, only .05 per cent of work time was lost to strikes. The consistent pressure for sizable wage and other benefits led to public reaction after the war.

There were also many abuses of union power. In an age when industrial processes are large-scale, interdependent, and complex, labor disputes are generally conceded to be more vitally affected with the public interest than in a simpler day. One strike can today tie up a vital industry nationwide, or slow the economy of a vast metropolitan area.

Certain types of industrial disputes seem far removed from labor–management conflicts. Jurisdictional disputes can ruin an employer even though the protagonists are unions, struggling for job control. Unions have resorted to strikes and boycotts as a means to win interunion arguments. Or again, secondary boycotts have been pressed against third parties not directly involved in a dispute. It appeared in 1946 that the public had no protection against oft-times ruthless and arbitrary power of large scale unionism.

A second source of public concern over union power in the immediate postwar period stemmed from the issue of Communist influence within the union movement. The leadership of several CIO unions had displayed a record of shifting their positions of support of the "party line" and were blatant in promoting Soviet views.

A third reason for the reaction to the power of labor may be sought in the growth during the war of greater political activity on the part of the unions. The CIO started the PAC (Political Action Committee) in 1943 to press for favorable legislation. Labor's League for Political Education was started in 1947 as a parallel organ in the AFL.

Opposition to the growing trend of union power was not long in appearing. The strike record of 1946, the Communist question, the favorable legislative and judicial actions, and the more objectionable practice of unions showed the need for a redress of the balance of economic power.

The Labor–Management Relations Act of 1947 (the Taft–Hartley Act) was the result. In sum, the Act tried to resolve the issues of union power. Some of its provisions dealt with the procedure for handling strikes affected with the public interest. Others sought to remedy what were held to be abuses of union power such as the secondary boycott, the closed shop, and jurisdictional disputes. Still others were directed to the question of Communist-dominated unions. And where the Wagner Act had spelled out unfair practices of management, Taft–Hartley enumerated a series of unfair labor practices from which firms could seek relief through the NLRB (National Labor Relations Board). One feature of the Act particularly objectionable to unions was the inclusion of a clause which allowed states to adopt legislation more restrictive against union membership requirements than was provided by federal law.

Among other things, the Taft–Hartley Act: (1) banned the closed shop, (2) outlawed secondary boycotts and jurisdictional strikes, (3) instituted a 60-day cooling off period before a strike could go into effect, (4) permitted an eighty-day injunction in any dispute which the President feels will affect the health or safety of the nation, (5) made dues checkoff voluntary with the individual worker and not part of the collective bargain, (6) required that union dues and initiation fees be "reasonable," (7) prohibited payments for certain services not actually performed, (8) required that union officers sign non-Communist affidavits, (9) revived the injunction for enforcement of certain phases of the Act, (10) forbade strikers who had been replaced from voting in a representation election.

Labor dissatisfaction with Taft–Hartley did not result in a scrapping of the legislation, which passed over President Truman's veto. The subsequent experience with the law showed that it did not directly impede union growth as much as had been anticipated. Nonetheless, the state "right-to-work" laws which followed on the heels of the Taft–Hartley Act do hamper union effort to some extent.

The issue of Communist-dominated unions ended early in the 1950s when the CIO expelled nine Communist-dominated unions. With regard to feather-bedding, several Supreme Court decisions have gone far to reduce the scope of the anti-featherbedding provisions of the Taft–Hartley Act. Newspapers, for example, can be compelled to pay for the setting of type not used, and a local standby orchestra must be paid when a traveling orchestra is hired for an engagement. Neither instance, asserted the Court in 1953, represents a violation of the featherbedding ban.

## The Labor–Management Reporting and Disclosure Act, 1959

Some of the gains made by unions are responsible for further problems. The growth of huge welfare and pension funds presented a prime opportunity for unscrupulous persons within the union movement to divert these funds for personal gain. Also, the gains at the bargaining table may have spurred management efforts to seek means to automate and thus to contribute to some of the nagging unemployment.

The AFL–CIO approved a Code of Ethical Practices to govern the administration of health and welfare funds and to set high standards of conduct for union affairs. To implement the Code, an Ethical Practices Committee was made a permanent part of the federation's administrative machinery. Where undesirable practices are found the Committee can recommend expulsion of the union from the federation and the establishment of competing unions to absorb membership.

When the issue of corruption and malfeasance broke, the union movement took steps to solve its own problems. The Ethical Practices Committee held an investigation. As a result the Teamsters were expelled from the federation and the Distillery Workers put on probation.

The hearings by the McClellan Committee of the United States Senate (Select Committee on Improper Activities in the Labor–Management Field) also disclosed flagrant abuses of positions of trust. Gangsterism was unearthed within the union movement (and among management personnel). Rights of individual union members were denied; members were intimidated; and elections rigged.

The McClellan hearings terminated in the 1959 Labor–Management Reporting and Disclosure Act (Landrum–Griffin Act). This legislation regulates the internal affairs of unions in many respects and approaches making unions quasi-public bodies. According to the Act, facts on labor organization must be reported to the Department of Labor: constitution and bylaws, lists of officers, qualifications for membership, and many other facets of union practices thus come under public scrutiny. Financial reports must be submitted disclosing the assets and liabilities of the union, and union officers and employees must report many types of their personal financial transactions. Those who handle finances must also be bonded. The Act finally details many provisions aimed toward assuring the democratic behavior of unions. No Communist and no crook can hold union office; fair and frequent elections must be held for union officers; members must be assured of free speech and of the right to nominate and vote as they wish without intimidation. Provisions such as these, it is hoped, will terminate the abuses found by the McClellan Committee.

The American labor movement has been referred to as "business unionism," a term which implies that the main function of the union is collective bargaining. Since the securing of a contract is foremost, let us see what the typical contract contains.

The range of the modern contract is very broad. If there has been an NLRB certification, the bargaining unit has already been defined. The bargaining unit is the groups of workers to be covered by the collective contract. If no NLRB certification has been made, then the bargaining unit will be spelled out in the contract. From there the agreement will move on to include causes governing union security, wages, hours, overtime, vacations and holidays, seniority provisions, grievance administration, discharge and discipline, management prerogatives and union rights, safety, health and welfare, severance allowances, strikes and lockouts, and, finally, provisions for renewing the contract. Naturally, not all the above areas will be included in every contract.

The issue of union security is of high importance to the union. The union wishes to assure that it shall be the exclusively recognized bargaining unit and that all employees in the bargaining unit are members of the union. The closed shop is the ultimate in union security. Where it prevailed, the firm could employ only those persons already union members, and nonunionists could not work for the firm. This arrangement is presumably outlawed by the Taft–Hartley Act. The polar extreme would be the open shop, where the employer hires whomsoever he wishes and the worker is free either to join or not to join the union as he sees fit.

Between the extremes of closed and open shop lie a host of compromise arrangements. The *union shop* is the closest thing to a closed shop. Under this arrangement, the firm is free to hire anybody it wants to with the stipulation that the person must join the union within a given time-period. The *preferential shop* gives preference to union members with regard to hiring, promotion, and layoffs. In the maritime unions, preferential hiring resulted in the unions running a hiring hall through which the employer obtained labor. The *modified union shop* permits a worker to drop out of the union if he wishes to do so and still retain his job. Under the union shop this would not be possible. Maintenance of membership is a form of union security that emerged under wartime conditions. In a tight labor market the union risked losing members, and to offset this, the maintenance of membership agreement stipulated that persons belonging to the union at the beginning of a contract must remain members throughout the period of the contract. The *agency shop* agreement requires that the worker need not join the union but he must pay a fee to the union for bargaining services rendered. This amount will approximate union dues, but the worker is not entitled to vote in union elections except perhaps when a strike is at issue.

In the postwar period, the battle for union security has been over the union shop. Many states have outlawed the union shop by enacting right-to-work laws which eliminate union shop clauses from collective bargaining contracts. Employers and their organizations poured in vast sums to have such laws passed and unions did likewise to prevent their passage. The eighteen or so states which have such laws are mostly agricultural states in the Southeast and West. The only industrial state to have a right-to-work law is Indiana.

Supporters of these enactments against union security argue that the union shop deprives the individual of his right to work, since union membership becomes a condition of employment. Unions reply that there are lots of other conditions for employment which the worker must be able to meet, such as educational and experience requirements. Nor may the worker by given free choice in such matters as the type of clothing he will wear on the job. The supporters of right-to-work laws assert that required union membership is undemocratic. Unions reply that the majority-rule concept is most democratic. Since the Taft–Hartley Act requires that the union serve as the bargaining agent for *all* employees in the bargaining unit, the unions argue that all workers in the unit should be required to contribute their support, financial and otherwise, to the union. Fundamentally then, this issue becomes one of determining the boundary between free individual choice and the interests of the group, the perennial problem of democratic process.

Financial security is a matter of concern to the union. The dues-checkoff provision in the contract, if it can be obtained through bargaining and if the state laws allow it, requires that the employer deduct union dues from the wage-earner's paycheck and give the sum to the union treasury. In the absence of the checkoff, the shop steward has the task of making the rounds regularly on payday. The checkoff thus makes dues collection automatic and assures a steady income to the union. It is frequently argued that this financial security makes the union less responsive to the needs of desires of the membership and thus contributes to a decline of union democracy.

With a contract providing for union security in the form of the union shop and the dues checkoff, the union no longer has to fight for its existence. Unions

assert that a beneficial result from this is that the union can be more "responsible." The union will be more willing to see uncooperative workers disciplined.
It will not countenance the pressing of phoney grievances and will be able to
assist management to solve its problems. This line of reasoning may be true in
some cases, but it may also be true that the tranquility following upon a strong
contract is the result of capitulation on the part of management.

The seniority clauses of a contract are one way in which control over the
job is maintained by the union. Seniority rules can vary in numerous ways. All
the provisions have the effect of requiring that length of tenure should determine
order of priority for promotion, layoffs, and the like. Management, naturally,
prefers to base such matters on skill, capability, and productivity rather than on
length of service. Very often then, seniority provisions are coupled with clauses
allowing efficiency of the workers to play a role.

Job security is also involved in the clauses of the contract setting forth the
conditions under which a worker is subject to discipline or discharge and still
more importantly in the clauses governing work rules. To what extent is management free to reclassify jobs? To change wage rates? To schedule production
as it sees fit? To transfer workers? To alter work procedures? To what extent will
the union participate in the preparing of job descriptions? In these and other
areas, job security plays a dominant role.

Management frequently complains that many of the job-security provisions
are featherbedding on the part of the union. That is, the union may require that
unnecessary tasks be undertaken and paid for, or that necessary tasks be done
in an inefficient manner simply for the sake of making work. One current example is seen in the attempts of the railroad firemen to keep firemen in the loco-
motive when the job of the fireman no longer exists on modern locomotives.

It is sometimes charged that unions act as a drag on technological change
by their hamstringing rules and regulations. While at the national level, the
AFL–CIO stands in favor of automation and technological change, the practices of many unions are not consistent with this position. No one likes to see *his*
job automated out of existence. To combat the adverse job impact, union leaders lobby for greater social security and for legislation allowing for retraining
and relocation of workers affected by shrinking job opportunities. They seek to
bargain for extended supplementary unemployment benefits and larger amounts
of severance pay to make the costs of replacing labor by machines higher for
management. They urge that innovations introduced by the firm be phased-in at
a rate consistent with the natural attrition rate of labor through retirement,
death, and voluntary quitting, so as not to cause labor displacement.

Beyond the issues of union security and job security the union contract is vitally concerned with wages. Fundamentally, there are two types of wage-payment systems—per unit of time and per unit of work.

Generally unions are in favor of having the same rate of pay for each individual doing the same job when an hourly rate system is in effect—equal pay for equal work. But equal hourly rates may not result in equal work, depending on the efficiency of those doing the job. The effective worker may turn out more work in an hour than his less diligent brother. The reason for union insistence on equal hourly rates for all workers on the same task is that, in the absence of this, the better worker might be able to bargain with the firm for a pay differential reflecting his superior skills. Were this to happen, the union might begin to appear less desirable in the eyes of the workers. If they believed that they could do better for themselves through individual bargaining, the unions would be weakened.

For piece rates, wages based on output, union attitudes vary. Where incentive systems are in effect, the union likes to be in on the rate-setting and standard-setting, and see to it that reasonable work loads are assigned. If the standards are set too high, the worker might have to work too hard or too fast ever to get his output into the zone where the incentive pay would be realized. Or he might receive too low a weekly paycheck if the standards exceed his physical capacities.

Where unions are willing to go along with incentive systems, they do so for any of several reasons: they recognize the workers' desire for higher earnings; or they hope to see costs per unit of output lowered for the firm so it will be in a better competitive position; or the work itself may not be such that hourly rates are practicable.

Frequent objections are raised by the union to incentive systems: that management is trying to break the "solid front" of the union; that the firm will set unreasonable standards of performance; that the workers, if the flow of materials is interrupted for reasons lying beyond their control, will lose out in terms of pay (this might occur, for example, if a machine were to break, or if delivery of materials were interrupted); that some jobs are not suitable to piece rates. Where the machine sets the pace, or where the contribution of one worker cannot readily be ascertained, incentive systems are difficult to devise.

With respect to relative wage rates within a plant or between crafts and skills, unions prefer to maintain the existing rate pattern. Relative wages are an important determinant of social status. If one group of workers finds that the members of the "poorer" craft or skill are gaining on them, invidious comparisons are made and agitation soon begins for the traditional differential to be maintained. In like manner, the bottom groups do not want to see the favored groups pull still further ahead. As a result, the entire rate structure tends to move in the same direction about the same time. Market forces tend to work to the same end. If one skill-group gets too far out of line, workers may shift their occupations, thus tending to bring the customary wage pattern about through the forces of demand and supply.

Since World War II, wages have been supplemented by a host of fringe benefits for which unions have bargained. This movement started at a time when direct wage increases were severely restricted. These fringe benefits do several things, First, they reallocate the time-stream of the worker's income so that for his work now, he will be compensated later. Paid vacations and retirement benefits are cases in point. Second, some part of the fringe benefits is on an insurance-on-contingency basis so that no one worker will ever be sure he will appropriate the sums representing the time he worked. Unemployment benefits, sickness, and severance pay are examples. Third, fringe benefits represent implicit hourly wage increases, although they are not stated as such. Paid rest and wash-up periods are illustrations. These and other fringe benefits make a real contribution to the level of living and are now an important part of the worker's income. On the other hand, they do sometimes raise the cost of investment, and hence discourage growth. Fringe benefits presently average over 20 per cent of total payroll for all industries across the nation. They thus are a significant element of total cost to the firm.

Several other compensation innovations deserve brief mention. During and shortly after World War II, the guaranteed annual wage proposal elicited much discussion. According to this scheme, the employer would guarantee that specified workers in the firm would receive pay for at least a minimum number of hours per year. In effect, covered hourly rated employees would become "salaried" in a sense. The guaranteed wage proposal never went far in its original form, but the supplementary unemployment benefits (SUB) provisions and increased severance pay are related schemes. The final compensation technique we will mention here is the profit-sharing plan. This not a new idea. Procter and Gamble has had such a plan since the 1920s. More recently, Kaiser Steel Corporation negotiated a profit-sharing (or saving in production costs) plan with the steelworkers.

### Trends in Labor Regulation: Summary

At the present time, discussion of labor legislation seems to be following a reverse pattern from that of the anti-trust laws. The anti-trust laws began with an attempted blanket onslaught upon the mere *fact* of market power. Later development has largely concerned itself with the spelling out of permissible and nonpermissible types of action. Union regulation, on the other hand, since the

Wagner Act, has gone the other way. At first there was a well-nigh blanket endorsement of union power as such. This has been followed by two Acts: the Taft–Hartley and the Landrum–Griffin Acts, which have spelled out nonpermissible actions. But there is increasing discussion of how much power *as such* can be permitted.

Although the labor movement at the present time contains only about one-third of the labor force, and this proportion may have declined slightly in the last few years, this proportion does not, it is said, represent the real force of labor power and the strategic nature of its location. In trucking and in railroads and also in shipping the unions have almost air-tight control. In steel, automobiles, the building trades, and other strategic industries, power is almost equally great. Though the *total* labor share has not changed greatly through the rise of unions, and though the rate of increase of total average real wages has not increased, this tells us little about what individual pressure groups have accomplished. A few examples may be helpful:

Professor John Maurice Clark in Chapter 18 of *Competition as a Dynamic Process* (Brookings Institution, 1961) points out that between 1955 and 1959 productivity in "all manufacturing" rose an average of 9.3%, but wages rose by 20%, output by only 12%, and prices by 10.6%. However, this is an average figure. For the same period productivity in electrical machinery rose not at all, output by 5.4%, wages by *19.5%*, and prices by 20.7%! For iron and steel productivity rose by 11.3%, output by 11.6%, wages by *34.8%*, and prices by 26.5%. For automobiles productivity *declined* by 1.7%, output by 25.1%, but wages and prices *rose* by 17.1%. There can be little doubt, if the student recalls the principle of substitution and relative costs, that we have here one of the main reasons for automation, and also for the high costs that underlie the gold outflow, though for these the "stabilization" of farm prices also plays a major role.

There is a fundamental social issue raised here. We have seen that mobility is a basic quality for the growing society. If the market system is to continue its marvelous productive record it cannot be tampered with too much. But if political power is invoked to control pressure groups it will soon control the whole society. Wages, for example, cannot long be fixed without prices. Next, output has to be manipulated to give a satisfactory total, and so we find ourselves in a generally controlled society. At some point the power issue must be faced. But here we reach a state in our discussion at which the question of alternative economic systems must be discussed. We do this in the next chapter.

# ✦✦✦ XXVIII ✦✦✦

## Comparative Economic Systems

In Chapter I, in defining economics, we pointed out that many economic disputes are not disputes of economic theory at all but disputes over social goals. We have managed to dodge most of these questions of social goals, so far, but now we reach a point at which we must discuss the principal alternative types of social-economic systems advocated in the world today. It must be understood that the question of comparative economic systems involves a far broader range of problems than mere technical economics. Nevertheless, although the technical economist, as such, cannot settle these questions of social philosophy, he has to know about them, since variations of social philosophy greatly affect the type of practical policy and the type of wants which people are trying to implement by their particular economic system. We will divide the topic up into four main heads: First we will discuss Marxism with its many ramifications. As the most comprehensive statement of the anti-capitalist position we will devote most of our space to it. In evaluating Marx one by implication discusses most of the main economic points of the other socialist schools also. Next, we will discuss what is called third-force socialism, or non-communist socialism. The next heading will treat of cooperatives and the back-to-the-land movement—the so-called distributivist movement. Finally, we will mention such topics as indicative planning and controlism, or what the French call *dirigisme*. Under third-force socialism, we will also mention something of the various brands of welfare state.

### Marxism

The first thing to remember about Marxism is that it is not a single coherent body of teaching. There are almost as many kinds of Marxists as there are Christians or Muslims or Hindus, and the differences between various groups can be profound. The Marxist movement, in fact, can be approached in three ways: (1) according to the tactics advocated, (2) according to the political authority which is invoked to manage the social experiment, (3) according to the type of economic teaching which is embodied in the particular group or country. All Marxists claim to take their departure from Karl Marx, but the divergencies are indeed wide. On tactics the principal question is between the notion of democratic evolution on one side or violent revolution on the other. The so-called social democrats, or revisionist Marxists have always been advocates of peaceful democratic evolution rather than revolution. The disciples of Lenin, on the other hand, have taught that violent revolution was at some point inevitable. But this is only the beginning of the differences between the various Marxist groups, and before we go further it may be well to say something about the background of the movement and its founders.

## Karl Marx and Friedrich Engels

Karl Marx was the son of a Jewish official in the Rhineland possessions of Prussia in the early nineteenth century, who was converted to the Christian faith when Karl was about six years old. Marx was raised as a very devout person and never succeeded in completely escaping the influence of his early religious environment. He grew to manhood at a time when German philosophy was enormously influenced by the great philosopher, Hegel; and although Marx eventually repudiated Hegel's teaching, he never really escaped from its influence either.

Marx early became a radical and was compelled to take refuge in England, where he passed the rest of his life. He had earlier formed a friendship with a fellow student named Engels, the son of a rich manufacturer. Engels was an extremely successful businessman, although deeply interested in radical social movements; and he furnished Marx with a great part of his financial support during the rest of his life.

In 1848, at a time of general democratic, capitalist revolution against feudalism, Marx and Engels were among those who sought to give the reform movement a more radical turn. They issued in that year the famous *Communist Manifesto* in which they jointly set forth the principal elements of their teaching. Later, after Marx's death, there came increasing pressure to revise some of the elements of his dogma, and there was particular dissatisfaction with the idea of inevitable revolution. Engels in his old age actually went so far as to say that it might be possible to have a development into Communism without a revolution, though Marx had never been willing to hold out more than a faint possibility that, perhaps, England might become Communist without violence.

## Lenin, Stalin and Co.

The next great figure in the development of Communist thought is Lenin. The Marxist movement has always suffered from a certain ambiguity concerning the question of democracy. Some Marxists talk at times as if their eventual ideal state would be brought about by the voluntary action of the workers themselves. Other Marxists, on occasion, talk as if only leaders could bring about the necessary reconstruction. Lenin was emphatically of the second opinion. He broke entirely with those intellectuals who were laying the foundations for the "social democratic" or peaceful evolutionary type of Marxism. Instead, in *State and Revolution* he set forth a doctrine of rigid dictatorship by a trained elite, and necessary revolution. We will have more to say about this later.

Lenin played his important role in connection with the Russian revolution. Russia had been a very backward nation, both industrially and politically, although a small capitalist sector had made a good start at development. When, at the end of World War I, the Czarist monarchy began to crumble, most Marxists were the so-called "Mensheviks." They felt that the country was not ripe, economically, for true Marxist institutions. They advocated instead a cautious type of evolutionary socialism. Lenin, completely disregarding many of the fundamental teachings of his own system, as we shall see later, advocated immediate revolution; and with the aid of his partner, Trotsky, successfully carried it through.

Lenin found that attempts to usher in immediate total socialism resulted in economic chaos, and accordingly he embarked upon the so-called NEP or New Economic Policy, which was one of limited capitalism. This proved enormously productive and, shortly after Lenin's death, power passed to his disciple, Stalin. Trotsky fled to Mexico where he was eventually murdered. Stalin, on the other hand, decided to begin upon a regime of all-out socialism, on the basis of the capital which had been accumulated during the NEP period. By frightful sacrifices and desperate costs of famine and dislocation, drastic reorganization of Russian life was carried through; and the capital stock in the heavy industries greatly increased. But all this was accompanied by constant terror and purges.

After Stalin's death, power eventually passed into the hands of Khrushchev, who has attempted some relaxation of the iron rules of the Leninist state. In the meantime, however, several national Communisms have arisen. These are nations which claim to be Leninist, but do not accept the final authority of the Kremlin. The most important of these today are China and Yugoslavia, and the political rift has been accompanied by great difference in the application of Leninist teachings in and between the national Communist countries.

In the meantime, in Western Europe, the social democratic or revisionist Marxists continue to have great influence. But in most places Social Democracy has become steadily more conservative. This is especially true of West Germany, where recent statements of social democratic principles have removed all but a mere vestige of Marxist teaching. However, the social democratic movement is always a difficult thing to pin down, and contains many variations and potential reaction toward greater economic radicalism. But let us go on to specific Marxist–Leninist teaching.

## Leninism

In order to avoid becoming lost in a maze of qualifications and sectarian differences, we will concentrate here for a moment upon the pure theory of what might be called classical Leninism. The two books upon which we will draw the most are Marx's *Communist Manifesto* and Lenin's *State and Revolution*. To those who really want to understand the ideas that have fundamentally shaped Russian history during Stalin's regime, there is no substitute for *State and Revolution*. The theory of Leninist Marxism may be described as three-fold. There is the theory, first, of history; second, of economic exploitation and reorganization; and, third, of political salvation. We will begin with the economic theory, pass on to the theory of history, and, finally, consider the theory of political salvation. At the end we will evaluate the theory as a whole. The word "salvation" is used advisedly, for Leninism, as we will see later, is little short of a search for an alleged kingdom of God on earth—without God.

Although we begin now with the economic theory of Marxism, it is very difficult to disentangle any one aspect of Marxian theory from the remainder. In particular, certain philosophical and almost religious aspects of the case are deeply imbedded in the analysis, and perhaps it will be as well to explain the manner in which Marx's economic thought evolved. Strangely enough, he begins with some of the evangelical Christian writings of the philosopher Hegel.

## Religious Roots of Marxism

Hegel, using German Lutheran terminology, had spoken in terms of a triad of conflicting values. These were called "alienation," "objectification," and "coming to one's own." Alienation, in the language of German theology, meant the feeling of being estranged and condemned by God's moral code so that the sinner felt that he was lost in hopeless condemnation. Objectification meant that the law, the moral code, stood over against the sinner in separate and complete condemnation. Coming to one's own, again using the language of German theology, meant that through faith in Christ the sinner was reconciled to God. In terms of the Epistle to the Ephesians 2:14 it might be said, "For he is our peace, who has made us both one." Such religious language may seem remote from Marx, the eventual atheist. Yet it is from these classifications that he first took his departure. But Marx reduces them to extremely down-to-earth economic terms. Alienation, instead of meaning the feeling of loneliness of the soul, becomes the frustration of the workman who is condemned to work to supply the demands of the market rather than occupying himself, artistically, doing the thing which he loves. It might be pointed out that this alienation is not necessarily a function just of capitalism; it is rather a product of the division of labor. Marx feels that the truly free man is free to work on whatever task he chooses, and is not obliged to pick a type of labor needed to meet the requirements of the market. This romantic view of the productive process, Marx never wholly abandoned.

It has therefore been pointed out by several writers that the real evil in this analysis is not capitalism. For any society in which people concentrate on a particular skill, demanded by the market as a whole, rather than laboring artistically on what they choose, is a society in which men are alienated, if we follow Marx's analysis. But, to continue, Marx feels that the alienated workman comes to see the market in which his goods are exchanged as if it were an objective fact created by natural law. Marx calls this attitude, among many other uncomplimentary names, "commodity fetishism." Those economists who spend "all" their time studying exchange relationships in the market, so Marx says, are "commodity fetishists," for they treat the market, which should be regarded merely as a convenience, as if it were some eternal decree of the Almighty. And Marx regards this attitude toward the market as "objectification."

The next aspect of Marx's analysis is to reduce "coming into one's own" to economic terms. He holds that society comes into its own when the people are no longer content to be "subordinated" to the market, but instead seize it and twist it to their own uses. Marx hoped by the "productivity of planning" to create a society so rich that labor would once more not be a necessity but a pleasure and a privilege. People would work not because they had to but because they loved working. In one of his more eloquent early passages he speaks of the people who will hunt in the morning, fish in the afternoon, breed cattle in the evening, and criticize literature after dinner. The American, working at hobbies on his long weekend, may thus be considered a *capitalist* version of Marx's goal. But Marx seems sometimes to have in mind an eternal weekend! However, he gradually switched emphasis from alienation to a more specific economic analysis—exploitation.

**Exploitation**

It will be pointed out later, from the foregoing analysis, that had Marx followed his line of thought logically, he would have wound up by condemning economic growth, industrialism, and the principle of market exchange. For all these demand some conformity to market needs and changes in needs, rather than personal impulses of workmanship. But, instead, Marx switched to a quite different analysis. Whereas the alienation–objectification concept dealt with the conflict between the individual instinct of workmanship and the demands of the market (a conflict which we analyzed at length in Chapter II, and which we will return to later) the exploitation classification deals with the conflict of two allegedly irreconcilable social classes—the bourgeois and the proletariat—usually, though not quite accurately, equated with the notion of the rich and the poor. But before discussing these classes and Marx's idea of the class struggle, let us summarize the theory of exploitation.

### Labor versus Labor Power

In terms of Marxian analysis all economic value is created by the number of hours of socially necessary labor time embodied in the commodity produced. Machinery cannot, he says, create any more "value" than goes into making it. He regards machinery as so much "canned labor," or as like a cake of ice which in melting gives off no more water than went into freezing it. But at this point one encounters a basic distinction.

Marx's whole exploitation analysis rests on the distinction between "labor" and "labor power." By "labor" he means the actual day's work, or hour of work done. By "labor power" he means the *capacity to be worked*. When a man works an hour, he has produced an hour's labor, but when a man hires himself to *be* worked, then he is selling his labor power. Now, says Marx, labor power is a commodity as much as anything else and what is its economic value? Its value, according to Marx, is determined by the same laws which determine the value of everything else; namely, the number of hours of socially necessary labor time needed to produce it. In more concrete terms this means the number of hours needed to support the workman and reproduce him; that is, raise his family. And Marxian analysis usually equates this with a "subsistence" wage, or the "iron law" of wages.

In other words, Marx feels that the laborer in hiring himself out by the day or week is selling his commodity—labor power—and this commodity labor power is paid for by the same market laws as determine everything else, namely, the number of hours of labor needed to produce it. In other words, the laborer receives for his labor power that minimum value which serves to support him and his family—the subsistence wage. We are here of course cutting through a great fog of elaborate terminology.

### The Source of Exploitation

But at this point, says Marx, we encounter a special problem. Although the employer may pay the worker the true market value of his work, that is to say the subsistence wage, or the value of the number of hours needed to produce the worker and reproduce him, the employer can nevertheless work the employee a *longer* number of hours than those whose value he has paid over to the worker. Let us put the matter a little more concretely. Suppose the worker is working an eight-hour day, suppose that after five hours he has produced enough, in value, to pay his daily wage. But he does not stop working at this point. Instead, he goes on and works for three more hours. Part of this three hours will go for depreciation. That is, it will offset the wearing out of the machinery with which the laborer is working. But the remainder (let us say it is two and one half hours) will go to the benefit of the owner of the factory. It is these hours which are not needed to replace machinery or to pay the laborer's wage which the Marxist calls surplus value, or exploitation. Marx regards them as the source, in the aggregate, of all profit, and he considers the scramble for surplus value, or profit as the ultimate source of all social conflict and dislocation.

### The Economic Theory of Crisis: "The Industrial Reserve Army"

Now we must ask a question: Why does not the process of competition bring wages up (in the way we described in this book) and, furthermore, gradually eliminate all profit? Marx, it is true, admitted that competition would not eliminate "rent" for the reasons we have given in Chapters IX and X. But he thought that the state might seize the rents and redistribute them through some species of national dividend, or otherwise handle the problems through price control. What really concerned him was the question of profit. Why would wages remain at subsistence, as he mistakenly supposed they would. Why would not profit disappear?

Marx might have taken refuge in a usual Malthusian idea of population growth, but that would have made the laborers, or proletariat responsible for their own condition, and he repudiated Malthus' ideas as a libel on the human race. Marx, further, had noticed that there did seem to be a connection between profits and technical change. But he could not give this insight a favorable interpretation if he wished to retain his generally hostile attitude toward the capitalist system. Instead he worked out a theory which he called "the industrial reserve army." Technical change, he said, is introduced not to raise efficiency, but to create unemployment! By creating unemployment the bargaining power of labor is weakened and wages fall. The fall in wages creates higher profits or, in terms of Keynesian analysis, a greater marginal efficiency of capital. Investment starts up once more and a boom begins. As the boom continues the economy gets nearer and nearer full employment, labor becomes scarce, and wages rise. Profits, "therefore," he mistakenly says, *must* begin to fall, and with falling profit we have another crisis and more unemployment. In other words, technical change creates unemployment, which creates low wages, which in turn creates high profits, which starts a boom, which causes high wages, which makes profits low, which causes a slump, and so on indefinitely. It will be seen that this entire analysis rests on the idea that high wages must inevitably mean low profit—a point we have seen to be untrue. But before going into detail, let us seek an over-all picture by discussing the Marxian theory of history.

## The Marxist Theory of History

In dealing with Marx, as distinguished from Lenin, we are dealing with a man whose mind is broader than his own system. That is to say that Marx from time to time could not help seeing and noticing exceptions to his own idea. Somewhere in Marx's voluminous writings one will find qualifications and admissions concerning almost everything that he taught. But the "cutting edge," as it were, of his doctrine lies in the black-and-white simplicity of much of it, and we will give here the basic Marxist teaching as it usually appears in propaganda writings all over the world. The Marxist theory of history is a particularly interesting example of cut-and-dried reasoning. Marx, in his more unguarded moments, holds that history is entirely determined by economics, and economics is entirely determined by technology. "Your very ideas," he exclaims in the *Manifesto,* "are but the outgrowth of the conditions of your bourgeois production and your bourgeois property." Thus, according to the mainstream of Marx's teaching, stated as simply as possible, productive methods determine social systems and social systems determine culture and ideas. As one person has put it, to Marx feudalism is the hand mill, and capitalism is the power mill. The individual is essentially shaped by his society and society by production methods. When methods of production change, society changes, and when society changes, Marx says, people change. But there is one vital question, we will find, which the Marxist does not ask: that question is, Why do methods of production change? We will come back to this question and we will see that sometimes social systems cause changes in method, not the other way round. But what we are interested in here is the Marxist theory of history and of the decline of capitalism. Marx holds that as society becomes richer— capitalist society, that is—and the quantity of capital relative to labor becomes greater, the profit rate must necessarily fall as the capitalists compete with one another for the scarce labor supply. We have already sketched the basis of this analysis in the sections on "exploitation" and "the industrial reserve army." It is important to remember that he does not feel that profits, in the aggregate, can be made from anything except the working of human beings;

that is, working living labor, and paying it a subsistence wage while pocketing the remainder of the output.

But now comes his theory of history and of capitalist revolution. As society gets richer, and the rate of profit consequently falls, crises will get worse and worse. Finally the people will be forced into such misery that there will be a violent revolution and the "dictatorship of the proletariat will ensue." Once this occurs society will move toward the ideal Utopia. But let us now criticize the basic historical idea.

### The Marxist Theory of History Criticized

The first thing to realize about the Communist theory of history and "economic determinism" is that it has not worked, even on its own terms. From our account you will see that Marx expected a revolution to occur in those countries which were highly developed. The more the stock of capital increased, and the more the rate of profit fell, the greater, he said, the increasing misery of the workers, and this was expected to produce more or less automatically the eventual revolution. Had this theory been correct the United States today would be the citadel of Communism and Russia and China would be the citadels of capitalism. For clearly Marx intended Communism as the answer to the contradictions of a developed capitalism, and not as a means of developing society. The revolution should have broken out in New York, and not in Moscow or Peking. The Russian Mensheviks were thus better Marxists than Lenin, but Lenin, nevertheless, ranks among those outstanding figures in history who, by sheer will power, have, for good or ill, changed the course of history. In the language of the Victorians, he was a "hero." This epithet need not mean anything complimentary. It is only the designation used by the Victorian Thomas Carlyle, for those outstanding figures who greatly influenced the development of history. But as a "hero," using the word in Carlyle's terms, Lenin's figure is an outstanding contradiction of the whole philosophy for which he stood. For he lived a life of voluntary action far *ahead* of any of the economic trends of his country, far beyond the demands of any necessity of economic determinism.

We thus have a first-class, factual refutation of the Marxist theory of history drawn from the history of Marxism. Economic relationships do affect history, but so does character, and so do ideas. The Communists have covered reams of paper with attempts to explain away this glaring contradiction but the fact remains that Marx, the infallible prophet, was wrong about the future of his own movement.

Similar mechanical weakness is found in the theory of surplus value, exploitation, and the business cycle. The whole weakness of his position lies in the assumption that capital is only canned labor and that surplus value can be created only by the employment of living labor. The basic failure of the theory lies in Marx's unwillingness to realize the productive power of the individual idea. In a developing capitalism, we have seen earlier in this book, a newly produced capital instrument is usually not just canned labor, but the vehicle for expressing a new technical idea, and the idea itself, may be so productive that it can at one and the same time raise the incomes of both capital and labor. Thus wages have not remained "subsistence," nor is unemployment necessary for the existence of profit. All that *is* necessary is mobility and enterprise. A people must be willing to allow the new ideas to be adopted, and this means constant disturbance of the noneconomic dimensions of life, but it does not mean lower wages.

There is a curious arithmetical error here. Marx only noticed that the value of the capital stock, relative to the number of *workers,* was rising, and he supposed the rate of surplus value—the proportion of wage to nonwage income—would remain the same. But he further assumed that wages could not rise. However, if we allow the productivity of the new idea plus investment to raise total income, and it is shared in a constant proportion, then labor gets a constantly *rising* wage, a constant share of a growing total, and this corresponds pretty closely to what the actual statistical trends show. Furthermore, while the total *absolute* value of the capital stock rises, the statistics show a long-run tendency for the average capital-output ratio in value terms to remain fairly steady, on average, at about 3 to 1. The result is that the ratio of total nonwage income to the capital stock, in value terms, remains the *same* on average. There is no falling rate of profit. Some businesses are losing out, and others are making abnormal profits, but the average total value relations remain unchanged. Marx was subconsciously relating the number of *men* to the value of the capital stock, and he assumed labor's wage to be unchanged. But he should have compared the value of the total capital stock to the value of a rising labor income and, had he done so, he would have found no necessary fall in the profit rate, even on his own terms. In missing the possible increases in productivity from new ideas, he missed the essence of the problem. However, in realizing once more the importance of change, we are at this point in a position to describe the Marxist claim to political salvation, Utopia, and the "withered state." An evaluation requires a return to the idea of the "class struggle" and of "bourgeois" versus "proletariat."

## Bourgeois versus Proletariat

By "bourgeois" and "proletariat" Marx means, in the strict technical meaning of his language, people, on the one hand, who live on the proceeds of machinery and equipment; that is to say, who derive their income from surplus value; and people, on the other hand, who live by the sale of their labor power. The *bourgeoisie,* to Marx, are the people who live by the ownership and control of industry. The proletariat are the people who live by selling their labor power. And Marx, in some of his more unguarded expressions, attributes not just some but all social conflict to the eternal conflict of *bourgeoisie* and proletariat for the share of total output. It must be pointed out, however, that his classification contains a number of ambiguities. In the first place, most people think of the bourgeois as the rich and the proletariat as the poor but in strict Marxist terminology this is not correct. The retired schoolteacher, living on invested earnings, may be very poor but he would nevertheless, in strict terminology, be a bourgeois, for he lives through the ownership and benefits of property. On the other hand, the vice president of some great industrial corporation with an income of $300,000 a year, who, by some accident has not bothered to accumulate any private fortune or capital, would be, strictly speaking, a proletarian—for his entire income would be derived from the sale of his labor power. He is a salaried worker albeit a tremendously well-paid one. Thus the classification of bourgeois and proletarian, in strict Marxist technical language, is not the same thing as the classification of rich and poor. Nevertheless, for ordinary purposes of propaganda, most Marxists use the two ideas interchangeably and speak as if a bourgeois were necessarily wealthy and a proletarian were necessarily poor. But now let us consider the "class struggle" and the "withered state" concepts.

**The Theory of Political Salvation and the "Withering Away of the State"**

We said earlier that the basic notion of Marxism, particularly Leninist Marxism, is an attempt to achieve the kingdom of God on earth without any God. By kingdom of God on earth is meant the type of rule of absolute righteousness, lack of conflict, and justice referred to in the Old Testament, particularly in the promise of the new covenant: "Behold the days are coming, says the Lord, when I will make a new covenant with the house of Israel . . . , not like the covenant which I made with their fathers. . . . I will put my law *within them,* and I will write it upon their hearts. . . . And no longer shall each man teach his neighbor and each his brother, saying 'Know the Lord', for they shall all know me from the least of them to the greatest" (Jer. 31: 31–34, RSV; italics added). This passage may be compared with a passage from Marx quoted in Lenin's *State and Revolution* in which he says there will eventually come a new generation who will obey the requirements of civilized life "without force and without compulsion."

But how are we to reach the reign of absolute righteousness in which the lion will lie down with the lamb, and, as Marx puts it, the state will "wither away"? To understand we must know why Marx thinks the world at present is evil. We saw earlier that Marx in the notion of alienation seemed to put the blame on the forces which made a man work for the market rather than for his own pleasure. But we also saw that instead of following out this line Marx increasingly emphasized the notion of exploitation, and the conflict of bourgeois and proletarian. In the mature Marxist teaching, the source of evil becomes not so much alienation as the fight between the two great single classes of bourgeois and proletariat over the share of social output which they will receive. We have seen that Marx thought that this would "inevitably" lead to revolution and the "dictatorship of the proletariat." But what happens then?

## The Dictatorship of the Proletariat

It is true that Marx supposed that with the abolition of private property, or "socializing of the means of production," the basic drive toward evil and conflict would be eliminated. But one must not be so naïve as to suppose that the dictatorship of the proletariat, in Communist language, has anything to do with self-government by the actual worker. On the contrary, the dictatorship of the proletariat means the rule *of* the proletariat by a certain indoctrinated elite, the members of the Communist Party. Party members, by their special wisdom, are supposed to know what should be done. They seize power in order to administer the economy for the *"benefit"* of the proletariat—something very different from rule by the proletariat. As Lord Lindsay of Birker has put it, "discussion for us is very different from discussion by us." It is true that the basic source of all evil as set forth in Lenin's *State and Revolution* is the competition of bourgeois and proletariat, for income, in a regime of competitive private property. And it is true that, to the Leninist, when a revolution ends the competitive system, this is, in effect, like pulling the infected tooth.

But just as a doctor, after the infected tooth has been pulled, may treat the rheumatic patient to a course of purges and hot baths in order to get the remaining "poison" out of his system, so it is felt, in Leninist terms, that society must, as it were, be put into trusteeship after the revolution. For there will be left over from the evils of capitalism any number of "bad" ideas and attitudes. Society must be sweated to remove evil from it. The dictatorship of the proletariat is regarded (most truly) as a sort of purgatory to which society is submitted in order to achieve a state of righteousness. Let us describe this in more detail.

Russia does not today claim to be a "Communist" country in their technical meaning of the term. Neither does China nor Yugoslavia nor any existing Communist nation. All of these countries are treated by themselves as being in what is called the "socialist" phase. That is to say, they are considered by themselves to be in the interim condition of trusteeship or social purgatory by which they are being cleansed of the evil left over from capitalism. On the one hand, economic development is going forward and, on the other, society is being conditioned into an "eventual" state of complete justice and righteousness. But the goal has not been reached—yet!

## The Leninist View of Human Nature

The Leninist view of human nature is that a man is shaped by his surroundings as a medal is struck from a mold. If you want to get a good man, put him in good surroundings and vice versa. The idea is that if people have never heard evil (by evil is meant whatever the ruling group thinks is evil) and if the basic source of temptation, which is private property, is eliminated, then there will come a point at which they will forget that evil is possible. People will be so conditioned, or so brainwashed, if one wishes to put it in an unfriendly way, that it will no longer be possible for them to think of anything different from what the good society requires. Up to this point compulsion will have to be used, for only by careful social censorship can this state of innocence be achieved. But it is supposed that after so long a time the great work of social conditioning will be completed. The new generation spoken of by Lenin will have been reached and at that point it will no longer be necessary to use any violence or compulsion. Everybody will know the law. In the words of the Old Testament, it will be "written on their hearts" and everyone will follow the conditions of civilized life without force and without subjection. Parallel to this state of complete righteousness the economy will become so wealthy that people will no longer have to work to suit the market. In terms of a recent American writer, they will "be released from the thraldom of productive efficiency" and labor will no longer be a disagreeable necessity but a pleasant privilege. Such is the idea of the eventual withered state. But, before becoming enthralled with such an alluring prospect, two questions must be asked: (1) Can one ever reach a withered state, and (2) How do the Communists attempt to find it?

## Can a "State" Ever Wither Away?

We come now to one of the most important questions of all political theory: Can society ever exist without a state? By "state" is meant, in Communist literature, not the ordinary apparatus of government, but the apparatus of "coercion" and "suppression." They object not to the post office, but to police, courts, sheriffs, and armies. The aim is a society in which men are good spontaneously "without force and without compulsion." In other words there will be no conflicts which courts, police, or armies will have to suppress.

There are two fundamental ways, however, to obtain a conflict-free state (remember that they are not aiming for a society in which men are merely afraid to fight, but for one in which nobody *wants* to fight, or has to use force). One way to avoid conflict is to have everybody in agreement on everything. The other way is to have them agree to disagree. If I do not care what my neighbor does, as long as he leaves me alone, and vice versa, we can get along quite happily, though with the most wildly different ideas. Or if we have the same ideas we can get along. Trouble begins, however, when he feels that I *ought* to have his ideas, even when I do not want to have them, and starts trying to force me to share his convictions.

It is fundamental in American constitutional literature that men have a "propensity to disagree." As Alexander Pope, the English poet, put it:

> Tis with our judgments as our watches, none
> Goes just alike, but each believes his own.

In other words we assume that men of good will and equal education and information will still disagree. Accordingly, the "limited" or "liberal" state seeks to obtain, or approximate, peace by keeping the area of enforced unanimity as small as possible. But the Russian approach is different. Leninism believes that by "socializing the means of production" and by social conditioning, people can be shaped to be spontaneously unanimous on all important points all the time. All men of good will and equal information will reach the same conclusion.

The Leninist believes that disagreement and conflict are based solely, in the last analysis, on conflict over shares of economic income. "When, in the course of development, class distinctions [bourgeois and proletariat] have disappeared, the public power will lose its political character. . . . the free development of each will become the condition for the free development of all." But we saw in Chapter II of this book how many possible sources of conflict can survive even in a society in which everybody has equal money income and all industry is owned by the state. Furthermore, the problem of conflict far transcends the question of selfish egotism of any type. All the football team wants the team to win—but they can still come to blows as to whether or not to buck center or throw a forward pass. The true, ultimate source of conflict is a difference of opinion backed up by deep emotion. And one source of deep emotion may be a passionate, unselfish desire to see the right idea prevail!

But cannot men be conditioned into unanimity? Never completely. Why not? Because the human personality is never a completely closed system, limited in its thoughts to what it has heard or experienced. The mind has a creative character and its creations vary from person to person. We will see how this works scientifically in discussing the theory of invention, but its repercussions on political theory are evident: "Compulsory unanimity of opinion achieves only the unanimity of the graveyard" as Mr. Justice Jackson once put it. There will always be a dissenting minority which the monolithic state must suppress. And even the liberal state cannot tolerate indefinite and complete disobedience. The ultimate tragedy is the need to coerce the "altruistic" dissenter. At some point he must be lifted off the rails that the trains may run— however "altruistic" his motive for demonstration. The conclusion is that the "state," in its Marxist meaning, can never wholly wither away under any system. A minimum of coercion always survives. This point is particularly important when we attempt a final evaluation of Leninist theory and of the long-run growth prospects of Russia.

### Final Evaluation of Leninism

Much is said today about the growth of Russia, although it must be realized that the capitalist economies of West Germany, Japan, and Italy have grown faster. But when we attempt to evaluate the long-run prospects for Russian growth we come up against the fundamental weakness of the whole Marxist-Leninist idea. It should be evident from Chapter II, that, over the long run, the nation will grow fastest which both has the most active flow of new productive ideas, *and* succeeds in implementing them most promptly.

We asked earlier about the means to be used by the Leninist to arrive at his supposed withered state. This involves an understanding of what the Leninist calls the "socialist phase." The socialist phase is that period of social purgatory and sweating we described earlier. It is important to realize that during the socialist phase "anything goes." Leninism promises eventual tolerance and equality, but only some day. During the socialist phase there is a more or less rigid conditioning and only minor criticism is permitted. Leninism often means, in practice, slavery today in the name of "freedom" tomorrow. The one thing the system finds hardest to handle, in practice, is differences of opinion, for all men of good will are supposed to come, if they have the facts, to the same opinion. In short a Leninist state in its socialist phase is, even in its own theory, an unmitigated despotism. What does this mean for growth?

Despotism, in the short run and on subordinate issues, has many advantages mechanically speaking, as far as growth goes. Authority can quickly settle the pressure-group problem. Any labor leader in Russia attempting one-twentieth of the obstruction habitually used in the United States, would be shot. But though authority, when it is efficient, can quell all subordinate pressure groups it cannot quell or police itself. Continued development requires a flow of really new ideas. Authority can put resources at the disposal of men, but it cannot put elasticity into men's minds. We are obliged here to take a short detour into the theory of scientific discovery.

## The Theory of Scientific Discovery

Many people feel that scientific discovery is simply a matter of accumulating "facts." Pile one fact upon another fact and eventually you have a new "law." Marxist writings incline toward this view. The attempt is to portray discovery as largely a routine, mechanical process. More money for facts equals more new laws. Unfortunately life is not that simple. The step omitted is the operation of the brain in deciding what facts to look for. Without individual brains capable of constructing, in advance, productive, new hypothetical models of how the world works, in the case under study, mere facts will not lead to much. Facts are useful (1) in suggesting models to the creative mind, and (2) in checking the hypothetical model to see if it is true. But the individual brain still counts. And brains differ.

We have seen that the basic assumption of the Marxist is that human nature is shaped by society and that the human mind is the outgrowth of the social relations around it. Such a view goes back to the seventeenth-century idea of the human mind as a mere blackboard or *tabula rasa* on which experience writes character. But the human mind is much more than a passive blackboard. It is a sort of computer or problem-solver complicated by emotional blocks and urges. The mind, though varying tremendously in power, from man to man, does not passively receive experience but instead meditates upon it and tries to work out explanations by constructing "models" or theories. Science shows us that embedded in reality are an apparently limitless number of hidden causal connections. These connections exist "objectively"—we do not just make them up—but they do not manifest themselves automatically. They are what the great philosopher Alfred North Whitehead calls "eternal objects." We need mean here only such things as the binomial theorem and other mathematical relationships. Implicit in any given happening is an apparently boundless number of these causal connections, and the mind in its computer or model-building aspect can formulate numerous models of how these causal connections are embodied in what is actually occurring. Through these models genuinely new ideas appear in the world. It is true that the social surroundings often shape the type of ideas and help to determine what situations appeal to the mind for thought. But the mind goes far beyond such limitations and in the hands of persons of strong and logical imagination it can reach far beyond the limitations of its own time. Such minds must be tolerated if invention is to occur. But here is a fundamental problem for the Leninist state. Once you start men thinking you cannot guarantee that they will always think your way! Since most men have in some degree this power of making contact with latent pattern inherent in the logic of the universe, and since brains and temperaments differ, we have the explanation of the American constitutional doctrine of the propensity of men to disagree. A society which believes in "agreement to disagree" as the approach to relative peace can adjust to differences of opinion within a wide range, but a society which believes in conditioned uniformity cannot. In this point we find the basic weakness of Leninist-Marxism.

It is submitted that history indicates that over time the centralized despotism does not grow. This is called the law of decay of self-perpetuating, non-competitive groups. Dictatorial development comes to be increasingly "one formula" development, a given set of scientific preconceptions is imposed throughout the system and those who disagree are not promoted. The Marxian philosophy reinforces this rule by the built-in idea of imposed uniformity. Many Communists of the Russian variety genuinely wish to escape from terror, or so we are told. But the fact is that, as society develops, and men are allowed more freedom they will, necessarily, develop deviant ideas, and these will lead to conflicts of authority. In a state to which a conflict of opinion is, past a certain point, anathema, and conflicts of authority are not permitted, suppression must be invoked. This suppression has not merely a political but also an economic aspect. The conflict may be over the best way to do something, the best scientific rules for example. Russia today is a continuation of Czarist despotism with one great difference. That difference is the attempt to educate the masses. But it is a difference which may well destroy the whole experiment. For as people are taught to think, especially as they are taught to think scientifically, they will inevitably form differing opinions and want to experiment with different possibilities. It is submitted that either the scientific development of Russia will blow up the mechanism of the Leninist state or the Leninist state will end scientific development. The two, over the long pull, are not compatible.

### Non-Marxist Socialism and the Welfare State

We have seen that over the long pull Leninism is likely to perish from its own narrowness. But what of non-Leninist socialisms? In its modern development Marxist social democracy has become more and more assimilated with non-Marxist socialism and, indeed, with many reform movements. We may therefore go on to discuss non-Marxist socialism since it presents the most definite alternative pattern.

Non-Marxist socialism as distinguished from mere "planification" represents a revolt against the necessities of the Industrial Revolution. It tends toward the "alienation" side of Marx's thought, but with an emphasis on a static instinct of workmanship. As we saw in the chapter on labor the aim is equality of income, intimacy, "democracy" of corporate management, and general security. History has not borne out the conviction of the English socialists that nationalization plus equal money income would bring about general good feeling, reduction of caste barriers, removal of strikes and pressure groups, and more rapid development. On the contrary, there have been as many strikes under socialist government as under capitalist government, and caste barriers are not notably affected.

But the great weakness of a non-Marxist socialist is that it calls for tremendous outlay in the form of pension and other welfare services while at the same time largely hamstringing economic development through the refusal of individual pressure groups to yield to the public welfare. The slogan of security and intimacy serves to underwrite continued adherence to obsolete methods, and greatly to retard the rate of industrial progress. At the same time the removal of inequality of income cuts down on the rate of voluntary saving, while the consumption outlays fostered by welfare expenditure rise rapidly. The result is tremendous pressure toward inflation and this has not been lacking in the non-Communist socialist states. To check the inflation, controls of various sorts are invoked which in turn increase the industrial rigidity. In a celebrated editorial the *London Economist* summed up the problem in its famous parable of the carrot and the stick. In order to achieve output the workman needs two things—the carrot of reward and the stick of loss. Under capitalism the carrot is profit or promotion and the stick is demotion and loss. Under communism the carrot is income rewards, plus titles, and the stick is exile and possible death. But, says the *Economist,* third-force socialism has neither the carrot nor the stick. For differential rewards are cut down very far, and, on the other hand, all the penalties of striking and poor workmanship are largely eliminated through the universal security of the welfare state. Thus the short-run performance of non-Communist socialism is far less than that of either capitalism or communism, namely, the lack of independent opportunity.

Far more logical, therefore, than the non-Communist socialists are those who explicitly oppose the industrial revolution. This school is mostly lumped under the name of "Distributivist" and it has many adherents in Catholic countries particularly. The trouble, however, with abolishing technical change is the population problem. Since it is the inventor and investor who, by keeping ahead of the "stork," have prevented the emergence of Malthus' problem in the West, to stop the inventor is to invite famine. In addition to the Malthusian problem, is the problem of creativity. Where all social relationships are fixed in the name of intimacy and security, there cannot be any large-scale manifestation of creativity. There might still be such special cases as miniature painting or fine handwriting, for example, which do not disturb the general social technical picture, but no major change in science. But to those who believe in the creative development, which the West has so far shown, such a society of Chinese immobility would be stultifying.

Finally, there has been a vogue, in Europe particularly, of what may be called "indicative planning," and of the Beveridge-type control of social organization. Here the idea is not to abolish private property but merely to direct it. The individual manufacturer is still allowed to call his plant his own, and to pay taxes on it, and to have a certain amount of authority within the plant. But the general direction of his output, his prices, and so forth, are set by the state. In indicative planning this setting is ostensibly not compulsive. However, the state is in possession of so many potential weapons, and can bring so many indirect pressures against the noncooperative producer that very few people would have the courage to oppose the "indicated" plan. In the Beveridge-type society, the controls are explicit and potentially very severe. Both societies suffer from the same fundamental weakness. There is no adequate independent social opportunity, or social mobility, over the long run. For since the central control decides what shall be produced, it also decides who shall hold power and what ideas shall be adopted. The frontier of independent change and the independent mobility which have been the leading characteristics of the capitalist state are lacking.

In this chapter we have summarized some of the major conflicts of value in modern society. It is necessary to make such a summary before attempting a final discussion of economic policy. We have now reached a point in which we may go ahead to a final policy discussion.

# Concluding Outlines of Economic Stabilization and Economic Policy

We end our survey of economics by drawing our threads together, and discussing the general outline of economic policy as modern economic analysis would set it. We first review the problem of stabilization purely technically, but we will soon find that technical analysis cannot carry us very far without a discussion of social conditions and social values. Accordingly, in the second half of the chapter we will summarize those alternative social standards among which an intelligent policy must somehow choose if it is not to be self-defeating. Economic analysis cannot, as such, make the choices for us. But it can show that the choices must be made.

## A First, Technical Summary of the Problem

The main points in the problem of economic stability have been stated repeatedly in this book, but it will help to sum them up once more. Growth, we have seen, comes through change and causes change. As output expands, the pattern of wants constantly changes, and also the pattern of production. Over the long run consumption seems to parallel output, more or less smoothly, and there is some evidence to show a long-run stability in the relationship between the stock of equipment and the level of output. Thus the economy need never reach complete saturation, and, barring the intervention of special social attitudes and forces, new frontiers of investment and consumption keep opening out. But all these comfortable relationships are long-run affairs. In the short run things are not nearly so neat. Even if the total of consumption and investment were rising smoothly, there still would be disturbing changes *within* the total. And even if we keep our minds on aggregate output alone, and forget about the problems of individual groups, there still is no particular reason, in the short run, to expect the total of individual changes *always* to add up to a smooth, steady growth. Sometimes the totals of expansion and change do not absorb the full flow of current planned saving, and then a slump begins. Sometimes the totals call for more than full employment, and then we are likely to have an inflation.

The question for this chapter is: What do we do about these instabilities? First, we will state briefly the nature of the problem, both for inflation and for unemployment. Then we will review the various control methods that can be used in each case.

## Depression

The best way to summarize the depression problem is to say that a depression begins when some important industry or industries slow down expansion or even cease to expand, without offsetting growth elsewhere. The *effect* of this stoppage in expansion is to create a net drop in income payments, which in turn will probably be multiplied into a more general decline of both payments and employment.

Crises of this sort can arise for a tremendous number of reasons. Short-run consumption may be lagging, or an industry may simply have caught up with its backlog or frontlog, and new lines are not being expanded fast enough. The social atmosphere via taxes and other controls may have become so hostile that sufficient private investment will not be forthcoming. Money wages may have been forced up too fast—or they may have lagged too far, producing a consumption lag. The international demand for the products of one of a country's major industries may have suddenly fallen off. Too generous a credit policy may have permitted such a rapid rate of expansion, plus inflation, that costs have got out of line with the long-range expectations which initiated the boom. The banks may run out of reserves. A speculative bubble may burst. These are some of the *possible* sources of a collapse. But the social process has a tremendous variety—and the chances are that a complete catalogue can never be made.

## Inflation

Inflation comes when an important part of the community is trying to buy more than can be produced and has somehow got hold of the necessary funds to bid up prices. The excess purchasing power can come from increased bank lending, changes in velocity or "dishoarding," government printing press operations, and wild-eyed private credit extension—a great increase in installment buying, for example.

The feeling of *scarcity* which usually underlies and induces the monetary disorganization may be due to war, government extravagance, accumulated backlogs or frontlogs, excessive money wage increases (if reinforced by monetary expansion), sudden inflows of credit from abroad due to an export boom, and attempts to industrialize too rapidly. But again, we are never likely to have a complete catalogue of all possible reasons. Let us now see what can be done about both depression and inflation.

### Anti-Depression Weapons: General Advance Direction of Growth

One anti-depression weapon would be trying to make sure *in advance* that depressions would never happen, by ensuring that the total of industrial changes could always be guaranteed *in advance* to match up. This is essentially the plan advocated by Lord Beveridge in *Full Employment in a Free Society,* and largely followed in a United Nations Economic and Social Council (ECOSOC) report on unemployment. The method consists of setting up a board to forecast and license all important change. Industry need not be nationalized, but all important projects for expansion and change would have to be cleared through the planning authority. This planning authority would draw up, in advance, an investment and consumption budget, and might be given authority to start some projects of its own in case the number of spontaneous applications seemed insufficient—though anyone familiar with politics is not likely to be worried about the dangers of too few requests.

The main objections to the Beveridge and ECOSOC proposals are: First, the immense concentration of political power that is implied, and second, the tendency toward rigidity. We have seen that change can never be completely foreseen and that the unexpected is always likely to happen. The central planning group, no matter how high-minded, would inevitably be tempted to greater and greater extensions of its control of expansion, merely to prevent unforeseen disturbances. Add to this the actions of rival pressure groups seeking to protect their special routines, plus simple mistakes and delay, and it will easily be seen what an immense force for stagnation the system could become. The effects would be particularly serious on international trade, for each security-conscious country would try to reduce external shocks to a minimum. This usually would lead to a reduction in international trade and to intense control of what survived. We will come back to these points in the final section.

For the reasons just given, we will not here further develop the Beveridge-type plans even in their "indicative" version. Our aim will not be to show how to plan economic life in advance, but rather to discuss methods of stabilizing, within reason, a system that is spontaneously expanding under highly competitive conditions.

### Stimulating Consumption

Because a drop in purchasing power or in consumption is the first thing about a depression that the general public is likely to feel, a great many people are inclined to think that the stimulation of consumption is the first and, indeed, the only policy to use in overcoming unemployment. But employment is determined by *both* the inducement to invest and the propensity to consume, nor are the two mechanically related. There is, therefore, just as good reason for stimulating one as the other. Thus, though we begin now with a list of weapons to stimulate consumption, we will also consider the stimulation of investment.

The first method of stimulating consumption, and the one that is likely to happen in any case, is the incurring of government deficits. In earlier chapters we showed what a great influence government had on the flow of credit and the money supply. When government fails to cover its current expenses by taxes, the difference is usually made up by borrowing from the banks, and if (as will probably be the case once a depression has started) the banks are not lent up to the full amount permitted by reserve requirements, the government borrowing operates as a net creation of new bank deposits in the hands of those who are paid by, or sell to, the government.

What usually happens is that tax revenues fall off as depression spreads, and even though government may not increase its spending, or may even cut it, a net deficit is nevertheless likely to appear. But sometimes a government which wishes to stimulate consumption will act more directly. Taxes, especially sales taxes and other taxes on consumption goods, may be reduced while expenditure is maintained or expanded. In that case the deficit increases faster (and with it the rise in deposits that the public can spend) while the lowering of taxes also stimulates buying. Finally, the government may pass out the borrowed money directly to consumers on relief. Again, some extremists have advocated giving money to everyone during a depression in order to get them to spend.

So far we have talked of tax reduction. But there are some who advocate *raising* certain taxes in a depression in order to increase consumption. Proposals of this sort come under two main heads. The first type wishes to tax "idle hoards" in order to stimulate spending and increase the velocity of money. If we could be sure that our taxes *were* only falling on idle cash some money outlay would result. But would employment rise? We cannot be sure. It seems a bit hard to tax a man's money savings in a time of crisis. Nor can one forget the general repercussions on confidence involved. We will come back to these points later.

The second type of increased taxation that is often advocated is the taxation of the upper-income groups on the ground that they save more, and that therefore a redistribution of income in favor of the poor will increase spending. Two things, however, may be said about this plan. First, the evidence is not very definite as to whether the marginal propensity to spend of the upper-income groups is much different, in the short run, from that of the poor, so that the factual basis of this idea is shaky. But even if it were true, the trouble is that the taxes which redistribute income are the taxes which fall most heavily on the marginal efficiency of capital. *Total* employment may not be increased if we lower the inducement to invest at the same time that we raise the propensity to consume.

Turning now from direct government action to other fields, another method of (temporarily) increasing consumption would be to give more generous installment-buying terms. It is not at all clear, however, whether we do the individual a favor by encouraging him to load himself with debt, and unless we keep extending repayment dates further and further the stimulus will be temporary.

There remains a final and much disputed method often advocated for increasing consumption. This is raising money wages. It is often argued that a wage increase swells the size of the total national paycheck, which increases spending, which will help to bring on recovery. There are two things to recall before we accept the wage-increase argument. First, we must remember the difference between wage *rates* and labor's total net earnings, or take-home pay. It does not do a man any good if he gets twice as much money per hour, *but* only gets half as much work. Thus, if a rise in money wage rates simultaneously cuts employment, it *need* not increase the total incomes of labor at all. Second, even if there is some increase in spending, the increase in costs which follows a wage increase may so diminish the marginal efficiency of capital that the inducement to invest may be lowered just as much as the propensity to consume is increased. As already said, we will come back to these points later.

## Stimulating Investment

One way in which government can stimulate both investment and consumption—provided other policies do not neutralize the effect—is by investing directly in public works and social services, deficit financed. If they are not deficit financed, no net monetary stimulus is given the economy. One difficulty with this policy is that if the government begins to parallel private investment with public plants, the private investment may be scared off and there will be no net gain. Thus it is important to concentrate on *public* works. A more complicated argument is the idea, often expressed, that the mere existence of a deficit will so frighten businessmen and undermine confidence that it will discourage investment.

A third way to encourage investment is to lower the rate of interest, increase bank reserves, and try to persuade the banks to give more generous credit terms. In some extreme cases the government has set up credit bureaus of its own when the risks are so great that private credit is unobtainable. Such plans, however, can lead to rather important misdirection of investment, and easy money can be quite inappropriate in some foreign trade difficulties.

Another method of stimulating investment is the removal of barriers to foreign trade. High tariffs may sometimes prevent a foreign nation from selling enough to the United States to be able to keep its economy on an even keel and to make it a good prospect for long-run investment. On the other side of the picture, foreign nations, by unduly penalizing investors, may prevent the United States from lending as much as it would like. Again, if exchange rates and domestic wages are out of line, a readjustment of wages or costs may stimulate a country's investment and foreign trade generally.

As in the case of consumption, we thus wind up with the very controversial problem of wages. Many economists feel that *reducing* money wages in a slump may stimulate investment. In this connection we should remember that lower wage rates do not necessarily mean lower take-home pay, any more than higher rates necessarily mean higher pay. The question is: How quickly will a reduction in wage rates stimulate employment? There definitely can be times in which wage reduction will have very favorable results. The case is especially strong if instead of cutting *all* money wages we pick those in which high labor costs are particularly important in restricting demand and the holding back of employment. But a full treatment of this problem must be reserved for our summary.

### Anti-Inflation Weapons: Restricting Consumption

Just as in the case of depression policy, it is not enough to talk about consumption alone. Inflation, in the first instance anyway, can be caused by too much investment just as easily as by too much consumption. However, as before, we will begin with consumption.

One of the most obvious methods of helping to reduce consumption is by taxing it. And the best method of taxing consumption is a sales, or purchase, or excise tax. Of course many people object to taxing sales because such taxes do usually burden mass consumption. But that is precisely why a sales tax is so powerful a means of fighting inflation. If you object to taxing food and other necessaries, a sort of halfway measure is provided by levying high taxes upon luxury consumption goods. But, as these do not usually make up a very high percentage of total outlay, luxury taxes are not usually very effective.

Another important way of cutting consumption is by balancing the government budget or (better still) running a surplus. In fact all that merely *balancing* the budget does is to stop the increase in bank deposits resulting from government borrowing. Total outlay is not decreased. Indeed, if the proceeds of a sales tax are immediately spent by the government, total money outlay would be the same as before—though, as we will see in connection with investment, the general situation might nevertheless be helped by such a measure.

Another method of cutting consumption tried during World War II, and again when the Korean War began, was the curtailment of installment buying. If stricter terms are demanded of consumers, this obviously can greatly reduce their buying power.

A final method of cutting consumption and stimulating saving has been tried quite often in Europe but not in this country. It consists in reducing taxes on *saved* income. Holland has managed to work out effective ways of administering such a tax, and it would seem to be a potentially very effective weapon. Many people, however, object that such a policy does not really help, because the money that is saved may be invested and then (as in the case we mentioned of a sales tax used to finance government outlay) total money income will not be reduced. This leads us on to the whole problem of investment.

### Restricting Investment

In the chapter on business cycles we saw how the attempt to invest faster than consumers were willing to save could, when financed by extra bank credit or government printing press money, lead to inflation. We will not repeat the analysis here, but from the explanation there given it can easily be seen that a reduction in consumption brought about through voluntary saving or taxation would help to divert resources into investment, and to ease the urge to expand by "stuffing the economic ballot box" in favor of the investment industries. However, some people have asked: Why cut consumption? Why not cut investment instead?

If we look only at the immediate problem this point of view is an understandable one. But suppose the attempt to invest rapidly is due to an intensely felt shortage of, say, housing. Clearly the only way this shortage is to be remedied is by building new houses. And if we cut the rate of investment in order to prevent inflation, we will actually be keeping the economy from supplying an intensely felt need. The same thing is true if the acute shortage is one of general equipment and plant.

Let us assume that we have done all we can to stimulate saving, but that investment demand is still too great to be met by voluntary saving, or without further injections of money. What shall we do then? We can express this problem graphically in terms of Figures 20 and 21. In effect, we can think of the problem as a rise in the marginal efficiency of capital schedule without an offsetting shift of the savings line. Only two things are possible if we wish to prevent further injection of credit. One is raising the rate of interest to the equilibrium level. The other is rationing credit—that is, allotting only certain amounts to various types of banks and various kinds of investment. But rationing credit easily leads into exactly that central planning of the investment flow which we wish to avoid. Thus, if we do not wish to keep on planning the flow of investment and still want to prevent inflation, a higher interest rate is (barring controls) the only alternative.

## Wage and Price Controls

Many people feel that wage and price controls are a workable alternative to the measures we have enumerated here. We have discussed this problem earlier and need not repeat the discussion here. We have seen that they entail disadvantages of their own, and are never a permanent substitute for more basic restrictions of the money supply, consumption, or investment.

## General Summary of Economic Stabilization

The trouble with a catalogue such as we have been outlining is that it is apt to give the impression that the economic stabilizer, practically speaking, will be confronted by two clearly defined, easily recognizable, and independent conditions labeled "inflation" and "deflation." Also that any one of a long list of cures is available for these ailments, in much the same way we can go into a drugstore and ask for a salve for poison ivy.

But the problem, as it is actually presented, is never so simple. Since there are always some movements up and down among the economic indices, and since they seldom all move together, a forecaster is not apt to be sure which condition the economy is really moving toward until things are far along. He is even less apt to be certain what is causing the decline (or expansion)—except in such clear cases as wars—until long after the movement has begun, or even after it is over. The stabilizer's job therefore, in the first instance, is rather like treating a man for a disease which he may not have and which (if he does turn out to have it) is due to an unknown infection. And, finally, if we mistakenly or excessively correct for one disease we run the risk of infecting the patient with another. The immediate, commonsense piece of advice which emerges is, therefore, not to be in too big a hurry to do anything. One cannot, however, end with so purely negative a conclusion. In addition, the situation is not quite so vague as we have sketched. Let us therefore try to outline a general framework of policy which will tie together both the inflationary and the deflationary problems.

In order to make a comprehensive policy outline we have first to agree upon our basic assumptions. The writer submits that these should be twofold. First, we should act on the assumption that unless we adopt measures hamstringing the economy and undermining incentives, adequate new investment outlets will soon be forthcoming spontaneously. This means that, in spite of the fact that (in a depression) hoarding may be taking place, we will soon once more be wanting people to save. And in any event we will certainly be wanting (in depression) to encourage them to invest. Second, the economic stabilizer ought, we believe, to say that indefinite deflation will *not* be permitted. In other words, there ought to be general confidence that the bottom is not going to drop out of the economy. There is not much trouble today in carrying out the second recommendation.

## Policy

The Great Depression of 1929 and the years which followed has left deep in the public mind the advisability of preventing prolonged deflation. But this fact is far from removing all the complications of modern policy. Two points remain to be considered. First, why has investment slacked off? What has happened to reduce the marginal efficiency of capital relative to the rate of interest? The second question is very closely connected with it. It is: Would employment actually increase if spending increases? We have seen that an increase in spending does not necessarily result in either an increase in employment or an increase in output. It is at this point that we have to consider social attitudes. Napoleon has been portrayed as saying, "Economists are blockheads who make financial plasters to cover the running sores of the body politic. They do not understand that a nation can have a sick soul."

This means that if the social attitudes of a country (we do not need to give an explicitly theological interpretation) are such as to prevent growth and mobility then mere injections of money will have little effect in bringing about a genuine state of economic vigor. Financial manipulation may still keep us from experiencing a sudden crisis, but without more searching methods and examination the economy can enter into a condition of prolonged convalesence or unsatisfactory performance. Let us therefore discuss some more fundamental aspects of the problem.

## Social Choices behind Public Policy

In the world today the real source of unemployment in most countries is the failure to form capital as fast as the population is growing. If the capital stock is not big enough then a reduction of money wages even below the level of subsistence would not give jobs for everyone. Thus for most of the world today the problem of Malthusian welfare—that is, living standards—and the problem of employment are the same, and both depend upon the rate of capital formation. But when one attempts to do anything to stimulate investment, whether in the wealthy industrial societies or in the undeveloped countries, the immediate social problem which emerges is that of the distribution of wealth. For if private capital formation is desired the two prerequisites are, first, security of property and, second, incentive, which means differential rewards for special effort. A man will not save if he knows that his capital is going to be confiscated, nor will he work at the height of his power without some differential reward. Some saving and some work may be accomplished with very little incentive or security of property, but to get as much saving and as much work as we wish there must be real incentive and security. Translating these words into more specific economic terms, this means that there must be inequality of income and of property. This brings us to the question of the basic meaning of democracy.

Does democracy mean literal equality or a fair chance? It will be found if one makes any research at all into the constitutional literature of the United States that neither Thomas Jefferson nor John Adams nor any of the other Founding Fathers believed in the literal equality of men. Jefferson, in fact, was quite explicit. He believed in what he called "the natural aristoi," those who by "virtue and talent" commanded more influence than others. There were two ways, he and Adams agreed, to misunderstand the nature of the good society: The first misunderstanding was to think that the good society consisted of the rule of the single philosopher king, or tight little group of elite statesmen, self-perpetuating and all-powerful. Even if such a group thought that it was acting for the benefit of the rest of society such a society was not, Jefferson and Adams considered, truly free.

The other way of misunderstanding democracy was to think that it consisted of holding everyone down to the same level—in other words, rule of a mere mass kept anonymous and literally equal. Such a society cuts off the superior man and prevents the emergence of any type of leadership or achievement. The solution which Jefferson and Adams advocated was a *fluid* society, one in which new men and new families continually emerge, as less efficient men and less efficient families decline. And this fluidity was largely underwritten by the presence of private property plus minimum social services—education, for example—plus competition.

One thing must be faced. Whatever we think of this solution it remains true that even an approximation of literal equality of opportunity can be achieved only by destroying the family. We would come nearest having literal equality of opportunity if all children were taken from their parents and raised in identical state orphanages. However, modern medical science has made it quite clear that the institutionalized rearing of children is both physically and psychologically extremely harmful. The family appears to be an indispensable part of civilized life. But once one has a family one has the possibility of the transmission of private traditions and private attitudes, and these private traditions and private attitudes may have a tremendous effect upon the achievement of the children. Mere brains and brawn are not enough for success. Social attitude is possibly even more important, and some of the most valuable moral instruction may be given at home.

We are thus, if we preserve the family, thrown back once more on the notion of a fair chance. Perhaps the most important aspect, stressed in our society, is the notion of independent opportunity, a chance to rise on independent terms. To the believer in a fixed social structure the "natural" solution would be competitive examination. Would not universal competitive examination furnish the fairest opportunity for all? Unfortunately the trouble with competitive examination is the examiners. Men are expected to write "correct" answers and if their answers happen to disagree with those who are examining them, they will not be promoted. Yet sometimes it is the examiners who are later found to have been wrong. A society in which promotion comes through competitive examination, administered from above, slowly moves into a state of social stagnation. For such a framework is intensely hostile to independent experiment. But the competitive pluralism of a vigorous capitalism furnishes precisely that independent opportunity and *in*security of social status needed to give a fair chance all round. People speak of the top 200 businessmen in America and of the top 200 leaders in Russia but there is a tremendous difference between them. The top 200 leaders of Russia are a single, cooperating, coordinated institution acting as a definite unit. They may have disputes among themselves but it is a single organization. The top 200 businessmen in the United States are simply a statistical aggregate. They do not act together to any great extent, nor are they allowed to act together. America is far from perfect mobility but it has had a nearer approach to social turnover in its society than has almost any other. This is at once the secret of American democracy and past development.

### Social Services

Let us turn next to the other side of the picture. If the state is not to give literal equality, nevertheless, it has to see to it that there is a fair chance. In the United States the notion of public education is a very old one. For example, the University of Georgia—the first state university chartered in the United States

—was chartered in 1785. England did not have public education until 1870 on any broad scale. Furthermore, the physical vulnerability of the modern suburbanite and his technological helplessness in case of unemployment all require that we take some steps to protect people from the worst vicissitudes of the moving society.

Many people, however, feel that the provision of basic social services somehow requires a heavy taxation of the wealthy. This is a mistake. There is no necessary connection between a reasonable minimum of welfare and the plunder of the rich. In the first place, the yield from the high brackets of progressive taxation is extremely small. The real money comes from the taxation of the middle- and lower-income groups. It would make very little difference to the finances of the United States if the income tax brackets from 50 per cent on were leveled out. But the one thing that the provision of modern social services does require is economic growth. Even minimum social services are very expensive, nor are they necessarily met by setting up so-called "reserves." In the true insurance principle, the premiums paid by the people insured are used to erect office buildings, to make loans to factories, and otherwise to increase the productive potential of the country. In the Social Security reserves the money is invested merely in the I.O.U.s of the government. Social Security payments come in as part of the current receipts of the government and are used for current expenses. Of course, to some extent this is also true of private insurance, since the private insurance company also buys government bonds and government bonds are also merely a lien on the future. But in both cases the paper assets thus accumulated are not, for society as a whole, any necessary increase in its productive potential. It is as if a man were to provide for his old age by borrowing his *own* I.O.U.s. When he became old, the only thing he would have would be the collection of his own I.O.U.s and they would be worth no more than his *then* ability to produce—probably zero.

It is here that a basic social problem obtrudes. To keep the welfare state solvent we must have growth. But growth, we have seen, requires both mobility and enterprise. If people are as well taken care of when they are not working as when they are, they will frequently not bother to work. If people find their marginal efforts taxed practically completely away, again, they will not bother to exert themselves. Thus the effort to insure a man from all risks, and to obtain literal equality of income, results in social stagnation. Add to this the pressure for literal job security, and one has a pattern which could scarcely be more hostile to future development. Yet if development does not take place, on an adequate scale, the burden of welfare expenditure becomes inordinate, and inflation is the usual result.

## Creativity

There is one aspect of this case which must also be stressed. Would people really be happy in a riskless society? The answer is not as easy as one might think. The urge to use one's brains and one's talents, to express them creatively is deeply seated in man. The perfectly secure, perfectly unchanging society—even if it happens to be solvent—will nevertheless be very hostile to the creative artist and the creative scientist. Indeed, without some sort of technological inquisition such as is spoken of by Samuel Butler in *Erewhon* it is difficult to see how perfect stability could exist.

Our discussion thus brings out two of the basic choices of modern society. Shall our aim be democratic choice, or shall we turn over society to the rule of a cultural elite? The second point is, do we value the long-run productivity of spontaneous development more than the short-run efficiency of expert government? If we settle for a great deal of spontaneous development and creativity, then we are necessarily limited as to the amount of insulation from risk which we give the individual.

## Pressure Groups

Reinforcing the drive toward literal equality and extravagant welfare is the desire to underwrite job security throughout the economy. We have seen that one thing which modern society cannot give is security in work routine. Some approach to security of income is possible, if we are willing to pay the social price of it, but security in work routine is absolutely impossible if there is to be development in *any* type of society. In the same way, some scope of authority is inevitable if there is to be development. For society cannot be governed by a collection of independent parish councils. The total of effort must be tied together by the pricing system, or tied together by a planning board. But to have a rule by independent, uncoordinated, and secure small village or planning groups, total change must be stopped.

Without some realization of the social usefulness of *in*security people often fail to realize the potential selfishness of a supposedly unselfish group. The altruistic labor leader who sees the swings and the playgrounds and the pensions which he has achieved for his rank and file finds it hard to think of himself as an exploiter and yet it is quite possible that the economic situation has been such that these concessions have been wrung for the most part from other laborers. The union may have stopped growth for its own benefit, and thus denied others opportunities. There are many lines of work today, for example, which would be open to the moderately educated teenager at wages which he would consider very good but which are closed to him because those callings have been rendered too expensive to be used any more. For example, in one city which the author visited not long ago there were unemployed teenagers in the square outside while nearly all the services in the hotel were automated. But automation did not come down from heaven. It is the natural result of a high price of a given factor. The economic principle of substitution works universally and quite impartially.

### Advertising and the Cultural Aspects of the Market

Shifting to a more cultural criticism, one of the things frequently urged by the intellectual against the functioning of the capitalist market is advertising and the alleged vulgarity of the market. That there is plenty of vulgarity goes without saying. That some advertising is bad also goes without saying. But does one automatically get a higher cultural life by abolishing advertising and the market? That by no means necessarily follows. For example, the relative stagnation of Soviet art is a good case in point. The Soviet artist is subsidized by the state, to be sure, but experiment is limited. Nor is there any necessary improvement between hanging glaring *political* slogans around a square, and hanging *advertising* slogans. The true problem of democratic progress is the problem of persuasion of a free people through education, religion, and ethics. When the attempt is made to substitute force for persuasion, the best that can be hoped for is tyranically imposed cultural stagnation, and the worst may be tyranically imposed cultural barbarism.

### International Maladjustment and Economic Policy

It is in the light of considerations like these that we come to grips with the basic problems of international adjustment and unemployment. When a nation becomes a part of the world market, in the sense of drawing many of its basic resources from foreign countries, it automatically assumes an obligation to keep up technologically with the other nations of the world. One cannot be a part of the world market and also feel "release from the thraldom of productive efficiency." If a nation becomes too complacent, and too security-conscious, its over-all productivity will lag. Its prices will get out of line and it will experience both gold outflow and unemployment. But these monetary difficulties are mere symptoms of more fundamental social problems. Nor can one deal successfully with them by making "financial plasters"—such as deficit finance or devaluation. More basic social reorganization to curb pressure groups, to re-create incentives, and to induce greater flexibility must be carried through.

# Discussion Questions

## Chapter I

1. Would there be any use for "economics" in a planned economy?
2. Does a free public park have any costs?
3. If economists were so scientific that all men believed their predictions, would the predictions be correct?

## Chapter II

1. "If the output of every industry were increased 10 per cent, our standard of living would be bound to rise 10 per cent." Is this correct?
2. Does a socialist country need entrepreneurs?
3. If the United States lends money to a country to build a steel plant, will that country's economy be bound to grow?

## Chapter III

1. "Since a modern citizen is so dependent on the market for his goods, he cannot possibly be personally independent." Is this correct?
2. How does a market economy seek to get capital formation?
3. How were specialization and ownership related to the growth of the market?

## Chapter IV

1. "The most usual type of American firm is a large corporation." Is this correct?
2. If a business is receiving many orders, will that make it easier for the business to pay its bills?
3. "Bonds are good investments but common stocks are not." Provide definitions, and comment on the statement.
4. What is the fundamental advantage of a partnership? Disadvantage?

## Chapter V

1. Does a socialist manager have any labor problems? Any problems of external strategy?

2. If a man's account books show a 10 per cent profit can the economist still say the man is losing money?
3. You are introducing a new product. How would you decide what price to put on it?

*Chapter VI*

1. How can we say that goods are scarce when all the stores are filled with goods?
2. Why is the law of diminishing marginal utility important?
3. If a study of an industry showed that sales increased when its prices were highest, would that contradict the law of demand?
4. Would the principles of economic theory be of any use to you in buying a new car?
5. Give a series of price and sales figures for an elastic demand curve. An inelastic curve.

*Chapter VII*

1. " 'Short-run' price means the price that prevails for a short time." Is this correct?
2. Which way do the following curves slope: Average fixed cost? Average variable cost? Marginal cost?
3. "The law of variable proportions means that output grows just as fast as employment increases." Is this correct?

*Chapter VIII*

1. If there are large numbers of small competitors, can you say that there is pure competition?
2. What is meant by "maximizing"?
3. If a producer produces beyond the intersection of marginal cost and marginal revenue, will he go bankrupt?
4. Where is the marginal revenue curve under pure competition, and why?

*Chapter IX*

1. Are profits a cost of production?
2. "If the market worked perfectly it would not work at all." Explain this statement.
3. "Under monopolistic competition prices are higher, output less, and profit higher than under pure competition." Is this correct?
4. Will a purely competitive producer always know what the market price is going to be?

## Chapter X

1. Can equilibrium wages ever be above subsistence?
2. Do wages rise without unions? If so, how?
3. What is the difference between contractual and economic rent?
4. Is there anything in this chapter that is important in analyzing automation?

## Chapter XI

1. What is the difference between profit and the marginal efficiency of capital?
2. Is a poor country poor because its interest rate is high or is the interest rate high because the country is poor?
3. Is modern industrial interest the same thing which medieval writers condemned as usury?

## Chapter XII

1. How does the "economic election" shape the flow of investment in full employment?
2. Can statisticians measure output either by incomes earned or by the value of goods produced?
3. Does a socialist economy need private saving?

## Chapter XIII

1. What is the difference between gross national product and national income?
2. Can disposable income rise when gross national product is falling? If so, how?
3. What is meant by "imputation"?
4. If a man marries his cook, what is the effect on gross national product?

## Chapter XIV

1. Give a definition of inflation.
2. What are some of the main problems in compiling a price index?
3. Why is the concept of velocity important?

## Chapter XV

1. "A bank can have deposits though no one has deposited a dollar." Explain.
2. How can the banking system create credit though no banker is conscious of lending more than he has received? Is it correct to say "create credit"?
3. "A bank's lending power can be reduced by an increase in deposits." Explain.

*Chapter XVI*

1. What advantages does an individual bank receive from belonging to the Federal Reserve System?
2. What is meant by "open market operations"?
3. Can all the debts in a country be repaid at once?

*Chapter XVII*

1. Planned saving can be greater than planned investment. How then do economists sometimes say that savings and investment are always equal?
2. Can a planned economy inflate as much as it chooses and never be forced to stop?
3. If consumption is rising, will there always be enough investment for full employment?

*Chapter XVIII*

1. Explain the "backlog" difficulty.
2. Why are rates of change of output sometimes more important than absolute amounts?
3. Do most industries rise and fall at about the same time? Why or why not?

*Chapter XIX*

1. Define "full employment."
2. "You get full employment only when consumption is high." Is this correct?
3. Can a rise in profit expectations affect the rate of interest?
4. Can a fall in the propensity to consume affect the rate of interest without causing unemployment?

*Chapter XX*

1. If current consumption falls, must investment fall?
2. "Since the multiplier holds good without time lag, a government deficit will immediately increase employment." Is this correct?
3. When can a reduction in money wages increase employment? When not?
4. Does international trade ever limit employment policy?

*Chapter XXI*

1. Why do we have international trade?
2. "The United States does not need to import anything important." Is this correct?
3. Is it correct to say that we get the greatest world output if each nation makes the product that it can produce most efficiently?

## Chapter XXII

1. Is there any connection between the rise of the union movement and the fall of the Gold Standard?
2. What is the difference between the balance of payments and the balance of trade?
3. What is meant by "purchasing power parity"?
4. Why does a country receiving capital usually have an adverse balance of trade?

## Chapter XXIII

1. If a devaluation of currency helps exports, why does not everyone devalue?
2. What is meant by the "transfer" problem?
3. What is meant by "blocked balances" and how do they operate?
4. Why bother to have fixed exchange rates?

## Chapter XXIV

1. Does a purely competitive producer ever expect prices to change?
2. Can you give the argument for "good" monopoly? Against it?
3. Is pure competition always the best way of economizing natural resources?

## Chapter XXV

1. If a firm makes 90 per cent of a product, is it a monopoly?
2. Do a number of small businesses necessarily produce more than a few large ones?
3. Does big business have any risks?

## Chapter XXVI

1. What makes wages rise?
2. Do differences in wages serve any purpose?
3. Is there any connection between the noneconomic aims of unions and the rate of economic growth?

## Chapter XXVII

1. Who were the "Knights of Labor"?
2. What is the difference between the CIO and the AFL?
3. Give some arguments for and against the closed shop.

## Chapter XXVIII

1. Can the "state" wither away?
2. If everyone had equal money income, would there be any social conflict?

3. What are the main differences between the Communists and the Social Democrats?

*Chapter XXIX*

1. Can you always cure unemployment by running a deficit?
2. What are the arguments for and against central planning?
3. How would you reconcile stability and growth?

# Bibliography

In the following lists some seminal books are identified by their first year of publication, and the name of the publisher at that time. Library cards or reserve shelf copies will often show the publishers as they appear in the lists below, although mergers (examples of economic growth) have produced new names of some firms.

## Chapter I

Heilbroner, Robert L. *The Making of Economic Society.* Englewood Cliffs, N.J.: Prentice-Hall, 1962 (paperback).
James, Clifford L. *Principles of Economics.* 9th ed. New York: Barnes and Noble, 1963 (paperback)
Robbins, Lionel Charles. *The Nature and Significance of Economic Science.* London: Macmillan, 1932.

## Chapter II

Bauer, P. and Yamey, B. S. *Economics of Underdeveloped Countries.* Chicago: University of Chicago Press, 1957 (paperback).
Black, Eugene R. *The Diplomacy of Economic Development.* New York: Atheneum, 1963 (paperback)
"Frontiers of Human Progress." Symposium, *General Electric Forum,* V (January–March 1962).
Okun, B. and Richardson, R. W. *Studies in Economic Development.* New York: Holt, Rinehart and Winston, 1962.
Rostow, W. W. *The Stages of Economic Growth.* Cambridge, Eng.: Cambridge University Press, 1960 (paperback).
Wright, David McCord. "True Growth Must Come through Freedom," *Fortune,* LX (December 1959).

## Chapter III

Evans, W. Duane and Hoffenberg, Marvin. "Interindustry Flow of Goods and Services by Industry of Origin and Destination, 1947." Table, *Review of Economics and Statistics,* XXXIV (May 1952).
Heilbroner, Robert L. *The Making of Economic Society.* Englewood Cliffs, N.J.: Prentice-Hall, 1962 (paperback).
Katona, George. *The Powerful Consumer.* New York: McGraw-Hill, 1960.
Mulcahy, R. E. *Readings in Economics from Fortune.* New York: Henry Holt, 1952.
Wright, David McCord. *Capitalism.* Chicago: Henry Regnery, 1962 (paperback).

*Chapter IV*

Bonneville, Joseph Howard, Dewey, Lloyd E., and Kelly, Harry M. *Organizing and Financing Business.* Englewood Cliffs, N.J.: Prentice-Hall, 1955.
Drucker, Peter. *Concept of the Corporation.* Boston: Beacon Press, 1960 (paperback).
Mason, Edward S. (ed.) *The Corporation in Modern Society.* Cambridge, Mass.: Harvard University Press, 1960.

*Chapter V*

Clark, J. M. *The Economics of Overhead Costs.* Chicago: University of Chicago Press, 1923.
Dean, Joel. *Managerial Economics.* Englewood Cliffs, N.J.: Prentice-Hall, 1951.
Friedman, Milton. *Price Theory.* Chicago, Aldine, 1962 (paperback).
Madeheim, H., Mazze, E. M., and Stein, C. S. *Readings in Organization and Management.* New York: Holt, Rinehart and Winston, 1964 (paperback).

*Chapter VI*

Boulding, K. E. *Economic Analysis.* New York: Harper, 1955.
Friedman, Milton. *Price Theory.* Chicago: Aldine, 1962 (paperback).
James, Clifford L. *Principles of Economics.* 9th ed. New York: Barnes and Noble, 1963 (paperback).
Schultz, T. W. *Agriculture in an Unstable Economy.* New York and London: McGraw-Hill, 1945.
Shepherd, G. S. *Agricultural Price Control.* Ames, Iowa: Collegiate Press, 1945.
Stigler, George J. *The Theory of Price.* New York: Macmillan, 1946; rev. ed. 1962.

*Chapter VII*

Boulding, K. E. *Economic Analysis.* New York: Harper, 1955.
Clark, J. M. *The Economics of Overhead Costs.* Chicago: University of Chicago Press, 1923.
Friedman, Milton. *Price Theory.* Chicago: Aldine, 1962 (paperback).

*Chapter VIII*

Boulding, K. E. *Economic Analysis.* New York: Harper, 1955.
Chamberlin, E. H. *The Theory of Monopolistic Competition.* 6th ed. Cambridge, Mass.: Harvard University Press, 1948.
Friedman, Milton. *Price Theory.* Chicago: Aldine, 1962 (paperback).
Schultz, Henry. *Statistical Laws of Demand and Supply.* Chicago: University of Chicago Press, 1928.

*Chapter IX*

Boulding, K. E. *Economic Analysis.* New York: Harper, 1955.
Chamberlin, E. H. *The Theory of Monopolistic Competition.* 6th ed. Cambridge, Mass.: Harvard University Press, 1948.

Clark, J. M. *Competition as a Dynamic Process*. Washington, D.C.: Brookings Institution, 1961.
————. *The Economics of Overhead Costs*. Chicago: University of Chicago Press, 1923.
Fellner, W. J. *Competition among the Few*. New York: Knopf, 1949.
Wright, David McCord. "Some Notes on Ideal Output," *Quarterly Journal of Economics*, LXXVI (May 1962).

## Chapter X

American Assembly. *Automation and Technological Change,* ed. John T. Dunlop. New York: Prentice-Hall, 1962 (paperback).
Clark, J. B. *The Distribution of Wealth*. New York: Macmillan, 1914.
Douglas, P. H. *The Theory of Wages*. New York: Macmillan, 1934.
Dunlop, J. T. *Wage Determination under Trade Unions*. New York: Macmillan, 1944.
Hicks, J. R. *The Theory of Wages*. London: Macmillan, 1963.
Leiter, Robert. *Labor Economics and Industrial Relations*. 2nd rev. ed. New York: Barnes and Noble, 1960 (paperback).

## Chapter XI

Clark, J. B. *The Distribution of Wealth*. New York: Macmillan, 1914.
Fisher, Irving. *The Theory of Interest*. New York: Macmillan, 1930.
Keynes, J. M. *The General Theory of Employment, Interest and Money*. New York: Harcourt, Brace, 1936.
Schumpeter, Joseph A. *The Theory of Economic Development*. New York: Oxford University Press, 1961 (paperback).
Stokes, William S. and Schoeck, Helmut. "The Politics of Economic Stagnation," *Foreign Aid Reexamined*. Washington, D.C.: Public Affairs Press, 1958.

## Chapter XII

Bailey, Martin J. *National Income and the Price System*. New York: McGraw-Hill, 1962.
Powelson, John P. *National Income and Flow of Funds Analysis*. New York: McGraw-Hill, 1960.
Wright, David McCord. *The Economics of Disturbance*. New York: Macmillan, 1947.

## Chapter XIII

Bailey, Martin J. *National Income and the Price System*. New York: McGraw-Hill, 1962.
Kuznets, Simon. *Income and Wealth of the United States*. Cambridge, Eng.: Bowes and Bowes, 1952.
"National Income, 1954." Supplement, *Survey of Current Business*. Washington, D.C.: U.S. Department of Commerce, 1954.
Ruggles, Richard. *An Introduction to National Income and Income Analysis*. New York: McGraw-Hill, 1949.

U.S. Department of Commerce. *Survey of Current Business,* XLIII (July 1963).
"U.S. Income and Output." Supplement, *Survey of Current Business.* Washington,
    D.C.: U.S. Department of Commerce, 1954.

## Chapter XIV

Chandler, Lester V. *The Economics of Money and Banking.* 3rd ed. New York:
    Harper, 1959.
————. *An Introduction to Monetary Theory.* New York: Harper, 1940.
Friedman, Milton (ed.). *Studies in the Quantity Theory of Money.* Chicago:
    University of Chicago Press, 1956.
Halm, George. *Monetary Theory.* Philadelphia: Blakiston, 1942.
Harriss, C. Lowell. *Money and Banking.* Boston: Allyn and Bacon, 1961.
Patinkin, D. "Price Flexibility and Full Employment," *Readings in Monetary
    Theory* (selected by the American Economics Association). New York:
    McGraw-Hill-Blakiston, 1957.
Pigou, A. C. "The Value of Money," *Readings in Monetary Theory* (selected by
    the American Economics Association). New York: Blakiston, 1951.
Ritter, Lawrence S. "Income Velocity and Anti-Inflationary Monetary Policy,"
    *American Economic Review,* XLIX (March 1959).
Robertson, D. H. *Money.* Chicago: University of Chicago Press, 1959 (paperback).
Selden, Richard T. "Monetary Velocity in the United States," *Studies in the
    Quantity Theory of Money,* ed. Milton Friedman. Chicago: University of
    Chicago Press, 1956.

## Chapter XV

Chandler, Lester V. *The Economics of Money and Banking.* 3rd ed. New York:
    Harper, 1959.
*Money—Master or Servant?* New York: Bulletin of the Federal Reserve Bank of
    New York, May 1955.
*Essays in Commercial Banking.* Kansas City: Bulletin of the Federal Reserve Bank
    of Kansas City, August 1962.
Goldsmith, R. W. *Financial Intermediaries in the American Economy since 1900.*
    Princeton, N.J.: Princeton University Press, 1958.
Harriss, C. Lowell. *Money and Banking.* Boston: Allyn and Bacon, 1961.
Hart, Albert Gailord and Kenen, Peter B. *Money, Debt and Economic Activity.*
    3rd ed. Englewood Cliffs, N.J.: Prentice-Hall, 1961.

## Chapter XVI

Burns, Arthur F. and Mitchell, Wesley C. *Measuring Business Cycles.* New York:
    National Bureau of Economic Research, 1946.
Friedman, Milton. *A Program for Monetary Stability.* New York: Fordham
    University Press, 1959.
*The Federal Reserve System, Purposes and Functions.* Washington: Board of
    Governors of the Federal Reserve System, 1961.
*Open Market Operations.* New York: Bulletin of the Federal Reserve Bank of
    New York, January, 1963.

Roosa, R. V. *Federal Reserve Operations in the Money and Government Securities Markets.* New York: Federal Reserve Bank of New York, 1956 (paperback).
Simons, Henry. "Rules versus Authorities in Monetary Policy," *Readings in Monetary Theory* (selected by the American Economics Association). New York: McGraw-Hill-Blakiston, 1957.
Smith, Warren L. "On the Effectiveness of Monetary Policy," *American Economic Review,* XLVI (September 1956).

## Chapter XVII

Haberler, G. *Prosperity and Depression.* New York: Atheneum, 1963 (paperback).
Hayek, F. A. *Prices and Production.* 2nd rev. ed. London: Routledge, 1935.
Keynes, J. M. *The General Theory of Employment, Interest and Money.* New York: Harcourt, Brace, 1936.
Pigou, A. C. *Industrial Fluctuations.* London: Macmillan, 1927.
Robbins, L. C. *The Great Depression.* London: Macmillan, 1934.
Wright, David McCord. *The Economics of Disturbance.* New York: Macmillan, 1947.

## Chapter XVIII

Haberler, G. *Prosperity and Depression.* New York: Atheneum, 1963 (paperback).
Hicks, J. R. *Contribution to the Theory of the Trade Cycle.* Oxford: Oxford University Press, 1950.
Keynes, J. M. *The General Theory of Employment, Interest and Money.* New York: Harcourt, Brace, 1936.

## Chapter XIX

Keynes, J. M. *The General Theory of Employment, Interest and Money.* New York: Harcourt, Brace, 1936.
Wright, David McCord. *Capitalism.* Chicago: Henry Regnery, 1962 (paperback).
———. *The Keynesian System.* New York: Fordham University Press, 1962.

## Chapter XX

Fayerweather, John. *Facts and Fallacies of International Business.* New York: Holt, Rinehart and Winston, 1962.
Haberler, G. *Prosperity and Depression.* New York: Atheneum, 1963 (paperback).
Keynes, J. M. *The General Theory of Employment, Interest and Money.* New York: Harcourt, Brace, 1936.
Wright, David McCord. *The Keynesian System.* New York: Fordham University Press, 1962.

## Chapter XXI

Haberler, C. *The Theory of International Trade.* London: Hodge, 1956.
Harrod, R. F. *International Economics.* Chicago: University of Chicago Press, 1958 (paperback).
Kenen, Peter B. *International Economics.* Englewood Cliffs: Prentice-Hall, Inc., 1964 (paperback).

Ohlin, Bertil. *Interregional and International Trade*. Cambridge, Mass.: Harvard University Press, 1933.
Young, John. *The International Economy*. 4th ed. New York: Ronald, 1963.


## Chapter XXII

*International Economic Papers* (translations prepared for the International Economics Association), ed. A. T. Peacock *et al*. New York and London: Macmillan, 1951–date.
Jacobson, Per. *The Market Economy in the World of Today*. Philadelphia: American Philosophical Society, 1963.
Meade, J. E. *The Balance of Payments*. London: Oxford University Press, 1951.
Federal Reserve Board. "U.S. Trade and Payments in 1963," Federal Reserve Bulletin, Washington, D.C., April, 1964.
Mikesell, R. F. *Foreign Exchange in the Post-War World*. New York: Twentieth Century Fund, 1954.
Triffin, Robert. *Gold and the Dollar Crisis*. New Haven: Yale University Press, 1961 (paperback).


## Chapter XXIII

Einzig, Paul. *Exchange Control*. London: Macmillan, 1934.
Haberler, G. *The Theory of International Trade*. London: Hodge, 1956.
Harrod, R. F. *International Economics*. Chicago: University of Chicago Press, 1958 (paperback).
*International Economic Papers* (translations prepared for the International Economics Association), ed. A. T. Peacock *et al*. New York and London: Macmillan, 1951–date.
Kindleberger, C. P. *Foreign Trade and the National Economy*. New Haven, Conn.: Yale University Press, 1962 (paperback).
Meade, J. E. *National Income and Expenditure*. Cambridge, Eng.: Bowes and Bowes, 1952.
Mikesell, R. F. *Foreign Exchange in the Post-War World*. New York: Twentieth Century Fund, 1954.
Ohlin, Bertil. *Interregional and International Trade*. Cambridge, Mass.: Harvard University Press, 1933.
Young, John. *The International Economy*. 4th ed. New York: Ronald, 1963.


## Chapter XXIV

Clark, J. M. *Competition as a Dynamic Process*. Washington, D.C.: Brookings Institution, 1961.
Fellner, W. J. *Competition among the Few*. New York: Knopf, 1949.
Wright, David McCord. *Capitalism*. Chicago: Henry Regnery, 1962 (paperback).
———. "Some Notes on Ideal Output," *Quarterly Journal of Economics*, LXXVI (May 1962).

## Chapter XXV

Adams, Walter (ed.). *The Structure of American Industry.* 3rd ed. New York: Macmillan, 1963.

Clark, J. M. *Competition as a Dynamic Process.* Washington, D.C.: Brookings Institution, 1961.

Jewkes, John, Sawers, David, and Stillerman, Richard. *The Sources of Invention.* New York: St. Martin's Press, 1958.


## Chapter XXVI

American Assembly. *Automation and Technological Change,* ed. John P. Dunlop. Englewood Cliffs, N.J.: Prentice-Hall, 1962 (paperback).

American Economic Association. *Readings in the Theory of Income Distribution.* Philadelphia: Blakiston, 1948.

Clark, J. B. *The Distribution of Wealth.* New York: Macmillan, 1914.

Douglas, P. H. *The Theory of Wages.* New York: Macmillan, 1934.

Dunlop, J. T. *Wage Determination under Trade Unions.* New York: Macmillan, 1944.

Hicks, J. R. *The Theory of Wages.* London: Macmillan, 1963.

Leiter, Robert. *Labor Economics and Industrial Relations.* 2nd rev. ed. New York: Barnes and Noble, 1960 (paperback).

Slichter, Sumner. *Union Policies and Industrial Management.* Washington, D.C.: Brookings Institution, 1941.

Wright, David McCord (ed.). *The Impact of the Union.* New York: Kelley and Millman, 1956.


## Chapter XXVII

American Assembly. *Automation and Technological Change,* ed. John P. Dunlop. Englewood Cliffs, N.J.: Prentice-Hall, 1962 (paperback).

American Economic Association. *Readings in the Theory of Income Distribution.* Philadelphia: Blakiston, 1948.

Clark, J. B. *The Distribution of Wealth.* New York: Macmillan, 1914.

"Crisis in the American Union Movement, The." Symposium, *Annals of the American Academy of Political Science,* CCCL (November 1963).

Douglas, P. H. *The Theory of Wages.* New York: Macmillan, 1934.

Dunlop, J. T. *Wage Determination under Trade Unions.* New York: Macmillan, 1944.

Hicks, J. R. *The Theory of Wages.* London: Macmillan, 1963.

Leiter, Robert. *Labor Economics and Industrial Relations.* 2nd rev. ed. New York: Barnes and Noble, 1960 (paperback).

Perlman, Selig. *A History of Trade Unionism in the United States.* New York: Macmillan, 1922.

Slichter, Sumner. *Union Policies and Industrial Management.* Washington, D.C.: Brookings Institution, 1941.

Webb, Sidney and Beatrice. *The History of Trade Unionism.* New York: Longmans Green, 1955.

Wright, David McCord (ed.). *The Impact of the Union*. New York: Kelley and Millman, 1956.

*Chapter XXVIII*

Crossman, R. H. S. (ed.). *New Fabian Essays*. London: Turnstile Press, 1952.
Halm, G. N. *Economic Systems*. New York: Holt, Rinehart and Winston, Revised Edition, 1961.
Lenin, N. *State and Revolution*. New York: International Publishers, 1935.
MacIntyre, A. *Marxism; An Interpretation*. London: Student Christian Movement Press, 1953.
Marx, Karl. *Capitalism* (Any standard edition).
Schumpeter, Joseph A. *Capitalism, Socialism and Democracy*. 3rd ed. New York: Harper, 1950 (paperback).
Wright, David McCord. *Capitalism*. Chicago: Henry Regnery, 1962 (paperback).

*Chapter XXIX*

Haberler, G. *Prosperity and Depression*. New York: Atheneum, 1963 (paperback).
Parkinson, C. Northcote. *Parkinson's Law*. Boston: Houghton Mifflin, 1957.
Wright, David McCord. *Capitalism*. Chicago: Henry Regnery, 1962 (paperback).
———. *The Keynesian System*. New York: Fordham University Press, 1962.

# APPENDICES

All Appendices are from the *Federal Reserve Bulletin* for April 1964

# APPENDIX A (for Chapter XIII)

## NATIONAL PRODUCT AND INCOME

### GROSS NATIONAL PRODUCT OR EXPENDITURE

(In billions of dollars)

| Item | 1929 | 1933 | 1941 | 1950 | 1959 | 1960 | 1961 | 1962 | 1963 | 1962 IV | 1963 I | 1963 II | 1963 III | 1963 IV |
|---|---|---|---|---|---|---|---|---|---|---|---|---|---|---|
| Gross national product | 104.4 | 56.0 | 125.8 | 284.6 | 482.7 | 502.6 | 518.2 | 554.9 | 585.1 | 565.2 | 571.8 | 579.6 | 588.7 | 600.1 |
| Personal consumption expenditures | 79.0 | 46.4 | 81.9 | 195.0 | 313.5 | 328.2 | 336.8 | 355.4 | 373.1 | 362.9 | 367.4 | 370.4 | 374.9 | 379.9 |
| Durable goods | 9.2 | 3.5 | 9.7 | 30.4 | 43.6 | 44.9 | 43.6 | 48.2 | 51.5 | 50.5 | 50.6 | 51.0 | 50.8 | 53.6 |
| Nondurable goods | 37.7 | 22.3 | 43.2 | 99.8 | 147.1 | 151.8 | 155.1 | 161.4 | 167.1 | 163.6 | 165.3 | 165.9 | 168.6 | 168.7 |
| Services | 32.1 | 20.7 | 29.0 | 64.9 | 122.8 | 131.5 | 138.0 | 145.7 | 154.5 | 148.9 | 151.4 | 153.5 | 155.5 | 157.7 |
| Gross private domestic investment | 16.2 | 1.4 | 18.1 | 50.0 | 72.7 | 71.8 | 69.0 | 78.8 | 82.3 | 78.8 | 77.8 | 80.7 | 83.7 | 87.1 |
| *New construction* | 8.7 | 1.4 | 6.6 | 24.2 | 40.2 | 40.7 | 41.6 | 44.4 | 46.6 | 45.0 | 43.7 | 45.8 | 47.9 | 49.2 |
| Residential, nonfarm | 3.6 | .5 | 3.5 | 14.1 | 22.3 | 21.1 | 21.0 | 23.2 | 25.0 | 23.7 | 22.7 | 24.8 | 25.9 | 26.8 |
| Other | 5.1 | 1.0 | 3.1 | 10.1 | 17.9 | 19.7 | 20.5 | 21.2 | 21.6 | 21.2 | 21.0 | 21.0 | 22.0 | 22.4 |
| Producers' durable equipment | 5.9 | 1.6 | 6.9 | 18.9 | 25.9 | 27.6 | 25.5 | 28.8 | 30.9 | 29.9 | 29.0 | 30.7 | 31.6 | 32.5 |
| Change in business inventories | 1.7 | −1.6 | 4.5 | 6.8 | 6.6 | 3.5 | 1.9 | 5.5 | 4.7 | 4.0 | 5.1 | 4.3 | 4.2 | 5.4 |
| Nonfarm only | 1.8 | −1.4 | 4.0 | 6.0 | 6.5 | 3.2 | 1.5 | 4.9 | 4.2 | 3.2 | 4.3 | 3.6 | 3.7 | 5.1 |
| Net exports of goods and services | .8 | .2 | 1.1 | .6 | −.8 | 3.0 | 4.4 | 3.8 | 4.5 | 3.3 | 3.6 | 4.8 | 4.3 | 5.4 |
| Exports | 7.0 | 2.4 | 6.0 | 13.1 | 22.9 | 26.3 | 27.5 | 28.9 | 30.7 | 28.8 | 28.6 | 30.7 | 31.4 | 32.3 |
| Imports | 6.3 | 2.3 | 4.8 | 12.5 | 23.6 | 23.3 | 23.1 | 25.1 | 26.2 | 25.5 | 24.9 | 25.9 | 27.1 | 26.9 |
| Government purchases of goods and services | 8.5 | 8.0 | 24.8 | 39.0 | 97.2 | 99.6 | 107.9 | 117.0 | 125.1 | 120.2 | 123.0 | 123.8 | 125.7 | 127.7 |
| *Federal* | 1.3 | 2.0 | 16.9 | 19.3 | 53.6 | 53.1 | 57.4 | 62.4 | 66.3 | 63.6 | 65.5 | 66.5 | 66.4 | 66.6 |
| National defense | 1.3 | 2.0 | 13.8 | 14.3 | 46.2 | 45.7 | 49.0 | 53.3 | 56.7 | 54.3 | 56.4 | 56.7 | 56.7 | 57.2 |
| Other | | | 3.2 | 5.2 | 7.9 | 8.0 | 8.9 | 10.0 | 10.5 | 10.4 | 10.1 | 10.6 | 10.8 | 10.4 |
| Less: Government sales | | | | .1 | .5 | .6 | .6 | .8 | 1.0 | 1.1 | 1.0 | .8 | 1.2 | 1.0 |
| State and local | 7.2 | 6.0 | 7.8 | 19.7 | 43.6 | 46.5 | 50.6 | 54.6 | 58.8 | 56.6 | 57.5 | 57.3 | 59.4 | 61.2 |
| Gross national product in constant (1954) dollars | 181.8 | 126.6 | 238.1 | 318.1 | 428.6 | 439.9 | 447.7 | 474.8 | 492.9 | 481.4 | 485.3 | 489.4 | 495.1 | 501.7 |

NOTE.—Dept. of Commerce estimates. Quarterly data are seasonally adjusted totals at annual rates. For back data and explanation of series see *National Income 1954 Edition, A Supplement to the Survey of Current Business*; *U.S. Income and Output, A Supplement to the Survey of Current Business* (1958); and the July 1963 *Survey of Current Business*.

## NATIONAL INCOME
### (In billions of dollars)

| Item | 1929 | 1933 | 1941 | 1950 | 1959 | 1960 | 1961 | 1962 | 1963 | 1962 IV | 1963 I | 1963 II | 1963 III | 1963 IV |
|---|---|---|---|---|---|---|---|---|---|---|---|---|---|---|
| National income | 87.8 | 40.2 | 104.7 | 241.9 | 400.5 | 414.5 | 426.1 | 453.7 | r478.2 | 462.2 | 466.7 | 474.6 | 482.0 | 489.3 |
| Compensation of employees | 51.1 | 29.5 | 64.8 | 154.2 | 278.5 | 293.6 | 302.1 | 322.9 | 340.4 | 327.7 | 332.0 | 338.7 | 342.8 | 347.9 |
| *Wages and salaries* | 50.4 | 29.0 | 62.1 | 146.4 | 258.5 | 271.3 | 278.8 | 297.1 | 312.3 | 301.5 | 304.5 | 310.8 | 314.6 | 319.4 |
| Private | 45.5 | 23.9 | 51.9 | 124.1 | 213.1 | 222.9 | 227.0 | 241.6 | 253.0 | 244.7 | 246.7 | 252.2 | 255.2 | 258.1 |
| Military | .3 | .3 | 1.9 | 5.0 | 9.9 | 9.9 | 10.2 | 10.8 | 11.0 | 10.5 | 10.7 | 10.8 | 10.8 | 11.8 |
| Government civilian | 4.6 | 4.9 | 8.3 | 17.3 | 35.4 | 38.5 | 41.6 | 44.7 | 48.3 | 46.3 | 47.1 | 47.8 | 48.7 | 49.5 |
| *Supplements to wages and salaries* | .7 | .5 | 2.7 | 7.8 | 20.1 | 22.3 | 23.3 | 25.7 | 28.0 | 26.2 | 27.5 | 27.9 | 28.2 | 28.5 |
| Employer contributions for social insurance | .1 | .1 | 2.0 | 4.0 | 9.7 | 11.3 | 11.9 | 13.7 | 15.4 | 13.8 | 15.0 | 15.3 | 15.5 | 15.7 |
| Other labor income | .6 | .4 | .7 | 3.8 | 10.4 | 11.0 | 11.4 | 12.1 | 12.6 | 12.3 | 12.4 | 12.6 | 12.7 | 12.8 |
| Proprietors' income | 14.8 | 5.6 | 17.4 | 37.5 | 46.5 | 46.2 | 48.1 | 49.8 | 50.5 | 50.3 | 50.7 | 50.0 | 50.5 | 50.8 |
| Business and professional | 8.8 | 3.2 | 10.9 | 23.5 | 35.1 | 34.2 | 35.3 | 36.5 | 37.7 | 36.9 | 37.2 | 37.4 | 37.8 | 38.2 |
| Farm | 6.0 | 2.4 | 6.5 | 14.0 | 11.4 | 12.0 | 12.8 | 13.3 | 12.8 | 13.4 | 13.5 | 12.6 | 12.7 | 12.6 |
| Rental income of persons | 5.4 | 2.0 | 3.5 | 9.0 | 11.9 | 12.1 | 12.1 | 12.0 | 12.1 | 12.0 | 12.0 | 12.0 | 12.1 | 12.2 |
| Corporate profits and inventory valuation adjustment | 10.1 | -2.0 | 14.5 | 35.7 | 47.2 | 44.5 | 43.8 | 47.0 | r51.1 | 49.3 | 48.8 | 50.1 | 52.2 | 53.4 |
| *Profits before tax* | 9.6 | .2 | 17.0 | 40.6 | 47.7 | 44.3 | 43.8 | 46.8 | r51.5 | 48.4 | 48.3 | 51.0 | 52.2 | 54.5 |
| Profits tax liability | 1.4 | .5 | 7.6 | 17.9 | 23.2 | 22.3 | 22.0 | 22.2 | r24.4 | 22.9 | 22.9 | 24.2 | 24.7 | 25.8 |
| *Profits after tax* | 8.3 | -.4 | 9.4 | 22.8 | 24.5 | 22.0 | 21.8 | 24.6 | r27.1 | 25.5 | 25.4 | 26.8 | 27.5 | 28.7 |
| Dividends | 5.8 | 2.1 | 4.5 | 9.2 | 13.7 | 14.5 | 15.3 | 16.6 | 17.8 | 17.1 | 17.1 | 17.6 | 17.6 | 18.8 |
| Undistributed profits | 2.4 | -2.4 | 4.9 | 13.6 | 10.8 | 7.5 | 6.5 | 8.1 | r9.3 | 8.4 | 8.3 | 9.2 | 9.8 | 9.8 |
| Inventory valuation adjustment | .5 | -2.1 | -2.5 | -5.0 | -.5 | .2 | .......... | .2 | -.4 | .9 | .4 | -.9 | .0 | -1.1 |
| Net interest | 6.4 | 5.0 | 4.5 | 5.5 | 16.4 | 18.1 | 20.0 | 22.0 | 24.1 | 23.0 | 23.3 | 23.7 | 24.3 | 25.0 |

NOTE.—Dept. of Commerce estimates. Quarterly data are seasonally adjusted totals at annual rates. See also NOTE to previous table.
r Revised

382

# APPENDIX B (for Chapter XIV)

## CONSUMER PRICES

### (1957–59 = 100)

| Period | All items | Food | Housing | | | | | | Apparel and upkeep | Transportation | Health and recreation | | | | Other goods and services |
|---|---|---|---|---|---|---|---|---|---|---|---|---|---|---|---|
| | | | Total | Rent | Home-ownership | Fuel oil and coal | Gas and electricity | Furnishings and operation | | | Total | Medical care | Personal care | Reading and recreation | |
| 1929 | 59.7 | 55.6 | ..... | 85.4 | ..... | ..... | ..... | ..... | ..... | ..... | ..... | ..... | ..... | ..... | ..... |
| 1933 | 45.1 | 35.3 | ..... | 60.8 | ..... | ..... | ..... | ..... | ..... | ..... | ..... | ..... | ..... | ..... | ..... |
| 1941 | 51.3 | 44.2 | 61.4 | 64.3 | ..... | 45.2 | 88.3 | ..... | ..... | 51.2 | ..... | 50.6 | 47.6 | 57.3 | 58.2 |
| 1945 | 62.7 | 58.4 | 67.5 | 66.1 | ..... | 53.6 | 86.4 | ..... | ..... | 55.4 | ..... | 57.5 | 63.6 | 75.0 | 67.3 |
| 1955 | 93.3 | 94.0 | 94.1 | 94.8 | 92.6 | 91.9 | 94.9 | 97.3 | 95.9 | 89.7 | 91.4 | 88.6 | 90.0 | 92.1 | 94.3 |
| 1956 | 94.7 | 94.7 | 95.5 | 96.5 | 94.1 | 95.9 | 95.9 | 97.3 | 97.8 | 91.3 | 93.6 | 91.8 | 93.7 | 93.4 | 95.8 |
| 1957 | 98.0 | 97.8 | 98.5 | 98.3 | 98.2 | 98.0 | 96.9 | 99.4 | 99.5 | 96.5 | 97.0 | 95.5 | 97.1 | 96.9 | 98.5 |
| 1958 | 100.7 | 101.9 | 100.2 | 100.1 | 100.4 | 99.0 | 100.3 | 99.9 | 99.8 | 99.7 | 100.3 | 100.1 | 100.4 | 100.8 | 99.8 |
| 1959 | 101.5 | 100.3 | 101.3 | 101.6 | 101.4 | 100.2 | 102.8 | 100.7 | 100.6 | 103.8 | 102.8 | 104.4 | 102.4 | 102.4 | 101.8 |
| 1960 | 103.1 | 101.4 | 103.1 | 103.1 | 103.7 | 99.5 | 107.0 | 101.5 | 102.2 | 103.8 | 105.4 | 108.1 | 104.1 | 104.9 | 103.8 |
| 1961 | 104.2 | 102.6 | 103.9 | 104.4 | 104.4 | 101.6 | 107.9 | 101.4 | 103.0 | 105.0 | 107.3 | 111.3 | 104.6 | 107.2 | 104.6 |
| 1962 | 105.4 | 103.6 | 104.8 | 105.7 | 105.6 | 102.1 | 107.9 | 101.5 | 103.6 | 107.2 | 109.4 | 114.2 | 106.5 | 109.6 | 105.3 |
| 1963 | 106.7 | 105.1 | 106.0 | 106.8 | 107.0 | 104.0 | 107.9 | 102.4 | 104.8 | 107.8 | 111.4 | 116.7 | 107.9 | 111.5 | 107.1 |
| 1963—Feb | 106.1 | 105.0 | 105.4 | 106.4 | 106.1 | 104.8 | 108.0 | 102.1 | 104.0 | 106.8 | 110.1 | 115.6 | 107.3 | 110.0 | 105.7 |
| Mar | 106.2 | 104.6 | 105.7 | 106.4 | 106.5 | 104.8 | 108.0 | 102.3 | 104.2 | 107.0 | 110.2 | 115.8 | 107.3 | 110.1 | 105.7 |
| Apr | 106.2 | 104.3 | 105.8 | 106.5 | 106.9 | 104.2 | 107.5 | 102.3 | 104.4 | 107.0 | 110.7 | 116.1 | 107.6 | 111.0 | 105.8 |
| May | 106.2 | 104.2 | 105.7 | 106.6 | 106.7 | 102.4 | 107.4 | 102.3 | 104.3 | 107.4 | 110.7 | 116.4 | 107.8 | 110.7 | 106.0 |
| June | 106.6 | 105.0 | 105.9 | 106.7 | 106.8 | 102.1 | 108.1 | 102.4 | 104.5 | 107.4 | 111.4 | 116.8 | 107.8 | 110.9 | 106.0 |
| July | 107.1 | 106.2 | 106.0 | 106.7 | 107.1 | 102.3 | 108.1 | 102.4 | 104.5 | 107.8 | 111.7 | 116.9 | 108.0 | 111.5 | 107.6 |
| Aug | 107.1 | 106.0 | 106.0 | 106.8 | 107.1 | 102.6 | 107.2 | 102.5 | 104.7 | 108.3 | 111.9 | 117.1 | 108.0 | 112.1 | 108.0 |
| Sept | 107.1 | 105.4 | 106.2 | 107.0 | 107.2 | 103.7 | 108.0 | 102.7 | 105.4 | 107.9 | 112.1 | 117.2 | 108.2 | 112.3 | 108.0 |
| Oct | 107.2 | 104.9 | 106.3 | 107.1 | 107.4 | 104.5 | 108.1 | 102.6 | 105.9 | 109.0 | 112.1 | 117.4 | 108.4 | 112.7 | 108.0 |
| Nov | 107.4 | 105.1 | 106.6 | 107.2 | 108.0 | 105.4 | 108.0 | 102.7 | 106.1 | 109.1 | 112.3 | 117.5 | 108.4 | 112.8 | 108.2 |
| Dec | 107.6 | 105.4 | 106.9 | 107.3 | 108.4 | 105.8 | 108.1 | 102.9 | 106.1 | 108.9 | 112.4 | 117.9 | 108.8 | 113.1 | 108.3 |
| 1964—Jan | 107.7 | 105.8 | 106.9 | 107.3 | 108.5 | 106.6 | 108.1 | 102.7 | 105.0 | 109.4 | 112.7 | 118.2 | 108.5 | 113.1 | 108.3 |
| Feb | 107.6 | 106.0 | 106.9 | 107.5 | 108.8 | 106.6 | 106.2 | 102.7 | 105.1 | 108.6 | 112.9 | 118.5 | 108.4 | 113.3 | 108.4 |

NOTE.—Bureau of Labor Statistics index for city wage-earners and clerical workers. The new series index begins with January 1964.

# APPENDIX C (for Chapter XXII)

APRIL 1964

## U.S. BALANCE OF PAYMENTS

### U.S. BALANCE OF PAYMENTS

(In millions of dollars)

| Item | 1961 | 1962 | 1963[p] | 1962 III | 1962 IV | 1963 I[r] | 1963 II[r] | 1963 III | 1963 IV[p] |
|---|---|---|---|---|---|---|---|---|---|
| A. Transactions other than changes in foreign liquid assets in U.S. and in U.S. monetary reserve assets, and other than special U.S. Govt. transactions—Seasonally adjusted | | | | | | | | | |
| Exports of goods and services—Total[1] | 28,311 | 29,790 | 31,603 | 7,550 | 7,424 | 7,452 | 7,903 | 7,921 | 8,327 |
| Merchandise | 19,913 | 20,479 | 21,902 | 5,270 | 4,925 | 5,010 | 5,494 | 5,559 | 5,839 |
| Military sales | 402 | 660 | 632 | 141 | 216 | 181 | 203 | 292 | 156 |
| Investment income receipts, private | 3,464 | 3,850 | 4,067 | 946 | 1,060 | 1,059 | 969 | 993 | 1,046 |
| Investment income receipts, Govt. | 380 | 472 | 498 | 105 | 114 | 123 | 124 | 125 | 126 |
| Other services | 4,152 | 4,329 | 4,504 | 1,088 | 1,109 | 1,079 | 1,113 | 1,152 | 1,160 |
| Imports of goods and services—Total[1] | -22,867 | -24,964 | -26,118 | -6,282 | -6,341 | -6,270 | -6,453 | -6,694 | -6,701 |
| Merchandise | -14,497 | -16,145 | -16,962 | -4,127 | -4,046 | -4,014 | -4,182 | -4,392 | -4,374 |
| Military expenditures | -2,934 | -3,028 | -2,880 | -732 | -794 | -748 | -725 | -708 | -699 |
| Investment income payments | -882 | -995 | -1,196 | -245 | -265 | -278 | -287 | -309 | -322 |
| Other services | -4,554 | -4,796 | -5,080 | -1,178 | -1,236 | -1,230 | -1,259 | -1,285 | -1,306 |
| Balance on goods and services[1] | 5,444 | 4,826 | 5,485 | 1,268 | 1,083 | 1,182 | 1,450 | 1,227 | 1,626 |
| Remittances and pensions | -705 | -736 | -812 | -176 | -187 | -211 | -211 | -195 | -195 |
| 1. Balance on goods, services, remittances and pensions | 4,739 | 4,090 | 4,673 | 1,092 | 896 | 971 | 1,239 | 1,032 | 1,431 |
| 2. U.S. Govt. grants and capital flow, net, excluding advance debt repayments[2] | -3,370 | -3,520 | -3,789 | -849 | -911 | -871 | -1,199 | -784 | -935 |
| Grants[3,4] | -1,854 | -1,903 | -1,907 | -434 | -466 | -440 | -515 | -462 | -490 |
| Long-term loans and subscriptions[4] | -1,941 | -2,133 | -2,184 | -486 | -660 | -563 | -620 | -438 | -563 |
| Change in foreign currency holdings and short-term claims, net (increase, —)[2,4] | -261 | -248 | -441 | -74 | 28 | -50 | -260 | -30 | -101 |
| Seasonal adjustment on three preceding items combined | | | | -50 | 14 | | 41 | -78 | 37 |
| Change in associated liabilities | 80 | 147 | 94 | 65 | 25 | 31 | -1 | 46 | 18 |
| Scheduled loan repayments | 606 | 617 | 649 | 130 | 148 | 151 | 156 | 178 | 164 |
| 3. Private capital flows, net, excluding foreign liquid assets in U.S. | -3,507 | -3,118 | -3,690 | -708 | -902 | -956 | -1,468 | -338 | -928 |
| U.S. direct investments abroad | -1,598 | -1,557 | -1,799 | -359 | -493 | -501 | -488 | -209 | -601 |
| U.S. long-term capital, other | -1,011 | -1,209 | -1,641 | -188 | -335 | -512 | -620 | -294 | -215 |
| Foreign long-term investments in U.S. | 466 | 271 | 387 | -10 | 20 | -9 | 203 | 112 | 81 |
| U.S. short-term capital | -1,541 | -507 | -642 | -164 | -39 | 84 | -626 | 29 | -129 |
| Foreign short-term capital[5] | 177 | -116 | 5 | 13 | -55 | -18 | 63 | 24 | -64 |

| Item | 1961 | 1962 | 1963[p] | 1962 | | 1963 | | | |
|---|---|---|---|---|---|---|---|---|---|
| | | | | III | IV | I[r] | II[r] | III | IV[p] |
| 4. Errors and unrecorded transactions | -905 | -1,025 | -495 | -469 | -492 | -135 | 121 | -386 | -95 |
| Balance of A (= 1+2+3+4) | -3,043 | -3,573 | -3,301 | -934 | -1,409 | -991 | -1,307 | -476 | -527 |
| Less: Net seasonal adjustment | | | | 337 | -95 | -181 | -94 | 364 | -89 |
| Balance of A before seasonal adjustment | -3,043 | -3,573 | -3,301 | -1,271 | -1,314 | -810 | -1,213 | -840 | -438 |

B. Changes in foreign liquid assets in U.S. and in U.S. monetary reserve assets, and special U.S. Govt. transactions—Not seasonally adjusted

| Item | 1961 | 1962 | 1963[p] | 1962 | | 1963 | | | |
|---|---|---|---|---|---|---|---|---|---|
| | | | | III | IV | I[r] | II[r] | III | IV[p] |
| Total | 3,043 | 3,573 | 3,301 | 1,271 | 1,314 | 810 | 1,213 | 840 | 438 |
| Advance repayments on U.S. Govt. loans[6] | 668 | 666 | 325 | 471 | 142 | 25 | 34 | 241 | 25 |
| Advances on U.S. military exports, net | 5 | 470 | 359 | 107 | 223 | 20 | -5 | [p]105 | 239 |
| *Sales of nonconvertible nonmarketable securities,[7] net* | | 251 | -43 | | 251 | 63 | -10 | -95 | -1 |
| Dollar securities | | | 31 | | | 58 | 19[8] | -45 | 8[8] |
| Foreign currency securities | | 251 | -74 | | 251 | 5 | -29 | -50 | -9 |
| *Sales of convertible nonmarketable securities,[7] net* | | | 702 | | | 350 | 152 | 175 | 25 |
| Dollar securities | | | 150 | | | 125 | | 25 | |
| Foreign currency securities | | | 552 | | | 225 | 152 | 150 | 25 |
| *Change in U.S. short-term liabilities reported by U.S. banks[9] and foreign holdings of marketable U.S. Govt. bonds and notes* | 1,764 | 653 | 1,580 | -188 | 309 | 320 | 918 | 187 | 155 |
| International and regional organizations[10] | 407 | 213 | -225 | -107 | 109 | -64 | -48 | -19 | -94 |
| Foreign private holders excluding banks[11] | 81 | 134 | 394 | -137 | -42 | 74 | 115 | 93 | 112 |
| Foreign commercial banks | 595 | -147 | 434 | -214 | -132 | 384 | 75 | -36 | 11 |
| Foreign official holders | 681 | 453 | 977 | 270 | 374 | -74 | 776 | 149 | 126 |
| *Change in U.S. monetary reserve assets (increase, —)* | 606 | 1,533 | 378 | 881 | 389 | 32 | 124 | 227 | -5 |
| IMF position | -135 | 626 | 30 | 331 | 14 | -46 | 2 | 59 | 15 |
| Convertible currencies | -116 | 17 | -113 | 104 | 351 | -33 | 6 | -28 | -58 |
| Gold | 857 | 890 | 461 | 446 | 24 | 111 | 116 | 196 | 38 |

[r] Revised
[p] Preliminary
1 Excludes military transfers under grants.
2 Includes also very small amounts of changes in "misc. Govt. nonliquid liabilities."
3 Includes military grants.
4 Not seasonally adjusted separately.
5 Other than foreign liquid assets in U.S.
6 Includes sell-offs.
7 With maturities over 12 months.

8 Certificates sold abroad by Export-Import Bank.
9 Includes official liabilities.
10 Includes, for International Monetary Fund, only changes in its holdings of income earning U.S. Govt. securities.
11 Including undetermined holders.

NOTE.—Dept. of Commerce data. Minus sign indicates net payments (debits); absence of sign indicates net receipts (credits).

# APPENDIX D (for Chapter XXVI)

APRIL 1964

## LABOR FORCE, EMPLOYMENT, AND UNEMPLOYMENT

(In thousands of persons unless otherwise indicated)

| Period | Total non-institutional population | Total labor force | Civilian labor force | | | | | | Not in the labor force | Unemployment rate[2] (per cent) S.A. |
|---|---|---|---|---|---|---|---|---|---|---|
| | | | Total | Employed[1] | | | Unemployed | | | |
| | | | | Total | In nonagricultural industries | In agriculture | | | | |
| 1957 | 120,445 | 70,746 | 67,946 | 65,011 | 58,789 | 6,222 | 2,936 | 49,699 | 4.3 |
| 1958 | 121,950 | 71,284 | 68,647 | 63,966 | 58,122 | 5,844 | 4,681 | 50,666 | 6.8 |
| 1959 | 123,366 | 71,946 | 69,394 | 65,581 | 59,745 | 5,836 | 3,813 | 51,420 | 5.5 |
| 1960[3] | 125,368 | 73,126 | 70,612 | 66,681 | 60,958 | 5,723 | 3,931 | 52,242 | 5.6 |
| 1961 | 127,852 | 74,175 | 71,603 | 66,796 | 61,333 | 5,463 | 4,806 | 53,677 | 6.7 |
| 1962 | 130,081 | 74,681 | 71,854 | 67,846 | 62,657 | 5,190 | 4,007 | 55,400 | 5.6 |
| 1963 | 132,125 | 75,712 | 72,975 | 68,809 | 63,863 | 4,946 | 4,166 | 56,412 | 5.7 |
| 1963—Mar. | 131,590 | 74,382 | 71,650 | 67,148 | 62,812 | 4,337 | 4,501 | 57,208 | 5.7 |
| Apr. | 131,740 | 74,897 | 72,161 | 68,097 | 63,434 | 4,673 | 4,063 | 56,843 | 5.7 |
| May | 131,865 | 75,864 | 73,127 | 69,061 | 63,883 | 5,178 | 4,066 | 56,001 | 5.9 |
| June | 132,036 | 75,901 | 75,165 | 70,319 | 64,365 | 5,954 | 4,846 | 54,135 | 5.7 |
| July | 132,196 | 77,917 | 75,173 | 70,851 | 64,882 | 5,969 | 4,322 | 54,279 | 5.6 |
| Aug. | 132,345 | 77,167 | 74,418 | 70,561 | 65,065 | 5,496 | 3,857 | 55,178 | 5.5 |
| Sept. | 132,497 | 75,811 | 73,062 | 69,546 | 64,220 | 5,326 | 3,516 | 56,686 | 5.5 |
| Oct. | 132,682 | 76,086 | 73,344 | 69,891 | 64,541 | 5,350 | 3,453 | 56,596 | 5.6 |
| Nov. | 132,853 | 76,000 | 73,261 | 69,325 | 64,548 | 4,777 | 3,936 | 56,852 | 5.9 |
| Dec. | 133,025 | 75,201 | 72,461 | 68,615 | 64,576 | 4,039 | 3,846 | 57,824 | 5.5 |
| 1964—Jan. | 133,200 | 74,514 | 71,793 | 67,228 | 63,234 | 3,993 | 4,565 | 58,685 | 5.6 |
| Feb. | 133,358 | 75,259 | 72,527 | 68,002 | 64,071 | 3,931 | 4,524 | 58,099 | 5.4 |
| Mar. | 133,519 | 75,553 | 72,810 | 68,517 | 64,500 | 4,017 | 4,293 | 57,965 | 5.4 |

1 Includes self-employed, unpaid family, and domestic service workers.

2 Per cent of civilian labor force.

3 Inclusion of figures for Alaska and Hawaii beginning with 1960 increased population by about 500,000 and total labor force by about 300,000. Most of the increase was in nonagricultural industries.

NOTE.—Information relating to persons 14 years of age and over is obtained on a sample basis. Monthly data relate to the calendar week that contains the 12th day; annual data are averages of monthly figures. Bureau of Labor Statistics estimate. S.A. (seasonally adjusted)

## HOURS AND EARNINGS OF PRODUCTION WORKERS IN MANUFACTURING INDUSTRIES

| Industry Group | Average hours worked (per week; S.A.) | | | | Average weekly earnings (dollars per week; N.S.A.) | | | | Average hourly earnings (dollars per hour; N.S.A.) | | | |
|---|---|---|---|---|---|---|---|---|---|---|---|---|
| | 1963 Mar. | 1964 Jan. | Feb.p | Mar.p | 1963 Mar. | 1964 Jan. | Feb.p | Mar.p | 1963 Mar. | 1964 Jan. | Feb.p | Mar.p |
| Total | 40.5 | 40.1 | 40.6 | 40.7 | 98.09 | 99.90 | 101.15 | 101.40 | 2.44 | 2.51 | 2.51 | 2.51 |
| Durable goods | 41.0 | 40.8 | 41.3 | 41.3 | 106.49 | 109.21 | 109.88 | 110.56 | 2.61 | 2.69 | 2.68 | 2.69 |
| Ordnance and accessories | 40.7 | 40.6 | 40.2 | 39.9 | 118.20 | 121.18 | 119.80 | 119.10 | 2.89 | 2.97 | 2.98 | 2.97 |
| Lumber and wood products | 39.9 | 39.2 | 40.5 | 40.7 | 77.81 | 79.90 | 82.39 | 82.61 | 1.98 | 2.07 | 2.07 | 2.06 |
| Furniture and fixtures | 40.7 | 40.1 | 41.3 | 41.1 | 79.19 | 79.59 | 82.01 | 82.42 | 1.97 | 2.02 | 2.02 | 2.03 |
| Stone, clay, and glass products | 41.4 | 40.7 | 41.6 | 41.5 | 99.47 | 99.50 | 101.50 | 101.34 | 2.45 | 2.50 | 2.50 | 2.49 |
| Primary metal industries | 40.5 | 41.0 | 41.1 | 41.0 | 122.91 | 125.77 | 126.18 | 126.48 | 3.02 | 3.06 | 3.07 | 3.07 |
| Fabricated metal products | 41.2 | 41.3 | 41.8 | 41.9 | 105.67 | 108.79 | 109.18 | 110.39 | 2.59 | 2.66 | 2.65 | 2.66 |
| Machinery except electrical | 41.6 | 41.9 | 42.5 | 42.4 | 115.51 | 118.71 | 120.84 | 121.13 | 2.77 | 2.84 | 2.85 | 2.85 |
| Electrical machinery | 40.3 | 40.0 | 40.3 | 40.6 | 97.84 | 100.40 | 100.65 | 101.40 | 2.44 | 2.51 | 2.51 | 2.51 |
| Transportation equipment | 41.8 | 42.0 | 41.9 | 41.5 | 123.85 | 127.41 | 127.71 | 126.68 | 2.97 | 3.07 | 3.07 | 3.06 |
| Instruments and related products | 41.0 | 39.8 | 40.7 | 40.6 | 101.18 | 99.90 | 101.40 | 101.81 | 2.48 | 2.51 | 2.51 | 2.52 |
| Miscellaneous manufacturing industries | 39.6 | 38.8 | 39.8 | 39.7 | 80.39 | 79.87 | 82.16 | 82.58 | 2.03 | 2.08 | 2.08 | 2.08 |
| Nondurable goods | 39.8 | 39.1 | 39.9 | 39.8 | 86.68 | 87.85 | 89.04 | 89.44 | 2.20 | 2.27 | 2.26 | 2.27 |
| Food and kindred products | 41.1 | 40.7 | 41.0 | 40.9 | 93.32 | 95.91 | 95.68 | 96.08 | 2.31 | 2.38 | 2.38 | 2.39 |
| Tobacco manufactures | 39.2 | 37.6 | 36.2 | 39.0 | 73.11 | 72.69 | 68.25 | 73.83 | 1.96 | 1.97 | 1.95 | 1.99 |
| Textile-mill products | 40.7 | 40.4 | 41.2 | 41.1 | 68.51 | 70.40 | 71.98 | 71.63 | 1.70 | 1.76 | 1.76 | 1.76 |
| Apparel and other finished textiles | 36.5 | 34.7 | 36.4 | 36.3 | 62.59 | 60.00 | 64.61 | 64.79 | 1.71 | 1.77 | 1.78 | 1.78 |
| Paper and allied products | 42.8 | 42.5 | 42.9 | 42.6 | 104.13 | 106.09 | 106.85 | 106.60 | 2.45 | 2.52 | 2.52 | 2.49 |
| Printing, publishing, and allied industries | 38.4 | 38.1 | 38.4 | 38.4 | 110.21 | 110.67 | 111.63 | 113.28 | 2.87 | 2.92 | 2.93 | 2.95 |
| Chemicals and allied products | 41.6 | 41.2 | 41.5 | 41.8 | 111.37 | 113.85 | 113.99 | 114.82 | 2.69 | 2.77 | 2.76 | 2.76 |
| Products of petroleum and coal | 41.3 | 41.4 | 42.3 | 41.7 | 128.61 | 132.16 | 132.39 | 129.47 | 3.16 | 3.20 | 3.19 | 3.15 |
| Rubber products | 41.1 | 40.7 | 41.0 | 40.8 | 100.12 | 101.25 | 100.85 | 100.19 | 2.46 | 2.50 | 2.49 | 2.48 |
| Leather and leather products | 36.9 | 36.5 | 37.8 | 37.4 | 64.58 | 66.95 | 68.58 | 67.32 | 1.75 | 1.79 | 1.80 | 1.80 |

S.A. (seasonally adjusted)
N.S.A. (not seasonally adjusted)

NOTE.—Bureau of Labor Statistics; data are for production and related workers only.
p Preliminary

# INDEX

# Index